Get the eBook FREE!

(PDF, ePub, Kindle, and liveBook all included)

We believe that once you buy a book from us, you should be able to read it in any format we have available. To get electronic versions of this book at no additional cost to you, purchase and then register this book at the Manning website.

Go to https://www.manning.com/freebook and follow the instructions to complete your pBook registration.

That's it!
Thanks from Manning!

Data Privacy

Data Privacy
A RUNBOOK FOR ENGINEERS

NISHANT BHAJARIA
FOREWORD BY NEIL HUNT

MANNING
SHELTER ISLAND

Manning Publications Co.
20 Baldwin Road
PO Box 761
Shelter Island, NY 11964

Development editor:	Ian Hough
Technical development editor:	Michael Jensen
Review editor:	Aleksandar Dragosavljević
Production editor:	Rachel Gibbs
Copy editor:	Andy Carroll
Proofreader:	Jason Everett
Technical proofreader:	Jon Riddle
Typesetter:	Gordan Salinovic
Cover designer:	Marija Tudor

ISBN 9781617298998

Printed in the United States of America

brief contents

contents

foreword

I met Nishant while I was leading the product and engineering team at Netflix, where I had been since the beginning of the company. The team was about 500 strong, and while we had had early brushes with security challenges, we had not tackled privacy in a significant way until we faced blowback from the Netflix Prize, and then GDPR and CCPA in quick succession. We were building out the team, the philosophy, and the deliverables at the same time, and Nishant was a key part of that team—someone who spoke both engineering and privacy, who understood the pragmatics, the needs of the business, the limits on engineering effort, and the commitments we had made (and needed to make) to our customers and how to fulfill them.

For the Netflix Prize, 2006–2009, we wanted to publish a large dataset of 100M ratings from 500k users (e.g. user N liked title T with 4 stars) and offer a $1M prize for the team who could best build a prediction engine to predict ratings on a test set held back from the competitors. Obviously we needed to anonymize the dataset, but James Bennett, who ran the prize effort for me, also took a sophisticated approach of randomizing a percentage of the ratings so they could not be matched to other public sources. However, Arvind Narayanan and Vitaly Shmatikov at the University of Texas at Austin wrote a paper showing that statistical re-identification techniques could match ratings to IMDB and expose the identities of several individuals—a possibility we hadn't sufficiently thought through. This was a wakeup call for me.

Around this time, there were an escalating series of breaches at various other companies, disclosing personal information including names, addresses, SSNs, credit cards, etc. It was easy to view these as security problems, but in many cases, the breach was less a penetration of defenses, but was by or through an insider, or an accident. As we studied how to avoid being hit ourselves, it became clearer and clearer that while we needed to have strong security measures, it would also be necessary to design our IT systems to limit and segregate personal information so that accidents were unlikely, insiders had less chance (and more incentive) to avoid a leak, and hackers would have to work much harder to put the pieces together.

Then came the GDPR regulation, as a harbinger of many new privacy regulations that are still rolling out as I write this in 2021. GDPR (and later CCPA) added the new consideration that individuals should have the right to know what data was collected, to be able to see that data, to fix it if incorrect, and to delete it if they wished. This further reinforced the need to design our systems with privacy in mind, to make all these things easier to accomplish.

For Netflix, this meant segregating our personally identifying information in tokenized data stores, ensuring that all references were indirect, and adding policies, controls, and auditing around access to those stores. Accomplishing this on a system running at scale, without impacting performance, was a significant challenge, and one in which Nishant was a key leader. It made me wish that we had planned more for this when starting out, and that we didn't have to build it after the fact—and I started to think and communicate about principles of design for privacy with my team.

This book takes that thinking further and deeper. It is written for professionals in technology companies facing the same challenges that we faced then, but in an ever more stringent and demanding environment when privacy matters more to individuals and thus regulators, when more data is stored and more breaches and disclosures happen all the time, when technology platforms are less monolithic and more bolted together from various partnerships and services, and public opinion about technology companies has turned increasingly negative on their use and abuse of private data.

Your digital exhaust can be incredibly valuable, and can be used to pay for services and products which are offered for free (or to boost revenue for products sold for a fee). Free (or reduced cost) has always been an attractive model to consumers, but now people are becoming more savvy and demanding about what is done with their data, and companies are being more aggressive about deriving maximum value from that data to pay for ever richer and more interesting products.

But your private information linked to behavior is increasingly used in services or systems that are unavoidable: from government services, health, banking, travel infrastructure, to third party infrastructure like ratings agencies. These systems, being non-optional, have an even bigger responsibility to use your personal information safely, since you can't "vote with your feet" and avoid companies that abuse your trust.

This requires that companies think clearly about what they will do with the data, are clear and up-front about it with their users, and do it in a safe way that restores some of the lost trust.

Executing on those requirements starts with the people: inculcating a privacy sensitivity, a state of mind, that makes privacy a first-order topic throughout an organization.

Then it requires thoughtful product and service design, thinking about what is needed, and for how long, and what to do with it afterwards, and the ability to clearly communicate that with users.

And then it requires technology design and implementation that makes it possible to comply with the promises made and the regulations that need to be followed, without becoming a burden on the organization preventing productivity, agility, and the ability to deliver value. The design needs to anticipate future privacy needs that will come in evolving public expectations and future privacy regulations that will inevitably arise as the public concerns develop.

This book will give you a better appreciation for what privacy is and why it matters; with frequent examples of breaches and leaks, it provokes you to think about what if that were my organization; how can I take steps to lower the risk?

Nishant describes methodologies for classifying and talking about data with differing privacy sensitivities, where that data goes and what it is used for, and prompts you to ask the questions: Is it necessary for the purpose? Is it what I would want as a customer? Is it ethical? Is it compliant with our policies and with regulations? Then he considers sharing with other parts of the organization, and (increasingly important) with partners, suppliers, and vendors, and how to ask the right questions of those other organizations before you trust them with your users' data.

A big part of the book is about technical design to make it easy to keep private information private. Techniques include encryption, hashing, tokenization, and ways to segregate data to secure the private data. Another aspect is avoiding informal data collection (such as logging or debug streams) that inadvertently capture PII in an insecure way. This requires tooling to support collecting useful data without PII, and educational programs that ensure that engineers are mindful of the need to take care.

So much of privacy depends upon what data is collected. Thus an important part of design for privacy is ensuring that there is justification for collecting and for keeping data, and making sure that it is not collected if not needed, or removed when no longer necessary. Defining *need* matters too—there's the data you find that you need in the future that you wish you had collected when you had the chance, and there is the data that you *need* yesterday that doesn't really add much value, and probably wasn't that important in the first place.

The new privacy regulations introduce user rights to know, to view, to correct, and to delete their data; this can very quickly become an impossible task unless data collection is designed from the start with an ability to find everything about an individual, and an ability to selectively delete individual records without leaving inconsistencies in the data (such as audit trails for transactions that point to deleted customer records).

Privacy is joined at the hip with security. Without strong identity/authentication and (appropriately fine grained) authorization, it becomes impossible to keep control of, or audit access to private information, and without good controls around unauthorized access, it becomes easier for an intruder to compromise privacy.

The book closes with thoughts on scaling—that is, matching the resources and team focused on privacy to the size and maturity of the organization and the task it is facing. It is easy to undersize the effort and fail to achieve the goals; it is also easy to oversize the effort, waste resources, slow things down, and kill the value that the organization seeks to deliver. Finding the right effort level is a challenge!

I wish I had had this text in 2015 or 2016 at Netflix when we started working on GDPR readiness. It would have been helpful in 2008–2012 in a time of significant architectural evolution of our technology, when we could have implemented some of the ideas much more easily. I would have benefited from the text as far back as 2006 thinking about the Netflix Prize, or even before as we laid the foundations for Netflix in the late 1990s. And now, I find the text valuable as I work on AI in healthcare, where the opportunities for data-driven medicine are so huge but regulatory and public scrutiny are especially prominent, if dated and hard to interpret in the modern era of privacy in technology.

I frequently encounter teams who have ignored or dismissed privacy as something for later, and this text is both a good antidote to that kind of thinking, and also a good primer on how to make progress getting where they need to be, in a balanced and cost-effective, value-enhancing way.

Enjoy your read!

NEIL HUNT

CHIEF PRODUCT OFFICER, NETFLIX 1999–2017

preface

There are known knowns. These are things we know that we know. There are known unknowns. That is to say, there are things that we know we don't know. But there are also unknown unknowns. There are things we don't know we don't know.
—Donald Rumsfeld, Former United States Secretary of Defense

The above quote by Donald Rumsfeld often came to mind during my early days as a security and privacy engineer. Seemingly trivial problems—locating data, verifying user acceptance, and deleting data—often revealed themselves as unimaginably more complicated than they should have been. The same instincts of data collection and dissemination that served me well in my previous incarnation as an engineer and product manager boomeranged on me in my role as a privacy leader.

I remember looking for resources online and coming up empty. Most frustrating were the moments when those of us working on privacy were deemed by the business to be blockers. The lack of any data hygiene among engineering teams made it hard for me to offer clear and verifiable answers to attorneys representing us in court.

The onset of privacy regulation and scrutiny has led to improvements at companies that use customer data. Even so, existing privacy laws are too segmented and often too confusing. Unsurprisingly, the ambiguity hurts businesses that lack the resources that the bigger companies have. The relationship between businesses and privacy regulators ranges from distrust to disgust, and the consumer is poorer for it.

My favorite example from my Netflix days: The Video Privacy Protection Act (VPPA) was passed by the United States Congress in 1988. It was the outcome of the contentious Supreme Court nomination of Judge Robert Bork. Judge Bork stated that

"Americans enjoy only those privacy protections conferred by legislation." In response, Michael Dolan, a freelance writer for the *Washington City Paper* talked a video store clerk into giving him Bork's rental history.

Congress passed the VPPA to regulate data around our viewing history decades before streaming platforms like Netflix and Amazon Prime existed. These platforms, nonetheless, are impacted by the VPPA's stipulations. Newer privacy laws suffer from flaws, as well, in that they often do not account for the complexity of building technical privacy solutions.

Also, engineering teams increasingly operate in silos with bespoke processes. That has made it increasingly difficult to execute privacy controls in a way that is scalable and measurable. Companies and governments have feasted on too much data for far too long, with too little restraint.

In 2019, I decided to help other engineers and leaders who were trying to solve problems similar to the ones I had wrestled over the years. I started teaching courses on this topic on LinkedIn Learning, and those were well received. My insights and experience were soon sought after by startup founders, mature companies, venture capitalists, and members of the cybersecurity community at large.

I found that my esoteric skills—a mix of engineering, data protection, regulatory policy—enabled me to run massive and impactful privacy programs. If I could aggregate all my learnings, victories, and missteps as a reference for companies, they could start building privacy into their products from the beginning rather than bolting it on at the end.

There is a need in the market, and in government, for a framework that combines business and policy context with hands-on technical skills. I decided to write a book to offer just that.

Over the span of one year when data was spreading worldwide while most of us were locked in place at home, I wrote this book to increase the number of "known knowns" and decrease the number of "known unknowns" and "unknown unknowns."

acknowledgments

This book would not have been possible were it not for the growing cybersecurity community, of which privacy and data protection are a key part. Engineers who constantly strive to protect customer data made for an inspiring target audience as well as north star. The many industry experts who have offered solutions and commentary are too numerous to list, but that does not diminish their contribution.

I want to thank the people at Manning who made this book possible: Publisher Marjan Bace, Editor Ian Hough, Acquisitions Editor Michael Stephens. Candace Gillhoolley and Beth Faris from marketing, and others on the editorial and production teams who worked behind the scenes. A heartfelt thanks also to Michael Jensen for technical reviews that made the book more focused on helping its core engineering constituency.

Sincere gratitude is also in order to mentors and experts in industry who helped my career grow in this space and whose contributions have enriched this book: Anthony Dupre, Larry Drebes, Anne Bradley, Jason Chan, Benjamin Malley, Patrick Mueller, Neil Hunt, Naresh Gopalani, Russell Lewis, Charles Smith, Vikram Khare, Vinay Goel, John "Four" Flynn, Yong Qiao, Ruby Zefo, Derek Care, Uttara Sivaram, Michelle Dennedy, Melanie Ensign, Simon Hania, Mohammad Islam, Catherine Nelson, Peter Dickman, Kim Lucy, Bryan Casper, Ben Feinstein, Engin Bozdag, Calvin Seto, Matt Olsen, Ayana Miller, Ahmed Ibrahim, Avni Verma, Latha Maripuri, Nicolas Lidzborski, Zhengquin Luo, and others.

To all the reviewers: Benjamin Lampert, Brian Liceaga, Des Horsley, Diego Casella, Doniyor Ulmasov, Floris Bouchot, Håvard Wall, Jean-François Beauchef, Jens Gheerardyn, Joe Ivans, John Tyler, Jon Riddle, Jonathan Bourbonnais, Marc Roulleau, Marcin

Sęk, Matthew Todd, Maytham Fahmi, Michael Langdon, Nadia Noori, Osama Khan, Paul Love, Peter White, Pietro Alberto Rossi, Tim Wooldridge, and Willem van Ketwich, your suggestions helped make this a better book.

about this book

This book is intended to serve two purposes. First, it is intended to be a stepping stone for engineers looking to solve privacy problems using tools, automation, and process. I have provided not just hands-on implementation techniques, but also the business context that is critical in fast-moving companies. Second, the book is supposed to help decision-makers in companies, governments, and media provide the right guidance to help businesses thrive as well as protect customer data.

Who should read this book

This book's primary audience is engineers who work with data, especially in highly distributed architectures. They have to solve complex problems and have lacked the framework to embed privacy engineering into their system designs and implementations. This is the first book in the era of cloud computing and identity graphs to help engineers implement complex privacy goals like data governance, technical privacy reviews, data deletion, consent management, etc.

This book will help engineers regardless of whether they choose to build these solutions in-house or onboard third-party solutions. Engineers can also use this book to find overlaps between privacy and security risks, a key consideration given our present threats of ransomware, breaches, and email fraud.

Executives would also benefit from reading this book. While some of the technical details would be out of scope, these readers will be able to partner with engineers more effectively after having read this book to solve privacy problems and make informed decisions.

I also hope that members of the media, regulators, and attorneys use this to build a baseline of knowledge. This will enable them to offer commentary and analysis rooted in context and expertise.

How this book is organized: A roadmap

This book is organized in four parts and 11 chapters. The bookends, i.e. the first and fourth parts, offer contextual guidance and will help engineers develop a scalable privacy program. The second and third parts offer hands-on skills that focus on data governance and tooling respectively.

Part 1 focuses on how privacy engineering fits as part of a company's overall innovation ecosystem:

- Chapter 1 explains how privacy is impacted by the flow of data through the tech stack and storage, and how a company can develop programmatic controls accordingly.
- Chapter 2 explains how data can create privacy risk because of breaches, misuse, and regulations.

Part 2 focuses on data governance so as to enable engineers to manage better the data they collect and its attendant risk:

- Chapter 3 focuses on classifying data with cross-functional partners so as to align with privacy risk.
- Chapter 4 is a deep-dive on data inventory, which entails categorizing data using a mixture of manual and intelligence-powered classification.
- Chapter 5 offers techniques to anonymize datasets and measure privacy impact, using data sharing as a use-case.

Part 3 will help engineers develop mission-critical privacy tooling aimed at improving privacy compliance as well as building customer trust:

- Chapter 6 will help engineers set up a technical privacy review and consulting process to front-load privacy guidance and reduce the strain on the privacy legal team.
- Chapter 7 will walk through a sample architecture for data deletion, a core requirement for data risk minimization as well as for several compliance regimes.
- Chapter 8 will help readers design a data export capability so as to help fulfill "Data Subject Access Requests" or "DSARs."
- Chapter 9 offers a sample design for a Consent Management Platform (CMP) so that businesses can meet this new requirement that is being enforced by regulators and corporations.

Part 4 will help build on the earlier portions of the book and help engineers scale their privacy program:

- Chapter 10 aligns privacy risks to security risks, and offers best practices to mitigate those risks.
- Chapter 11 helps engineers plan maturity models for their privacy offering and their staffing models.

If you are a hands-on engineer, parts 2 and 3 are more directly in line with your imminent needs. More senior engineers will benefit from a fuller reading of the book given their responsibilities often cover the full span of the organization. For executives, members of the media, and regulators, I'd recommend a deep dive in sections 1 and 4, while a more self-paced reading of the more technical middle sections could suffice.

About the code

This book contains examples of source code both in numbered listings and in line with normal text. In both cases, source code is formatted in a `fixed-width font like this` to separate it from ordinary text.

In many cases, the original source code has been reformatted; we've added line breaks and reworked indentation to accommodate the available page space in the book. In rare cases, even this was not enough, and listings include line-continuation markers (➥). Additionally, comments in the source code have often been removed from the listings when the code is described in the text.

You can get executable snippets of code from the liveBook (online) version of this book at https://livebook.manning.com/book/data-privacy. The complete code for the examples in this book is available for download from the Manning website at https://www.manning.com/books/data-privacy.

liveBook discussion forum

Purchase of *Data Privacy* includes free access to liveBook, Manning's online reading platform. Using liveBook's exclusive discussion features, you can attach comments to the book globally or to specific sections or paragraphs. It's a snap to make notes for yourself, ask and answer technical questions, and receive help from the author and other users. To access the forum, go to https://livebook.manning.com/#!/book/data-privacy/discussion. You can also learn more about Manning's forums and the rules of conduct at https://livebook.manning.com/#!/discussion.

Manning's commitment to our readers is to provide a venue where a meaningful dialogue between individual readers and between readers and the author can take place. It is not a commitment to any specific amount of participation on the part of the author, whose contribution to the forum remains voluntary (and unpaid). We suggest you try asking the author some challenging questions lest his interest stray! The forum and the archives of previous discussions will be accessible from the publisher's website as long as the book is in print.

about the author

Nishant Bhajaria has a Bachelor's and a Master's Degree in Computer Science. He has been part of the cybersecurity and privacy community since 2010 and has led teams of various sizes in these areas at Nike, Netflix, Google, and Uber, where he currently leads the privacy engineering organization and reports to the CISO. The organizations he has led have included engineers and architects, data analysts and privacy consultants, as well as product managers and incident response specialists.

After having started his career building teams and programs, he has pivoted to building more strategic programs that enable privacy maturity, partnerships with core engineering and data platform teams, and tighter alignment with the legal and PR teams. His areas of impact range from helping the board of directors make data-driven decisions to coaching product management to operate with fairness and trust as a consideration.

Nishant is also active on the cybersecurity circuit with published white papers on privacy and multiple speaking engagements for industry bodies. He advises startups on data protection strategy and teaches courses on LinkedIn Learning on data privacy (https://www.linkedin.com/learning/instructors/nishant-bhajaria) as well as other areas that include career development and inclusivity in tech staffing. He also partnered with researchers at MIT to draft the first-ever privacy principles for COVID-19 contact tracing (https://law.mit.edu/pub/commentaryoncovid19contacttracingprivacyprinciples/release/1) in the early days of the pandemic.

This eclectic set of contributions map back to his days in college, when he was the rare engineer who wrote editorials for the college paper, was part of the debate team, and worked for political science professors.

Outside of work, there are several causes close to his heart and they center on wild-life. Helping to rescue dogs from kill shelters, fighting back against wildlife smuggling, and protecting elephants from poaching and abuse serve as his moral purpose.

about the cover illustration

The figure on the cover of *Data Privacy* is captioned "Paysanne des Environs de Berne" or, a peasant from the area around Bern, Switzerland. The illustration is taken from a collection of dress costumes from various countries by Jacques Grasset de Saint-Sauveur (1757–1810), titled *Costumes civils actuels de tous les peuples connus,* originally published in France in 1788. Each illustration is finely drawn and colored by hand and the rich variety of drawings in the collection reminds us vividly of how culturally apart the world's regions, towns, villages, and neighborhoods were just 200 years ago. Isolated from each other, people spoke different dialects and languages. In the streets or in the countryside, it was easy to identify where they lived and what their trade or station in life was just by their dress.

Dress codes have changed since then and the diversity by region, so rich at the time, has faded away. It is now hard to tell apart the inhabitants of different continents, let alone different towns or regions. Perhaps we have traded cultural diversity for a more varied personal life—certainly for a more varied and fast-paced technological life.

At a time when it is hard to tell one computer book from another, Manning celebrates the inventiveness and initiative of the computer business with book covers based on the rich diversity of regional life of two centuries ago, brought back to life by pictures from collections such as this one.

Part 1

Privacy, data, and your business

The target audience for this book is engineers, and this book will also be helpful to leaders in management, media and government as well. However, it is critical that all readers are able to place privacy and data protection in context. They need to understand how software engineering has changed in practice, and the corresponding change in business risk. This will help them avoid mistakes that prove to be hard to undo.

Chapter 1 will serve as an advisor on data flow so that technical leaders can understand how their architecture and data work in conjunction. We will also look at the regulatory risks and dive deep into emerging privacy tech players. This context will help the reader approach their privacy challenges with a clear-eyed and informed lens.

Chapter 2 will explore how various business stakeholders have varying interests in data processing. We will also examine high-profile privacy incidents, thereby giving the reader a sense of the vulnerabilities they need to watch for. Finally, there is context on how to monitor investments and build a program that can scale in line with the business.

Privacy engineering: Why it's needed, how to scale it

This chapter covers

- What privacy means
- How privacy is impacted by the flow of data through your tech stack and storage
- Why privacy matters and how it affects your business
- Clarity on privacy tooling, especially the "build vs. buy" debate
- What this book does not do
- How the role of engineers has changed in recent years

Over the last few years, privacy seems to have been front and center in the news. There is talk of new laws aimed at protecting customers from harm and reports of data breaches and fines being levied upon companies.

People at all levels of business are finding this unsettling, and understandably so. Many company founders are engineers or technologists; they are finding it hard to assess risks related to products that depend on data collection. There are other mid-level engineers in companies who write code and build other automation. They make many smaller decisions, and their technical outcomes, when multiplied by scale, can create shareholder and investor risk. Such tech leaders are right to wonder, "what decisions am I making that may have a privacy impact down the line, just as my strategy is about to bear fruit?"

Anyone in a position that will directly or indirectly impact user privacy will benefit from being conversant around privacy as a concept and as a threat vector. Such people need clear hands-on skills for implementing privacy controls. These skills will help them embed privacy engineering and tooling into a company's technical offerings, as well as create privacy controls that break through the silos that typically define tech companies.

Too often, businesses fall into the trap of pitting innovation against privacy, where they build digital products on a foundation of user data, only to play catch up on privacy several cycles later. By this time, there has often been privacy and reputational harm. *Privacy harm* is an all-purpose term that captures the impact of data leakage, exfiltration, or improper access through which a user's privacy is compromised. The loss of privacy protection implies that the user has been harmed; hence the use of this common term. These business leaders then have to find resources and bandwidth to staff a privacy program, prioritize its implementation, and alter the rhythm of business to adapt to privacy scrutiny.

This book will help you avoid this false choice and allow readers—ranging from technical department leaders to hands-on technologists—to think and speak of privacy from a place of knowledge and vision, with an understanding of the big picture as well as brass tacks. After the tools, techniques, and lessons of this book sink in, leaders will be able to adapt to a privacy-centric world. Beyond that, they will also find synergies in their operations to make their privacy posture a competitive differentiator.

In this chapter, we'll begin with the fundamentals: what "privacy" actually means, the privacy implications of data flow within a company, and why privacy matters. The latter part of the chapter will take a brief look at privacy tooling, discuss what this book does *not* do, and consider how the role of engineers has evolved in recent years—an evolution bringing with it implications for privacy. Let's start simple; what is privacy?

1.1   *What is privacy?*

In order to understand privacy, it helps to first refer to security. Most companies and leaders have some sort of security apparatus and at least a superficial understanding of the concept.

For readers of this book, many of whom may need to do double-duty as privacy and security specialists, this is an important insight. If you end up with a security issue, it probably includes something along one of these lines:

- An employee or equivalent insider accesses sensitive business or customer data when they should not have.
- A business partner obtains business or customer data at a time or in a volume that affects the privacy of the customers or the competitive advantage of the business.
- Data that was collected for a benign, defensible purpose gets used for something more than that. For example, data collected for fraud detection by verifying that the user is real rather than a bot then gets used for marketing, because the access control systems were compromised.

Each of these examples started with a security compromise that led to the user's privacy being compromised, besides any other damage done to the business and its competitive advantage. Any time you have a security issue, there is a strong possibility that there will be a privacy harm as well. This is critical for leaders to understand, lest they take a siloed approach and think of these concepts as disconnected and unrelated. In subsequent chapters, the privacy techniques you'll learn will aim at improving both privacy and security, thereby helping companies protect their competitive intellectual property, as well as their user data.

IT security involves implementing a set of cybersecurity strategies aimed at preventing unauthorized access to organizational assets. These assets include computers, networks, and data. The integrity and confidentiality of sensitive information is maintained by validating the identity of users wishing to access the data and blocking those who do not have access rights. You can read more about this from security sources such as Cisco Systems. Cisco defines IT Security as "a set of cybersecurity strategies that prevents unauthorized access to organizational assets such as computers, networks, and data. It maintains the integrity and confidentiality of sensitive information, blocking the access of sophisticated hackers."[1]

Note that the definition covers access to computers (or more broadly, anywhere data can live), networks (where data moves in transit from computer to computer), and the data itself. The goal here is to avoid the data being leaked, modified, or exfiltrated by external bad actors, popularly known as hackers. This definition also introduces the concept of sensitive information, which means different things when it comes to data that belongs to a human being versus data that belongs to a corporation.

As a leader in the privacy space, I have always built privacy programs by adapting and repurposing security tools. This means that I would place an external bad actor (such as a hacker) on the same mental plane as an insider who may knowingly or unknowingly use data inappropriately. As a result, the goal is protecting the data by managing the collection, access, storage, and use of this data. In that sense, rather

[1] "What is IT security," *Cisco*, http://mng.bz/Koag.

than recreating tools and processes for privacy, you can start by adapting the structures aimed at data security, and adjusting them to provide privacy capabilities.

As an example, if you detect unauthorized access from an outsider, you might shut down that account temporarily to investigate whether the account holder is posing a risk or whether the account has been breached. You may also suspend other accounts associated with the same email address, IP address, etc. With an internal user, you may be able to suspend access for just that account and that database, in the event that you find this was not a malevolent act but an incorrect use of access rights. What you have done is deployed security tools with an explicit goal of enhancing privacy and tracking the privacy impact of data access. This creates a sense of continuity and allows for the efficient use of existing tools and relationships rather than creating unneeded tools and processes that could be disruptive.

Let's consider the first of my favored definitions of privacy. According to *The Privacy Engineer's Manifesto*, "Data privacy may be defined as the authorized, fair, and legitimate processing of personal information."[2] Privacy is closely related to security. Without security, there is no privacy, since any access that breaches security protections will be, by definition, unauthorized, unfair, and illegitimate. Where privacy goes a step beyond security is that *security* primarily guards against external bad actors, while *privacy* requires processes and systems to protect data from such misuse internally as well. In that sense, privacy starts once optimum security is in place. As a candidate who I recently interviewed told me, security is a necessary but insufficient condition for privacy.

Implementing such a program requires a level of creativity, since your strategy will impact how your teams operate on an ongoing basis. Rather than try to stymie external threats, privacy controls will seek to influence how your teams connect with users and use their data. This involves, for example, what data you are able to collect, how you affix risk to various types of data, and how you address these questions at scale while petabytes of data course through your systems.

On to a second definition of privacy that I like, since it gives the user a sense of agency even when you use their data in their absence. According to the International Association of Privacy Professionals (IAPP), "Information privacy is the right to have some control over how your personal information is collected and used."[3] We will touch upon this in detail in subsequent chapters, but as privacy has moved front and center in the public imagination, it has empowered users to hold businesses accountable.

However, many feel that there is a need for more accountability. It is likely that public pressure will raise the bar on the privacy protections that are required and the repercussions of failing to meet those requirements. The lessons this book will offer in building your program will help you meet this moment in a scalable fashion that will help your business in the long run.

---

[2] Michelle Dennedy, Jonathan Fox, Tom Finneran, *The Privacy Engineer's Manifesto* (Apress, 2014), p. 34.

[3] "What does privacy mean?" *IAPP*, https://iapp.org/about/what-is-privacy/.

For the purpose of this book's hands-on audience, here is a definition of privacy we will move forward with, integrating the concepts we have discussed: "Data privacy refers to the tooling and processes necessary to protect user data from being processed/accessed in a way that is different from the user's expectation." This definition is important and a personal favorite since it puts the obligation for privacy where, in my opinion, it belongs: on the companies that collect user data and benefit from it.

And while this entire book will focus on the privacy tooling mentioned in the preceding definition, here is a small sample of the topics we will encounter along the way:

- *Data classification*—Defining privacy risks associated with different types of data.
- *Data inventory*—Tagging the data across the storage systems to reflect their classifications.
- *Data deletion*—Deleting data after a predetermined use is complete.
- *Data obfuscation*—Using various anonymization techniques to reduce the likelihood that the data could identify a user. As you will see in chapter 5, the key value privacy engineers can provide is to obfuscate data to preserve privacy while preserving the utility of data for legitimate uses, like using de-identified medical records for aggregated research.

Now that you have a basic understanding of privacy, we'll look at the challenges engineers and technical leaders will face when it comes to data and modern engineering. The next section of this chapter will discuss how technical systems and processes optimized for innovation create data sprawl. After all, we can't effectively plan to manage our data in a privacy-centric manner unless we first understand how that data is ingested and moved throughout companies.

1.2   How data flows into and within your company

Understanding how data flows through an organization is critical, since engineers in many companies are incentivized to focus on their tools and products, and are also allowed their own custom tech stacks, code repositories, and DevOps processes. As a result, they often do not understand the full flow of data and how it spreads in a company's storage systems.

Figure 1.1 illustrates how data enters a company via "producers," which is to say that APIs and other services ingest data in a company. From the perspective of the rest of the company and downstream services, the data could enter the company from customers, third parties, data providers, governments, etc. Typically, this occurs via an API gateway that serves as a single point of initial collection. However, behind the API gateway there are a slew of microservices—a concept we will discuss in detail in subsequent chapters—that process and infer data, and I am, therefore, calling this layer of data collection "producers."

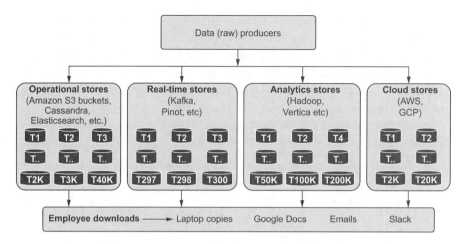

Figure 1.1   Data flow in a company's storage systems: ingestion, stores, and downloads

From the initial "producers" layer, data flows to several layers:

- Operational databases like Cassandra, where data can be stored and accessed rapidly by other applications
- Real-time stores like Kafka, Pinot, and other distributed event-streaming platforms used by companies for high-performance data pipelines, streaming analytics, data integration, and other mission-critical applications
- Analytics stores like Hadoop, Vertica, and others, from which data analysts and data scientists run queries for business intelligence purposes
- Cloud stores like Amazon Web Services (AWS), Google Cloud Platform (GCP), and others, where data can be stored and archived

However, as the diagram shows, data also makes it into other systems that may be hard to manage and audit, such as employee laptops, productivity software like Google Docs and Microsoft Word, emails, and chat channels. Simply put, in a modern business, it is critical to realize that the instincts and best practices that have accelerated innovation—decentralized development, distributed and redundant data storage— make it harder to build at scale the privacy tools I referenced in the last section, be it data deletion, access control, risk mitigation, and the like.

The spread of data also inevitably inflates the volume of data across the organization. Figure 1.2 shows that a high volume of data ingestion and distribution leads to a large number of data stores, tables, and files, and to maybe even upwards of an exabyte of data.

When technical leaders try to build privacy tooling and technical processes, they need to also ensure that their tooling applies to the massive volumes of data described previously. To do so, they will need a catalog or inventory of data so that they can deploy their tooling in a targeted fashion (chapter 4 will cover that topic). Technical leaders need to take this into consideration as they build privacy tools, seek buy-in for these tools, and budget to scale their efforts. Merely projecting privacy as an altruistic

Number of data stores: 10+
Hadoop, Schemaless, Cassandra, etc.

Number of tables ~ 300K

Number of files: 800M+

Data at rest ~ 1EB

Figure 1.2   A company's storage systems that house distributed data

nice-to-have is a missed opportunity to deliver tangible benefits for your business. Simply put, privacy engineering is a lot cheaper if you build it in instead of trying to bolt it on, given the spread of data in your systems.

In the next section, we'll dive deeper into why privacy matters for your business. The arguments and examples we will examine will help connect the work of engineers to the legal angle of privacy and then to overall business growth. This will help you make the case for better privacy within your own context.

1.3   *Why privacy matters*

I expect readers of this book will range from the doers to the dreamers. The *doers* include the technical program managers, engineers, data architects, cloud and DevOps specialists, and the leaders who wear many hats but have a singular goal: to maintain business operations continuity and predictability. The *dreamers* include the technically oriented startup founders, the technologist disrupters, and the venture capitalists who will fuel tomorrow's ideas.

Dreamers optimize for delivery and rapidity, while doers optimize for execution and consistency. All these goals could be thwarted if or when privacy issues stop companies in their tracks. However, as stated previously, too many leaders, fueled by achievements in other areas, believe themselves invulnerable and impervious to privacy risks. They also believe that governmental enforcement muscles have atrophied, owing to politicians' reluctance to stymie the entrepreneurs who create untold amounts of wealth and work for the United States and other countries worldwide. That confidence may be unfounded.

1.3.1   *The fines are real*

The passage of legislation like the EU's General Data Protection Regulation (GDPR)—which we will look at in subsequent chapters—has allowed regulators to fine companies found to be wanting in privacy.

Figure 1.3 shows one way in which privacy issues impact businesses. The financial penalties enforced by government authorities on companies are real and consequential. Large businesses with proven profit models may be able to endure the financial burden of such fines, but smaller companies may find them debilitating. Startups may find that resources dedicated to funding new initiatives and hiring key personnel may get diverted to these fines. Venture capitalists may find their investment and prestige attached to a stillborn venture that will struggle to take off amid a financial cloud.

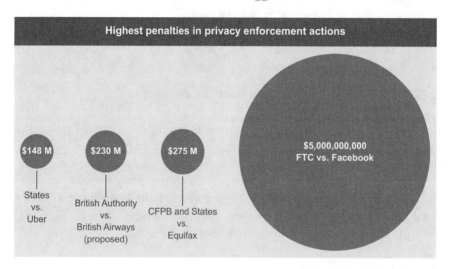

Figure 1.3   Highest penalties in privacy enforcement actions[4]

No business is outside of the risk of having their privacy compromised or beneath the attention of regulators. Penalties could fall upon the head of any business, and that is why these fines are important to consider. In some cases, the fines are revised downward—the British Airways fine shrank to $20 million,[5] but it is unwise to depend on luck or clemency, especially if you are a company that lacks deep clout or roots.

One of my industry mentors recently told me that Equifax should have been fined more aggressively after its famous 2017 breach.[6] The credit agency has the power to collect my intimate financial details without my consent and to drive decisions around my creditworthiness. Equifax then leaked so much of that data through processes that were so sloppy and inappropriate that even a junior privacy or security engineer could have identified them as risky. It is especially galling that consumers like you and I have to pay about $120 per year to lock down credit reports, not to mention the costs to businesses who have to absorb such costs as well.

---

[4] http://mng.bz/9aZq.

[5] "ICO fines British Airways £20m for data breach affecting more than 400,000 customers," *ICO*, October 16, 2020, http://mng.bz/WBWl.

[6] Josh Fruhlinger, "Equifax data breach FAQ: What happened, who was affected, what was the impact?" *CSO*, February 12, 2020, http://mng.bz/80A5.

Why should engineers have to worry about fines? Isn't their job to build stuff and fail fast, while the folks in legal and compliance manage the business risk? Besides the obvious answer—that no company has endless resources to pay fines—it is vital that engineers understand that their work now involves more than building features, driving engagement, and monetizing data. They need to understand the permissibility of their actions as well as the downstream impacts of present-day decisions.

The next subsection will discuss an example where well-meaning customer-driven decisions made early in the innovation process caused privacy headaches downstream.

1.3.2 Early-stage efficiency wins can cause late-stage privacy headaches

During the early stage of innovation, and even when companies try to drive product adoption, engineers make a number of decisions to appeal to venture capitalists (VCs) as well as business-to-business (B2B) and business-to-consumer (B2C) customers. That makes sense, because funding and early adoption are necessary, if insufficient, conditions to the sort of transformative change that engineering leaders seek. Let's look at a scenario in which a lack of long-term strategy led to some serious issues for a company.

GAMESBUSTER: A CASE STUDY

There was a company—let's call it *Gamesbuster*—that built video game apps for smart TVs. The goal was to engage the user as soon as the smart TV turned on. In order to achieve that goal, it was critical that the app be ready as soon as the TV turned on, because the user might otherwise move on to other apps.

To guarantee that the app would launch with low degrees of latency upon the smart TV turning on, the engineers at Gamesbuster conceived of automation logic called "Boot to Suspend" mode. This was a persistent background mode initiated on device boot that would communicate regularly with Gamesbuster servers to receive updates and keep the application in a "ready for use" state.

In order for Boot to Suspend mode to perform its function, it was necessary for Gamesbuster servers to receive information from the devices, including IP addresses, which was automatically sent via standard internet communication protocols. It was critical to collect these IP addresses, the engineers reasoned, since location information inferred from the IP addresses would enable them to personalize the app for users.

This feature was the brainchild of two engineers who wanted to make sure that the games they featured were not abandoned by their target audience while their much-desired features loaded: young folks who were not exactly known for their patience. These engineers did not comprehend the nature of the data that would change hands when the devices communicated with the Gamesbuster servers. This was a page out of the "fail fast and make things" handbook.

As Boot to Suspend caught on, it went from being a strict engineering idea to a possible business growth opportunity. Sales teams saw an opportunity to ensure that partners who carried Gamesbuster apps were aware of this option and supported it.

Based on their contract negotiations, partners that preloaded the Gamesbuster app on their devices were strongly encouraged to implement Boot to Suspend. In time, the number of devices supporting Boot to Suspend, the number of users, and, in turn, the amount of data streaming into Gamesbuster servers grew explosively. This meant significant revenue upside for Gamesbuster's engineering founders, as well as its innovative technical workforce. Investors noticed this success and poured more money into Gamesbuster's coffers.

Investors were not the only ones noticing, however. Regulators who were charged with protecting privacy rights of users were concerned that Gamesbuster was collecting location information from customers. The data may have been collected by the engineers without malicious intent, but it was collected by them while their app was running in the background (which is essentially what Boot to Suspend was); the data, therefore, was collected before the user signed in and accepted the privacy policies and other disclosures that typically allow companies to collect user data.

The regulators demanded that Gamesbuster stop collecting IP addresses without consent, and if it absolutely needed to collect them, their engineers needed to store them in separate databases with very limited access and to automate deletion once the app launched and the data had been used for its intended personalization purposes.

In order to ensure that they could detect exactly what data they were collecting, the engineers who pioneered Boot to Suspend created filters that would detect fields named "IP address." However, a few months later, when the regulators audited the data warehouses in Gamesbuster's systems, they found millions of IP addresses that were retained for months. This was in clear violation of the commitments Gamesbuster had made to the regulators.

How did this happen? There were two key reasons:

- The filters the engineers built would have detected values like IP addresses as long as they were in a structured data format, where each entity was defined as a key/value pair. As it turned out, an increasing number of partner devices that preloaded the Gamesbuster app transferred data to the servers in the form of JSON blobs. For the purposes of this example, a *JSON blob* is a single field with JSON-format text stored in it. Ergo, the database had no real knowledge of any of the keys in the blob or their values. This meant that the Gamesbuster filters could not detect the IP addresses; rather than storing them in special limited-access tables, the Gamesbuster systems allowed these IP addresses to mingle with other data and to be stored alongside other data that was permitted to be used freely.

- When such IP addresses were successfully intercepted and were logged in the one permissible table, they were stored for 30 days' use. However, the engineers granted access to this table to the security team for critical security purposes, such as preventing and researching DDOS attacks and other security-related incidents. However, it turned out that various automated scripts queried this table as a source, and IP data was then copied and stored in other tables for longer than 30 days. In other words, neither tight access controls nor retention periods were enforced as was promised to the regulators.

The auditor investigation threatened the company's business model, since a company under investigation for misuse of location data would struggle to find partners willing to host the app. This would lead to a slowdown in customer growth and engagement, which in turn would lead to a slowdown in ad revenue. As a result, the company had to take several remedial actions:

- First, they had to delete IP addresses en masse, which meant that in some cases they had to be overcautious and even delete IP addresses that had been collected legitimately. It was impossible to be certain which IP addresses were collected in Boot to Suspend mode, and the lack of a data inventory hampered what could have been a more targeted deletion effort. In later chapters I'll discuss how a front-loaded governance program could help.
- Second, this effort led to a disruption of new feature development, since the company could not rely on existing data and revenue streams until the investigation concluded. As a result, several product roadmaps were impacted, and ambitious engineers whose promotions depended on building new features left for newer companies with less regulatory scrutiny.
- Third, the company had to create a restrictive compliance regime that hurt the speed with which products could be deployed and built. The "move fast and make things" model was replaced by the "fill forms and check things" model.

The lessons for engineers are clear: building new data-driven features without a privacy lens carries significant risks. It behooves engineers and technical leaders to build privacy tooling and processes as they develop core products and features. Later in this book, we will dive deep into a detailed engineering-focused privacy review process that will help protect data privacy while empowering engineers to be ingenuous and productive as they innovate.

Just as the fines can be financially crippling for companies, so can the investigations themselves. It is critical that engineers and technical leaders (founders and their funders) understand the potency of regulatory attack on their roadmaps. We'll consider this in the following subsection.

1.3.3 *Privacy investigations could be more than a speed bump*

Regulations around privacy and security are relatively new, and knowledge among regulators about privacy technology can be fairly embryonic, given the novel concepts involved. Additionally, millions around the world are connecting to the internet for the first time, and companies are inferring information about users by combining data from different databases and identities that were out of their reach a decade ago.

Just as the potential of techniques like artificial intelligence and machine learning grows by the day, so does the potential for abuse and investigations. It is hard to predict the impact such investigations and audits will have on qualitative innovation, but I want to offer an example of a far-reaching governmental investigation that stifled the plans of one of America's most successful companies and altered the trajectory of technology.

Antitrust laws ensure one company doesn't control the market, deplete consumer choice, and inflate prices. In the late 1990s, the US Department of Justice accused Microsoft Corporation of trying to create a monopoly that led to the collapse of rival Netscape by providing its browser software for free. Charges were brought against the company, which was sued by the Department of Justice in 1998. Until this investigation, Microsoft seemed unstoppable.

That investigation disrupted Microsoft's business model and its day-to-day operations. In a recent interview, founder and business icon Bill Gates stated that Windows could have been the world's dominant mobile operating system had it not been for the antitrust case the US Department of Justice brought against Microsoft.[7]

"There's no doubt the antitrust lawsuit was bad for Microsoft, and we would have been more focused on creating the phone operating system, and so instead of using Android today, you would be using Windows Mobile if it hadn't been for the antitrust case," Gates said at the New York Times' DealBook conference in New York. Microsoft remains dominant with Windows on desktop PCs and in other categories like commercial productivity software, but it no longer works on Windows for phones. Alphabet's Google currently has the most popular mobile operating system, with Apple's iPhone in second place.

"Oh, we were so close," Gates said about the company's miss in mobile operating systems. "I was just too distracted. I screwed that up because of the distraction." He said the company was three months too late with a release Motorola would have used on a phone. "Now nobody here has ever heard of Windows Mobile."[8]

As I write this book, the most far-reaching privacy laws are less than five years old, but Gates's comments have a clear implication: major cases against today's technology companies could have negative market implications. Lest you think Microsoft was an anomaly, consider this: antitrust laws grew from theoretical to directly impactful over many years. Privacy could follow a similar trajectory in today's political climate.

Let's look as some other more recent fines and sanctions. In 2017, before its troubles with Cambridge Analytica, Facebook faced multiple fines within a 24-hour window:

---

[7] Jordan Novet, "For a sense of what Elizabeth Warren's antitrust crusade would do to tech, look back at Microsoft," *CNBC*, March 9, 2019, http://mng.bz/EDvX.

[8] Jordan Novet, "Bill Gates says people would be using Windows Mobile if not for the Microsoft antitrust case," *CNBC*, November 6, 2019, http://mng.bz/N4pv.

- WhatsApp was fined €3M by the Italian antitrust regulator for "inducing" WhatsApp users to share data with Facebook (that is, they had to share data or lose access to the app).
- The next day, the European Commission fined Facebook €110M in an antitrust action for providing inaccurate information about its ability to automatically correlate Facebook and WhatsApp user accounts. Facebook said in 2014 it couldn't, but then in 2016 it suddenly could by leveraging common phone numbers.
- That same day, France, Belgium, and the Netherlands each announced that Facebook had violated their respective data privacy laws in connection with Facebook's 2014 global revision of its user agreements, through inappropriate data collection and use practices. France imposed a fine of €150K (the current maximum); Belgium and the Netherlands may impose fines. Spain and Germany announced investigations into the matter.

It is helpful to understand some details about how these investigations blurred the lines between antitrust and privacy.

€110M EUROPEAN COMMISSION FINE FOR WHATSAPP DATA MISREPRESENTATIONS

During the antitrust regulator's review of the $19B acquisition deal, Facebook claimed twice in 2014 that it could not "establish reliable automated matching" between Facebook and WhatsApp accounts. Then, in 2016, WhatsApp announced updates to its TOS and privacy policy, including linking WhatsApp to Facebook accounts via phone numbers. The Commission cried foul and imposed the large fine but agreed not to revisit the merger approval. The fine could have ranged up to 1% of global revenue (approximately $270M based on Facebook's 2016 numbers).[9]

- *Key insight*—EU antitrust regulators believe that consumer data use rights and promises are important in analyzing mergers and enforcing competition law. Also, the EU appears ready to impose large fines against US tech companies. Time will tell if the EU data-protection authorities leverage their ability to do so under GDPR (fines up to 4% of global revenue).
- *What engineers and technical leaders need to know*—It is impossible to know for certain how engineers at Facebook had stored phone numbers in their databases, what corrective controls existed (if any) to prevent the linking of accounts based on phone numbers, and how those controls were overcome to then link those accounts.

    What is true, however, is that European authorities considered the commitment that the two databases would be kept separate to be ironclad. That turned out not to be the case. Engineers often find value in linking two sets of data

---

[9] Mark Scott, "E.U. Fines Facebook $122 Million Over Disclosures in WhatsApp Deal," *New York Times*, May 8, 2017, http://mng.bz/DKnA; "Mergers: Commission fines Facebook €110 million for providing misleading information about WhatsApp takeover," European Commission press release, May 18, 2017, http://mng.bz/l9md.

about the same user because the combined dataset provides better visibility for personalization and monetization, or they may have simply been able to secure the combined dataset better based on a unique value like a phone number.

Either way, an engineering decision to link two sets of data that in turn affected the privacy rights of those users was then viewed through the lens of a commitment made by Facebook during a merger/acquisition transaction. Technical founders and other such leaders must ask themselves, "What are the privacy implications of their data handling practices, and could they affect long-term strategic growth opportunities for their business?" How many such decisions are engineers making every single day with a very limited understanding of privacy that could then snowball into something larger down the line?" Having verifiable data cataloging could help mitigate some of these harms, and you will see how in chapter 4.

The key technical takeaway for engineers is that well-meaning decisions made with convenience in mind might run afoul of legal commitments and representations, so having solid data governance as well as tighter coupling between engineering and legal is critical.

€3M WHATSAPP FINE FROM ITALIAN ANTITRUST REGULATOR

At least one EU member state (Italy) decided to impose its own antitrust fine for the Facebook/WhatsApp account linking. The rationale in the decision focused on an important data protection concept: whether the WhatsApp users consented to their accounts being combined with their Facebook accounts. The regulator concluded that WhatsApp/Facebook placed "excessive emphasis" on the need to agree with the new TOS and privacy policy as part of an in-app upgrade.

- *Key insight*—Certain EU antitrust authorities appear willing to apply data protection and privacy principles when finding an anti-competitive harm has taken place.
- *What engineers and technical leaders need to know*—In this specific case, whether users had consented to a specific use of their data was an area of focus for investigators and regulators. The regulators also seemed to wish that users were not pressured to consent to terms of use and instead provided informed consent.

Engineers often believe in refactoring code to make it more efficient and scalable. They take a similar approach to disparate sets of data that describe the same users. The lesson for engineers and technical leaders is that while they may feel that a combined dataset could increase their understanding of the user, privacy-focused regulators wish to ensure that user rights are not violated. It is vital that engineers work closely with their legal counterparts to ensure users have consented to such data aggregation.

FIVE EU DATA PROTECTION AUTHORITIES PURSUE FACEBOOK FOR 2014 POLICY CHANGES AND OTHER DATA ACTIVITIES

The wheels of justice grind slowly. Although Facebook's 2014 changes to its privacy policy are long forgotten by most users, five EU data protection authorities (DPAs) took note and launched investigations. In May 2017, three of the DPAs announced their findings, while one other had previously announced a judgment (Hamburg, Germany) and the last (Spain) has an investigation pending.[10] Here is a breakdown:

- *France*—The DPA found these violations: (1) no legal basis to combine user information for online behavioral advertising purposes, (2) unlawful tracking via "datr" cookie, and (3) insufficient notice and consent for a Like button on third-party sites. They imposed a €150K fine.
- *Belgium*—The DPA concluded that Facebook violated and *continued* to violate Belgian data protection law through its use of cookies, social plug-ins, and pixels, such as by collecting excessive personal data, including from non-members. The DPA is seeking a court order to enforce the changes it seeks to impose on Facebook's practices.
- *Netherlands*—Among the more relevant findings in this case are the DPA's determinations (1) that it had authority over Facebook (rather than the Irish DPA), (2) that the Like button data collection and use practices are unlawful (a common theme among the DPAs) because they did not provide adequate notice around data collection, and (3) that Facebook's privacy disclosures are too deeply layered to be sufficient (I've seen the Dutch DPA raise this concern before, in a separate 2015 investigation). The DPA is assessing whether Facebook has changed its practices to comply with Dutch data protection law, and if not, it may seek fines.
- *Germany*—The Hamburg DPA previously ordered Facebook to stop combining data from WhatsApp users without their prior consent and to delete the data that had previously been shared.

So what do these country-specific outcomes teach us?

- *Key insight*—Even though Facebook vigorously argued that only the Irish DPA should have jurisdiction and only Irish data protection law should apply, all of the DPAs found that their local laws applied (the jurisdictional hook typically involved a local, in-country Facebook entity).
- *What engineers and technical leaders need to know*—There is often a substantial lag between engineering decisions and the privacy law implications. In the case of the Belgium investigation, the authorities contended that Facebook had collected "excessive personal data." Engineers have often followed an approach of collecting data with an eye toward the future, and retaining data for as long as

---

[10]"Common Statement by the Contact Group of the Data Protection Authorities of The Netherlands, France, Spain, Hamburg and Belgium," Autoriteit Persoonsgegevens, May 16, 2017, http://mng.bz/B16w.

possible with the belief that it may be of use at a later date. Authorities are now cracking down on data collection and retention unless there is a legitimate business purpose.

In the case of the Netherlands investigation, the level of transparency and visibility provided to users came under scrutiny. In order to prevent such adverse actions, it is vital that engineers are deliberate and that they communicate with their legal counterparts as well as UX designers so that users can be informed correctly about data collection.

Finally, in the Germany example, engineers had to delete data that they had previously collected and joined with other data. As you saw in the Gamesbuster example, these deletions can be prohibitively expensive and technically disruptive. Engineers should invest in deletion tooling so as to avoid inefficient and error-prone deletion, something we will dive into in subsequent chapters.

The lesson here is clear: decisions technical leaders make during early innovation, growth, and acquisition stages can lead to privacy harms, investigations, and fines downstream. This book is aimed at helping you solidify your technical privacy foundations so that the breezes of regulations do not send your monument crumbling down. Additionally, engineers can no longer just write code, collect data, and build features with scant regard for the regulatory implications of their actions. This book will help engineers build innovative systems with technical privacy controls in a manner that will accelerate their work without having to clean up after the fact.

So far, we have seen the importance of privacy from a defensive standpoint, whereby things can go sideways for companies because of long-ago technical decisions. Companies can, however, make correct decisions at the front end to put in place solid privacy practices. This could help unlock business opportunities and set the stage for future success.

1.3.4   *Privacy process can unlock business opportunities: A real-life example*

In 2012, I was employed by a small startup that sought to innovate in the digital identity space. Our products included a global openID that would allow you to authenticate with multiple websites without a username and password, and it allowed for federated sessions across different web properties and backend data collection for easy customer research.

As with most startups, we were idea-heavy and process-light. Engineers eschewed top-down mandates to document code, review data collection, and ensure consistency between public disclosures and privacy practices. In time, however, in order to raise our Series B funding, it became critical to sell to customers who themselves were tightly regulated and were often located in jurisdictions that were privacy-sensitive, like the European Union.

At the time, far-reaching privacy laws like the EU's General Data Protection Regulation (GDPR) did not exist, so demonstrating our maturity as a privacy-conscious company was to prove difficult. The company's senior vice president of engineering asked me to pursue an ISO 27001 certification: "ISO/IEC 27001 formally specifies an Information Security Management System (ISMS), a governance arrangement comprising a structured suite of activities with which to manage information risks (called 'information security risks' in the standard)."[11]

The ISMS would prove to our would-be customers that we had technical processes in place to manage data protection; this was critical, since our tools would enable our customers to handle data they collected from their customers. Without a solid technical framework in place, no major corporation would trust a small American startup with massive amounts of customer data. As a young engineer who sought to work on new technical skills as well as differentiate myself from my fellow engineers, I dove deep into the ISO standard.

The ISO/IEC 27001 standard has two distinct purposes:

1. *It lays out the design for an ISMS, describing the important parts at a fairly high level;*
2. *It can (optionally) be used as the basis for formal compliance assessment by accredited certification auditors in order to certify an organization compliant.*

The following mandatory documentation is explicitly required for certification:

1. *ISMS scope (as per clause 4.3)*
2. *Information security policy (clause 5.2)*
3. *Information risk assessment process (clause 6.1.2)*
4. *Information risk treatment process (clause 6.1.3)*
5. *Information security objectives (clause 6.2)*
6. *Evidence of the competence of the people working in information security (clause 7.2)*
7. *Other ISMS-related documents deemed necessary by the organization (clause 7.5.1b)*
8. *Operational planning and control documents (clause 8.1)*
9. *The results of the [information] risk assessments (clause 8.2)*
10. *The decisions regarding [information] risk treatment (clause 8.3)*
11. *Evidence of the monitoring and measurement of information security (clause 9.1)*
12. *The ISMS internal audit program and the results of audits conducted (clause 9.2)*
13. *Evidence of top management reviews of the ISMS (clause 9.3)*
14. *Evidence of nonconformities identified and corrective actions arising (clause 10.1)[12]*

As we started making progress on building these requisite tooling and processes, I noticed the following changes:

- The mere fact that we were pursuing the certification created more interest among VCs willing to fund us and support us.
- Conservative and risk-averse companies in the United States and Europe started using our tools, since they now had confidence that we could handle their data securely.

---

[11]ISO/IEC 27001:2013, Information security management systems—Requirements, second edition, www.iso27001security.com/html/27001.html.
[12]ISO/IEC 27001:2013.

- Engineers within the company came around to the fact that some of the tools and processes made their work more efficient and improved data quality, and they helped me shape some of my work; this, in turn, helped us create much-needed structure in a company that badly needed it.

Over time, this certification made us a more mature company, built a solid customer base, and got us through a difficult recession. Personally, the effort I put in to understand massive backend systems, data pipelines, and technologies like Hadoop and Kafka made me a better engineer. That enabled me to land very senior technical leadership roles at companies like Netflix, Google, and Uber, teach courses on LinkedIn, and then author this book on technical privacy.

The lesson for engineers is this: privacy is not just about avoiding fines and rework; when done right, it can differentiate your technical offering and boost your company as well as your career.

You have so far seen how privacy can impact companies in terms of regulatory fines and inefficiencies born of short-sighted technical decisions. You have also seen the salubrious effects of good privacy practices. How your performance in this space affects societal trust, safety, and relationships is critical for engineers to grasp. The following section will make all of this a little more concrete, as we consider how the workflow looks, first within a company not following good privacy practices, and then within a company that does follow good practices.

1.4   Privacy: A mental model

We have discussed why privacy matters, but to bring that home, let's consider a scenario in which a company is not following good privacy practices. Then we'll look at how things will change when good practices are followed. This section will give you a brief overview of some of the core tenets of privacy engineering, which I will expand upon as the book progresses.

Figure 1.4 shows a company that orchestrates privacy the wrong way. The company developed an app that runs on smart TVs, and the moment the customer turns on the TV, data starts flowing from the TV to the company's servers. Notice how data is ingested into the company. It is then shared, copied, multiplied, and stored across various systems, and it is not classified or inventoried until late in the workflow. By that point, it is possible that engineers and their tools will have used the data that causes privacy issues. The company is left with a real headache in organizing and dealing with this proliferated data. We will discuss this further in chapter 4, but for now let's consider the implications of collecting this much data, not knowing what portions of it cause privacy risks, and failing to protect it correctly. It is possible that many breaches, fines, and privacy abuses arise out of sloppy designs like this one!

In this book, my aim is to have you think about good privacy measures as a foundational component within your business. Data should go through privacy measures as soon as it enters the company, leading to much more effective data management, more control over who can access what, and a much lower likelihood of a privacy violation

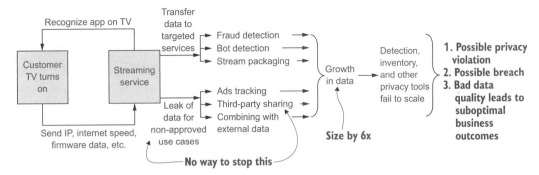

Figure 1.4 Privacy done wrong—data flows into a company and is not dealt with in a privacy sense until it has already proliferated throughout the company via sharing and copying. Privacy tools may not scale well for such a volume of data, and privacy violations become much more likely.

taking place. Figure 1.5 illustrates a company that is doing it right. Chapters 3–9 will equip you to view privacy the same way as this company does. You will learn to architect sound data governance to help identify privacy risks at the point of ingestion, and you will learn to build the right tooling, automation, and processes to enforce privacy protections. This sequence—governance followed by tooling—is important and will help engineers improve privacy while also enriching data quality and productivity.

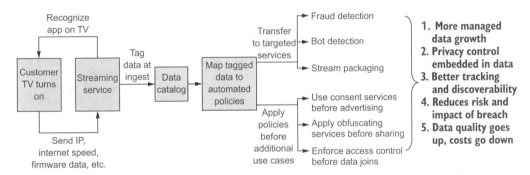

Figure 1.5 Privacy done right—data flows into a company and is immediately tagged and cataloged. Data becomes much more manageable, and privacy measures work effectively. Privacy violation is much less likely to occur.

Let's zoom in a little on the company in figure 1.5 and see the processes in play throughout the privacy process. Figure 1.6 demonstrates how tagging and cataloging is to work in this brave new world. We will discuss these techniques in a lot more detail later in this book, but this diagram shows how the values of individual data fields will change right after they enter our ecosystem. You can see that the fields are ingested with their core values, and then we append a tag that indicates their privacy risk. The box labeled "Data Tagging Service" is a simplistic placeholder for an entire data inventory infrastructure that you will learn about in great detail.

For now, the key takeaway is that this early-stage tagging will allow you to affix enforceable data handling policies (deletion, retention, etc.) to the data. This creates a privacy engineering architecture where privacy controls are baked in early, onto the data itself. The figure makes a simple point: there is no secret sauce to privacy—just timely identification and automated orchestration.

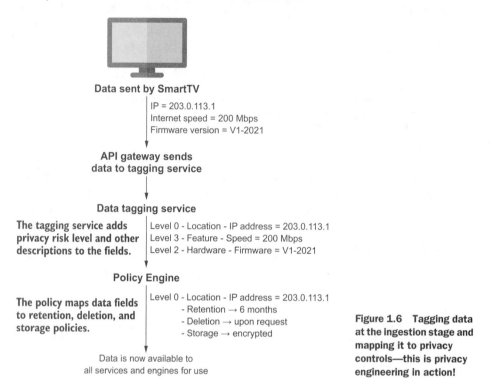

Figure 1.6 Tagging data at the ingestion stage and mapping it to privacy controls—this is privacy engineering in action!

We have considered the privacy workflow at a high level, and I will expand upon these themes over the course of this book. For now, I hope that this has given you a clearer idea of the privacy process, and the implications of both managing it poorly and managing it well.

Having considered the concrete implications of privacy engineering, let's continue and consider things in a slightly more abstract sense. The following section is aimed at engineers who feel like they have to choose between shipping a feature and earning trust.

1.5   *How privacy affects your business at a macro level*

Before you fall into the trap of making tactical adjustments for privacy and calling that a win, let's look at how major shifts in the business climate or regulatory sentiment could also affect privacy implementation at your company. We will look at two examples that are quite recent. First we will consider the fact that, as in our offline lives, our online lives and the ways in which we do business rely upon trust and safety. Following that, we'll consider the implications of privacy regulation upon the way your business should operate.

1.5.1   *Privacy and safety: The COVID edition*

In companies large and small, engineers and other technical leaders will ask questions like these:

- With finite resources and challenging roadmaps, why on earth are we dedicating so much time to privacy?
- Everyone collects data, and we have seen companies be really bad at privacy and their stock price seems to soar. Why care about privacy?

The answers may seem counterintuitive, but they are obvious once given some thought. Businesses operate based on predictability, and they prosper based on trust. When predictability is disrupted and trust is eroded, business viability tends to suffer.

We can draw an interesting parallel with the coronavirus. The pandemic changed how we lived our lives. Bustling streets, teeming sports centers, overflowing conference halls, glowing wedding venues—all of them went silent. Human connectivity has historically been a symbol of comfort and aspiration. In the times of coronavirus, it became a threat vector, an ingestion point for contagion.

Physical human mobility, and the commerce that stems from it, builds on a foundation of trust and safety. When those components disappear, our economic engines stop moving, atrophy, and start receding. In much the same way, the lives we live online are built on trust and safety.

When I first moved to the United States in 2000 as a teenager, I'd call my parents using expensive phone cards. Besides the cost, the process was painful: a toll-free number followed by a long PIN, which was then followed by a potentially unreliable connection. Adding funds to the card and procuring a new one were not trivial either.

Two decades hence, reaching my parents in Mumbai has gotten easier and cheaper. WhatsApp, Skype, and Google Meet allow data-driven connectivity that is reliable, fast, and cheap. It is ubiquitous and personal. I can see them, send them information mid-chat, and connect that conversation to other media. That connectivity and intimacy occurs on the foundation of safety, as do all my other online activities: ordering groceries, getting food delivered, hailing a rideshare, booking tickets. Online commerce relies on trust and safety.

If you are an engineer whose tools thrive on the exchange of goods, ideas, money, and information online, you benefit from this trust and, as such, are responsible for its safe upkeep. Just as the habits of a lifetime were paused by fear of a virus, online commerce is similarly vulnerable to a deficit of trust, and privacy is a component of this trust. If your customers feel like their data and their identity are not safe in your custody, their patronage will go elsewhere. That is why engineers need to care about privacy.

Then there is the matter of your reputation and legal compliance. Newly passed laws offer regulators the tools to peek into your privacy practices like never before. The ensuing scrutiny is likely to shed light on past decisions that were made based on a very different set of data but that in the present circumstances make for suboptimal privacy outcomes.

Privacy is no longer an altruistic endeavor that companies can optionally partake in; public awareness and concern with privacy is keener than it has ever been, and businesses are under ever-increasing scrutiny with regard to how they handle and protect their customers' data. Mistakes and bad decisions that companies make are more likely than ever to be brought to light. You should look at your privacy program as an investment that will enable you to protect your customers and that will promote your business as worthy of trust.

Having said all of that, the following subsection will explain why companies that use customer data need to think about public sentiment, laws, regulations, investigations, and business growth as interconnected, much like trust and business growth are interconnected. Many hands-on leaders are so busy with the day-to-day that they fail to find time to make these connections, and they feel like they are always in catch-up reactive mode, and never have time to set vision.

1.5.2   *Privacy and regulations: A cyclical process*

It helps to understand how and why privacy is so important for business success. Figure 1.7 shows an obvious first step, in which a government passes privacy laws.

Figure 1.7   In a general sense, a government produces privacy law and regulations.

However, figure 1.7 overlooks the fact that unlike tax law, where you have one law for the state where you live or where your company is incorporated and then one federal law, you could have several governments passing several privacy laws. To that end, figure 1.8 shows two influential jurisdictions with two privacy laws. For example, the EU passed the General Data Protection Regulation (GDPR) that has been in effect since May 2018, while California's law, the California Consumer Privacy Act (CCPA), has been in effect since January 2020.

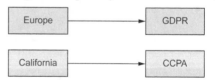

Figure 1.8   Things become complicated when we have multiple governments and authorities introducing different laws and regulations.

Once these laws are in effect, they are available to regulators and auditors. Regulators can launch investigations into companies and into practices of those companies that may even predate the passage of those laws. Simultaneously, companies could be subject to audits to prove compliance with these laws, and may need to demonstrate compliance before they can sign enterprise contracts or gain access to specific markets. Figure 1.9 makes that point.

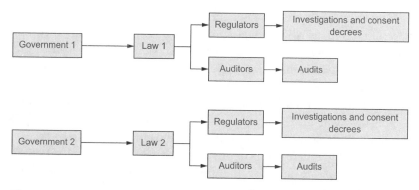

Figure 1.9   **The chain of events brought about by multiple governments producing their own laws and regulations**

As figure 1.9 shows, you could have several governments passing several different privacy laws, and these laws in turn could spur concurrent audits, investigations, and consent decrees (where a government and company agree to a specific outcome of an investigation). For small companies, where a few key team members handle IT, security, and privacy all at once, this can represent a significant operational burden. It will almost certainly impact productivity and throughput. This book focuses on hands-on skills aimed at preventing such harms as much as possible and mitigating those that occur as expeditiously as possible. Embedding privacy into the data and design of products is critical, and this book will dive deep into these techniques.

There is yet another layer to consider: Laws and regulations do not occur in a vacuum. When it comes to areas like security and privacy, they are often a response to events. Breaches, data leaks, inappropriate access to data, improper identification or re-identification of users, and other misuses of personally identifying information have occurred with some regularity over the last few years. After repeated incidents of this type, media and privacy activists start paying close attention to companies that are considered bad actors in privacy. Such attention leads to critical press coverage, which then leads to public awareness.

If you are a small company, this could result in loss of business and damaged relationships. For larger companies, this creates a reputational dark cloud that lingers even after the crisis passes. In either case, the hardening of public opinion and sustained press coverage leads to privacy laws. So, regardless of the size of your business, it is critical that you take steps early to address privacy gaps, lest they become chasms.

As any savvy PR expert will tell you, the best form of damage control is to control the extent of damage you cause. As a technical leader who wears many hats, you have to ask yourself, "When would you rather optimize for sound privacy and data governance?" Is it in the early days of the enterprise when you are organizing the strategy, will it be in reaction to the first privacy issue, or will it be when you are in crisis mode after your growth spurt has been stymied by shoddy privacy practices?

Today's technologists have the benefit of starting a bit ahead of zero. The past few years have offered many privacy data points, ranging from mishaps at companies and governments to tools built by privacy-focused vendors. Given this plethora of resources, today's leaders have the opportunity to devise privacy strategies that will avoid the setbacks that have hurt companies.

This book is aimed at helping you get your timing right in building privacy tooling. I often repeat a saying attributable to one of my mentors from my Netflix days: "The best time to do the smart thing is yesterday; the second best time is today."

We've talked at length about how privacy can affect your business. Let's now introduce some of the options on offer that will help you to address privacy issues and go about automating privacy processes and tooling.

1.6   *Privacy tech and tooling: Your options and your choices*

Given all the news and scrutiny around privacy, security, and risk, it is unsurprising that startups are springing up in the privacy tech space, with venture capital firms pumping more and more money into this mission-critical area. I have lost count of the number of VC firms that have sought my advice on the stickiness of products that represent potential investments for them. Just as numerous are the startups and early stage privacy tech companies that routinely contact me for a proof of concept and pilot as they seek high-profile adopters.

Engineers need to be able to think of privacy tooling in three buckets:

- *Know*—Know where you discover and locate sensitive data
- *Reduce*—Reduce where you minimize the surface area via obfuscation and deletion
- *Protect*—Protect where you enforce access control

When engineers buy or build tools, they need to understand what they are solving for and how a tool or approach under consideration would work toward that solution. They then need to make that critical choice: do they build privacy tooling in-house or do they buy third-party, off-the-shelf solutions that can range from comprehensive privacy platforms to more narrowly focused solutions? I use a framework similar to figure 1.10 to help my decision-making.

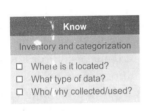

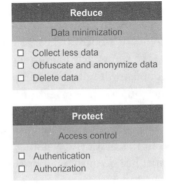

Figure 1.10   Framework for the "build vs. buy" privacy tooling debate

1.6.1   The "build vs. buy" question

"Build vs. buy" is a critical question for engineers to weigh in on. It is the engineers who will ultimately have to implement whatever solution is chosen, so it behooves them to have an informed perspective.

Engineers and technical program managers tend to lean toward the "build" option as a starting point for several reasons:

- Homegrown solutions will benefit from contextual and technical consistency with the company's existing tech stack and will potentially be easier to integrate within a distributed architecture.
- Engineers directly impacted by privacy tooling gaps and inefficiencies can build technical solutions more directly aligned with immediate needs.
- Building machine learning (ML) models based on customers and data germane to the company's business may be easier for in-home engineers already steeped in the details.
- Engineers often find resistance from leaders in finance when they wish to procure third-party tools. Companies have gotten wary of engineers buying too many tools with expensive licenses.

I agree with these arguments, but only in part. There are limitations to in-home solutions as well:

- As mentioned before, engineers are often siloed and rarely if ever consider the tech stack as a whole or the end-to-end data lineage. Rather, they tend to focus on the portions germane to their products. It is this prioritization of depth over breadth that blinds them to downstream privacy and security implications, so having the same engineers build privacy tooling that will have end-to-end coverage can be risky. I have observed such tooling to be hampered by recency bias, where the solutions solve for the most exigent recent issues rather than employing predictive analysis to prevent future privacy issues. The "build" solutions often optimize for "stop the bleeding" rather than "building muscle."
- Engineers often switch jobs and teams, and this can lead to maintainability issues. Privacy tooling often has to dig deep into data warehouses, data pipelines, and APIs, and it needs to support high levels of scale and availability. The lack of stable ownership can hurt a company's ability to build privacy tools in-house and to build the institutional memory necessary for a data-driven approach that can prevent and remediate privacy issues.
- Modern B2C services often optimize for availability over consistency (a service like Twitter or TikTok can often have backend errors that a user may never notice, given the volume of content available), while privacy tooling may need to support audits and reporting. These audits test precision and completeness, and it may be better to use established and benchmarked third-party tooling rather than risk an internal tool that may miss or misstate critical data in the event of a privacy incident.

There is no perfect one-size-fits-all solution in the "build vs. buy" debate, but as engineers explore options for automating and operationalizing privacy, the preceding considerations should serve as guiding principles. It is likely that unless you have a large number of engineers dedicated to building tools in-house, you will need to explore a third-party solution. The next subsection will explore some common tools in this space and offer a starting point for analysis and decision-making.

1.6.2   *Third-party privacy tools: Do they really work and scale?*

Given how long I have worked in the privacy field, I have a deep familiarity with several well-known and upcoming privacy tools. I have used several tools at various stages of their development and have evaluated several others. I want to offer my candid assessment of what purpose these tools serve, since the glut of privacy tooling has led to a lack of differentiation. The phrase "privacy tech" has become for engineers what "organic" is to food shoppers, in that it has been stripped of meaning due to overuse and abuse.

The lack of detailed awareness of privacy among engineers often makes the selection process onerous. Additionally, these tools need to be integrated into several touchpoints—APIs, data stores, endpoints, key management systems, etc.—and that process is expensive. Equally expensive is the process of extricating and replacing them, so it's important for engineers to understand the capabilities of some commonly discussed third-party solutions.

PRIVACY PLATFORM SOLUTIONS: BIGID AND ONETRUST

Engineers who often struggle with discovering sensitive data and therefore protecting it need tooling to start this discovery, and they also need to build tooling for data deletion, export, consent, obfuscation, sharing, and cataloging. The fact that engineers often start with privacy tooling after a chunk of data already sits in their warehouse means that they prefer using one platform solution that meets as many of their needs as possible.

BigID (https://bigid.com) has a significant edge in that the company was an early mover in this space and has therefore been tried and tested in massive cloud-based corporations. (Disclosure: I was part of the team that evaluated BigID at Nike in 2015.)

BigID offers several key capabilities:

- *Data inventory and cataloging*—As with the IP addresses in Gamesbuster, engineers need tooling to detect and index data at scale. BigID can help map sensitive and personal data, metadata, and documents using ML patterns and lineage.
- *Cluster analysis*—Based on its data catalog, BigID can provide you visibility into which data stores house sensitive data so that you can execute its deletion tools in a targeted fashion. This analysis also enables BigID to correlate data back to owners (so as to reduce the footprint of orphaned datasets), thereby reducing overall risk.

- *Data handling*—Having built an indexed catalog of your data, BigID tries to offer a centralized view into a subject's data index and API access to it. This enables a company to delete data and export it to meet requests from users based on laws like California's CCPA.
- *Compliance mapping*—For activities such as data transfers through partner platforms and other endpoints, BigID aims to map your privacy processes to the requirements of laws like GDPR, thereby accelerating your audit compliance.

BigID is an attractive product for companies that require end-to-end coverage for their privacy automation, but it lacks critical capabilities that define fast-moving companies:

- BigID operates at the tail end of the data pipeline, after the data has already been accessed and utilized, so it may provide privacy controls a tad late, after some privacy risks have already gone undetected.
- BigID is typically utilized at a stage when the data footprint has grown fairly large; its discovery processes make a necessary tradeoff between accuracy and performance. Based on my last experience, BigID relies on sampling in order to discover sensitive data. Therefore, you either deal with the approximation that is endemic to sampling or the latency that comes with more comprehensive coverage.
- Even though BigID's cataloguing supports data deletion, BigID's capabilities in validating third-party deletion are limited. This is a critical limitation, since questionable data-sharing with third parties has caused trouble for companies big and small. Validating third-party deletion is critical.

I have found that engineers have had to build custom tooling to discover metadata and to drive deletion in data stores like Hadoop to make up for the gaps created by BigID's shortcomings and the volume of data that companies have collected by the time they can use BigID. I have also observed that in-house engineers are able to build discovery tooling that worked better than BigID, since they were more aware of how their colleagues collected and used data. Their tools were therefore used more commonly than the ones supplied by BigID. This is not a criticism of the BigID offering, but it's something engineers need to know before selecting the tool.

OneTrust (www.onetrust.com) is a similar end-to-end data privacy platform that offers capabilities ranging from templates for automation of privacy reviews (a topic we will cover in more detail later in this book), performing vendor risk assessments, and responding to subject rights requests and data breach incidents. For other heavy-duty privacy obligations like Data Subject Access Requests (DSARs, something we will also cover in detail later in this book), OneTrust also provides templates to collect requests, track progress, and assign to internal resources.

OneTrust is very useful if your privacy operations are run out of a legal and/or compliance team with a workforce of contractors and engineers manually performing the operations. In other words, OneTrust provides a checklist interface so as to stop you from creating bespoke processes or overlooking steps in a by-the-book process. Put simply, OneTrust is *workflow automation* you can use to create repeatable automation so as to outsource the job of privacy verification to individuals not charged with building revenue-critical products. If your sole aim as an engineer is to not worry about privacy and to make it someone else's problem, then OneTrust is a great tool.

What engineers really need is a full mental model for privacy and governance whereby you have automation embedded into the data rather than shaping processes to address privacy. Hoping that OneTrust addresses your privacy concerns is like hoping that a band-aid can alleviate a brain tumor.

PRIVACY POINT SOLUTIONS: PRIVICERA, COLLIBRA, DATAGRAIL, INFORMATICA, SAILPOINT

Given that many companies are using vast amounts of data to conduct customer analysis and advertising, and also that they have varying cultures and equally divergent levels of privacy risk, it may not make sense for them to own platform tools like BigID.

For example, if you are an engineer or technical program manager at a health care company, you and your fellow engineers probably are more constrained regarding data collection than engineers at a social media platform; the very purpose of a social media platform tends to require collecting vast amounts of data to build predictive behavioral models. For engineers at health care companies, data discovery may not be the most pressing challenge, since there are guardrails to advise on who can collect what (and how much) data. The critical challenge for health care engineers may be managing access to sensitive health-related data about patients.

In this case, a point solution that offers access-control policy management and data encryption at the field/column level may be more apropos. A tool like Privicera (https://privacera.com/products/enterprise-grade-encryption/) may offer that, although I do not have enough experience with this product to vouch that it would scale for large volumes and varieties of data.

Another tool that focuses on access management is SailPoint (www.sailpoint.com); this tool optimizes for granular access management, user identity management, access lifecycle, and provisioning and compliance. This tool could be used not just for access management but to apply those policies to data in the cloud and data throughout its various lifecycle stages. The promise of this tool lies in applying identity-based access control to data and then using that identity to derive intelligence. This intelligence could include shadow IT, data quality, etc., thereby providing business and security benefits besides the core privacy benefit. Whether SailPoint can integrate across an entire ecosystem to deliver these benefits at scale is worthy of a proof of concept.

The benefit of point solutions is that instead of offering a full array of privacy tools, in-house engineers and technical leaders can optimize these solutions for present-day needs and even use them to understand the scale of the work. Once you have enough experience, your engineers can build internal tooling and get it right more easily, rather than wasting cycles.

There are solutions focused purely on data discovery as well. Collibra (www.collibra .com) offers the capability to gain visibility into all relevant data with its business context by tracking the data lineage. Similarly, tools like DataGrail (www.datagrail.io/platform/) and Informatica (www.informatica.com/products/data-catalog.html) offer data cataloging capabilities by looking at data upstream rather than in the warehouses when the volumes are large.

The reason I have dug into off-the-shelf tooling in detail is that engineers and technical leaders at small and large companies often have to make purchasing decisions under pressure and with limited budgets. It will help them to have a framework to match their needs with these tools; this is critical not just to make the right "build vs. buy" decision but also to be able to explain to their financial stakeholder why a specific course makes sense. Each choice has varying tradeoffs, and it is vital that companies avoid committing to an irreversible course of action, making expensive investments, and failing to reduce privacy risk.

Additionally, engineers and their partners in finance (who will need to approve any requisition of third-party tools) do not always have the same understanding of how these tools differ from each other. Also, in my experience, the budget for such tools typically opens up in a crisis, and it is hard to perform a clear-eyed analysis of which tool is appropriate for the moment. This is how companies end up buying the wrong tools, finding them unsatisfying, and then building hacked-up add-ons for bespoke internal teams. This lack of discipline leads to poor metrics and a feeling that privacy costs too much without fixing the problem.

Tools are a foundational aspect of privacy engineering, and now that you have had an introductory glance at the options in that area, we can talk about the risks of buying off-the-shelf solutions.

1.6.3 *The risks in buying third-party privacy tools*

Small and medium-sized companies, as well as bigger companies, often think of privacy as a disrupter that they can just hand off to a reputable third-party tool. We leverage this sort of thinking in doing our taxes—we leverage tax preparation software rather than doing our taxes by hand. There are two risks to this approach.

First, consider what happened in June 2021. According to reporting by Alex Hern at *The Guardian*, a massive internet outage, affecting websites including *The Guardian*, Amazon, and Reddit, was traced to a failure in a content delivery network (CDN) run by a company called Fastly. The outage resulted in visitors to a vast array of sites receiving error messages. Besides bringing down some websites entirely, the failure also broke specific sections of other services, such as the servers for Twitter that host the social network's emojis.

Fastly, a cloud computing services provider, runs an edge cloud designed to speed up loading times for websites, protect them from denial-of-service attacks, and help them deal with bursts of traffic. Fastly sits between most of its clients and their users; if Fastly's service suffers a catastrophic failure, that can prevent its clients from operating at all.

Having a critical link in your tech stack depend on a third party means that single points of failure can result in sweeping outages. In another example, a 2017 problem at Amazon Web Services brought down some of the world's biggest websites for several hours across the east coast of the United States. Given the scrutiny around privacy, do you really think it advisable to outsource critical data protection functionality to a third-party tool?

Second, given the variety in tech stacks and roadmaps from company to company, it is unlikely that a single off-the-shelf tool will work for most of today's businesses.

All of this is not to write off these tools, but to make the case that addressing today's privacy needs will require a level of involvement by a company's engineers, even after tooling is secured.

1.7 What this book will not do

While this book is designed to be an excellent resource for the strategic preparation of a business, it is not intended to be used as a tool for crisis management. In the event of an imminent crisis, you will probably need access to experts who will optimize rapidity of response over strategic investments in privacy. I am not a legal expert or an attorney. This book will explain how you can build operational and strategic privacy knowledge, but not legal expertise on interpreting laws and regulations.

1.8 How the role of engineers has changed, and how that has affected privacy

When I first started writing code in 2003, engineering had a predictable cadence to it, as did relationships between the professional enterprise and its customers. Work had a structured and top-down feel to it, with a sense of regimented discipline aimed at creating desired outcomes. Rather than the thrill of ingenuity, corporate leaders opted for the slow but certain harvest of discipline. This meant that my goals were derivatives of my manager's goals, and their goals were derivatives of the goals of the next level up in leadership. My role was to execute and implement rather than ideate and innovate.

Our work product, and the execution it took to produce it, was the fruit of this discipline. I remember the phrase "waterfall model" being used to describe it. Team A would produce something, hand it off to Team B, which after a preordained period of time, handed it off to Team C, and so on.

The relationship with customers was similarly void of suspense and replete with certainty. Customer asks drove my technical implementation; the flow of ideas was a one-way street. The companies that executed best came first. Emerging from the embers of the dot-com recession, the focus was on efficiency rather than imagination.

And then, after the great recession of 2008, there seemed to be a breach in the top-down leadership consensus and institutional trust. This was happening across society, with people of all stripes feeling like the experts they had trusted were pretenders. As jobs and incomes disappeared, so vanished the idea that an expert atop the food chain had all the answers.

From this unsettled dynamic emerged a new type of technologist. Engineers, regardless of seniority, became entrepreneurs who created a vision of bottom-up leadership. In this vision, disparate teams worked to create an ethos where three *D*s would shape a new interconnected innovation process.

The first *D* was *data*—data that would drive change, measure outcomes, and the analysis of which would shape products and experiences that would delight customers. The ensuing customer engagement would drive revenue for businesses.

The second *D* was *decentralization*, where multiple engineers built products based on their own ideas, tools, and visions. With each iteration of innovation, they'd create a fast feedback loop and grow their scope. Process was out, progress was in, and the product that earned customer trust shipped. In this Darwinian world, only the fittest survived.

The third *D* was *democratization*, where junior engineers and data scientists often had more influence and understanding of the product landscape than senior leadership. Rather than individual contributors having to pay obeisance to authority, managers had to demonstrate they had influence.

These three *D*s have empowered engineers and technical program managers to act with a greater sense of autonomy and agency than ever thought possible, even during the high tech heyday of the late 1990s. That led, however, to an attenuation of the authority typically vested in centralized teams like IT in controlling how engineers make decisions. This has meant that teams like cybersecurity and privacy have found it tough going to implement a sense of consistency and conformity. These are typically, and inaccurately, seen as hampering rather than helping the business. Figure 1.11 summarizes these challenges—I have often used this diagram in meetings with C-Level execs so that they understand how engineering causes predictable, and fixable, challenges for privacy.

Figure 1.11 How engineering challenges privacy engineering

The change in how the tech sector is viewed—from wealth-creating heroes to data hoarders, targets of opprobrium from everyone ranging from Bernie Sanders to Steve Bannon—stems from these underlying functional changes in the roles technical contributors make.

More specifically, these changes have sowed skepticism around how companies collect and use customer data. I sense that skepticism when friends and family members who do not work in tech ask me questions like, "How does company XYZ make money?" or "How do I know company ABC will not get breached like Equifax did?" or even "Does everyone at these big companies have access to intimate details about my life so they can make money off of me?" The much-discussed *techlash* is an expression of these questions.

In large companies, leaders and executives who often hail from the product development or finance arms of their company lack the technical knowledge and the instinct for privacy. Smaller shops, where budgets are lean, margins are leaner, and team sizes leaner still, face an even harder challenge in this domain. Technical leaders and architects have to wear several hats and often lack the bandwidth and authority to make the cross-functional changes that privacy requires, since most product teams operate in silos and are focused on their quarterly targets, with privacy a distant worry.

For most companies, questions around privacy arise after a period of growth and often after irreversible decisions have reached maturity. It is in this context that I write this book.

This chapter has given you a foundation for thinking about privacy and its attendant concepts. Additionally, you now likely have a better sense of how your product vertical teams operate—how their siloed and roadmap-driven approach helps your business grow while often creating downstream privacy challenges. All of this occurs as the relationship between the business and its customers has evolved amid a shifting societal landscape. With this background, the next chapter will dive deep into helping you build a privacy program that you can customize for your company and your customers.

Summary

- Privacy is personal and contextual and therefore can be hard for engineers accustomed to owning specific tools and tech stacks to implement at scale.
- It is critical for engineers to peek out of their silos and understand both the data flow across various systems and how it affects technical and non-technical stakeholders.
- Engineers also need to understand the risks and potential of privacy tooling— what getting it right can mean versus what privacy harms can portend.
- There is no easy answer to the "build vs. buy" debate when it comes to privacy tooling, but it is key that engineers understand their use cases and how off-the-shelf tools may or may not meet their needs.
- The increased need for engineers to understand data privacy is a reflection of how modern engineering has changed and of how the increased power available to engineers creates new cross-functional responsibilities.

Understanding
data and privacy

This chapter covers

- Why privacy is hard, and what happens when it is overlooked
- How data can help grow your business
- How data can be a risk when you handle privacy incorrectly
- The regulatory sentiment around privacy
- How customers understand and assess data privacy
- Building a privacy-first program and culture

In the last chapter, we started building a very high-level understanding of privacy and your business. In this chapter, we will go one level deeper; we will more directly connect privacy outcomes to how your business operates. More specifically, after reading this chapter, you will better understand how your business operations and privacy are connected in the context of the economy, the regulatory landscape, and customer sentiment. To this end, we will look at *data*.

2.1 Privacy and what it entails

Why do accomplished companies and brilliant engineers find privacy so hard? They have skills that lead to amazing products and growing profits—why can't they plan for privacy success as well? I have heard these questions asked not in the abstract but in real-life situations where companies with no malicious intent and a proven record of successful products made serious privacy mistakes.

It is time to set some context. Let's consider how modern engineering works, and how that poses privacy challenges.

2.1.1 Why privacy is hard

Just as I connected privacy to the human instinct of trust in the last chapter, we will now connect privacy outcomes to specific decisions about data that your company makes. Decisions like the following:

- What data to collect
- How to access it
- Who to share it with
- What to do with the insights that data allows us
- How to manage the risks appropriately

However, it would be helpful to first discuss how work occurs in the trenches, because the hands-on cross-functional leaders who drive privacy will need this information to implement the strategies and tools necessary for privacy.

For a while after the dot-com era, programming occurred within a sandbox. Directives made their way from the top down and engineers executed against them. Figure 2.1 shows clearly what was a very linear and predictable process—one that was inherently top-down.

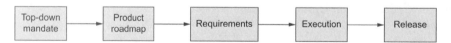

Figure 2.1   Traditional software development; a linear path

As figure 2.1 shows, the company's mission determined its product roadmap. The roadmap identified specific requirements for products and features, and the engineering teams executed on that mission. The product was then targeted for release.

The upside of this model was that it was predictable and repeatable. The downside was that you could invest a lot of resources and time building a product, and then you'd need to wait for feedback in terms of market acceptance or rejection.

Later in my career as an engineer, the development process became more innovative, unregulated, and unpredictable. Figure 2.2 paints a picture.

Toward the early 2010s, as trends like agile development and scrum started taking root, engineering innovation evolved as well. Companies could still adhere to the

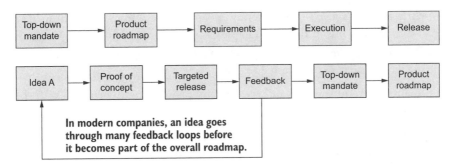

Figure 2.2 The modern dynamic innovation process; an ongoing cycle of feedback and new iterations

top-down development model, but alongside that, teams and engineers could experiment with ideas and innovate in byte-sized chunks.

As you can see in the top row of figure 2.2, modern businesses could build products in the traditional vein, where an SVP or C-Level leader could champion a product. Their vision would feed into the roadmap, and dedicated teams could dutifully execute it.

Concurrently, a team of engineers could explore a new idea, one that might or might not be related to the company's known area of expertise. This innovation often occurs on a piecemeal basis, with small bits of the product being released incrementally for feedback, possibly generating new investment. Such projects often do not follow the typical processes regarding how data and IT assets are handled. The second row in figure 2.2 shows this model.

Given the pressure to ship products quickly, drive engagement, and convert revenue, the second model is becoming more prevalent. This dynamic prevents executives and their technical leaders from overseeing all the smaller decisions that lead to any particular status quo. And it further complicates the task of centralized privacy and security engineers, since their plans have to account for the implications of these decisions across several disciplines over time.

Next we'll look at what technical leaders with new and evolving privacy goals face in a fast-moving company.

2.1.2 *Privacy engineering on the ground: What you have to accomplish*

In this subsection, we will look at what privacy engineers face at modern companies and what they need to accomplish. Against the backdrop we just saw, I will explain why their role is challenging.

Figure 2.3 shows how privacy engineering is an incarnation of the expectations that stem from regulations and industry best practices. The figure highlights four key privacy expectations that companies face:

- *Data protection*—Users and regulators expect you to protect customer data.
- *Right to know*—Companies are expected to provide copies of customer data upon request. We will be covering this in detail in chapter 8, which examines Data Subject Access Requests (DSARs).

- *Right to be forgotten*—This empowers users to seek erasure of their data. We will also look at this in detail in chapter 7.
- *Judicial investigations*—Companies need to manage what data they collect and retain for legal compliance reasons.

These abstract requirements map to specific privacy engineering tasks and technical controls:

- Data minimization, where you collect only what you need
- Authentication, which involves making sure you can validate the identities of employees and customers
- Authorization, which maps those seeking system or data access to a permission structure and policy
- Data inventory and categorization, which requires you to create a catalog of your data
- Audits, whereby you validate that privacy controls around deletion, retention, etc., are being enforced

Unlike when engineers collect vast amounts of data and iterate in silos, the privacy engineering work in figure 2.3 is cross-functional and requires alignment.

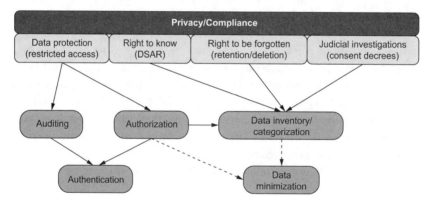

Figure 2.3   The four key privacy expectations that companies face and their associated privacy solutions

Privacy engineers, as they implement these privacy controls, will need to understand four key stakeholder perspectives they will encounter in their business, centering around data and its collection. Figure 2.4 identifies these perspectives. For example, the analytics teams optimize for maximal data collection to train their models and glean insights. These insights empower product managers and engineers to build products that drive engagement and revenue. Privacy engineers can expect significant levels of pushback from these stakeholders as they seek to reduce how much data is collected, reduce access to that data, and add steps to catalog the data and audit its usage.

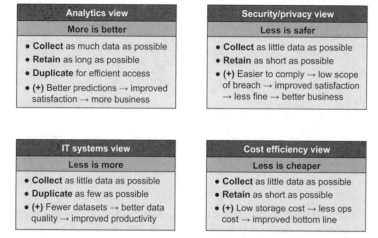

Figure 2.4   Lenses through which different stakeholders view data: analytics, security/privacy, IT systems, and cost efficiency

Fast-moving high-growth companies often face privacy challenges ranging from audits to internal misuse to breaches. That leads to difficult questions like "How did we get here?" and "Why did we not see this coming?" When teams conduct post-mortems, a lot of the answers to these questions come down to inconsistent decisions based on the contrasting perspectives highlighted in figure 2.4. It is important to be aware of these perspectives; privacy engineers should watch for them and factor them into data governance, privacy tooling, and reviews. This is especially the case with privacy; many companies do not think of privacy as an early investment. The habits and processes that lead to business success in tech do not necessarily encourage good privacy practices.

The next subsection will lay out the ground that privacy engineers must cover to automate privacy controls.

2.1.3   Privacy, data systems, and policy enforcement

Even after getting buy-in from stakeholders across the company, privacy engineers will need to apply their tools across the various systems that exist across the business. Figure 2.5 shows what such a landscape might look like.

In the previous chapter, you saw how data can spread across the company after ingestion. Figure 2.5 shows an example of the sorts of systems where that data might live. These systems range from

- Offline analytics data stores like Hadoop and Hive
- Operational data that serves real-time transactions and lives in structured and unstructured data stores
- Cloud data stores like S3 and GCP

System	Purpose
Offline data	Big data lake • Real-time stores: Kafka, Pinot • Analytics stores: Hive, Presto, Hadoop, Vertica, GCP BigQuery
Operational storage	Operational stores capturing transactional data • MySQL • Cassandra (C*) • Elasticsearch (inferred data) • MongoDB
Cloud stores	AWS S3 buckets and GCP Google Cloud Storage (GCS) buckets

Figure 2.5 Privacy and the spread of data

For data in all these data stores, privacy engineers need to apply automation to enforce controls like retention and deletion. When a predefined retention period expires, one or more of the following outcomes could occur:

- *Immediate deletion*—Complete deletion of a user upon request or for any reason on demand
- *Inactive user deletion*—Deletion of user data if the user has been inactive for a specified period of time
- *Data masking*—Disassociating content from the user, such as through partial anonymization, a topic we will cover later in this book
- *Preservation*—Preserving the data only for a specific use, such as encrypting the data to restrict access to the legal team after a retention period expires
- *Archiving*—Moving the data to an archival system for a defined period or future event

Privacy engineers may also need to manage access to data, such as by using encryption. This work involves several key steps:

- Identifying the level of encryption necessary (application level, at-rest, in-transit). This will require alignment between security, storage, data platform, and analytics teams.
- Building key management systems (KMS) to manage decryption keys, so that access can be granted or revoked using automation at scale.
- Configuring storage, data, and workload systems to get keys from KMS for access to data. That way, privacy engineers can ensure that their technical controls are mapped not to individual engineers and their whims, but to the systems and the data.
- Configuring business events and data lifecycle events to execute policies for encrypting and decrypting applicable data.
- Building immutable logging of access, including the actor, the target, and the data returned. You may need, for the purposes of security detection and audit response, logs that show who accessed what data, the corresponding decryption key, and what was done with or to the data upon access.

Be it data deletion or encryption, these technical controls need to be integrated as policies into the company's engineering workflow. This is critical, since enforcement at scale is only possible with automation and policy configuration. The following steps outline what such a workflow might look like:

- Setting up policies for applicable data set identification, after which data across the company can be identified based on its privacy risk.
- Extending the data platform tooling to hook into data lifecycle events, so that the policies can be enforced on data as it flows throughout the infrastructure.
- Rolling out integrations with storage, data, and extract, transform, load (ETL) tooling to emit lifecycle events, so that policies end up getting triggered and enforced. This is critical, because as data changes state, policies applicable to it will need to adapt. For example, if you end up combining data collected from your customers with third-party data, you may increase the risk that specific customers might be re-identified and suffer privacy harm. This, in turn, may require the enforcement of a stricter privacy policy. The change to the data would need to emit a lifecycle event so that appropriate policy changes could be enforced.
- Triggering the execution of policies to archive, delete, and/or encrypt applicable data. This represents the final step in ensuring that data privacy tooling can apply to the data at the appropriate time.

These steps will depend on the systems where the data lives being identified, the data being classified based on risk (so that more sensitive data is encrypted), and the data being tagged (so that policies around encryption can be enforced). We will be covering data classification and tagging in chapters 3 and 4 in detail.

Given that most companies start their work with limited privacy context and seemingly unlimited data, the preceding steps often represent a challenge. This is why privacy is hard, and we often end up with a scenario where the innovation and speed of development bears an inverse correlation to our ability to provide privacy and security to our customers. It is therefore imperative that privacy engineers automate as much of this as possible. This book will help you do just that.

Even so, privacy engineers will benefit from use cases where other companies have struggled. A more structured approach as outlined above will help them get buy-in to build privacy tooling and drive adoption across the company.

In order to understand how these high-level strategic directions map to operational decisions and details, let's consider how data and related decisions could help and then hinder your company, its growth, and its relationship with its customers.

2.2 *This could be your company*

It is one thing for technical leaders to know how the development world has changed in the macro sense, and quite another for them to know what trends and patterns to watch for before they cause privacy issues. To illustrate this, we will simulate the innovation process that you may well have participated in over the last few years. You will see how growth in ideas and the accumulation of data can lead to privacy problems and affect company growth. Consider the following scenario.

The whiteboard. The sticky notes. The user flow diagrams. The conceptual journeys. All the creative juices flowed to make your platform attractive. This was a perfect mix of great design meeting user interest and scaling up with the power of the cloud. Supply met demand, thanks to ubiquitous internet access in markets that had never seen this combination of customers and products.

A mere 18 months ago, you and your fellow engineers got together and created an engagement platform where like-minded individuals could get together and play video games. You would supply the initial video games, and they would attract a devout and animated following. Social media would allow your participants to share stories about their high scores, special tricks, and techniques.

Three months later, the platform was ready. You had all the golden oldies of the video game collection: Super Mario, Double Dragon, and many others. Gamers from all over the world could log in using their social media credentials, invite their friends (who could then invite their friends), compete against them, share their scores online, and form teams that could compete against each other in a round-robin format.

There would be concentric circles of social engagement, with people of all ages from all parts of the world playing their favorite video games from back in the day. Your platform would form the center of all those circles.

The data about your users—what they liked, how many games they played, who they invited, and other insights into your online arcade—would become the fuel for marketing and even building new games. You could even sell the platform to a major gaming company or a social media company.

You were experiencing the check-mark growth model (shown in figure 2.6), where after an initial dip in growth and revenue, both were spiking. The dip was during the period when you were building the platform, onboarding your first games, and hardening your first data storage systems. Once the users came, the data followed, which then enabled you to onboard more games and attract more users. From an economic and aesthetic standpoint, things checked out OK.

During this time, your team of engineers, data scientists, and product managers began to taste the power of data. The machine learning models they built using the data collected from your customers gave them powerful insights, which enabled them to attract even more customers. Your prodigies wondered, why not collect as much data as possible, even beyond what was immediately necessary. You could always use that data later, and if not, you could always delete it.

As it turned out, much like boxes that we never fully unpack when we move from one home to another, the unused data was never fully deleted. Newer engineers saw more experienced engineers collect data cavalierly and followed suit. Everyone could access whatever data they wanted, because the company's bottom-up innovation culture encouraged a "forgiveness rather than permission" approach, and after all, the

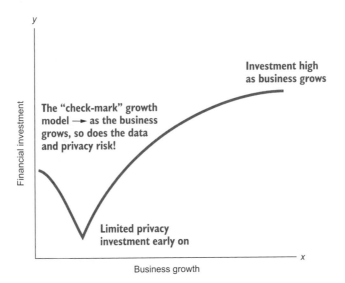

Figure 2.6 The check-mark growth model

faster you got more games on the platform, the more choices your users had. This was a self-reinforcing virtuous circle.

Over the next 15 months, your team started retaining more and more data, some of it very sensitive, in that it could identify users, where they lived, and how old they were. The comments feature, a crown jewel of the platform, could help infer details about your users, such as their body weight, sexual orientation, etc.

And then one day there was a breach. Hackers stole data about a significant chunk of your users from an unguarded database that was supposed to never have been created, then was supposed to have been retired, and then was supposed to have been deleted. None of those things happened, and the hackers were grateful for it. Because your team did not fix the roof while the sun was shining, it was now leaking data, and your company, your platform, and the trust of your users were all drowning.

Your business model went from the check mark to the inverted V that you can see in figure 2.7. The breach led to an erosion of trust and an exodus of users who previously thronged your website to play your games. That reduction in engagement led to fewer entrepreneurs willing to license their games on your platform, and that in turn helped dry up user engagement. You still had a self-reinforcing circle, but it's no longer a virtuous circle. It was a vicious circle.

NOTE Privacy issues are often a lagging indicator of real problems at a company. During high-growth cycles, companies tend to make mistakes in terms of how they collect, access, and store data; these mistakes often make it harder to continue innovating and growing. The sooner a company's privacy practices catch up with its ongoing innovation, the better.

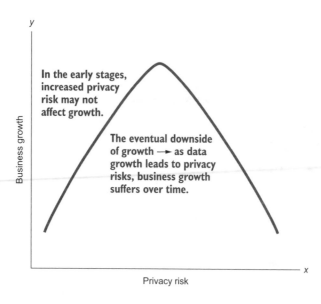

Figure 2.7   **How privacy problems cause growth to stop and fall**

This is not a hard scenario to imagine. In fact, given how common such a scenario is, it might be easy to dismiss it as something that happens to other people—people who are careless with data or who do not understand their users' need for privacy.

However, it is imperative that the lessons from this scenario are well absorbed so that cross-functional technical leaders do not find you repeating someone else's mistakes. Remember, in small companies, someone who wears many hats may have to step in and lead triage and rescue missions months—sometimes years—after privacy-adverse decisions are made, and they may not have the time or requisite context to address them.

The key takeaways for senior leaders are as follows:

- Data collection and analysis can lead to improved customer insight and innovation.
- This innovation can lead to faster product iterations and growing engagement.
- Often, in a decentralized and bottom-up culture, this trend can lead to sloppy privacy practices that often come to light much later.
- By the time a company discovers its privacy practices are suboptimal, it is possible that customers will have suffered privacy harm and that the company's trust is broken.
- This could happen during a time of growth and could slow down that growth, or worse, at a time of slowing growth when the benefits of initial growth could be lost.
- It is vital, therefore, that leaders account for the long-term privacy impacts of decisions that may be working well in the short term.

Data can be a powerful thing, providing many potential benefits both for businesses and customers alike. It's worth taking the time to appreciate the power of data before we get into a discussion about controlling the way we use or access it.

2.3 Data, your business growth strategy, and privacy

Data can help a business and solve real problems. This section will help establish that the scenarios and patterns we have seen thus far are predictors of real-world privacy harms.

Data may not feature on the balance sheet in a quantifiable sense, but it provides the ability to unlock insights and patterns around the behaviors and expectations of customers and potential customers. This could help you grow your business and make investments in ways that are likelier to succeed.

Platforms that track user mouse movements over time could be the first to notice symptoms of Parkinson's disease.[1] Data-powered artificial intelligence can improve shopping and social networks, provide clean energy, and better manage food supply and transportation systems. Data can help companies manage revenue with the goals of increasing economic prosperity and reducing layoffs created by uncertainty.

These capabilities require the collection of significant amounts of data over time, in order to study patterns and build models. Data that your tech tools collect in real time and in batches helps model human behavior, and those models set the tone for product designs and roadmaps. This is the heart of the work done by data scientists and analysts.

Privacy engineers need to understand how data collection can help your business, since they will need to understand why their colleagues in engineering, product management, and marketing tend to push back when it comes to privacy. Let's look at a real-life example to help explain.

Your online business could involve selling food, groceries, pet supplies, or services like ridesharing, hotels, etc. Regardless of the product, if you wish to grow your business, you need to

- Attract, and then retain, more customers
- Grow sales and revenue per customer
- Maximize profits using automation and scale

Your online business growth strategy will be based on several data points,[2] such as the following:

- Website traffic, which refers to the customer traffic your online presence generates.
- Traffic conversion rate, which refers to the portion of your traffic that converts to customers, sales, returns, etc.

---

[1] Roger McNamee, "A Brief History of How Your Privacy Was Stolen," *New York Times*, June 3, 2019, http://mng .bz/drRg.

[2] Si Quan Ong, "10 Crucial Ecommerce Metrics For Serious Entrepreneurs Only," *ReferralCandy*, June 13, 2017, www.referralcandy.com/blog/ecommerce-metrics/.

- Email opt-in conversion rate, which refers to the percentage of users who opt in to get email promotions, which in turn could help drive website traffic.
- Customer acquisition cost, which refers to the marketing and other costs associated with attracting and retaining customers.
- Average order value, which is self-explanatory.
- Customer lifetime value, which refers to how much revenue you will make per customer over time. This decision will influence how much you are willing to spend on customer acquisition costs.
- Percentage of returning customers, which is a key indicator of customer loyalty or "stickiness."
- Abandonment rate, which refers to the percentage of customers who start shopping on your website but do not complete the sale.

Each of these metrics serve as critical breadcrumbs for data scientists. The old way of building a product over months and quarters in an attempt to delight your customers has mostly fallen away; most companies collect large volumes of data, analyze them rapidly based on the preceding metrics, and improvise continually. This is where privacy is critical.

How safe your customers feel, and how much they trust you with their data, is a key driver for most, if not all, of these metrics. For example, if customers trust your privacy and data protection practices, that may lead to increased customer patronage and high website traffic (or app traffic, if we are measuring mobile data). It is also possible that if customers and potential customers do not trust your privacy practices, they may not show up in big numbers, might not spend as much, might not recommend your business to their friends, and might not return to buy more. All of this may lead to you having to offer them more discounts, spend more on marketing, and even create new after-the-fact privacy programs that are often seen as face-saving efforts rather than conscience-driven endeavors. Our online economy and individual online businesses, both of which make for a growing share of customer spending, depend on trust and privacy.

As a leader, you will find engineers and data scientists claiming that "more data is better" and "we can always use it later." An overly permissive regime regarding user data often yields to a careless set of practices for protecting that data. Examples of such sloppiness are legion.

2.4   *Examples: When privacy is violated*

When it comes to building a privacy program, leaders are often susceptible to the "it cannot happen here" syndrome, thinking that privacy incidents only "happen to the other side." This is how, combined with the creative sloppiness often inherent in bottom-up organizations, companies are often stunned by privacy issues. In reality, these issues are the accumulation of several mistakes of omission and commission. The following examples will help make that point.

These examples will also make clear another point we have discussed: when your security apparatus fails, privacy ends up buried in the rubble as well. When you fail to protect your data from a security standpoint, the users whose data it is will almost certainly find their privacy violated as well.

2.4.1 Equifax

Equifax, one of the three largest consumer credit reporting agencies in the United States, announced in September 2017 that its systems had been breached[3] and the sensitive personal data of 148 million Americans had been compromised.

The data exfiltrated included names, home addresses, phone numbers, dates of birth, Social Security numbers, and driver's license numbers. The credit card numbers of approximately 209,000 consumers were also breached.[4]

It is important to understand how this breached occurred[5]:

- The company was initially hacked via a consumer complaint web portal, with the attackers using a widely known vulnerability that should have been patched but, due to failures in Equifax's internal processes, wasn't.
- The attackers were able to move from the web portal to other servers because the systems weren't adequately segmented from one another, and they were able to find usernames and passwords stored in plain text that then allowed them to access still further systems.
- The attackers pulled data out of the network in encrypted form, undetected for months because Equifax had crucially failed to renew an encryption certificate on one of their internal security tools.

The breach cost Equifax $690 million in Q1 2019 to settle ongoing class action cases, as well as potential federal and state regulatory fines.

The ratings agency Moody's slashed Equifax's rating outlook, citing cybersecurity (and by implication, privacy issues) as a reason.[6] A Moody's spokesperson said the downgrade was significant because "it is the first time that cybersecurity has been a named factor in an outlook change." Moody's also stated that the cost of catching up would be a drag on Equifax's profits.

The lesson here is simple:

- If you think privacy and security programs are expensive, ignoring them is even more so.

---

[3] "Equifax Releases Details on Cybersecurity Incident, Announces Personnel Changes," Equifax Press Release, September 15, 2017, http://mng.bz/r6Xx.

[4] "Equifax Data Breach," *Electronic Privacy Information Center (EPIC)*, https://epic.org/privacy/data-breach/equifax/.

[5] Josh Fruhlinger, "Equifax data breach FAQ: What happened, who was affected, what was the impact?" *CSO*, February 12, 2020, http://mng.bz/VBjN.

[6] Kate Fazzini, "Equifax just became the first company to have its outlook downgraded for a cyber attack," *CNBC*, May 22, 2019, http://mng.bz/xXp7.

- It is important to get the details right, in terms of how data is protected and accessed.

- Just as there is no way to unring a bell, there is no way to unbreach the loss of data, and the damage to privacy and trust could similarly be irreversible.

It is bad enough that so much data that could personally identify people and their financial circumstances was exposed—this episode defines what privacy harm looks like. However, this breach also broadcast how much money these individuals made and what they owed to whom.

The only way this could have been worse is if someone could use this information to identify individuals in debt who also happened to be in positions of power. We will now look at another breach, and at how the data from that breach, when combined with the Equifax breach, could have privacy consequences with national security implications.

NOTE Small and nimble companies may often balk at the amount of work involved in building out privacy, since it forces teams to lose some agency and to collaborate. However, the examples of privacy breaches in this chapter show that a lack of privacy is often more expensive than privacy itself, and as you will see later, privacy can be a competitive differentiator for a business.

2.4.2 *The Office of Personnel Management (OPM) breach*

In April of 2015, IT staffers within the United States Office of Personnel Management (OPM), the agency that manages the government's civilian workforce, discovered that some of its personnel files had been hacked. Among the sensitive data that was exfiltrated were millions of SF-86 forms, which contain extremely personal information gathered in background checks for people seeking government security clearances, along with records of millions of people's fingerprints.[7] The OPM breach led to a Congressional investigation and the resignation of top OPM executives, and its full implications—for national security, and for the privacy of those whose records were stolen—may never be entirely clear.

Researchers have been able to piece together a rough timeline of when the breaches began and how the attackers gradually executed their plan.[8] The hack is thought to have begun in November of 2013, when the attackers first breached OPM networks. This attacker or group was dubbed X1 by the Congressional OPM data breach report. While X1 wasn't able to access any personnel records at that time, they did manage to exfiltrate manuals and IT system architecture information. The next month, in December of 2013, is when the attackers attempted to breach the systems of two contractors, USIS and KeyPoint, who conducted background checks on

---

[7] Michael Adams, "Why the OPM Hack Is Far Worse Than You Imagine," *Lawfare*, March 11, 2016, http://mng.bz/AO5e; Josh Fruhlinger, "The OPM hack explained: Bad security practices meet China's Captain America," *CSO*, February 12, 2020, http://mng.bz/ZxNN.

[8] Aliya Sternstein and Jack Moore, "Timeline: What We Know About the OPM Breach," *Nextgov*, June 17, 2015, http://mng.bz/RqzR.

government employees and had access to OPM servers (though USIS may have actually been breached months earlier).

In March of 2014, OPM officials realized they'd been hacked. However, they didn't publicize the breach at that time, and, having determined that the attackers were confined to a part of the network that didn't have any personnel data, OPM officials chose to allow the attackers to remain so they could monitor them and gain counterintelligence.

On May 7, 2014, an attacker or group dubbed X2 by the Congressional OPM data breach report used credentials stolen from KeyPoint to establish another foothold in the OPM network and install malware there to create a backdoor.[9] This backdoor could be used to gain illicit entry into the systems without proper authentication credentials. This breach went undetected, and OPM efforts to remove the attackers' access or the backdoor failed. In July and August of 2014, these attackers exfiltrated the background investigation data from OPM's systems.

By October 2014, the attackers had moved through the OPM environment to breach a Department of the Interior server where personnel records were stored, and in December 2014 another 4.2 million personnel records were exfiltrated. Fingerprint data was exfiltrated in late March of 2015. Finally, on April 15, 2015, security personnel noticed unusual activity within the OPM's networks, which quickly led them to realize that attackers still had a foothold in their systems.

The lessons from this specific breach are as follows:

- The more sensitive your data collection and the higher the volume, the bigger the attack surface for anyone to exploit. This could be an external hacker or an internal bad actor. In either case, the privacy implications for your users and on the trust between the company and the users is severe.
- Just as decentralized development expedites innovation, the sprawl in data and systems allows privacy harms to occur in disconnected systems and data stores, and it may take a while before the combined impact is understood. A central privacy team is critical to focus on the big picture, as opposed to the engagement-driven siloed approach that often drives individual tech teams.
- This privacy harm occurred due to security and network vulnerabilities. As stated before, security is a necessary precondition for privacy, and in subsequent chapters I will discuss how security practices and personnel will form key pillars of your privacy program.

The Equifax breach helped identify individuals and their financial circumstances. The OPM breach identified individuals and their power within government. An intersection of these two data stores would identify individuals in positions of authority in the US who may be in financial duress (see figure 2.8). In the wrong hands, this data could present an opportunity for blackmail or bribery, putting US national security in jeopardy.

---

[9] Josh Fruhlinger, "Malware explained: How to prevent, detect and recover from it," *CSO*, May 17, 2019, http://mng.bz/20Oo.

Privacy and security risks are often aggregated; engineers often believe that data they collect is not worthy of privacy protections, since they do not intend to act unethically. This example shows that accumulated privacy risks often show up at a later date, after a series of security incidents.

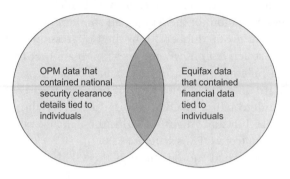

Figure 2.8 **How the OPM and Equifax breaches hurt privacy and national security**

Privacy may be contextual and personal, but the implications of privacy harms are rarely just that.

2.4.3 *LabCorp and Quest Diagnostics*

LabCorp, a medical testing company, said 7.7 million customers had their personal and financial data exposed through a breach. Quest Diagnostics suffered a breach that affected 11.9 million patients. That breach allowed an "unauthorized user" to gain access to financial information, Social Security numbers, and medical data. The common link: the breach occurred at a third-party billing collections company that served both LabCorp and Quest.

There are key lessons for businesses from these breaches:

- Even if you, as a company, do everything right, you are still vulnerable if one of your partners is impacted by a data breach.[10]
- In the coming years, as we escape the pandemic and as our population ages, protecting health care data will become even more critical.
- LabCorp claimed that the hackers did not obtain "any lab results," but it is almost impossible to prove that data related to health care was exfiltrated but somehow lab results were not. Getting breached is almost impossible to reverse, and its impact is almost impossible to mitigate.
- Finally, companies often over-index on protecting specific pieces of data but fail to afford the same level of consideration to others. This is how LabCorp may have allowed some data to be breached even as other data was safe. Leaders need to ensure that their company takes a holistic view rather than trying to score easy wins with privacy.

---

[10]Rachel Siegel, "LabCorp discloses data breach affecting 7.7 million customers," *Washington Post,* June 5, 2019, http://mng.bz/10eQ.

As we will discuss in subsequent chapters, it is key that your privacy program have a clear, objective, and scalable criteria for vendor assessment, methods to verify their privacy best practices before your engagement begins, and techniques to audit their methods after data starts changing hands.

These are just some of the relatively recent breaches that exposed the soft privacy and security underbelly of companies and governments. Additionally, each privacy incident shows different mistakes and vulnerabilities, all outcomes of the broader culture that seems to have valued velocity over alignment and innovation over detail.

As a result, a lot of recent regulation takes a more holistic view toward data protection. These laws combine privacy and security and are more comprehensive than any previous regime. The next section provides guidance on the broader landscape taking shape, with the caveat that the applicability of these laws to your business is for your legal department and outside counsel to assess.

2.5 Privacy and the regulatory landscape

Regulatory interest in privacy has grown in recent years. When I started my career in this space, most companies did not have to worry about multiple privacy laws or deal with empowered regulators. That has changed in recent years, and newly passed laws in various jurisdictions have created obligations for companies that collect data from their users.

Since I am not an attorney, I will advise that you speak to your legal team or outside counsel on the applicability of these laws. That said, I will touch on how laws like the European Union's General Data Protection Regulation (GDPR) have changed how companies interact with their customers. The GDPR gives customers more power and control over their data and makes companies responsible in a more granular fashion for how they access, process, and retain customer data.

I have a personal example of how the GDPR affected a business I patronized and the service it was able to offer me.

2.5.1 How regulations impact your product and their users

I used to work out at a gym where I could sign in using my badge at an electronic kiosk. Once I signed in, the cardio devices would display my name and my personalized workouts. All I had to do was click on my name; I did not have to worry about remembering my username and password.

Post-GDPR, even after I had signed in on the kiosk, the treadmills could not display my name. I had to enter my username and password all over again. I was told this was for privacy reasons. A lot of my friends saw the same thing.

I never found out why the connection between the treadmill and the kiosk was disconnected. It may have been that the legal teams felt there was a privacy concern, or the engineers who were cleaning up data for GDPR may have made that change for technical reasons, or a perhaps it was a combination of several reasons. Either way, such was the confusion and rush in the lead up to the GDPR that privacy was not always the focus in the changes that companies made and consumers experienced.

In any case, to avoid having to type their username and password, several gym users started using the guest mode. As a result, they could not use the personalized workouts they had created and that suited their weight-loss and muscle-development goals. They also could not, in guest mode, access their workout history. This was a critical metric for user satisfaction. This change in user behavior meant that the fitness company could not collect any data from the users either.

Now place yourself in the shoes of the gym owner or the manufacturer of the cardio machines. You are providing a product that helps individuals get fitter. You also hope to drive engagement and continued participation by collecting data that then helps you better educate your customers on how they can better handle their physical fitness. And then a complex piece of privacy legislation creates a wall between you and your users. In this case, neither the gym nor the users indulged in bad privacy practices, but there was enough concern around privacy practices in general that the GDPR became a reality, and in turn had outcomes beyond holding bad privacy actors accountable.

There are a few key lessons here:

- It is easy to point to examples of companies that do a bad job on privacy and get away with it.
- If companies collecting data won't do a better job on privacy, someone, somewhere, will pass a law that will hurt everybody's ability to connect with their customers.
- Privacy laws are often aimed at ensuring companies do right by their users, and that there is a safer exchange of data. In the case of the gym, the implementation of a specific law led to confusion and a suboptimal experience all around.
- Bad privacy practices are a lose-lose situation for everyone. This includes those in the industry who often do no wrong but are impacted by laws and the lack of trust that emanate from privacy harms.

From a non-legal perspective, the most effective privacy guidance I can give you is as follows: We are living in an age of institutional reaction. As awareness around privacy has increased, laws have sprung up in a rapid and somewhat disconnected fashion. It may take a while before there is alignment between determining which privacy protections are effective, getting them codified into law, converting them into enumerated instructions for implementation and verification, and then iterating them as customer needs evolve.

This example makes the case for the proactive privacy-by-design strategy this book advocates. Senior leaders are often upset when unplanned product changes lead to unwanted outcomes. This book will ensure that you sweat the details so that your customers at a gym don't have to be inconvenienced as they sweat it out.

2.5.2 *How your program should help prepare for changing privacy law*

The following examples show how you can create processes and tools to protect data privacy and improve your regulatory compliance:

- Build an access control regime to protect data without creating unnecessary and counterproductive bureaucracy. Such a system will tie data access to legitimate needs and put controls in place to prevent abuse.
- Align data retention and deletion with legitimate business needs and privacy commitments, which is to say that your company will not retain data in a way that abuses customer trust and leaves that data vulnerable to breach or exfiltration.
- Share data with external entities in a way that protects privacy. You'd share data using protected tools like encryption as well as by aggregating and/or anonymizing it so that individual users are not identified.

Subsequent chapters will discuss these concepts in much more detail.

This book will help you build a privacy program that will help you build trust with your customer by using the legal landscape as a floor rather than a ceiling. You will be able to relate to your customer's privacy needs because you value their trust, not because of regulatory pressure.

Having examined privacy through the lens of your business and the law, it is now important to add the third leg of this stool, and the most vital one: the next section will examine what privacy looks like to your customer.

2.6   *Privacy and the user*

It is often easy to lose sight of the fact that behind the petabytes, tables, and lakes of data, this is information about human beings. These human beings value their distinctiveness, their identity, and their privacy. Just as privacy and trust go hand in hand, privacy and respect go hand in glove. In order to explain this connection, a personal story from my own life is in order.

2.6.1 *Becoming an American, and privacy*

On May 6, 2013, I took my oath as a US citizen. It was a beautiful ceremony. After living in America for almost 13 years, I was officially an American.

But before that moving and momentous day, I had to go through a detailed process called naturalization. This process requires filling out multiple forms, providing tons of data about me, my family, and friends, giving my fingerprints, and being interviewed under oath where every possible question was on the table. During this process, I had to provide extremely personal information—financial, biographical, familial—and saying "no" was not an option.

I did not have the power to question why so much information was necessary to assess my eligibility for citizenship. For example, my maternal grandmother was born in a small village in India and died before my parents even met. The government wanted her birth certificate. Procuring this document was hard, since all those decades ago, the village where she was born did not even issue birth certificates.

Throughout this process, I had no visibility into how all my information would be used, who would have access to it or for how long, who it would be shared with, and how it would be protected. More than seven years later, I still do not. It would have been helpful if the government had explained to me why they needed all that documentation, some of which had not even a tenuous relationship to my application. While I understand that the authorities have a responsibility to protect the homeland and cannot share too many details, the whole exercise felt like a data grab and a reinforcement of the power asymmetry ... the government had something I wanted, and I had nothing to push back with.

I believe that privacy is about transparency and trust. Whether you are a business or a government, collecting data prudently, sharing it carefully, and protecting it always should be your key guiding principles. I have been leading privacy programs for a long time, and I bring to the table a sensibility that no user should feel as helpless as I did then.

2.6.2 *Today's users and their privacy concerns*

For engineers and other technical managers who need to justify privacy efforts to their executive and finance leadership, this section connects your goals of business success with your obligation to respect your customer. Building a privacy reputation and trust with your customers can help you achieve key business objectives such as

- Customer loyalty
- Business growth
- Brand differentiation

Research from SalesForce shows how important it is to build this trust. This research provides insights into customer behavior that may seem counterintuitive at first[11]: customers value personalized experiences, which require you to collect data, but customers also want you to respect their privacy. If customers trust you, they are more likely to be loyal to you with their dollars and recommendations. Especially critical in the research is the call-out regarding sharing; customers ranging from baby boomers to millennials to Gen Zs are more likely to share positive feedback about you if they trust you.

The research also indicates that customers' ability and willingness to trust a business is related to how that business handles their privacy. The customer sentiment is clear. Customers want you to give them control, to be transparent, not to take their consent for granted, and to treat their data with respect.

As you build your privacy muscle, you will notice that a lot of these expectations have been codified into laws. As with other social changes like marriage equality and

---

[11]"Research Brief: Trends in Customer Trust," *Salesforce*, http://mng.bz/PXV8.

pay equity, this is an example of laws catching up with social expectations. This is why, when it comes to operationalizing technical privacy, I have placed customer trust as your first privacy-related responsibility, ahead of legal compliance.

Senior leaders will understand by now that privacy is the thread that connects their success as business leaders, their ability to adhere to an expanding regulatory regime, and their ability to build an enduring relationship of trust with their customer base.

A functional and iterative privacy program can efficiently lead to a virtuous circle that will help you succeed materially as well as reputationally, where privacy is not seen as a blocker but an enabler and a differentiator.

All the challenges you have seen thus far help make a case for privacy tooling, and the subsequent chapters will discuss that. For now, let's look at how your program might scale once the tooling is in place.

2.7 *After building the tools comes the hard part: Building a program*

Privacy can be very personal and visceral for individuals, while also being very contextual. That means it is often hard to plan for, measure, and define in a common vernacular. Even when there is good faith and attempts to align on both sides (companies and customers), it can be hard to create a strategy. This book will help create a solid understanding of this complex domain and provide a game plan that you can improvise on based on your needs and organizational situation.

Based on my experience, the journey of privacy tooling and investment has three inflection points:

- There is an immediate surge of ideas and resources when privacy needs arise. In figure 2.9, you can see the spike in privacy investment; this spike is the first inflection point.
- There is a shortage of resources once the privacy threat recedes. This is where privacy investment is redirected to feature development, and you can see the corresponding dip in figure 2.9. You may even end up with less privacy spending than you had at the beginning.
- Then you end up treading water, making a series of privacy decisions to keep the company from getting into regulatory hot water. Spending in privacy picks up, but even as it recovers, it will remain short of the peak. This is the third inflection point, where the company accepts this status quo as its de facto risk tolerance level.

In such a scenario, the privacy program is front and center only when there is an imminent crisis. In a state of reactive panic, all hands are deployed to address privacy concerns.

Many companies that have had to respond to laws like GDPR will have faced a moment like this. The GDPR required companies to make several changes to their processes and tooling in early 2018.

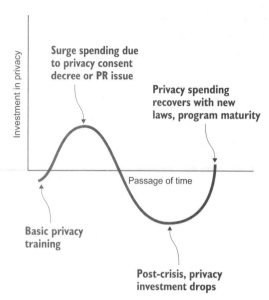

Figure 2.9 **Privacy investments: surge, drop and recovery**

For many companies, this represented a significant change to their regular operations. Many companies had to hire more staff, which was challenging, since individuals with deep privacy backgrounds are relatively rare. Other teams across the board were also impacted by this work. While many companies did try in earnest to meet their GDPR commitments, there was no long-term strategy whereby GDPR would be a stepping stone toward privacy maturity. Too many leaders saw GDPR as a capstone, after which employees would move on to business as usual. What ended up happening in too many instances was that employees kept getting pulled back to complete privacy work, leading to a sense of perpetual whiplash. In reality, leaders should have used, and can still use, GDPR as a foundation to build on. Subsequent chapters will provide you with hands-on skills for embedding privacy into the data and business processes that ensure privacy is a strategic accompaniment to your business endeavors rather than a fire drill that competes with revenue generation.

Customers were similarly confused. Many of us remember getting emails from just about every business we interacted with concerning changes they were making for GDPR. Many friends I talked with did not know what the fuss was about, while others were concerned that they did not understand how their life would be impacted by this law.

Given the sheer volume of work and reprioritization involved, it is hard to assess whether there was a greater alignment and trust between businesses and their customers. In subsequent chapters, we will look at how companies can better inform customers about privacy tools and decisions so that the work companies do for privacy is better understood. That in turn will help build trust and improve the company's brand, and it may even have the effect of reducing some regulatory pressure as well. This preemptive education is critical, since companies should use regulation as a floor rather than a ceiling—companies should do the right thing because it is the right thing for their customers, rather than convey the impression that they were dragged kicking and screaming by regulations.

In the period since the GDPR was enacted, many businesses have faced similar challenges with other privacy-related challenges. Many privacy endeavors require the redeployment of resources, and other work is deprioritized. Once the crisis passes, the status quo often reasserts itself and privacy finds itself resource-constrained, and the company settles into a rhythm where privacy programs tread water, borrowing resources on a case-by-case basis. Rather than strategically investing in making the program flexible, this approach is akin to going grocery shopping every time you get hungry, taking just enough money to pay for the next meal.

In the interest of long-term business success and building trust with your users, technical leaders should build a base of privacy knowledge that will help them manage and drive events rather than be driven by them. The good news is that other fields, like security, have gone through the same process of evolving maturity, so there is precedent on how privacy practices can improve.

The key responsibility of technical leaders who wear many hats is to make the business successful. This book will help you merge privacy into that success strategy by achieving the following goals:

- Build a strong understanding of terms like privacy, security, and compliance.
- Understand how the engineering innovation process has changed, and how a tension exists between data-driven innovation and privacy.
- Create a privacy governance program that will scale efficiently for a resource-constrained business.

With this knowledge in your leadership toolkit, your privacy program's consumption of resources will look less like the up-down-up sequence of figure 2.9 and closer to the graph in figure 2.10. Rather than lurching from spending a lot of resources to fend off a privacy crisis and then losing those resources once the crisis passes, you will build the expertise to operationalize and automate privacy at scale and yet retain the human intuition to do right by your users.

As your program starts out, you will need to expend significant resources to make up for decisions made during a period or growth. Over time, however, you will be able to build a program that will benefit from synergies with security, data platform, and data science. These efficiencies will help manage costs and prevent swings that hurt organizational predictability.

Figure 2.10 makes clear that, simplistically speaking, there is a negative correlation between experience and expenditure when it comes to privacy. This is true both for hands-on technical leaders and for your privacy program, which may include human investment and automation. The early stages of implementing privacy will be harder than when you build a product in your area of expertise, since the domain of privacy is not one that many multitasking technical leaders are deeply immersed in.

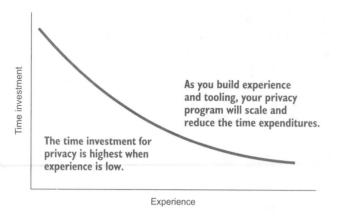

Figure 2.10 **Privacy experience and time investment are inversely proportional.**

While figure 2.10 demonstrates a downward slope in resource expenditure over time, getting started in the task of privacy engineering is initially going to feel like a tough mountain to climb. This book will serve as a base camp and provide you with a map and a ramp to the summit, while also helping you build the muscle for a steep and often unpredictable climb. The goal is not for engineers and architects to become privacy experts per se, but to become conversant enough that they can receive expert advice and incorporate it into business decisions that will have far-reaching implications.

2.8 *As you build a program, build a privacy-first culture*

At its core, this book has two main constituencies: technical leaders on one side, and engineers and cross-functional program managers on the other. In the real world, leaders may in fact travel back and forth between these groups. As such, this book has a broad audience and wide applicability.

Technical leaders at large data-driven businesses may not write code, but they do need to understand the tradeoffs and long-term implications of technical decisions. They have to weigh their decisions, considering how they impact measurable revenue/growth targets versus the more intangible trust/brand goals. These technical leaders—who in some cases may be executives—tend to operate at a high level with a strategic long-term vision. They fuse experience and instinct with data to make business decisions.

For them, privacy represents a disruption and a risk in that it affects their ability to connect to their customers, market to them, and retain them. Privacy goes to the core of how they handle data, how they keep it safe, and how they interpret complex regulations. Without the conceptual and technical understanding of privacy risks and controls, they are like architects who build tall technical structures and unknowingly walk to the edge without technical guidance.

This book will help such leaders do several things:

- Create a culture of "*teach, train, and trust,*" whereby they can *teach* their engineers to handle data with care, *train* them to work with interoperability rather than in siloes to protect customer data, and drive a *trust*-seeking culture rather than one that only craves engagement and monetization.

- Understand the complexity behind implementing privacy tooling at scale, as well as the necessity for their technical teams to have the political cover and budget necessary to get the job done.
- Be able to whiteboard technical privacy solutions and make data-driven decisions so that their teams have clear guidance.

These technical leaders are often founders or leaders charged with helping the company mature en route to an IPO or acquisition. It is vital that they build the hands-on skills to protect their investments and their users.

Understanding privacy will be equally useful to engineers and cross-functional program managers at small, medium-sized, and even large organizations. Such shops may not have dedicated functions and hierarchies, and functions like privacy may lack ownership. This book will provide hands-on tools and ready-to-implement privacy techniques. These tools will allow engineers and other technical leaders to operate on a small budget, avoid unnecessary processes, and produce privacy outcomes that are typically thought possible only in large businesses. As such, this book will enable such a shop to maintain privacy maturity and avoid falling behind, and to retain the option to invest further and turn privacy into a differentiator.

A leader reading this book will understand the general landscape around customer data and security. These are not strict requirements, since coherent strategic understanding of their own business is something this book builds on.

After reading this book, hands-on technical leaders will be able to complete the following tasks:

- Classify data based on privacy risk.
- Build a data catalog by embedding that classification into your data.
- Create privacy controls like data deletion, so that you can delete user data on demand or after the user cancels their account.
- Manage privacy risk by implementing Identity and Access Management (IAM) for your users.
- Run data minimization initiatives to reduce copies of sensitive data in your systems.
- Share data with privacy controls built in so that you can avoid harm to your users.
- Measure the privacy impact of techniques like data obfuscation, so you can qualify risk reduction as your privacy program matures.
- Conduct privacy reviews, ensuring that you can assess products and features with a legal/compliance lens as well as a technical lens.

Table 2.1 is a template for a typical privacy program for agile businesses in various life stages. It shows an abbreviated and somewhat simplistic privacy program, but it does indicate how a privacy program evolves. In its early stage, the program is very tactical and deals with damage control. There is also a substantial investment in understanding

Table 2.1 Stages of a privacy program

Privacy program stage	Components
Early stage	▪ Incident response ▪ Technical debt and discovery of data ▪ Understand legal compliance risk
Planning stage	▪ List the kinds of data being collected ▪ Classify data based on privacy risk ▪ Get signoff with legal and engineering on data classification
Execution stage	▪ Data cataloging ▪ Privacy reviews (prerelease) ▪ Manual data deletion
Maturity stage	▪ Classify and inventory new data ▪ Automate deletion ▪ Ability for exporting and sharing of data in a compliant fashion ▪ Ability to collect user consent ▪ Minimize data collection by building common data stores ▪ Build access controls
Audit-ready stage	▪ Map privacy controls to laws like GDPR and CCPA ▪ Map privacy controls to contractual commitments

the space, since technical leaders in a company will need to pair their broad coverage of the business with more in-depth expertise of specific domain areas.

As the program grows, the company will be able to build tools and processes to classify data, catalog it, and then protect it with privacy-preserving methods like deletion, access control, and minimization. These tools and others like them will form the core of subsequent chapters of this book.

Summary

- The modern engineering processes that drive innovation also tend to make the enforcement of privacy controls more difficult.
- When used correctly and prudently, data can empower and enable your business. If used incorrectly, data can hurt your relationship with your customers, possibly direct the ire of regulators, and hurt your business.
- Privacy is really about data, and how you handle data will help determine how much you can protect user data privacy and your business.
- There is a significant overlap between customer expectations and regulatory sentiment around privacy.
- The regulatory reach around privacy is increasing, so building a program that can protect your business and your users is critical.
- Your users are your customers, and when they use your services, they trust you to protect their interests. Ensuring their privacy is a demonstrable way to do just that.

Part 2

A proactive privacy program: Data governance

This part will help engineers think of privacy engineering not as a series of tools and point solutions but as a platform that leads to sound governance. Given the interconnectedness of the tech ecosystem, engineers will need to build privacy across the stack. This section will provide engineers with hands-on skills to embed privacy into the data.

Chapter 3 focuses on classifying data with cross-functional partners so as to align with privacy risk. Without data classification, you can neither quantify risk nor begin to enforce automated controls. There are also examples on offer to help engineers build instinct and muscle memory for their jobs.

Chapter 4 is a deep-dive on data inventory, so that engineers can affix data classification into the data that lives in their systems. We will architect a system that will inventory and index data using a mixture of manual and intelligence-powered categorization.

Chapter 5 will enable engineers to share data with privacy protections built in. It will educate the reader with techniques to anonymize datasets and measure privacy impact. That way, they can tailor data sharing to business risk appetite, regulatory commitments and customer trust.

Data classification

3

This chapter covers

- Data classification: what it means for your customers
- Why data classification is necessary
- How you can implement data classification
- How data classification can help satisfy your compliance challenges
- How data classification can work cross-functionally
- An end-to-end data classification process

In the first two chapters, I introduced the basics of privacy and what it means for your business. We then built a mental model that connects privacy to trust and safety, so that rather than an altruistic abstraction, privacy becomes a critical business goal.

Subsequently, we identified data as the building construct for privacy because of

- Its power to identify individuals
- Its abundance, thanks to ubiquitous internet connectivity, universally accepted IDs like Google, Facebook, and other device IDs

- Its ability to shape and influence behavior by way of machine learning and artificial intelligence
- Its potential to create often irreversible harms if used inappropriately or exfiltrated

Since protecting user privacy is critical for your company to maintain trust with users and maintain credibility with regulators, media, and privacy activists, it follows logically that your privacy-related efforts need to focus on data. To protect data from being used incorrectly in a way that hurts privacy, engineers need a holistic strategy on how best to understand data. The first part of that strategy is *data classification.*

Before we get into data classification and its details, it is useful to understand how data classification can help improve the overall relationship between the source of the data (the users and customers) and the recipients of the data (the companies that use the data to innovate).

3.1   *Data classification and customer context*

It is impossible to discuss privacy meaningfully without considering the context of the *techlash.* Gradually but certainly over the last 15 years, the tech sector has gone from being the crown jewel of the economy to being the entitled relative who comes to the potluck empty handed and yet grabs seconds and thirds before everyone else has had firsts.

As I wrote on LinkedIn in 2015, unlike traditional sectors like agriculture, infrastructure, and healthcare, technology is inherently different in terms of the relationship between output and labor. In those sectors, you need a lot of workers to consistently convert plans into products. That is not the case with tech jobs, where one of the main appeals of technology is using automation to do more with less labor and fewer iterations.[1]

For example, when Facebook acquired WhatsApp for $19B, WhatsApp employed just 55 employees.[2] This purchase was great for WhatsApp employees, but it did not create any profit or income for anyone outside of those 55 people.[3] Similarly, when Yahoo bought Tumblr, about 40 employees made millions and about 178 employees made about $300K.[4] There are similar examples all over the world.

As far as the tech sector being a jobs engine is concerned, the reputation is not always the reality. As advertised, technology creates great wealth; that wealth, however, is distributed among a small slice of society. There is a bright green line between those who make millions and the remaining "minions." Put simply, the tech sector can create wealth without creating a lot of work, and the average person may feel left out of the economic benefits of the tech boom as a result. As we saw with the recent WeWork

---

[1] Nishant Bhajaria, "Why isn't the tech boom helping the economy?" *LinkedIn*, May 5, 2015, http://mng.bz/v4j1.

[2] Adam Hartung, "Three Smart Lessons From Facebook's Purchase Of WhatsApp" *Forbes*, February 24, 2014, http://mng.bz/4K0D.

[3] "WhatsApp's 55 Employees Are Rich. So Now What?" *NBC News*, February 20, 2014, http://mng.bz/QqAR.

[4] Sam Gustin, "Inside Yahoo!'s Tumblr Deal: Here's Who Hit the Billion Dollar Jackpot" Time, May 21, 2013, http://mng.bz/voNm.

fiasco, the founders exited the company with generous packages, while the rank and file employees received next to nothing.

The ability of the tech sector to optimize everyday life using data is a source of this wealth. The titans of tech position themselves as disruptors of the status quo, but this disruption also often causes societal and social displacement. The contextual and cultural gap between the service economy and rest of the economy that we have witnessed over the last five years stems in part from this phenomenon. That some players in the industry have collected more data than they may have needed, handled it more cavalierly than they should have, and shared the data in a fashion more profligate than was appropriate adds insult to injury.

When users complain about "companies collecting too much data," it is this larger asymmetry that is at work; they feel like companies collect their data, and the benefits of that data collection vest disproportionally with the company. The company can make the argument, often credibly, that this data collection helps build better products for users. The problem is that these features may provide negligible benefits for the users even as they become sources for more data for the company. The character of Leo McGarry from *The West Wing* TV show spoke for many when he expressed his disappointment with the modern tech sector, asking where the moon colonies he was promised were.

Data classification is a critical step that aims to add discipline to the relationship between this sector and the users who ultimately are identified by this data. The process, and the outcome, will help companies evaluate their data collection from the point of view of the users whose data they collect. Data classification could help the company avoid possible privacy issues, demonstrate to outside stakeholders that the company does not see its users as commodities, and enable the company to handle the data more carefully (or delete it more quickly) in line with what the classification says about the data. While classification may not address the larger question of economic wealth inequality, this process will provide data-driven companies a more human lens through which to look at the data and the users represented by it.

In subsequent sections of this chapter, I will address in more detail the "why" and "how" of data classification, but senior engineers need to view this work as part of an overall investment in treating their users with respect and building trust.

3.2 *Why data classification is necessary*

At its core, data classification will answer the following questions for each type of data that is or might be collected or stored:

- What sort of data is this in terms of volume and definition?
- Why do we need to collect it?
- What does it tell us about our customers and our business?
- What would happen if this data were to be mishandled?

When I have to make a business case for data classification for C-level leaders, I tell them that data classification and inventory offer critical benefits to companies, including

- Insight into how a distributed and democratized engineering community uses data
- Continuous alignment between organizational data use and requirements under data protection law
- The ability to tailor data protection techniques and tools and inform engineering roadmaps

Let's add some context to this high-level summary.

3.2.1   *Data classification as part of data governance*

You have already seen that digital businesses face some key challenges:

- Massive growth of and dependence upon data collection
- A confusing and growing regulatory challenge in the US, the EU, and emerging markets

To add to that, we now have yet another challenge: most companies have no process to manage their data collection and identify how much risk that data poses to security and privacy. The author of *The Privacy Engineer's Manifesto*, Michelle Finneran Dennedy, recently stated that on the balance sheets of today's consumer-driven companies, data is both an asset and a liability.

In the absence of sound data governance, you cannot make informed decisions about what to keep and how to best protect it from external attack and internal misuse. Industry experts agree that data classification is step 1 in your journey toward maturing as a company regarding data privacy.

In Microsoft's landmark white paper "Data classification for cloud readiness," the company stated

> *Data classification provides one of the most basic ways for organizations to determine and assign relative values to the data they possess. The process of data classification allows organizations to categorize their stored data by sensitivity and business impact in order to determine the risks associated with the data. After the process is completed, organizations can manage their data in ways that reflect its value to them instead of treating all data the same way. Data classification is a conscious, thoughtful approach that enables organizations to realize optimizations that might not be possible when all data is assigned the same value.[5]*

According to the white paper, it is critical that senior leaders be deeply familiar with data classification. This includes "consultants, security specialists, systems architects, and IT professionals who are responsible for planning application or infrastructure development and deployment for their organizations."

---

[5] "Data classification for cloud readiness," *Microsoft*, http://mng.bz/Xrvl.

These roles include the following common job descriptions identified in the white paper:

- "Senior engineers, business analysts, and business decision makers (BDMs) who have critical business objectives and requirements that need IT support"
- "Architects and planners who are responsible for driving the architecture efforts for their organizations"
- "Consultants and partner organizations who need knowledge transfer tools for their customers and partners"

In previous chapters, we discussed how an increasingly decentralized and democratized organization, powered by a bottom-up innovation ethos, now can make decisions around vast volumes of data. Those decisions involve collecting, accessing, sharing, processing, modifying, and obfuscating data. It is next to impossible to make decisions about how to make these decisions without simultaneously understanding the level of privacy risk attached to the data.

Put simply, data classification is about ranking data in tiers based on risk. To understand why this is important from a prioritization standpoint, let's correlate the classification of data to the classification of human needs.

3.2.2 *Data classification: How it helps align priorities*

There is an inherent tension between finite engineering and data science resources on the one hand and prioritizing your efforts to protect data on the other. You cannot deploy all your resources to protect everything—all data is not equal. There is data that requires the most rigid protection under all circumstances, while other data can require less protection. This section will help engineers approach this prioritization process more systematically.

UNDERSTANDING HOW YOU PRIORITIZE DATA PROTECTION

Figure 3.1 shows Maslow's hierarchy of needs. At the very bottom, it shows how human beings first must provide for their basic needs like breathing, food, water, etc. These are physiological needs. Once those are accounted for, humans need health and employment, as well as physical and reliable security.

Building on that, humans crave love and belonging, the reassurance provided by friends, family and community. Once safety around material and external connections is accounted for, humans seek confidence and self-esteem; this is where they build their own self-worth. At the apex, humans build on their need to live the life of their truest and highest potential.

It is clear that the hierarchy diagram in figure 3.1 is also a prioritization diagram. At the very bottom, human beings prioritize their most existential needs. Once those needs are met, human beings work their way up the hierarchy to meet the next level of needs.

What does Maslow's hierarchy of needs have to do with data privacy? Maslow's hierarchy makes the point that our human needs are not met in one go, and as we meet

Figure 3.1   Maslow's hierarchy of needs

one need, we feel more aware of a more advanced need. Similarly, a company with finite resources, thinly stretched technical leaders, and an urgent need to meet privacy requirements must prioritize. It makes no sense to throw all your resources toward protecting all data equally. This is critical, since companies often overcorrect; after ignoring privacy to their detriment, companies tend to overcompensate by investing wastefully in privacy tools.

Data classification is about ranking data to apply privacy protection to it, much like Maslow's hierarchy ranks needs for fulfillment. Companies can then protect the most sensitive data first, and with lessons learned and tools created, they can then protect data that is of slightly lower sensitivity.

It is instructive to look at figure 3.2 for a simplistic example of what a data classification structure might look like.

> **NOTE** Data classification is about understanding what data you have and what privacy risks it poses, and then dedicating resources to protecting data by prioritizing the data that poses the most consequential privacy risks.

An organization might collect large volumes of data. The level of risk attached to different types of data will vary significantly depending on what might happen were that data to

- Leak (i.e., get exfiltrated outside the company or accessed by unauthorized persons)
- Get combined with other data available elsewhere, internally or externally
- Be shared with another partner

Levels	Definition
Restricted	Personal or business data that is subject to the strictest handling requirements due to its sensitivity and its risk to the business and to customers if mishandled
Confidential	Personal or business data that is subject to strict handling requirements due to its sensitivity and risk if mishandled
Internal	Data that is available to employees and affiliated partners under NDAs solely as a result of their employment with your company, and which is not categorized as confidential or restricted
Public	Business data that is publicly available, including business data disclosed to the public, and which is not subject to handling requirements

Figure 3.2 Sample classifications of data

As such, the resources you dedicate to protect the data should depend on the risk to privacy. In your hierarchy of data, you would want to dedicate a significant chunk of your resources to data that is highly sensitive—labeled as Restricted in figure 3.2. It would stand to reason that such data might identify your customers and their behaviors, but it may also include business-critical data.

The next level of data that you'd want to protect may not be as sensitive as what you have in the Restricted bucket. You will want to calibrate your strategy to protect this data accordingly.

Using figure 3.2 as our reference, it is critical to understand that organizations cannot just declare data to be Confidential because they find the security and privacy protections required for the Restricted classification to be too onerous. Data that is classified as Restricted tends to meet at least a subset of the following criteria:

- It uniquely identifies a specific individual. This is a subjective criterion; a name like "John Smith" does not uniquely identify someone unless accompanied by other data like a home address, but a name like "Nishant Bhajaria" offers a much higher level of identifiability.
- It is possible to join this data with other data that is easily available to identify a specific individual and their activities or preferences.
- Information about an individual made available in this data places them in a unique bucket. For example, suppose a company named 12080 Inc. manages an online pharmacy and stores a table containing data about people taking blood pressure medicines. In the table, the users are identified via random IDs so as to not name them. Such a table might be privacy-safe when it contains data for all of New York City, given the potentially high numbers of people. The same table, if it were to contain information about people living in Beatty, OR, might present a privacy risk since the town of Beatty has fewer people.

Simply put, Restricted data tends to be individualized while Confidential data tends to be more aggregated. Because of the attendant privacy implications, Restricted data has tighter access controls and lower retention timelines, whereas Confidential data could have looser access requirements and longer timelines for retention.

DATA SEGMENTATION

The previous subsection provided us a framework for classifying data based on risk. However, data classification exercises are not just about understanding the privacy sensitivity of the data itself; the classification exercises can help you reduce privacy risk by helping you modify the data itself.

It is relatively straightforward to classify data by categorizing as Restricted any data fields that privacy and security engineers deem sensitive. However, companies often automate policy enforcement based on such classifications. For example, all data marked as Restricted may be encrypted at rest and in motion. In such situations, it may be possible to be more flexible and balance data privacy right alongside accessibility. Privacy engineers can segment data such that only data that is truly sensitive gets stringent privacy protections, while other data can be more freely accessed.

Companies could segment data along the following lines:

- *Data about individuals*—This data would describe specific people who could be personally identified and therefore harmed if their privacy is violated. This data could further be segmented as follows:
  - Employee data
  - Contractor data
  - Customer data
  - Unregistered user data

  Data about individuals would be subject to privacy protections, but a company may wish to offer varying levels of protection to different kinds of individuals. For example, registered users (or customers) may be entitled to stringent privacy protections. On the other hand, employees may be subject to tracking to mitigate insider risk and information theft.

  If all data belonging to individuals were classified the same way, you would end up with a "one size fits all" approach that would either overprotect or underprotect data.

- *Data about things*—Companies also need to secure data that identifies objects like products, designs, places, etc. This data could be mission critical to the business and key to its profits and competitiveness. However, the data may not be subject to privacy-centric controls like deletion, obfuscation, etc.

  For example, for the US government, the location of a missile may be Restricted data and should not be accessible to all federal employees by default. However, the classification exercise must allow for that data to be identified, tagged, and protected differently than if it were customer data. You still need to protect business IP data, but in doing so you are protecting your business. In the case of customer data, you are being compliant with regulations and protecting customer trust.

Even in this case, a caveat is in order. It is possible that data about things could be associated or joined with data that identifies individuals. Therefore, classifying this data granularly could help implement and track privacy protections down the road.

- *Data in aggregation*—Data privacy risk is not immutable and static. As you aggregate data and obfuscate it, the privacy risk may discernibly decrease, as you will see in chapter 5.

  For example, a cohort of user records that doesn't include specific user identifiers (like names) but includes the home address for each user may normally be marked as Restricted. However, you may be able to reduce privacy risk by aggregating users based on the ZIP code they live in, excising the home addresses from the data set. You could retain only those user records that are in a cohort of 100 or more per ZIP code. This may enable you to run experiments tailored to aggregated data sets without subjecting those data sets to the same rigorous privacy precautions that are better suited to data about individuals.

  You may also be able to aggregate data based on timelines, trends, etc. The key takeaway is this: transforming datasets from ones that describe individuals to ones that look at a collective could help classify them as having lower privacy restrictions.

I added the preceding context around data segmentation because fast-moving companies without deep privacy expertise often are tempted by extremes. They are either overcautious and classify large volumes of data as Restricted or are overconfident in their sense of virtue and underestimate privacy risks. Looking at data more contextually enables a classification that is more accurate and enforceable.

Such an approach is also more reflective of how modern engineering works. Data, infrastructure, and microservices are tailored to fit their purposes. It is critical that privacy engineers classify data in a way that balances the needs of the business while placing data protection at the apex of their priorities.

In order to help this concept sink in, a small exercise is in order.

DATA PROTECTION EXERCISE: PRIORITIZATION AS A LENS

Let's assume you manage a company that analyzes the purchasing of medicine to advise a pharmacy so that they can plan for new orders. As such, you have access to the prescriptions that have been filled, with the names of patients, their birth dates, their genders, addresses, etc. Compiling these prescriptions over a period of time will give you a sense of what the demand looks like. Based on that demand forecast, you can plan for future orders from drug manufacturers so that you can make sure future prescriptions can be filled promptly.

In your database, the information that personally identifies the patients and what medicines they take would fall in the Restricted category. Under most laws, this information is extremely sensitive, and even beyond the regulatory angle, people are extremely protective of information that deals with their health care. It stands to reason that data in this bucket will be tied to strict access controls and constrained retention periods.

However, in this use case, you have no reason to focus on individual users and their health or medical situations. You are more interested in the aggregate prescription information over time, so you can plan for the future. As such, you could modify your storage patterns. The two tables that follow explain how.

Table 3.1 represents a database in which you have names of individuals listed with the medicines they ordered at a pharmacy. This information could uniquely identify individuals and hence would be classified as Restricted.

Table 3.1   Individual prescription listing

Name	Medicine	Date
Josh Smith	Ritalin	12/1/2019
Karen Jones	Ritalin	12/7/2019
Oona Blair	Losartan	12/8/2019
Vikram Khanna	Ritalin	12/15/2019
Tony Brown	Losartan	12/18/2019
Theresa Johnson	Losartan	12/22/2019

For your purposes, you may want to retain this data for longer than normally allowed or to allow more people to access it. In table 3.2, you can see a database that has redacted the names of the patients and yet retained the data you really care about—how many times specific medicines were purchased in the pharmacy. You could make an informed argument that the absence of personally identifiable information in this table means that it could be classified as Confidential, which means you could retain it for longer, perhaps to compare December 2019 to December 2018.

Table 3.2   Aggregated prescription listing

Medicine name	Number of prescriptions	Date range
Ritalin	3	12/1/2019–12/31/2019
Losartan	3	12/1/2019–12/31/2019

Figure 3.3 shows how transitioning from table 3.1 to table 3.2 is a win for privacy, cost savings, and security as well. This is an oversimplified example, but the takeaway is that data classification allows you to understand your use case better and to manage the data protection techniques more prudently.

Name	Medicine	Date
Josh Smith	Ritalin	12/1/2019
Karen Jones	Ritalin	12/7/2019
Oona Blair	Losartan	12/8/2019
Vikram Khanna	Ritalin	12/15/2019
Tony Brown	Losartan	12/18/2019
Theresa Johnson	Losartan	12/22/2019

Medicine name	Number of prescriptions	Date range
Ritalin	3	12/1/2019-12/31/2019
Losartan	3	12/1/2019-12/31/2019

The data for each user is individually listed. This means less privacy, higher storage costs, and expanded security attack surface.

The data is aggregated based on a shared attribute (medicine name). This means more privacy, lower storage costs, and reduced security attack surface.

Figure 3.3   Changing data for better privacy and lower costs

The thinking and collaboration required in transforming a table with individual data into a table with more aggregated data will ensure you are more thoughtful and proactive about what you collect and how long you keep it. The potential savings in storage costs and the reduction in risk are benefits that will accrue over time, and you will be able to build a credible narrative that you are collecting data for legitimate business reasons without being careless about user privacy.

Later in this chapter, we will look at a detailed example of how you'd want to classify data.

3.2.3   *Industry benchmarking around data classification*

As you have previously seen, data classification is the first step in an overall data governance program. Before we go deeper into data classification, it is vital for engineers and aspiring engineers to understand that, even as privacy has been top of mind in the tech industry and other data-driven sectors, companies have a lot of catching up to do in the data governance space.

In my professional travels, I hear a common theme. We do not know where to start with data governance. Gartner's research (titled "Guidance for Addressing Risks with Unstructured Data") bears that out.

- 25% of respondents do not have a formal program.
- Nearly 38% have a program that could be described as "early stage."
- Nearly 37% have a program that is functional on a regular basis.

If you don't have a fully functional program, you are hardly alone. But that will not make the challenge go away.

This is especially a problem for unstructured data, which is a big portion of what companies store in their data warehouses for analysis.

3.2.4   *Unstructured data and governance*

Unstructured data is data that can't be easily stored in a traditional column/row database or spreadsheet (such as a JSON blob). I once had an engineer tell me that they had no sensitive data in their Cassandra database, and then we discovered that in nested JSON objects there were IP addresses that could be used to identify some users. Unstructured data, though it's often overlooked, can be misused and thus should be governed with the same care as structured data (data stored in a traditional column/row database).

By contrast, structured data is data that adheres to a predefined data model and is aimed at use cases that require straightforward analysis.[6] Structured data normally conforms to a tabular format with a defined relationship between different rows and columns, such as a SQL database.

According to *Forbes*, the unstructured data collected and stored by businesses is growing at 55–65% each year.[7] According to TechRepublic, 80% of the data companies process is unstructured.[8]

Because of its nature, unstructured data is more difficult to analyze than structured data and it's not easily searchable, which is why it wasn't useful for organizations until recent years. Today, however, we have unstructured data analytics tools powered by artificial intelligence (AI) that were created specifically to access the insights available from unstructured data.

Organizations need to understand the types of unstructured data they are accumulating and the best ways to process and store this data. This is especially true since unstructured data will make it harder to implement the requirements of several privacy laws.

The Gartner white paper also explains how companies that struggle with data governance face a particular challenge regarding unstructured data.

- For 75% of respondents, identifying locations where unstructured data was stored represented a business challenge.
- For 63% of respondents, removing unstructured data after the expiration of retention periods was challenging.
- For 37.5% of respondents, getting business leadership buy-in was a challenge.

A lot of unstructured data ends up in logs or nested JSON blobs, where data is often buried. While it was easy to use tools like REGEX to detect sensitive data like IP addresses, if an IP address is buried deep in unstructured data, you may never detect it and therefore fail to delete it on time. While REGEX patterns can match unstructured data, the sheer volume of data being collected could lead to algorithms timing out before that data can be discovered and identified as sensitive personal data.

---

[6] "Data Types: Structured vs. Unstructured Data," *Enterprise Big Data Framework*, January 9, 2019, http://mng.bz/yJlo.

[7] Bernard Marr, "What Is Unstructured Data And Why Is It So Important To Businesses? An Easy Explanation For Anyone," Forbes, October 16, 2019, http://mng.bz/MvND.

[8] Mary Shacklett, "Unstructured data: A cheat sheet," TechRepublic, July 14, http://mng.bz/aZW9.

Remember, all these challenges exist even as companies are collecting more and more unstructured data. Such companies could end up not capitalizing on the unstructured data they collect and storing more unstructured data than they really need, thereby running up data center costs and adding to their privacy and security risks.

> **NOTE** Unstructured data is an example of how techniques that improve innovation—high speed and availability—could pose privacy risks. The nature of data empowers engineers and data scientists, but it makes life difficult for privacy engineers.

So, besides privacy, it is vital that the company have a sound data governance strategy for unstructured data, since a lot of this data may contain insights that could help business competitiveness. The cross-functional process of data classification will shed light on the data your company has collected and stored across all its systems and on how that data is used.

I'll revisit this in chapter 4 and explain how the data science, business development, and privacy teams can work together to inventory the data, which is another key part of data governance.

3.2.5 Data classification as part of your maturity journey

I'd be remiss if I made the case for data classification without connecting it to your organizational maturity and the journey it takes to get there.

WHAT IS ORGANIZATIONAL MATURITY?

Engineers and other technical leaders expect to help improve the quality of organizational output and then scale their organizations to help deliver that output more efficiently i.e. help get to a higher maturity level.

Organizational maturity is especially important for technical initiatives. This is where the model to measure and guide an organization to a higher level of maturity is useful.

According to TechTarget, "the Capability Maturity Model (CMM) is a methodology used to develop and refine an organization's software development processes. The model describes a five-level evolutionary path of increasingly organized and systematically more mature processes."

According to the TechTarget article, "the CMM is similar to ISO 9001, one of the ISO 9000 series of standards specified by the International Organization for Standardization (ISO).... ISO 9001 specifically deals with software development and maintenance." The two systems have differences as well: "ISO 9001 specifies a minimal acceptable quality level for software processes, while the CMM establishes a framework for continuous process improvement and is more explicit than the ISO standard in defining the means to be employed to that end."[9]

---

[9] "Capability Maturity Model (CMM)," *TechTarget*, https://searchsoftwarequality.techtarget.com/definition/Capability-Maturity-Model.

Without getting too deeply entrenched in the details, figure 3.4 shows the various levels of evolving capability and maturity. As you can see, software development processes range from unpredictable and poorly controlled to mature enough to allow for improvement and refinement. During the ideation phase of software development, it is common to have very few controls on code quality, documentation, deployment cadences, etc. This helps developers release early versions quickly with room to iterate, and the progress helps fledgling companies raise money. As companies mature, however, it is vital to create processes that can help scale technical work and improve quality.

Maturity level characteristics

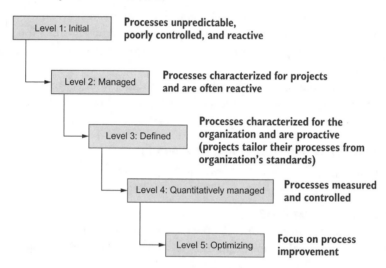

Figure 3.4   A Capability Maturity Model

In the early days of product development, it also makes sense to gather data in order to harness your roadmap and guide your execution. Left unchecked, however, this approach can lead to accumulation of risk and the possible violation of customer trust. In that sense, data classification can help your organization mature in its ability to secure the appropriate data, build trust with your customers, and possibly gain favor with stakeholders in markets where organizational credibility gets a special premium. Good privacy is good policy.

DATA CLASSIFICATION AND ORGANIZATIONAL MATURITY

In many cases, highly autonomous and decentralized engineering teams may blanche at the requirement that they label their data and handle it based on the risk that the classification implies. After having years of free rein to collect and access data, this step may reek of bureaucracy and process.

Before you dismiss their concerns, understand that these engineers are held to tight deadlines and aggressive roadmaps that executives or aspiring executives have set up. The same business forces that drive data-powered innovation ask the same engineering teams to show rigor and prudence in data handling. The former ask creates an incentive for moving fast with data and being creative, while the latter serves to rein in that exact mandate.

These contradictions often create tension between the teams that have to execute on regular deliverables, which is why classifying data early and cross-functionally is critical. Otherwise you will see endless churn, with the privacy team becoming the face of dysfunction.

Engineers and other technical leaders need to assist privacy teams when they impress upon their company the following realities:

- The concept of data classification is not a novel one. The highly regimented practice of coding documents as "sensitive" or "classified" has been commonplace in the military and in government for decades. This process was adapted by financial and commercial sectors as a way to protect valuable business data and prevent data exfiltration by outsiders as well as insiders.
- While governments and smaller companies can make do with high-level classification, companies that change their business lines often (such as entering new markets) and adapt to new use cases (such as supporting new user devices), may need granular and more flexible classifications. For example, a government can define "ID" as a tier to include anything that uniquely identifies an individual. This could include an email address as well as something like a Social Security number. However, a more data-driven company could create two classes like "Personally Identifying IDs" and "Government IDs," in which case an email address would map to the former, while a Social Security number would map to the latter.
- In order to prevent the data classification process from becoming siloed like many existing product and engineering teams, you'll want to avoid creating classifications for different use cases, such as one set of classifications for data that needs encryption, and another for data that needs to be deleted, etc. You want your classification to drive outcomes, rather than have outcomes dictate the data classification. The examples in the next section will show, for example, how changes in data classification could impact how you manage access to the data.
- Finally, the bottom-up democratic decision-making process that enables product innovation does not often work with privacy initiatives like data classification. You will want a model where engineers and data scientists have a voice, since they will make tactical decisions related to data. However, you will want senior leadership to make the final call on classification and to own the risks attendant to it. Discussions and debate must yield to decisions.

These lessons are important, since data classification is costly, as well as being the foundation of several future privacy decisions. The role of technical leaders who lead engineering and product teams is to provide their teams enough political cover and to incentivize them to be strategic. This will help ensure that engineers and product managers think beyond the next week or month, and produce outcomes that help privacy, data quality, and security, as well as help the overall maturity of the company.

In the next section, we will examine how data classification can be implemented through various lenses.

3.3   *How you can implement data classification to improve privacy*

As stated before, data classification helps rank your data based on business and privacy risks. As a practical matter, whether you have a usable and updated classification of your data has meaningful consequences ranging from your ability to protect data to matters as quotidian as how your employees access data.

3.3.1   *Data classification and access options*

When I started my career as an engineer at Intel, managing data access was a top priority for the company. I wrote code for the next-generation test chips, so I had access to device designs and formulas that were top secret. As such, I had to enter several different passwords and change them routinely to maintain my access to critical systems. I never complained, since I recognized the criticality of protecting the company's research. However, if the same rigor were applied to accessing noncritical data, it would hinder productivity. Additionally, modern engineers are extremely ingenious and can find ways around systems they deem to be needlessly bureaucratic. Data classification is critical in tailoring data access strategies to the risks inherent in the nature of the data itself.

Privacy programs can take two approaches:

- Lockdown
- Tooling, training, and trust

The *lockdown* model requires engineers and others to go through stringent controls to access data. While this may be practical in some companies, it can have unintended consequences. In a fast-paced environment, as the scale of data grows and as several distributed teams work together, this approach may slow down the business even if the data being accessed is not privacy-sensitive. For example, I have a friend who works in customer service. She tells me that callers often get annoyed when they have to verify their identity before getting access to their financial details.

While strict access control is absolutely essential for financial and health data, you need to apply privacy protections that are proportionate to the sensitivity of the data. Records around purchasing history, when all traces of user identity have been wiped out and there is no way to link that data back to a human being, require a lot less protection than records where the purchasing history includes IDs that can be mapped to another table where IDs are stored alongside user names and emails.

The *tooling, training, and trust* model is, as the name implies, a combination of three *T*s:

- Tools (encryption, multifactor authentication, deletion APIs, etc.)
- Training
- Building an overall culture of trust that will honor user privacy

The right approach is often a combination of both approaches. You will want to lock down some data that is extremely sensitive and that, if leaked or improperly accessed, could hurt your customers and their trust in your business. For the remaining data, you will want protections mapped to risk and use cases. For an overall program to work at scale, you need to classify all the major types of data you collect as a business.

There is a reason I am using *access* as a key vector to make a case for data classification. Companies can address the risk around sensitive data in three ways. First, they could clamp down on data collection. This is a strategic initiative and will take a focused and long-term investment, given the decentralized nature of data collection we have already discussed. While vital, this approach is unlikely to offer the centralized control that can meaningfully help privacy.

Second, companies could delete data that is critical or past its sell-by date. Deletion is a very useful privacy fix, in that it is often irreversible and the closest you can get to the guaranteed reversal of having identified a user.

However, deletion is not the catch-all solution many may wish it to be. It can be expensive, given that most companies start building deletion tools after having collected a fair amount of data. Additionally, it is very difficult to meaningfully target data for deletion unless you can optimize for risk.

Even powerful tools can suffer from timeouts and out of memory errors because the volume of data in your systems may be too large to discover, let alone delete. For engineers and other senior leaders, it would be problematic to declare that they have deleted data only to later find out that copies of the data still exist in some peripheral system that an engineer did not include in the system architecture.

Furthermore, in some cases, regulatory requirements for taxes, legal holds, etc., may require you to retain some records. I have also seen data retention periods tied to enterprise contract requirements, depending on advice from counsel.

Third, companies could manage access based on the privacy risk. This is a practical solution, since companies can classify data based on risk, label the data in the system using a process called data inventory, which we will discuss in the next chapter, and then apply access controls. This investment will also substantially help the deletion process.

If executives want to minimize and mitigate the privacy risk that emerges from engaging with customers and collecting their data, classifying it is a must. To understand how data classification can help protect privacy, let's look at an in-depth example.

3.3.2   *Data classification, access management, and privacy: Example 1*

This example deals with an issue that most companies face: how to verify that users trying to access sensitive data are who they say they are. The tools to help solve this are authorization and authentication (also known as *authn* and *authz*).

For data that is less sensitive, simply verifying user identity—that the user is an employee of your company, for example—may be sufficient. You can do this using *authentication.*

Authorization is the next step after *authorization.* As companies build up sensitive data, they need to build an access management regime that is fine-grained. The decision to grant access to specific data or combinations of data may need to be made at scale; authorization refers to the orchestration of access management. This enforcement can occur for automated interactions between two or more services, as well as interactions between the user and a service. For example, an engineer who maintains a specific service may be authorized to deploy to a staging environment with synthetic data but not to production environments with real user data. Authorization is a *bout setting access policies and enforcing them at scale.*[10]

Figure 3.5 explains how authentication provides privacy from an overall system standpoint, while authorization provides privacy on a layer-by-layer and system-by-system basis.

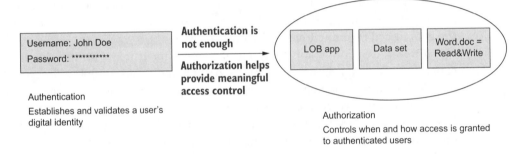

Figure 3.5   Authentication and authorization

You can see why authentication and authorization are critical for privacy, since the more sensitive the data, the more you'd want to use more than just authentication. However, privacy engineers need to understand that data classification can help you deploy these tools more strategically.

More and more companies are moving to a DevOps model, which has changed digital business in important ways. DevOps has come to describe companies that automate the deployment of code as well as aggressively develop capabilities and store data in cloud instances. More specifically, there is a push to move away from on-premises IT and toward a cloud-first future. This has made storing data easier, and as a result, companies collect more data.

Further, in the DevOps model, the infrastructure is powered by code rather than purely by hardware. This shift enables operations teams to configure machines as code. These machines need access and privileges to do what they were programmed to do, and it is increasingly difficult for security teams to keep track of who or what has access,

---

[10]John Walsh, "Distinguishing Authn and Authz," *DZone,* April 4, 2018, http://mng.bz/g1Z8.

especially in cases where machine access starts to exceed human access. You can see how data classification could help protect data in such a dynamic environment.

With a data classification system in place, you can deploy a hybrid strategy that might look like the following:

- Implement role-based access controls (RBAC) for user-to-system and system-to-system permissions management.[11]
- Keep critical access keys out of code, off of hard drives, and out of code repositories such as GitHub and GitLab.
- Generate audit reports to demonstrate regulatory compliance around access and authorization.
- Manage SSH keys and/or secrets at scale across dynamic systems.
- Gain visibility into the total set of cloud systems in use and see who has access to them.

These are all extremely critical points and appropriate for sensitive data, but *not for all data and all systems.*

A prudent and practical approach would have you apply authorization to sensitive data, while other data (like meeting agendas, public earnings reports, user data that is de-identified) could get by with just authentication, where anyone whose identity you have verified can access them.

3.3.3 *Data classification, access management, and privacy: Example 2*

As you may have picked up on, a sound data classification scheme enables you to protect data by managing access to it. In the previous example, we looked at one strategy that manages access to data by splitting access levels based on authentication and authorization. That approach makes decisions around access control at the system level; the system decides who can enter (authentication) and what they can access (authorization).

You could alternatively use data classification to tie the access control decision to the data. For example, if data is classified at the highest level of sensitivity, you could mandate tight requirements for how it can be transported between systems or stored in systems owned by the company. For example, let's assume that as we go from tier-1 to tier-n, the privacy sensitivity of the data decreases (tier-1 is the most privacy-sensitive data with arguably the most stringent data protection requirements). These requirements could look like the following:

- Access controls besides the traditional username/password combination (like multifactor authentication). In this case, the data may not need to be encrypted.
- Password-protected account/link and tier-1 data being encrypted in transit.

---

[11]Ellen Zhang, "What is Role-Based Access Control (RBAC)? Examples, Benefits, and More," *DataInsider*, December 1, 2020, http://mng.bz/5Z97.

- End-to-end transit encryption at the service layer with mutual TLS where technically feasible. Where mutual TLS is not feasible, you can mandate that engineers must use regular SSL/TLS, since unencrypted HTTP is not permitted.
- For data stored in the public cloud, tier-1 data must be encrypted using client-side encryption.

The final requirement is for protecting data at rest in general; it's not specific to data transmission with third parties. Whether or not highly sensitive data is shared with third parties, if that data is stored in public clouds for an extended period of time, it needs to be encrypted using client-side encryption.

An example of a threat vector is as follows: an actor employed by your public cloud provider may obtain the credential of a service account that has access to an S3 bucket and could use that service account credential to access your data in that bucket. Merely attempting to address privacy with server-side encryption doesn't protect against this threat. While you may not be versed in the technical details here, the key takeaway is that you need to think about access management even when data leaves your systems, since the trust relationship with your users and their privacy depends on how your partners access the data you send them. Be sure to take a holistic view of privacy, beyond just protecting data while it's in your system perimeter.

These restrictions may slow down access to your data. Having in place a solid data classification scheme will help you understand how sensitive different components of your data are, who accesses them, and for what purposes. That way, you can deploy these techniques more selectively and in a more targeted fashion. The process of classifying the data will be an education in itself.

3.4 How to classify data with a focus on privacy laws

So far, you have seen how data classification can help you deploy tools to better address privacy needs. Now we'll examine how you can classify data in a way that helps eliminate some of the confusion from new privacy laws and prevents varying interpretations of these laws from affecting your ability to protect your data.

3.4.1 Data classification as an abstraction of privacy laws

As I've previously mentioned, I am not an attorney, so my interpretation of privacy laws is based on my interaction with legal experts and should not be construed as legal advice. You will want to consult with in-house and outside counsel to interpret the applicable laws and remedies.

We have previously examined the rapidly evolving legal landscape around privacy and looked at why it is critical for engineers to build a baseline of knowledge around privacy. However, any time you have several laws emerging concurrently across the world, there can be unforeseen complications in how they apply to a company's ability to handle user data and its obligations under the law.

For the purposes of privacy, a key concept is *personal data* or *Personally Identifiable Information* (PII), but definitions vary and can be vague. Getting this definition right can be challenging for anyone trying to manage user data. There is no universal approach to PII in the United States or in the jurisdictions overseas that have adopted comprehensive privacy regulation. NIST defines it as "information that can be used to distinguish or trace an individual's identity."[12] This definition requires a case-by-case assessment of the specific risk that an individual can be identified.

California's CCPA defines "personal information" much more broadly. It includes

- IP addresses
- Commercial information like records of personal property, products considered, etc.
- Biometric information
- Internet browsing and search history
- Geolocation data
- Audio, electronic, visual, thermal, and olfactory information

Since defining PII is a challenge for companies that have historically collected vast amounts of data, it is key that companies are purposeful about what data they collect and how they protect it. Thus, it is vital any company that wants to scale their privacy efforts create a data classification system that can map to the critical mass of privacy laws.

The legal landscape around privacy is complex, but it also represents an opportunity. A company that can create a data classification that evolves from and scales with shifting privacy laws may not have to play catch up once the authorities start enforcing the laws. In that sense, implementing data classification is akin to having your own version of tax preparation software, which is in essence an abstraction of tax laws that regular taxpayers may never comprehend.

3.4.2 *Data classification to resolve tension between interpretations of privacy laws*

Another challenge these privacy laws pose is for data security. Just as privacy laws often have confusing and conflicting guidelines, they often make what is already hard even harder: protecting customer data.

On one hand, privacy begins only when adequate security is in place. Without security, you cannot have any meaningful privacy. On the other hand, sometimes the need for privacy can make security harder. We are starting to see this as privacy laws become more expansive.

For example, the WHOIS system makes the identifying and contact information of end users publicly available, and WHOIS data has been an important tool for security and fraud prevention, and in tracking down bad actors on the internet. The broad scope of GDPR may have created problems in administering this vital tool.

Data portability, as required by several privacy laws, has created privacy challenges of its own. Prominent individual rights granted to individuals in privacy proposals include the ability to access, correct, transfer, or delete information about them. California's CCPA requires that businesses make information available in a usable format

---

[12]PII definition, *NIST*, https://csrc.nist.gov/glossary/term/PII.

so a consumer can transmit the data to another entity. And Europe's GDPR introduces a right for individuals to have personal data erased. The right to erasure is also known as "the right to be forgotten."

Questions around these access and portability rights include how to securely transfer data to consumers. As privacy advocates like the Electronic Frontier Foundation have explained, "ported data can contain extremely sensitive information…, and companies need to be clear about the potential risks before users move their data to another service."[13] Risks include the theft or exposure of data that has been centralized for sharing, or transferring it to the wrong individual.

In addition to previously discussed problems around data deletion, there are a few more complications to consider:

- Deleting data can also affect the quality and breadth of underlying data sets, on which innovation and security will increasingly depend.
- If individuals or groups of individuals remove data from data sets, it will almost certainly hurt the quality of the data sets or the reliability of the output.

For example, the permanent deletion of records related to a particular user's activities—even where those activities are non-identifying—could prevent the type of long-term analysis of behavior that is increasingly used to identify new potential cybersecurity threats. This lack of historical data could create or perpetuate significant potential security vulnerabilities.

Given the complexity inherent to data from its collection through to its deletion and the privacy implications of data being mishandled, it is vital that companies not wait for regulatory clarification to start their privacy programs. Forward-thinking companies will do well to classify their data at an early stage, using existing legal frameworks as the floor and customer trust as the ceiling they want to reach for.

3.5   *The data classification process*

Now that we have set the stage for why you need to classify data, let's discuss what data classification looks like. In modern businesses, data classification is typically the outcome of detailed investigations and negotiations. The key players include

- Privacy legal
- Technical privacy
- Security
- Engineering
- Product management
- Data scientists

Although privacy is widely seen as a legal area, it would be a huge mistake to only let the legal team drive this classification process.

---

[13]Gennie Gebhart, Bennett Cyphers, and Kurt Opsahl, "What We Mean When We Say 'Data Portability'," *EFF*, September 13, 2018, http://mng.bz/6mWR.

The lawyers may take an overly defensive approach by applying the law without business context or may give engineers too much of a free hand, believing in their own ability to win in court. Either approach is suboptimal.

I have implemented the data classification process at three companies, all having very different cultures, using the same three steps at all three. Let's look at these steps.

3.5.1 Working with cross-functional stakeholders on your data classification

In step 1, I worked with privacy legal to get a sense of how they would classify data. Concurrently, I was working with engineering, product management, and data science to understand what data they needed for legitimate operational and analysis purposes.

It is critical to understand why you want input from this diverse set of stakeholders as part of your data classification. A practical example will help shed some light.

Let's assume you are the privacy lead at a company that provides an app called "Directions" that helps drivers navigate their travel. A typical use case would involve starting at location A, entering the address for destination B, and the app would then provide you with directions to help you get from A to B. At the backend, you would have a database that might look like table 3.3.

Table 3.3 Backend database for Directions app

Name	Email	Starting address (Lat/Lon)	Ending address (Lat/Lon)
Josh Smith	jsmith@gmail.com	5 decimals	5 decimals
Karen Jones	kjones@live.com	5 decimals	5 decimals
Oona Blair	oblair@msn.com	5 decimals	5 decimals
Vikram Khanna	vik@yahoo.com	5 decimals	5 decimals
Tony Brown	tony@tonybrown.co	5 decimals	5 decimals
Theresa Johnson	tjo@yahoo.com	5 decimals	5 decimals

The legal team would argue that each row of this table would uniquely identify an individual and focus on two reasons:

- The email addresses for users of the app uniquely map to specific individuals. The email could be linked with other data about the users on the internet and create a detailed profile about the user. Given the potency of such data, this would greatly increase the impact of a breach or misuse.
- The addresses—both starting and ending—are very precise. With GPS locations, the more decimals you have in the address, the more precise the location.

The legal team could come back with their assessment that each record (each row in the table) be called Restricted, with tight controls on who can access them, as well as requiring a short retention period.

The data science team might push back, since their ability to analyze trips, mine that data for advertising, update maps based on street usage, etc., depends heavily on collecting this data over time and observing what patterns emerge. They might argue that the database and the data contained therein be classified such that it can be retained for longer and with fewer restrictions.

I have been in many meetings where the legal team feels like the engineers and data scientists are being overly careless with the sensitivity of data, while the engineers and analysts accuse the lawyers of being intransigent and divorced from how common data access is across the industry—what I like to call the "our competitors do it already" argument.

The engineering team may propose a solution that looks like table 3.4, where fields that could uniquely identify an individual—their names and emails—are obfuscated using a technique called hashing. It may be worth pointing out that while emails do uniquely identify the specific person who created the account, names are not unique. But if you have a name like mine (Nishant Bhajaria), it is possible that very few, if any, individuals have the same name. That said, in the interest of avoiding records that would uniquely identify a specific user, the engineering team could obfuscate both the names and the email addresses.

Table 3.4   Backend database for Directions app

Name	Email	Starting address (Lat/Lon)	Ending address (Lat/Lon)
(hashed)	(hashed)	3 decimals	3 decimals
(hashed)	(hashed)	3 decimals	3 decimals
(hashed)	(hashed)	3 decimals	3 decimals
(hashed)	(hashed)	3 decimals	3 decimals
(hashed)	(hashed)	3 decimals	3 decimals
(hashed)	(hashed)	3 decimals	3 decimals

In order to make the location less precise, the engineering team could reduce the number of decimal points in the GPS addresses retained for analysis. The limited precision could mean that the starting and ending addresses describe a much larger geographic area. That makes it less likely that a given address would uniquely identify a specific home or office location.

The collective changes could mean that the data, as a whole, is now less sensitive, and that the database records as listed in table 3.4 are Confidential rather than Restricted.

This does leave open a question: what if there are use cases that need precise addresses and identities? For example,

- The safety team may need access to granular location and contact information data in the event that a customer complains they got into an accident due to bad directions.
- You may wish to launch premium versions of your app where a user's entire ride history is available to them for a small fee.

In this situation, you could retain both versions of the data, albeit with qualifications:

- Table 3.3 would be available to a small set of engineers with access controls, so that they would have to request access with a business justification, and their access dates would be logged.
- Table 3.4 would have less stringent requirements and be more open in terms of access and retention periods.

NOTE The preceding example casts engineers as less conservative on privacy, but in a truly bottom-up startup culture, engineers may take on a "conscience of the customer" activist role for privacy, while attorneys may be content with a "compliance first" approach. A solid data governance strategy will provide you flexibility to allow for the human dimension that is inherent in something as contextual and personal as privacy.

Step 1 represents the ideation phase, where you collect data from varying perspectives. However, in a real-world scenario, you will need to formalize a data classification scheme somewhat rapidly, since engineers and data scientists will depend on it to make decisions. Accordingly, I have customized steps 2 and 3, which follow, to allow for a scenario where you need an operative data classification system even as you work to evolve it with new information and use cases coming in.

3.5.2   *Formalizing and refactoring your data classification*

In step 2, I would produce an initial classification system based on the regulation-focused input from legal and real-word guidance from other stakeholders.

This is where engineers and aspiring engineers need to empower their privacy leadership to ensure that there is a conscious decision around how different risk levels are created and how different data components are mapped to those risk levels. This is the phase where many companies end up with either a half-baked data classification scheme that covers only the most urgent use cases, or several different versions of data classification that are bespoke to teams, geographies, etc.

While either of these may be great in the short term, fast-moving companies may find that the "urgent replaces the important" phenomenon takes over, in which case the company settles on a half-baked classification with a commitment to finalize it, but never gets around to it. At the same time, multiple engineering and data science teams end up making possibly irreversible decisions, thereby entrenching this data classification.

To avoid this, as a privacy leader, I work with my engineering and legal counterparts to create a biannual cadence for data classification, whereby we release our classification, V1 for example, as an official artifact while opening up a copy of the same document in draft format to collect comments. This is, in effect, the third step.

In step 3, the goals are to

- Identify stakeholders who may not have weighed in during steps 1 and 2, thereby making sure the process is truly inclusive and representative of the disparate work and product silos.
- Ensure that any new use cases that come up with business growth and other changes are assimilated on an ongoing basis into a data classification that is a truly living and breathing document, much like the company's products and technology stack itself.

The third step is critical, since you will uncover areas where key stakeholders may disagree on how privacy-critical a particular data element is.

Let's assume your company owns a platform where app developers can build video games. You may come across a use case where the engineering team wants to join internal IDs with external data about the customer to track which customers bought products by clicking on ads displayed in the game.

You may find that the engineering team believes that such an ID is not privacy-sensitive, since it is internal to the company and will not identify a customer externally. The legal team may disagree, since it may be possible to join this ID to information that will personally identify a customer, like an email address. The legal team may also contend that such data could create re-identification risks, especially in cases where customers request a copy of their data.

3.5.3   *The data classification process: A Microsoft template*

The three-step process I've just described represents the most effective and iterative incarnation of data classification that I have deployed at companies of various sizes. However, it is only fair that I present you with alternatives, especially from stakeholders I deem credible.

Microsoft has identified a model that I have found useful to replicate in organizations that are large and sprawled out, as well as in companies that are smaller and where specialized roles around privacy may not exist.

In their white paper "Data classification for cloud readiness,"[14] Microsoft introduced a *Plan, Do, Check, Act* model (see figure 3.6):

1. *Plan*—Identify a key individual from a central privacy team whose role would include identifying data systems, data collection points, the systems through which data flows (for example, Kafka Pipelines), the systems where data is stored (unstructured databases like Cassandra, structured databases like

---

[14]Microsoft, "Data classification for cloud readiness," http://mng.bz/o8XD.

MySQL), various teams that use the data, etc. This person will create a profile of the data that helps the company operate by working with the cross-functional stakeholders that I listed before.

2. *Do*—After data classification policies are agreed upon, this individual will own the deployment of data classification, which could include governance documents, system controls, etc.

3. *Check*—Merely classifying the data is not sufficient; you'd want to make sure that the privacy controls in your company as well as the products the controls apply to reflect the data classification. This is critical, since the purpose of data classification is to ensure that the data is treated in a meaningfully different fashion, especially from a privacy standpoint.

4. *Act*—Data classification is not a "once and done" effort. Companies grow and shrink, laws evolve continually, privacy activists and media ask questions, and engineering and product teams become creative in their data collection strategies. As such, the privacy team will constantly need to classify and reclassify data and adapt access control techniques accordingly.

Figure 3.6 explains the iterative nature of data classification, which is reflective of how the process will typically play out.

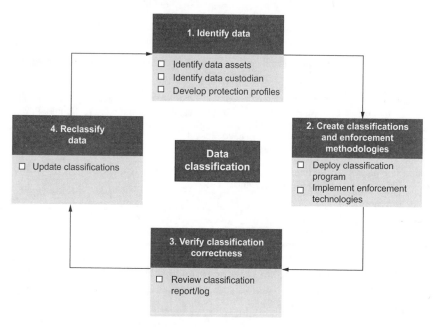

Figure 3.6 A model for data classification[15]

---

[15]Microsoft, "Data classification for cloud readiness."

It is now time for us to walk through an example of the data classification process in detail.

3.6　*Data classification: An example*

Let's look at a scenario reminiscent of what a real company may face in terms of its data. It is vital to remember that there may not be a single right answer to how data is classified—there may be differences in opinion between different teams and, as mentioned before, as the company iterates through this process, data elements may later be classified differently than they were before.

In this example, your company is part of a hospital where patients get treatment and are prescribed medicines. Your company also runs an online pharmacy and provides customers the ability to browse, compare, and buy medicines and then ship them to a specific address.

Customers can access these prescriptions via an app or the website. In order to conduct business, the company needs, as you can imagine, data from customers, such as the types of data described in table 3.5.

Table 3.5　Different categories of data

Type of data	Examples
Identity data	Name, email, address, gender, Social Security number, tax ID, passport number, driver's license number, income, marital status, occupation
Sensitive data	Medical history, prescription refill information, health care coverage information, preexisting conditions, etc.
Payment data	Credit card number (with or without expiration date), bank account and routing numbers, third-party payment service information (e.g., Venmo, PayPal)
Demographic data	Race, ethnicity, religion, sexual orientation/identity, political opinions or trade union membership
Transaction history	Services requested, services provided, date and time of service, amount charged and currency
Authentication and authorization data	Email (for authentication and login purposes, and to confirm order status), phone (for possible two-factor authentication, status updates, etc.), IP and device info (to check for fraud and other analysis)

Let's see what step 1 in the data classification process I described might look like for this business (the Plan phase, as described by Microsoft).

If you look at this purely from a legal and risk-based lens, you could make an argument for the lockdown model. For a specific customer, you would retain data for a specific order

- Only for as long as that order was in progress, and
- Only teams in charge of orders could access that data.

Once a customer receives their medicines and the refund period expires, the data would be deleted. In this context, all or most of these fields would be labeled, such that it reflects their privacy sensitivity.

In contrast, your marketing team may want to conduct analysis on purchases:

- What are the buying patterns based on demographics and location?
- What products are purchased regularly versus seasonally?
- How does use of the app versus the website correspond to purchases?
- How can we identify patterns of shoppers based on various income levels?
- How can we look at this data individually and in aggregate so as to provide better customer service and plan for inventory?

These insights, and others like them, will help drive future investments. And in order for these insights to be meaningful, you would need data from a lot of users over a protracted period of time.

As you can imagine, there is some tension between a very privacy-focused approach where you want limited retention and access, and a business-focused approach that requires higher levels of access and retention.

This is where the cross-functional and iterative approach to data classification can create a win-win situation:

- You could create an operational database with limited retention and access, where data is stored for individual users.
- You could then create an analysis database with longer retention periods and relaxed access, but with data aggregated for a large number of users.

As most seasoned leaders would agree, you should never need to look at a specific user's shopping habits in order to make strategic business investments. Besides being creepy from a privacy standpoint, you will likely end up with bad business decisions. By splitting the data and aggregating it, you can keep individualized data separate from aggregated data and use it appropriately. Good business and good privacy go hand in hand. Keep this in mind the next time someone tells you that privacy is a blocker.

So what does data classification look like in this brave new world?

Under Restricted, you could list individualized data that could specifically identify a user:

- Name
- Birthdate
- Address
- Email
- Phone
- IP and device info
- Payment information

In my experience, payment data is always rated at the highest level of sensitivity. The preceding data would be retained in the operational database for short periods of time with tightly controlled and audited access.

For the analytics database, you could aggregate purchases along the following lines:

- Birth years
- ZIP codes or GPS coordinates
- Phone area codes
- Device types
- Purchase date ranges

That way, you could perform the sort of analysis we described earlier without tying any of these purchases back to a specific user. You could store this data for longer periods of time and allow access to a range of stakeholders, from business teams in charge of inventory to security teams protecting the company from fraud. This is how a data classification process evolves to balance privacy needs and business goals.

At this point, you can use either the process I described to iterate on the data classification, based on new use cases, or follow the Microsoft process. In reality, step 2 as I described it combines the Do and Check steps in the Microsoft model, but I highly recommend tailoring a process that works for your team.

In either case, you will need to achieve two concurrent goals:

- Collect feedback on the most current version of your data classification with the goal of working toward the next iteration.
- Create enforceable and auditable controls to support the practical implementation of the data classification guidelines.

Some of the enforceable controls would be as follows:

- Encryption at rest (to be confirmed by an encryption expert)
- Encryption in transit (to be confirmed by an encryption expert)
- Limited and business-approved access by your own and third-party employees
- Compliance with user retention and deletion policy

Continual iteration on the individual data classifications and these controls will form the bulk of the work once an initial version is finalized. Note that the four controls in the preceding list are meant to be a starting point. I strongly encourage executives to look at the controls I have describe in this chapter and others more broadly as you develop your overall data governance.

Summary

- Data classification is a critical part of your overall data governance strategy; this is the process that helps you identify what you have and how it changes your overall privacy risk for your business and your customers.
- Data classification will help you build a solid data protection strategy to protect your business, scale your resources, and maintain user trust.
- As you classify data and revisit your classifications, you can more intelligently deploy tools and policies to handle various use cases without creating unnecessary bureaucracy and process.
- The complexity of privacy laws can be managed by a sound data classification process and the learnings that emerge from it.
- Data classification is a strategic investment in building a truly company-wide, cross-functional process to help drive privacy, since several teams will need to contribute to the end result.
- Ultimately, every company will need to create and customize its own data classification process.

Data inventory 4

This chapter covers

- What a data inventory is
- Creating tags and a baseline for a data inventory
- The technical architecture for the data inventory process
- Understanding your data better for a more accurate inventory
- Starting and adjusting the depth of the data inventory process
- Assessing the effectiveness of your data inventory outcomes

In the last chapter, we dove deep into data classification. We saw how the classification exercise helps build cross-functional context on privacy risk, how it changes based on data usage and context, and how it helps you tailor data protection methodologies. The process and outcomes equip engineering leaders and their lieutenants to make informed decisions around what data to collect and how to protect it.

However, the data classification process is just half of a larger data governance exercise. In order to right-size and scale your privacy and security tools, you need the right tooling to ensure that your data systems reflect your data classification. This chapter will help you accomplish just that by completing your data inventory. This is more important than most leaders realize.

When companies had tightly controlled top-down cultures, data collection operated in a need-based and awareness-centric paradigm. Engineers knew what they could collect, so the privacy and security controls were baked in by way of preemption. In a decentralized and democratized setup, data collection is ad hoc, automated, and voluminous. The preponderance of universal identifiers, mobile devices, and internet connectivity means that it is very difficult to control data intake. Having your data—in databases, data stores, and warehouses—reflect the data classification means that anyone seeking to access and process it will have a good sense of the privacy risk attached to that data. Building this automation into your data and your systems will ensure that you can proactively detect privacy risk even at scale. This is what a data inventory does. Based on my experience, it is unlikely that any manual process will enable you to sift through petabytes of data and identify the risk levels without either high error rates or significant delays in data flows to downstream users. Additionally, just as finding books in a library or emails in an inbox is that much easier when you have a label (some sort of index) attached to them, it is easier to locate data in your systems if the data has tags. This is critical, since you may need to locate data quickly and accurately when the need arises to delete it or to surface it to a customer by way of a Data Subject Access Request (DSAR). Those privacy requirements will be much harder to fulfill without a data inventory.

And that is why, once your data classification is complete, you will need the other half of the data governance offering—the data inventory.

4.1 Data inventory: What it is and why you need it

The process of adding tags derived from your data classification to your data systems is the data inventory process. As you build your data inventory, you are indexing the contents of your data stores and making individual components expeditiously searchable. Creating a data inventory is like building the backend of a search engine for your data, much like a team of smart engineers built the backend of tools like Google.

This explanation offers an intuitive explanation of a data inventory, but it is key that technical leaders understand the risk mitigation and business enablement that a data inventory makes possible.

In the lead-up to the GDPR, the International Association of Privacy Professionals (IAPP) provided an enumerated plan so companies could get a head start on compliance.[1] This was to be a checklist so that companies would know where to start and what structures and processes to create as they prepared for a post-GDPR world, one where privacy was to become front and center like never before. This list remains

---

[1] Rita Heimes, "Top 10 operational responses to the GDPR – Part 1: Data inventory and mapping," *IAPP*, February 1, 2018, http://mng.bz/AxDx.

fairly applicable, even as its individual components have become more complex to implement and there are more variations based on a company's use of data.

I have listed the plan here with my insights added:

1. *"Conduct data inventory and mapping."* This assumes that the starting point of a sound data protection program is the ability to classify, catalog, and discover data, such that the privacy risk is comprehensible at the time of data collection and access. This book provides a deep dive into data governance based on this time-tested guidance from industry experts.

2. *"Establish a lawful basis for data processing and cross-border transfers."* This is something your legal team should advise on, but how you can process data and where you can transfer it to may take on additional complexities when it comes to geographic boundaries. Making that assessment requires exactly the sort of insight and discoverability that data classification and data inventory make possible.

3. *"Build and maintain a data governance system, including establishing leadership (where appropriate, a data protection officer, setting forth policies and training personnel)."* This helps ensure that rather than allocating privacy responsibilities to engineering teams, it is preferred that privacy leadership be separate. This independence will allow for better tracking and accountability.

4. *"Perform data protection impact assessments, along with data protection by design and by default."* This typically refers to the privacy risk assessments and privacy reviews that your teams conduct on products and features. We will be looking at privacy risk assessments in chapter 6.

5. *"Prepare and implement data retention and record keeping policies and systems"* so that you can be transparent about what you collect and retain. These obligations could form a part of your audits, for which prudent bookkeeping is a prerequisite. Otherwise, your audit processes could become cumbersome and expensive.

6. *"Configure systems and put in place processes to accommodate data subjects' rights, including access, rectification, erasure, portability, objection to automated processing and revocation of consent."* As mentioned before, data subjects' rights (DSAR) are a key commitment for many companies thanks to laws like the GDPR and the CCPA. Having a data inventory is key to meeting these commitments at scale and with accuracy.

7. *"Prepare for security breach response and notification."* You will want your legal team and/or outside counsel to weigh in, but several jurisdictions in the United States and elsewhere have breach notification laws. These laws create expectations that companies that suffer from a data breach need to notify the impacted entities with specific pieces of information and within specific timeframes.

8. *"Have a sound vendor management protocol."* This step is critical, since vendors that may get access to your systems and your data could make decisions with privacy implications. Assessing both the ability of your vendors to follow your data protection guidelines and their past record is critical. As you saw previously,

companies may claim that data privacy issues occurred at third parties, but your stakeholders in the privacy community may hold you responsible nonetheless.

9. *"Establish systems and channels for communicating with your data protection authority."* It is possible that you will need to provide regulatory authorities with granular details around data, your decisions about handling it, and time-stamped records. A data inventory will enable and accelerate this disclosure process, and that could help build a strong trust relationship as well.

To engineering leaders who seek comfort from the fact that the only companies in the news for privacy breaches are the big tech giants, I have this to say: These high-visibility companies faced a moment of truth *after* rapid growth; at least they had the money to build privacy teams and retain lawyers to represent them in court. What if regulators or activist citizens come after a startup pre-IPO, and VCs fail to even get a basic return on their investments?

Additionally, the smaller your size and the more limited your resources, the harder it will be to adapt to a sudden regulatory change—I know of several small companies that found their roadmaps severely impacted. If you think privacy is expensive, the opportunity cost of not having privacy controls will almost certainly be higher. As a somewhat imperfect analogue, consider this: Bill Gates recently said that the antitrust investigation around Microsoft in the late 1990s affected the company's ability to effectively comprehend the threat posed by Google's SaaS model and Apple's mobile computing model, resulting in a lost decade for Microsoft. Why would you knowingly subject your company to such uncertainty, especially when doing the right thing with privacy will help your business build trust with your customers and help growth?

The data inventory process is a key part of your data protection program. Having established what a data inventory is and the reasons that it is key, we will now look at the foundational building blocks of a data inventory. The next section will look at data inventory tags.

> **NOTE** A data inventory is the act of making sure that your classification of data based on privacy risk is reflected in the physical data stored in your systems and data stores.

4.2 Machine-readable tags

Tagging or labeling is something we all do routinely in our lives to help locate important materials like our tax returns or medical records. However, this concept and process is key when it comes to data governance. In this section, we'll discuss in detail what data inventory tags are, and we'll look at a specific example of their use.

4.2.1 What are data inventory tags?

A data inventory is the process of applying your data classification onto your physical data stores. As you have already seen, the classification process is fairly cross-functional, and it forces teams to come up with labels that describe the nature of the data and the privacy risk attached to it. However, additional steps are required to ensure that your data inventory is functional and serves its purpose—you need to index the data, making it searchable and easier to protect.

The first step in this process—one that many companies tend to overlook, to their eventual detriment—is to come up with tags or labels. These tags are the machine-readable incarnation of the data classification. This may well be the first time a company has common definitions relating to the data previously collected by several teams across the company. The task of finalizing these tags can often be confusing, as teams may have gotten used to their own naming conventions.

To simplify this process, I'll provide some criteria for useable data tags that will help your data inventory process and outcomes:

- These data tags should be easily consumable by enforcement points like data loss prevention gateways or information rights management for actionable intelligence.
- The tags should be compatible with and support external regulatory requirements (e.g., GDPR, CCPA). There will often be occasions when you need to apply controls germane to specific legislation, so tagging your data appropriately will be helpful. (As an analogue, in Gmail you can tag a specific email with the labels "family vacation December 2019" and "Mom." In this case, a search for either term will surface that email.)
- Tags should be applicable to all data in these states: data at rest, data in transit, and data in use. When it comes to data, you will need to protect it regardless of its state, so the tags that enable you to locate it should yield similar outcomes regardless of whether the data is being transported between data centers or lives in a data warehouse.
- Tag definitions should be canonical, unambiguous, and machine-readable. They can be used either individually (such as for individual database columns or API parameters) or as a group, represented as comma-separated values where applicable (such as for an entire dataset or API).

This list is not exhaustive, but it should offer you a great place to start. It is vital that your team take seriously the exercise to come up with tag names. The process of applying these tags, as you will soon find out, can be extremely expensive. This is one area where weeks of planning will save you months and years of retagging or months and years of applying incorrect privacy protections.

4.2.2 *Data inventory tags: A specific example*

Now that you have a conceptual understanding of data inventory tags, looking at specific patterns and examples will help you form your own tagging strategy. This exercise will provide an educational view of the granularity and variety of data, as well as insight into why the tagging exercise is mission critical.

Since the data inventory extends the existing data classification, we will focus on a specific level of privacy sensitivity. Table 4.1 shows how you can create different kinds of tags for your most sensitive data (which I am calling level 1 data).

First, the format for a specific tag would be along the following lines:

```
(business|personal):[a-z]+(-[a-z]+)*
```

This regular expression provides a template for what the end result is allowed to be. This format achieves two goals:

- It provides a clearly identifiable signal to distinguish between business and user data; the former may have lower privacy risk but high security or IP risk, while the latter may have a high privacy risk in that it probably belongs to your customers.
- It includes a descriptive name that will identify, for consumers of that data, what is contained in the record.

Note that table 4.1 also contains the retention period and how the data is to be handled after the retention period expires. This is critical for engineers to absorb.

Table 4.1 Data inventory tag template (level 1 data)

Level	Business/personal	Description	Maximum retention period	Preservation requirement	Tag value (business|personal):[a-z]+(-[a-z]+)* Alternate value (e.g., GCP label) (business|personal)_[a-z]+(-[a-z]+)*
Level 1	Business	Board meetings	N/A	N/A	business:board-material *or* business_board-material
Level 1	Business	Non-public financial data	N/A	N/A	business:non-public-financial *or* business_non-public-financial
Level 1	Business	Security business data	N/A	N/A	business:security
Level 1	Personal	Location data	7 years	Delete (non-registered users); retain until retention period expires (registered users)	personal:level1-location
Level 1	Personal	Government identifiers	Life of application (LOA)	Delete (for non-registered users); 7 years (registered users)	personal:government-id
Level 1	Personal	Level 1 demographic data	LOA	Delete	personal:level1-demographic
Level 1	Personal	Biometric	LOA	Delete	personal:biometric

If you decide to categorize data at the tail end of the data pipeline, the volume of data makes it difficult to identify and classify, let alone automate policy enforcement, such as automated retention and deletion policies. Tailoring these policies in line with privacy risk at the categorization stage and then applying tags to the data at the point of ingestion will help scale privacy engineering for your organization. Let's assume, for example, that you have decided that a data field has a lower privacy risk than was previously thought. All you'd need to do is change the tag affixed to it, and the corresponding policy would then apply.

Now that you understand how tags are created in line with the regular expression format, we can examine how these tags are mapped to data that you need to store and protect. Let's look at different tags for a business that owns several restaurants and wants to build its data inventory.

Since your business owns restaurants, there would be a significant number of employees who work as cooks, delivery persons, and other staff. It is also likely that you'd support a vast number of different ways whereby people could prove their identity. Some of them might have a driver's license, while others may opt for a state ID.

Your use cases may involve

- Updating the database with employment verification records of new employees and supporting all forms of ID
- Searching for employees based on a specific ID criteria, such as all employees who are on a two-day probation after their first day, since they have not provided a government ID yet

In table 4.2, the tag format `(business|personal):[a-z]+(-[a-z]+)*)` allows you to provide a binary value (`True/False`). With this value you can discern which employees have provided a valid government ID (John Smith and Jane Doe) and which ones have not (Abe Linc). After the first three days of employment, you could run a query that searches for employees with "False" in their tags, and identify the employees who have yet to furnish an ID. This assumes that "government-id" is set to be a Boolean; alternatively, you could configure its value to be a number that would either match the pattern of a government ID (driver's license, passport, etc.) or be a sequence of zeros to indicate that a valid ID has not been provided.

The key takeaway here is that even if your data isn't in a structured data format, you can still use tagging to make the data searchable and identifiable.

Table 4.2   Basic data inventory tags with binary values

Tier	Business/ user	Description	Tag value (business|personal):[a-z]+(-[a-z]+)* Alternate value (e.g., GCP label) (business|personal)_[a-z]+(-[a-z]+)*	Tag example
Level 1	User	Govt identifiers	personal:government-id	John Smith:True
Level 1	User	Govt identifiers	personal:government-id	Jane Doe:True
Level 1	User	Govt identifiers	personal:government-id	Abe Linc:False

Now let's assume you want to identify employees who are on a work permit, and you therefore need to submit their passports to prove their eligibility to work in the United States. Table 4.3 shows how a data inventory can help. The second (`personal :government-id-passport`) and third (`personal:government-id-driverlicense`) rows have tag formats to allow for different kinds of IDs. Instead of a binary value of the kind in table 4.2, you can use regular expressions to map the value of the tag. That way, the tags will tell you whether a user has supplied a driver's license or a passport.

Table 4.3 Data inventory tags

Tier	Business/ user	Description	Tag value (business|user):[a-z]+(-[a-z]+):L|F Alternate value (e.g., GCP label) (business|user)_[a-z]+(-[a-z]+):L/F	Tag example
Level 1	User	Govt identifiers	personal:government-id-passport	Jerry Seinfeld:^d{10}
Level 1	User	Govt identifiers	personal:government-id-driverlicense	Jerry Maguire:^d{9}
Level 1	User	Govt identifiers	personal:government-id-passport	Jerry Tom:^d{10}

In table 4.3, the first and third users will match a request to identify employees with valid passports (on the assumption that passports have 10 numbers), while Jerry Maguire will match a user who still needs to supply a passport (since he has provided just a driver's license, which has 9 numbers).

In this way, you can use a data inventory to

- Come up with tags that make your data searchable and map the data to privacy sensitivity
- Extend the tags to meet diverse business use cases

The preceding example is a simplified exercise. Data inventory and real-world scenarios will get more complex and more diverse. The key takeaway is that you are far better off being able to search for, process, and delete data using the preceding inventory rather than searching for sensitive data in JSON blobs or other data formats. In that scenario, you may miss sensitive data or end up spending significant resources in the discovery process.

A data inventory ties in your privacy-centric understanding of your data (your data classification) to the data itself. This means that if you were to transfer your data from an on-premises environment to the cloud, or from MongoDB to Cassandra, you'd ensure that the data carried with it the identities and risk values you have attached to it. This will significantly help manage the privacy risk in a very decentralized and bottom- up data-driven company.

Now that you have the tags ready to apply to the data, we can create a baseline (a starting point) for your data inventory before using automation.

4.3   *Creating a baseline*

For any organization, getting a handle on its data will require a mix of human effort and automation. You will see in the next section how the process of applying the tags involves a combination of both, partly because of the volume of the data and partly because of its complexity.

Before you do that, however, you need a process for discovering your data. This is critical since, as you will see shortly, most companies start the data inventory process after a significant amount of data has already been collected. While this initial discovery represents an often unforeseen significant upfront expense, it also allows companies to build a baseline of their existing data.

What we are looking at is some initial legwork to collect information that is readily available but scattered across different teams or that is in the minds of engineers without being documented. This information is euphemistically referred to as "tribal knowledge," and turning tribal knowledge into communal understanding is what we mean by creating a baseline.

To create a baseline for a data inventory, engineers, data scientists, and others can come up with models and estimations of what data they have collected and where it lives. While these initial results may turn out to be incomplete or incorrect or both, this process can be useful in capturing known use cases and building machine learning (ML) models for additional discovery.

I recommend doing this pre-inventory by inspecting your data storage from two dimensions:

- Data inventory by storage systems
- Data inventory by data owner

In preparing your teams to inventory their data by storage system, you will want to hand them a template that helps them record what they find in their first manual inventory of the systems they can account for. For each storage system (e.g., Hive, Vertica, Kafka, SQL database, S3 buckets, etc.), data should be inventoried using the following attributes:

- Total size (storage volume)
- Structured/unstructured data by %
- Data classification tier (if your storage unit has data with multiple classifications, you should apply the highest risk tier)
- Whether or not the unit contains personal data

It is not sufficient to inventory your data by storage system, however. Storage systems are often owned by multiple stakeholders. You may also find that some storage systems are not owned by anyone, but multiple engineers use them to store data.

To get an accurate view of your systems, you will want to inventory your data by data owner as well. That way, orphaned data stores will find owners, and you can drive some accountability for privacy.

The attribute checklist for this second step would be similar to the first, and could look like this:

- Total size (storage volume)
- Unit count (# of services, users, accounts, or datasets)
- Structured vs. unstructured
- Data classification tier (if your storage unit has data with multiple classifications, you should apply the highest risk tier)
- Whether or not the unit contains personal data

Once these initial baselines are complete, you will have a sense of which business unit owns what percentage of privacy-sensitive data, and what systems the data lives in. This mapping is critical, and I have, on occasion, discovered data and systems that went undetected by automation; sometimes one reclusive engineer knows of an S3 bucket containing a table that maps home addresses to food deliveries.

Now that you have the tags ready to apply to the data, as well as an initial manual inventory, it's time to look at the technical and backend infrastructure required to execute the data inventory process.

4.4 The technical architecture

Many business leaders enjoy using phrases like "It costs money to make money." This typically refers to marketing, research, and other investments that are necessary for business growth. New products in new markets, for example, often require more expense in early stages before the product leads to revenue and profits.

There is a similar challenge with regard to data inventories. The business value add for a data inventory is that it attaches critical information to data, highlighting the privacy risk, and it also indexes the data for easy discoverability.

The engineering challenge in a data inventory involves a one-time expense in discovering the data so that you can index it and tag it; in other words, you have to first discover the data so as to make it discoverable. Note that this assumes you have a backlog of data already collected before the data inventory. In subsequent chapters, we will look at how you can time the data inventory process so as to minimize this backlog.

For the remainder of this chapter, we will be focusing on data discovery and ML-driven data categorization as key components for your data inventory. There is a clear implication in these terms that conventional tools are insufficient to discover such data.

4.4.1 Structured and unstructured data

I have had many business leaders ask me questions like, "Database A did not take long to process, so why is database B taking much longer, even though it has less data?" This is where the inherent difference between structured and unstructured data is key.

According to G2.com, a peer-to-peer review site,

> *Structured data is most often categorized as quantitative data, [and it is typically] data that fits neatly within fixed fields and columns in relational databases and spreadsheets. Structured data is highly organized and easily understood by machine language. Those working within relational databases can input, search, and manipulate structured data relatively quickly... This is the most attractive feature of structured data.*[2]

In figure 4.1, you can get a clearer sense of how structured data is created and how its components relate to each other. It shows a database that has tables for users (or more specifically, customers), the orders made by each customer, the composition of each order, and descriptions of the products themselves.

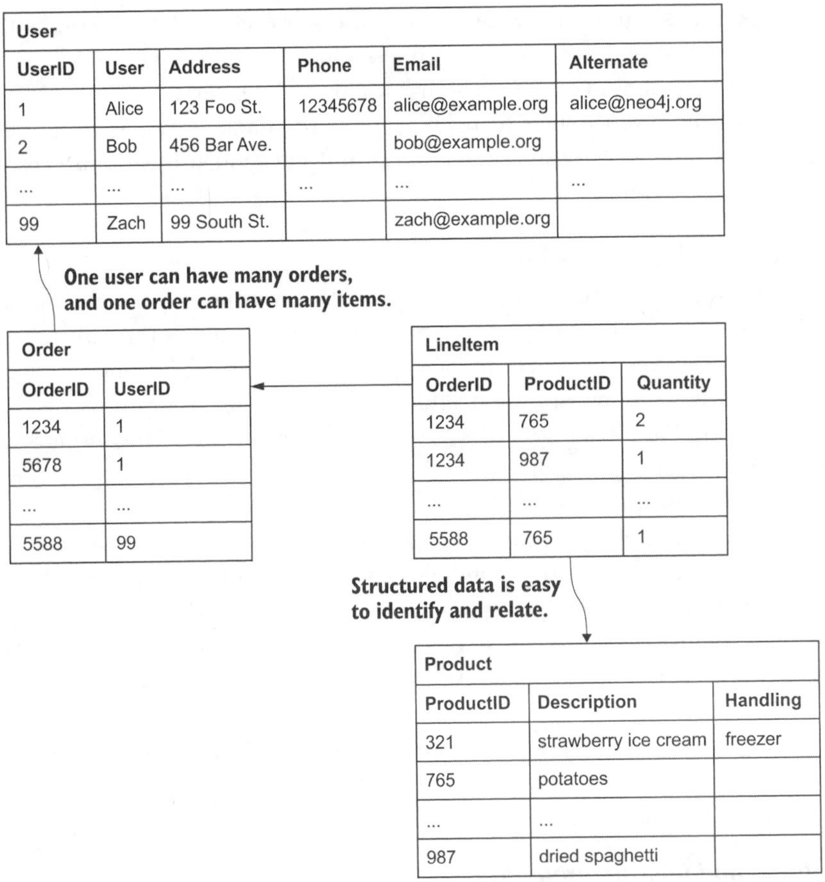

User

UserID	User	Address	Phone	Email	Alternate
1	Alice	123 Foo St.	12345678	alice@example.org	alice@neo4j.org
2	Bob	456 Bar Ave.		bob@example.org	
...	...	...	...	...	...
99	Zach	99 South St.		zach@example.org	

One user can have many orders, and one order can have many items.

Order

OrderID	UserID
1234	1
5678	1
...	...
5588	99

LineItem

OrderID	ProductID	Quantity
1234	765	2
1234	987	1
...	...	...
5588	765	1

Structured data is easy to identify and relate.

Product

ProductID	Description	Handling
321	strawberry ice cream	freezer
765	potatoes	
...	...	
987	dried spaghetti	

Figure 4.1   Structured data

---

[2] Devin Pickell, "Structured vs. Unstructured Data – What's the Difference?" *G2*, November 16, 2018, https://learn.g2.com/structured-vs-unstructured-data.

With figure 4.1 in mind, let's construct a database that will allow us to track orders for a retail business:

1. We will create a User table of users/customers.

   In order to send the merchandise to and possibly market to a customer, we will need to create a table that stores information about each user, like their name and contact information. Two things bear mentioning:
   - Each user's row contains personally identifiable information, like their address, email, etc.
   - Each row also contains a unique ID that can be used to associate a user's data in one table with other data about the user in a different table.

2. We will create an Order table that contains orders placed by a user.

   Since one user can place many orders, this table could have several entries for each user. Note that instead of using the user's name or email to link this table back to the main User table, we use the ID for two reasons:
   - This reduces the duplication of sensitive data in the computer systems for the company.
   - The ID can be numeric, and that could make matching easier for queries that are run for troubleshooting and analysis.

   Note that each order also has an OrderID, and that will help us further develop our database for the contents of the order.

3. We will create a LineItem table that contains details about the orders, so that we know what products are contained in an order.

   Just as each order has an ID, the products contained in the order also have an ID. In our LineItem table, we have a many-to-one relationship between products and orders, since each order could have zero or more products. The presence of a ProductID enables us to relate the LineItem table to a different table that contains details about the products.

4. We will create a Product table that contains details about the products themselves.

   This table links back to the LineItem table using the ProductID and contains details about the products themselves.

From the top down in figure 4.1, you can see that UserID 1 refers to the customer Alice, who had two OrderIDs of 1234 and 5678. Next, Alice had two ProductIDs of 765 and 987. Finally, we can see that Alice purchased two packages of potatoes and one package of dried spaghetti.

This data is organized very neatly and logically, but in modern systems the data does not often flow in with clear field and column delineations and logical correlations. In order to more accurately analyze your business performance, you need to account for data that does not follow the structured format. That brings us to unstructured data.

Unstructured data is often qualitative and cannot be processed or analyzed using conventional tools. The data management company NetApp identifies several examples:[3]

- *Rich media*—Media and entertainment data, surveillance data, geospatial data, audio, etc.
- *Document collections*—Invoices, records, emails, and productivity applications
- *Internet of Things (IoT)*—Sensor data, ticker data
- *Application logs*—Machine learning, artificial intelligence

These examples come under the umbrella of unstructured data because different service owners may define and store them differently. The interoperability between different apps and services means that a consistent key/value schema may not be possible.

The NetApp article points out that companies routinely collect and process large volumes of such data. This is unsurprising, given the proliferation of devices, internet connectivity, services, and identities that are available to engineers and customers alike. This means that the data itself could vary significantly across its various components, and inferences or changes to the data could lead to growth in its size. This data then proliferates across the tech stack, making it challenging in terms of size when it comes to privacy protections.

The difference between structured and unstructured data is instructive in terms of the value proposition for the company. The rigid schemas for structured data make discoverability easier but inhibit possible experimentation. The diversity of datasets within unstructured data creates new insights, but the volume makes maintainability and privacy harder. The value of the data is hard to quantify, and so is developing a tighter correlation between privacy risk and volume.

That said, given the autonomy that modern engineering teams possess, they opt to collect unstructured data not in response to a need, but in anticipation of needs down the line.

In subsequent portions of this chapter, you will note that expeditious discovery of this data for inventory purposes and methodical assessment of the privacy risk is key.

4.4.2   *Data inventory architectural capabilities*

It is now time to look at the technical implementation of data inventories. You need a data inventory architecture that can perform the following activities:

1. Crawl various known data stores.
2. Discover other datasets (especially unstructured data).
3. Make those datasets and corresponding metadata available for tagging.
4. Provide extensibility to add new metadata.
5. Support the categorization of personal data (privacy use case).

---

[3] "What is unstructured data?" *NetApp*, http://mng.bz/ZzwA.

In this list, the first three steps refer to data discovery and tagging. That core capability is at the heart of a data inventory. It is vital that your infrastructure be able to discover data spread out across your storage systems.

As I've mentioned, a significant chunk of data we collect tends to be unstructured. A chunk of data may enter your systems as JSON blobs, for example, so you will need tools like crawlers to crawl various data stores and discover datasets, and then apply the tags to the data at the right level of granularity. These data crawlers will use tools like regular expressions and data lineage to search for data and make it available for tagging. As you will see later, these tools will become richer as you discover more data, and, in that sense, a data inventory is a process that yields outcomes and improves based on those outcomes.

The fourth step in the preceding list, where your infrastructure allows engineers to enter additional metadata, is also important. Engineering leaders and the engineers they manage may ask, "Why invest in so much infrastructure only to include a manual process where engineers enter critical inventory information?" The reality is that, as you just learned, a data inventory is an evolutionary process that improves as you penetrate more systems and build relationships between different data. Until you reach data inventory maturity, a topic we will touch on shortly, it is vital that your process be as comprehensive as possible. You cannot rely on your engineers to inventory all your data, but you should allow them the option of entering the appropriate information via an API or some sort of UI. I have had the pleasant surprise, as I led data inventory programs into a stage of maturity, of engineers and data scientists volunteering to enter this information for data they had collected and knew about but that our scripts and tools had failed to detect.

You can then make a judgment call on whether to check their work using your tools or to divert your automation to other data stores.

Finally, as noted in the fifth step, your infrastructure should enable the categorization of personal data. This is where, having discovered your data, you will want to apply the tags. As I will explain shortly, this process requires infrastructure, automation, human judgment, and artificial intelligence.

The infrastructure for all this work will cost money, and the results will take some time to materialize. With tight budgets, many engineering leaders may wonder if the expense is worth it. As a privacy expert, as someone who sets a high bar on protecting user trust, and as someone who has had to work with regulators, I believe the data inventory is a bargain, considering the fines and reputational harm that privacy issues can cause.

Even so, it makes sense to look at the preceding list more holistically. Specifically, the first four steps are required by data science teams anyway, for improving data discovery and quality. Teams that guide business investment decisions need high-quality data that is correctly labeled. They typically avail themselves of such data in an aggregated form from the data warehouse. Having this data labeled and collated, with nonessential data deleted, will improve their analysis results and reduce the time it takes to run data retrieval queries.

Similarly, any time you discover too late in the process that you have retained data you shouldn't have, you have created work for teams like the data platform and warehousing teams. I once worked for a company where we unknowingly collected IP addresses from our users without their consent. The data made it to our warehouses in JSON blobs and was not discovered at the time of ingestion and initial storage. In order to delete this data, we had to take our databases offline, restate our tables (in essence, deleting them and rewriting them with less information), and re-run all our queries to derive analysis data. The entire data analyst team had to sit on their hands for three days while all available hardware was thrown at the problem to clean up the backend data. Besides the cost of deleting the IP address, we bore the opportunity cost of not being able to conduct data analysis for three days and losing out on legitimate data we could have collected.

I recommend that companies not make the privacy team the face of the data inventory. The data inventory is a business requirement, not a privacy requirement. In fact, the privacy, data platform, and data science teams should be able to split the costs, pool their abilities, and produce a better data inventory.

4.4.3   *Data inventory workflow*

Figure 4.2 outlines the flow of data and layout of systems for the data inventory infrastructure. It shows how the classification of data is followed by the creation of tags and their application to ingested data. Understanding this is critical for creating the tooling necessary to execute a data inventory.

Figure 4.2 zooms out a bit further on the data inventory workflow. I have labeled the boxes with numbers for easy reference, but please note that these actions are not always sequential. You will need to configure them to suit your needs.

The data inventory service (DIS, shown in box 6 in the diagram) is where the data inventory happens. This box represents the fifth step in the previous subsection, where you add tags to the data in line with your data classification.

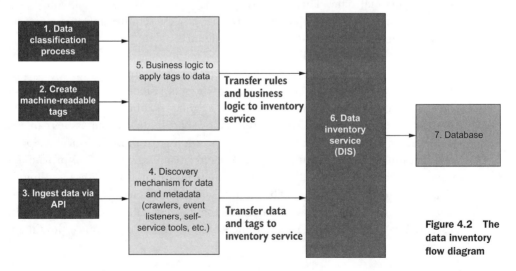

Figure 4.2   The data inventory flow diagram

Let's walk through this process in a bit more detail.

The data classification process is represented by box 1 in figure 4.2. This is where your cross-functional teams classify data based on regulations, usage, etc., with the intention of ending up with tags for your data. In a real-life scenario, this process will iterate and resurface repeatedly rather than be represented by just one box, but this diagram aims to simplify the process. Box 2 represents the creation of the machine-readable tags that you saw examples of earlier.

The data coming into your system is represented by box 3 at the bottom left. This diagram assumes you have one main API that makes all this data ingestion possible, though your infrastructure is almost certainly more complex.

The DIS can obtain all the data and related metadata via crawlers, event listeners, and other devices. All of this tooling is represented by box 4 in the middle section. I will explain this tooling more, shortly.

The data flow in figure 4.2 is logical in that it visualizes the steps ranging from the collaborative and manual (classifying data, planning the tags) to the automated (discovering data, affixing tags). However, there are some nuances to the process that call for further examination.

Figure 4.3 dives deeper and provides a technical view of the data flow ranging from discovery and ingestion to the classification, tagging, and additional processing tailored to the privacy risks represented by the tags. In order to perform a data inventory scalably and against the most comprehensive data set, it makes sense to consolidate as much of your data as possible before starting the tagging process.

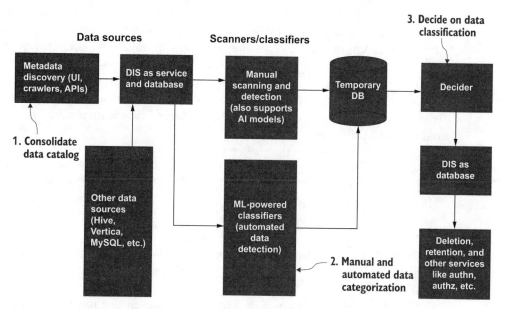

Figure 4.3 The data inventory system; consolidate your data before the tagging process.

Figure 4.3 shows how you can consolidate your data and metadata in one location (step 1 in the figure). You can do that using crawlers, event listeners, etc. These tools will use regular expressions and ML-based techniques to step through your data stores, sample specific databases, and look at the data lineage to infer the presence and risk of data. For example, in order to search for columns or rows with Social Security numbers, your crawlers could look for any piece of data that matches ^\d{3}-\d{2}-\d{4}$, whereby you will look for a pattern that has three numbers, followed by a hyphen, two numbers, another hyphen, and then four more numbers.

These tools will get more comprehensive and accurate with successive iterations of your data inventory process. You may also want to provide a UI portal for engineers to manually enter their data schemas, as we have already discussed.

The middle column of this diagram (step 2) highlights that

- Engineers and data scientists who know their data can manually categorize the data.
- This manual classification can be used to train ML-based models that will apply data classification tags to your data.

This combination of manual and ML-based data inventory will help reduce your dependence on manual classification

On the far-right of the figure (step 3) is the step of finalizing your data tagging after manual and ML-driven classification. The diagram shows DIS as a multidimensional system in how it instruments the data inventory process. DIS is both a service and a database. As a service, it feeds the data to be classified to the manual and ML-based classifiers. The classifiers are both human experts and ML-tools that infer what the data is and then assign a privacy classification and tag to that data. As a database, DIS provides information to classifiers such as column name, column type, manual personal data categorization, etc. The classifiers use this information to infer the personal data category type automatically. Manual classification is similarly enabled by this incarnation of DIS. In this way, DIS combines the data and the business logic to enable the actual tagging of this data. All the tagged data is then stored in a separate and temporary database.

Note that DIS also plays the role of a pure database on the far right. At this stage, it stores the data that has been tagged and processed through a "decider" process to make sure that the initial tagging was completed correctly. This decider could involve tooling to sample data, or it could allow for human verification to provide a sanity check. This is the judgment call I referenced earlier to ensure that you are not being overly conservative or cavalier in your tagging process.

Once all of this is complete, you can apply policies to protect your data. Remember, this is where you can programmatically apply policies like authentication, authorization, etc.

Now your data is ready to use, with appropriate protection embedded into the data. You may have heard industry buzzwords like "privacy by design." We have taken things a step further here with "privacy by data."

Since embedding appropriate controls into the data is critical for privacy, let's dive deeper into building a better understanding of the data.

4.5 Understanding the data

Key to successfully creating a data inventory is being able to recognize the data and infer what is contained in specific records. In order to get to this stage, you need to discover and assess all the metadata attached to the data.

4.5.1 The metadata definition process

You'll need a way to capture as much metadata as possible, so that data is classified correctly, and you'll need consistent metadata definitions across all your sources. Figure 4.4 shows the comprehensive nature of metadata collection that you will need. DIS needs to span not only datasets but all data entities. This means that merely locating data is not sufficient; you need to understand what service made that data available, where it was last located, and maybe even what the source of original ingestion was. All of this information, simplistically speaking, constitutes the *metadata*.

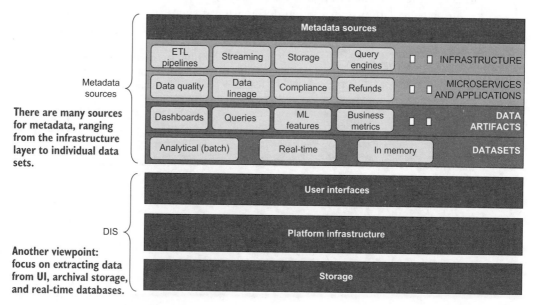

Figure 4.4 The metadata discovery system

The DIS needs to capture metadata about online, offline, and real-time datasets and other data artifacts such as ML features, business metrics, and dashboards. It must also collect information from services, such as data lineage and other infrastructure components.

Collecting this metadata reflects a singular priority: for years, companies have built infrastructure to harvest and consume data; the data inventory requires investing in handling this data based on what that data is and its attendant risk.

Because the DIS needs to understand the data it collects from many sources, you first need to establish a metadata definition, specifying what the metadata tells you about the data itself. Establishing such a definition will help distinguish your desired data from similar data found in different sources. If you lack a metadata definition, this may result in ambiguity within the information you are processing. For example, you will want metadata to distinguish between a valid credit card that needs to be protected and an expired gift card that poses less risk and may therefore need a lot less privacy protection.

The absence of a metadata definition may also lead to unstructured data being detected (and classified) incorrectly, since the definitions will vary across different searches. For example, credit card numbers and gift cards will ideally contain metadata that will help engineers differentiate between the two. It stands to reason that credit cards with a high limit would require more privacy protections than gift cards, whose value is presumably lower. Figure 4.5 illustrates how you can handle this problem. I recommend that you use a taxonomy-like structure with entity and value types to define the metadata. In figure 4.5, the MySQL and RelationalDB tables are defined as entity types with properties that define what they mean. Just as a human being has properties like height and weight, MySQL has properties like Name and Structure.

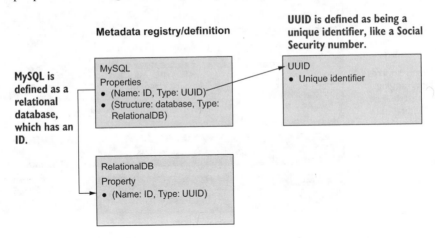

Figure 4.5   Metadata definition and registration

The MySQL table is defined as a relational database, and its ID is a UUID value by design. Every record in the MySQL database will have a unique ID, since the definition of the UUID guarantees as much.

Part of what DIS helps accomplish, besides discovering data, is correlating the metadata definition to the data. This way, we are able to standardize metadata across the board, from online schemas or offline Hive dataset schemas, from services or storage-level components. Once you have an understanding of how your datasets—which you have already classified conceptually—relate to each other, you can use tooling to inform the tagging outcome.

4.5.2 The metadata discovery process

Given the vast spread of data in your systems, you will need a mix of tools for data discovery. Figure 4.6 shows how you can use some of the tools we have already discussed to discover and collate your data and attendant metadata.

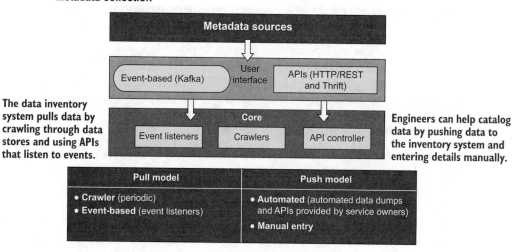

Figure 4.6   How a data inventory system can obtain data using the Pull and Push models

I recommend you use both the Pull and Push models to collect metadata from various metadata sources.

On the Pull model side, you have

- Crawlers that periodically collect information from metadata sources. Crawlers are very effective for collecting certain metadata types where the collection process needs to be throttled on the client side to avoid overloading target systems.
- Event-based listeners for near real-time metadata collection, to capture time-sensitive information such as data quality or metadata versioning. This way you can notify data users in a timely manner.

On the Push model side, things should be a bit more straightforward:

- You can use existing developer APIs and other tools engineers use to exchange data for discovery purposes.
- You can also use crowdsourcing to obtain humanly curated information, such as descriptions. This may sound basic, but you might be surprised by what you can get from engineers who have tucked away data on the premise that they *might* need it later.

It is reasonable to conclude that the Push model will lead to an inventory not just of the data but also of the pipes and vehicles that move it from system to system. In that way, the data inventory will help you build a better understanding of how data flows through your system in a way that very few engineers, if any, possess in modern businesses.

Now that you understand the logical and technical implementation of a data inventory, it is time to place this important activity in the ever-growing list of business priorities. The next section offers guidance on when to start your data inventory process.

4.6   When should you start the data inventory process?

Imagine asking someone for feedback on your cooking, only to be told something like, "It needs a little less salt." Some decisions are impossible to undo, and that is especially the case with data. This question—when is the right time to start a data inventory—goes to the heart of the second question, about why a data inventory is difficult; appreciating the first of those two questions tends to inform the response to the second.

4.6.1   Why is the data inventory process so hard?

Besides the technical details we have already seen, it is important to understand why the data inventory process is so complex to execute.

First, both as a business challenge and in the race for resources, privacy lags behind growth. In most companies, privacy/security specialists are never early hires. If engineers and data scientists are elephants in a circus, privacy and security specialists have the thankless task of trailing them with shovels. But more seriously, I have usually been hired at major companies *after* the company was hit by a fine or a consent decree, a lot of data had been collected, bad habits were formed, and there was a lot of catching up to do. At the same time, unless a company grows revenue and users, it cannot afford privacy specialists. Growth finances privacy, and privacy specialists need to remember that the business is not the enemy.

Second, as we have already seen, modern companies optimize for growth and build decentralized teams that chart their courses independently. Privacy, on the other hand, needs a centralized focus. Someone in France who uses the English version of your online service should get the same privacy protection as someone in France who uses the French version. This is challenging to enforce when various teams operate in their silos and make decisions around mapping artifacts to services in an inconsistent fashion. To that end, if any of your teams cause privacy issues, your company as a whole suffers, rather than just your payment team or billing team. You will need a sophisticated privacy program, since privacy not only lags behind growth but also requires a mindset different from the one that enabled you to grow.

Finally, there is procrastination. Too many companies wait until there is a major privacy incident or regulatory action before they start with privacy programs. By that time, data and risk have accumulated, and a fix needs to be put in place before the risk becomes financial and consequential. Engineers have gotten used to the "we have always done it this way" principle. In these cases, even mature and prestigious companies resemble data addicts. They feel a compulsion to keep going, to repeat the pattern again and again, because carrying on feels easier than stopping; stopping would mean a brutal audit of harm already done, money squandered, and trust destroyed. This moment of reckoning can be painful, but like getting a root canal, it's not one that can be postponed for long. Continuing this practice in the face of such risk would be doubling down on the sunk cost fallacy.

Given the costs of delaying the data inventory process too much, let's take a look at how you can place this critical step into your data lifecycle.

4.6.2 Data inventory: Sooner is better than later

A peer of mine from my Netflix days (where I started the privacy engineering program) had a pithy saying: "When it comes to protecting data, the best time to start is yesterday; the second best time is today."

To conceptualize an early stage data inventory process, think of data coming into your company as a funnel (figure 4.7). Once data enters your system, users will copy it, infer other data from it, and so on. As that data moves deeper into your system from left to right, it grows in size, just like the an inverse funnel. More than a few senior leaders may be too far removed from the front lines to appreciate this dynamic.

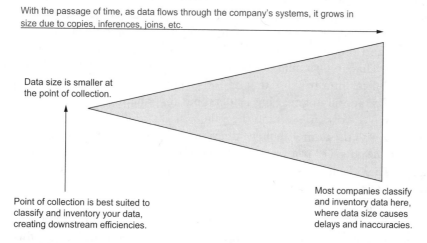

Figure 4.7 **Data inventory through the lens of a data funnel; as data flows through the company's systems, it grows in size due to copies, inferences, joins, etc.**

As engineers and data scientists have collected more data, cloud computing has made it easier to acquire more storage, compared to the early days when IT had to physically acquire more hardware. In much the same way, any time there is available storage bandwidth and computing power, creative engineers and data scientists will leverage them to conduct experiments with data that was previously not processed. The system is designed for growth: growth in data collection and growth in the infrastructural capabilities to process it. A colleague from my time at Google called this the paradox of "high availability, low visibility." This is how the funnel grows from left to right.

Recently published research by Gartner ("Guidance for Addressing Risks with Unstructured Data") explains how our IT infrastructure has become denser and more interconnected. This has had downstream implications on data. As companies grow and engineers become more empowered to manage their own services, the power of central IT teams to manage data and services tends to shrink. Individual engineers can provision services to automate their existing capabilities, optimize antiquated capabilities, evangelize new services to drive adoption, etc. This state of affairs means that creating a standard for data management becomes difficult. To make matters more complicated, sharing the data generated by these services with third parties complicates the task of maintaining a data catalog.

Bottom-up innovation offers teams across the company a lot of freedom, but freedom is not free. There is a cost-benefit balance to consider. The key goal of an in-house IT organization is to streamline the software and hardware procurement process. That discipline has the added benefit of helping the company manage data governance. However, as businesses have become more decentralized, the ability of IT to enforce this discipline has diminished.

There is no doubt that all the non-IT services help provide better experiences to customers and employees alike. After all, someone is paying for these enterprise accounts. These services could also help generate vast amounts of data to help drive marketing and product development. But they also make any kind of data management hard. That, in turn, makes risk measurement and data protection difficult. Creating a technical infrastructure that finds the right balance between these two systems is a challenge for all engineering leaders, but the data inventory process cannot be put off, given the risks inherent in the data.

To stick with the funnel analogy, the right time to inventory your data is as early in the funnel as possible. You want your data inventory to be as far left in figure 4.7 as possible. This will help you apply the optimum data protection techniques before engineers start using the data.

Engineering leaders often find it hard to make decisions about the timing for the data inventory when they face pushback from stakeholders across the business. Even as it makes sense to front-load the process, as described in figure 4.7, this requires additional expense (since most companies do not have the capability to tag the data at the ingestion point), and it may even slow the flow of data to downstream services, at least for some time.

A data inventory gets more and more accurate once engineers examine categorized data by sampling it for accuracy. The goal here is to build models that can be used to tag data at scale using automation. Until the data inventory process builds in enough models around data types and metadata, the inventory process may increase the time before your microservices can run low-latency queries like before.

In order to help drive that evolution and progress, figure 4.8 helps to explain how initiating data inventory early could demonstrably help manage and mitigate business risk. As you can see, unless you have inventoried your data, it is impossible to apply any meaningful controls to it. The message this diagram sends is that the moment you collect data

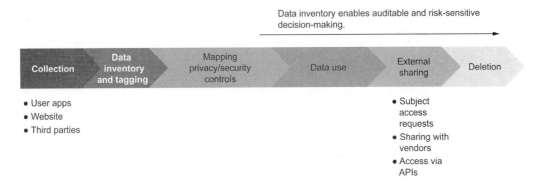

Figure 4.8 **The earlier you inventory the data, the more you help reduce risk.**

(in the far left panel), you'd ideally want to start the data inventory (the second panel from the left) so that you can finalize the logic around what data gets what protection via security and privacy controls (the third panel from the left). Once the privacy protections are tied to the data itself, you can move to data usage, external sharing, and eventual deletion, all of which are represented by subsequent panels.

The arrow that hovers over the rightmost three panels in figure 4.8 covers the parts that we are most familiar with: engineers running queries against data; modifying it; joining it; sharing it with vendors with tracking pixels, APIs, or file transfers; and finally deleting it. It is vital that you apply data governance, which includes classification and physical inventory, before your data enters this realm. This is where either your data will have built-in privacy controls, or it will not. The only way to be on the right side of that divide is having governance in place.

The use cases for data will keep increasing as innovation in the space grows; having your data classified, tagged, and protected in line with your privacy risk and trust metrics is critical. This is especially important, since data usage is irreversible; you cannot un-share data with a third party, so you will want to prioritize your data inventory so that you can make informed decisions around the use of your data.

4.7 A data inventory is not a binary process

Engineering leaders and their technical deputies will want to know how they can calibrate their data inventory in stages of maturity. It's not possible to inventory all or even significant chunks of data in one go, nor does all data need to be inventoried at the same time. To that end, I will present three stages of data inventory maturity. Besides allowing your teams to improve the reach and accuracy of your inventory process, this gradual maturing will allow your inventory process to evolve in line with specific business goals.

4.7.1 Data inventory level 1

Level 1 is the most basic level, where the data classification tags are applied at the database/bucket level. The results and key performance indicators (KPIs) of a level 1 data inventory are defined in table 4.4, but you will want to make changes as necessary for your business.

Table 4.4   Data inventory level 1

Data source	Results to be produced	KPI for measuring progress
Databases (structured data) in data centers	1. Total data volume (TB/PB) for each database instance 2. Data classification category tags for each database instance (i.e., what tags are represented in this specific database instance?) 3. Data tier composition for production data in production data centers: – % of total production data volume containing the most sensitive data – % of total production minus sensitive data – % of total production data volume containing public data	1. % of total production data volume in production data centers that has undergone a level 1 inventory 2. % of production database instances in production data centers that have undergone a level 1 inventory
Public cloud storage buckets (unstructured data; currently AWS/GCP)	1. Total data volume (TB/PB) for each bucket 2. Data classification category tags for each bucket (i.e., what tags are represented in this specific bucket?) 3. Data tier composition in production public clouds: – % of total production data volume containing the most sensitive data – % of total production minus sensitive data – % of total production data volume containing public data	1. % of total production data volume in production public clouds that have completed a level 1 inventory 2. % of buckets in production public clouds that have completed a level 1 inventory

As table 4.4 shows, a level 1 data inventory operates at the level of the storage container (the database or the bucket) and gives you a sense of the kind of data contained (by way of the tags present in the data) and the composition of the data itself (by way of the breakdown of the tiers of sensitive data).

As an engineering leader, you can get interesting insights from even this high level of data inventory:

- Buckets and databases that contain high volumes of data, but where only a small percentage of it is sensitive, could be split into two different databases or buckets with only the system containing sensitive data being subject to strict access controls.
- If a high percentage of a database instance has undergone the inventory process, but the portion yet to be inventoried contains a disproportionate share of unstructured data, the risk assessment could change. This could help you delay decisions around data sharing until fuller levels of inventory are achieved.

To address these concerns, and as your organization grows and privacy scrutiny increases, you may want even deeper insights. This is where the level 2 data inventory becomes critical.

4.7.2 Data inventory level 2

At level 2, tagging is much more fine-grained—either at the column level for structured data (such as a Hive database) or at the object level for unstructured data (such as AWS S3). The outcome of a level 2 inventory is that all columns in structured data stores and all objects in unstructured data stores are tagged. The results and KPIs for a level 2 data inventory are defined in table 4.5.

Table 4.5 Data inventory level 2

Data source	Results to be produced	KPI for measuring progress
Databases (structured data) in data centers	1. Total data volume (TB/PB) for each database instance 2. Data classification category tags for data columns in each column 3. Data tier composition for production data in primary production data centers: – % of total production data volume containing the most sensitive data – % of total production minus sensitive data – % of total production data volume containing public data	1. % of total production data volume in production database instances that have completed a level 2 inventory 2. % of production columns and objects that have completed a level 2 inventory
Public cloud storage buckets (unstructured data; currently AWS/GCP)	1. Total data volume (TB/PB) for each bucket 2. Data classification category tags for every data object (e.g., file) in each bucket 3. Data tier composition in production public clouds: – % of total production data volume containing the most sensitive data – % of total production minus sensitive data – % of total production data volume containing public data	1. % of total production data volume in production public clouds that have completed a level 2 inventory 2. % of buckets in production public clouds that have completed a level 2 inventory

As table 4.5 shows, a level 2 data inventory picks up from where the level 1 inventory left off and examines the spread, presence, and privacy-sensitivity of data one level deeper than database instances (by way of columns) and cloud buckets (by way of objects). This will help answer some of the previously raised questions around structured and unstructured data as well.

So far, we have examined data inventories from the perspective of discovering data and protecting it. However, if you want easy and expeditious retrieval of data based on privacy risk, you may want to go even one level deeper by indexing the data. This is where a level 3 data inventory becomes critical.

4.7.3   *Data inventory level 3*

The outcome of a level 3 data inventory is that, given some identifiers (UUID, name, phone, email, etc.) of a user, the underlying system should return pointers or references to all rows in each structured data store or objects in each unstructured data store that contain the user's data.

The results and KPIs of a level 3 data inventory are very similar to what you saw in tables 4.4 and 4.5, with the addition of an indexed database being the outcome rather than just tagged data.

This additional step will be time consuming, so you will want to understand the business forcing functions to help prioritize the inventory. In my mind, the following use cases would justify this expense:

- Supporting features like downloading personal data and DSARs
- Supporting features like data deletion
- Gaining insights about the business

Let's look at those each in turn.

SUPPORTING FEATURES LIKE DOWNLOADING PERSONAL DATA AND DSARs

Many data privacy use cases rely on access to account data on an individual basis, but most storage systems are not constructed to support such discovery at scale. A level 3 data inventory allows you to support these use cases without an infrastructure overhaul whereby entire databases would have to be re-created. This is particularly relevant as new privacy laws are coming online, which will almost certainly lead to an increase in the number and scope of user data requests. We will be looking at DSARs in more detail in subsequent chapters.

SUPPORTING FEATURES LIKE DATA DELETION

User account deletion relies on access to account data on an individual basis. Most systems are not constructed to support that at scale.

Currently, in order to delete data, many companies have a search mechanism such as a simple row-level Hive search that locates all records that match a user's UUID. For all those rows, data could then be obfuscated and rewritten in Hive tables.

This is a very limited search:

- It searches for records based only on UUID and ignores the fact that other transactions for the same user may not contain a UUID.
- It searches in specific Hive tables.
- It may be very slow.

We could use a level 3 search capability to aid the search by suggesting the table/row locations containing a vast range of data points present in database systems several layers deep. A deletion system backed by a level 3 inventory would also greatly improve your ability to audit the completeness and correctness of deletions.

Furthermore, as figure 4.9 shows, even when the number of breaches goes down, it is possible for bad actors to exfiltrate more and more data. With data inventory

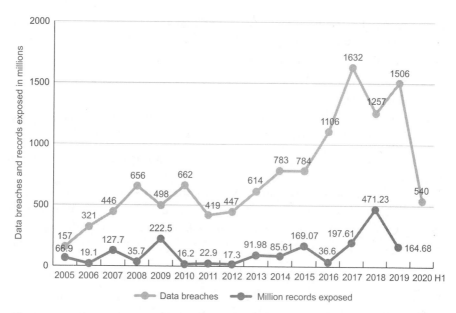

Figure 4.9   Annual number of data breaches and exposed records in the U.S. from 2005 to H1 2020[4]

insights, you can aim your finite deletion tools toward the most privacy-sensitive data and the locations that contain it. This may help reduce the likelihood of your sensitive data being affected by a breach, and it may help reduce the impact of such a breach were one to occur.

Most engineering leaders will understand that starting the inventory process early can prevent the buildup of data and allow for a more incremental and use-case based process as opposed to starting late and then trying to overdo it by opting for a level 3 inventory, as many organizations do.

GAINING INSIGHTS ABOUT THE BUSINESS

Your data inventory will offer you insights into the relationship between the growth of data and your business. Too often, companies have what one expert called "data envy," which is the belief that more data is a precondition to a deeper understanding of the business. On the flip side, news around privacy and security incidents could lead to an overcorrection in the opposite direction.

A data inventory can provide a more data-driven and trajectory-focused template with key data points:

- As the company grows, how does the growth in the customer base and revenue correspond to the growth in data?
- How fast is sensitive data growing relative to data overall?

---

[4] Joseph Johnson, "Annual number of data breaches and exposed records in the United States from 2005 to 2020," *Statistica*, March 3, 2021, http://mng.bz/REev.

You may also be able to reverse engineer the data sources and understand which teams are responsible for the growth in data size and risk.

The numbers may point to solutions:

- If the goal is to reduce cost and risk, you may want to delete data more aggressively.
- If the goal is purely to manage risk, you may be able to decouple portions of the data in a way that does not pose a privacy risk, while still retaining the data itself.

The information needed to drive these conversations can be derived from tables 4.4 and 4.5.

Remember, just because your business doubles in size, that does not mean your privacy team can double, so you need to ensure that your data and risk do not grow faster than your ability to manage them. Data governance, classification, and inventory go to the heart of scaling your business and spending your resources prudently.

4.8   What does a successful data inventory process look like?

A data inventory is like a medical treatment whose real effectiveness can only be assessed after the fact. Much like you can only assess the success of a kidney stone procedure after it is complete, you can only be certain about the effectiveness of your inventory when you try to, for example, delete at scale or identify what data was lost in a breach. In other words, success is proven based on an experience you'd rather not have to endure.

There are, however, several objective and subjective criteria that you can use to assess the efficacy of your data inventory outcomes. We'll look at them in the next two subsections.

4.8.1   Data inventory objective success metrics

Once you have a mature data inventory in place, you will be able to complete several key activities at scale and with increased accuracy.

You will likely build an infrastructure that has native connectivity and live integrations with AWS, Google Cloud, and Azure. This will help you dynamically categorize these cloud resources and leverage their native tagging infrastructures to speed mapping and duplication analysis. Rather than having to build crawlers and other tools, you will be able to use the capabilities these cloud providers sell and get more for the expenses you incur to store your data in the cloud.

One company I advised recently built workflows to understand the makeup of their on-premises and cloud data stores and the intention behind data usage. These workflows helped parse the data to find patterns and then label information. The ensuing data inventory led to a central, secure platform instead of the previous use of email or spreadsheets.

As I have mentioned, efforts toward privacy also help other business imperatives, especially if they need an improved understanding and quality of data. A data inventory enables you to automatically extract and map data lineage from various source systems and easily keep it up to date. This will help you track data as it flows through your systems and enforce privacy roles.

You will also be able to view indirect relationships that influence the movement of data, such as conditional statements and joins. All of this can help you make adjustments to protect data privacy. For example, if you had allowed a third party to access your data for analysis purposes via an API, and then you realized that they were accessing more data than permitted or using it for advertising or profiling, you could immediately constrain them by throttling and rate-limiting the API. This provides you with a single choke point for the data rather than requiring you to close multiple doors. This is a win for data privacy, as well as for your ability to protect business IP from leaking.

The detailed technical lineage made possible by a data inventory will allow you to drill down into table, column, and query level lineage, view transformations, and navigate through your data pipelines. This will help you understand how different feature and industry changes have affected your data in terms of both business value and privacy implications.

4.8.2 *Data inventory subjective success metrics*

A data inventory also offers some subjective metrics to help assess its efficacy. While these metrics may not be as instantaneous as the objective ones, they are often more revealing, since they are observed once the organization as a whole pivots and enough anecdotes surface.

Here are some anecdotal and cultural signs to look for, based on my years of experience in this domain:

- At what point do you have so much data that protecting it becomes prohibitively expensive?
- What do you do when your ability to delete data at scale is dwarfed by your data collection?
- When is the inflection point where you stop discovering data that ingenious engineers have tucked away?
- What does privacy do to help data quality—is there common cause to be made with data science teams?

The first two concern the consequences of having too much data. Once you have sound data governance, that should lead to more thoughtful data collection where you only collect what you know you need. Also, getting a sense of how much risk you are holding in your data should lead to timely deletion and anonymization. So if you see a reduction in the number of times you have to throw more money at security and storage to make up for your data collection, your data governance strategy may be starting to pay off.

This could point to a cultural change, where the company has realized how much work it takes to categorize data. Engineers often realize how much data they were needlessly holding on to while taking on risk. A data inventory may help reverse these long-entrenched habits.

The final two questions can speak for themselves. They point to not just better data handling practices but also an improved data privacy culture. When engineers and data scientists learn to abide by sound storage and collection practices, you should have fewer surprises. This could happen because they have realized how expensive the data inventory process is, and because they understand the risk so much better.

You may also see teams joining forces. The data science and privacy teams have a common interest in reducing their data footprint. The former cares about data quality, while the latter cares about risk and privacy. When you see these organic unions, you could be en route to a more mature and quantifiable privacy regime in your business.

Summary

- A data inventory is a critical part of your data governance, and it is the complement to your data classification process.
- A data inventory helps you apply your classification to the data and, as such, enables privacy by design.
- A data inventory involves automation at the data and infrastructural level, a process that can be refined continually as you understand your data better.
- The sooner you start the data inventory process, the less data you will need to clean up and the more effective you can be at managing privacy risk and building trust.
- There are several levels of data inventories, each with varying goals.
- There are several tangible and intangible metrics to help you measure the effectiveness of your data inventory.

Data sharing

5

This chapter covers

- Why companies share data
- How data sharing can create privacy risks
- Techniques to mitigate privacy risks during data sharing
- Measuring privacy risks before and after applying privacy techniques

We have so far worked to implement privacy engineering by focusing on data. In the preceding chapters, we have classified data based on risk and then tagged it using machine-readable tags. This process, both in its planning and execution, represents a significant investment. The reason for this effort is that data is used by humans and their algorithmic processes at scale to make decisions that impact the users whose data it is.

The other key benefit of this data governance is that companies can share data with privacy protections tailored to the risk. In this chapter, we will first take a look at why companies may share data. We will look at a use case that speaks to a key part of online commerce—the online ads ecosystem.

Then, we will look at a real-life scenario where data-sharing resulted in privacy risks. We will then explore techniques that will help reduce privacy risk when sharing data, and we'll explore the limitations of such privacy-preserving techniques. We will also explore how you can measure the privacy impact of sharing data and how such techniques can, in a numerically provable fashion, reduce privacy risk.

We will close with another real-life scenario related to data-sharing, except this one will offer two benefits. It will dive much deeper into individual components of data sharing, and it will highlight how the online targeting of users can be enabled by data, while also being sensitive to a user's data privacy.

Data sharing and its privacy implications are key for engineering leaders and aspiring leaders to understand, since a company's growth, user engagement, feature development and monetization, and compliance are all linked to its ability to move data from point A to point B.

5.1   *Data sharing:* **Why companies need to share data**

Before we discuss data sharing from a company's perspective, let's revisit the last time you called a business as a customer to get some service. Suppose you need to check your bank balance, and instead of going to a physical banking location or calling a customer support rep, you choose to check the account online. In order to access it, you will need information along the following lines:

- Your bank account number (assuming you already have an account with the bank)
- An email address, which will serve as your online login
- Personally identifiable information, like your Social Security number, home address, etc.

When you provide this information on the bank's website, that information goes to the bank's servers and enables you to access your account and view your balance. This simple transaction involves the following:

- Data sharing from the client (your computer or mobile device) to the server (the bank's databases) of information that identifies you
- Data sharing from the server to the client of your balance

This sharing of data creates privacy vulnerabilities both in terms of what happens to the data *at rest* (that is, when the data is stationary in a database), and what happens to the data *in motion* (when it moves over the wires between the client and server). These risks include erroneous and willful activity and will require compensating privacy controls. We will examine both these risks and mitigating privacy controls later in this chapter.

If something as basic as checking your balance online involves the sharing of sensitive data, you can imagine how complex sharing can get when it comes to massive companies whose entire business model depends on data. The next two subsections will look at two examples.

5.1.1 Data sharing: Taxicab companies

If you hail a car using a taxi or ridesharing app, it is possible, even likely, that the app is sharing some data with the city you are in. Such data sharing may also occur with cab companies or other transportation providers.

City planners and regulators need access to data from transport providers to inform and enforce policy decisions. For example,

- Cities need to understand the impact of transport services on traffic, parking, emissions, and labor practices.
- Municipalities and police need data to collect per-vehicle fees, enforce parking rules for shared bikes or scooters, and respond to service or safety issues.

There are some other valid data-sharing use cases in this context:

- Municipalities may ask cab companies to share drop-off geolocations to help them analyze the impact on parking and traffic flow. This data helps city governments analyze where people travel to and the routes they take. In real time, such data enables an understanding of traffic patterns and accidents, and in aggregate, such data enables infrastructure planning and other investments.
- Companies may also share trip telemetry data so as to help authorities detect when vehicles enter prohibited areas. Municipalities may use this data to issue enforcement citations. For example, if a vehicle that is not a school bus enters a loading zone beside a school, telemetry data could enable the government to issue a citation with evidence.
- Cab companies may also share vehicle or driver license numbers, and this data could enable municipalities to verify that all vehicles are permitted to operate within a city.

As you can see, there are perfectly legitimate functional reasons for companies to share data that they collect from users and customers, and these reasons don't always involve revenue.

I am using the example of taxi companies partly because I have worked for three companies that operate in the transportation and mobility space, but also because these companies' data combines identity with geolocation: who you are and where you are. Therefore, any data sharing needs to occur with careful consideration:

- Identify what data needs to be shared
- Determine the specific use case, so that the data use can be tracked and confined to that use case
- Protect the data at the transport layer (when it moves from the taxi company's systems and the recipient's)
- Ensure auditable access control even after the data leaves the taxi company's systems

Later in the chapter, you will learn that data sharing involves protecting the data at various levels, so understanding the risk vectors is critical. Focusing on a specific business will help us do that.

In the next subsection, you will learn how data sharing is optimized for revenue generation in the ad ecosystem.

5.1.2 *Data sharing: Online advertising*

The most common—and the most complex—example of online data sharing is online advertising. A lot of us are accustomed to seeing ads online that seem to intuit what we last purchased or browsed; that is, ads that are behaviorally targeted at us. It is important for leaders to understand with some level of detail the key players in the online advertising ecosystem and how data flows among them. This understanding will help engineers make intelligent decisions around data sharing as well as ensure that a promising revenue stream does not lead to abusive privacy habits.

Just as was the case with the taxi example, I have chosen the example of advertising consciously. In this section, you will learn in some detail how the ads ecosystem works, and I will demystify some of the concepts. Later in this chapter, we will revisit advertising and look at privacy controls that make advertising-related data sharing much safer from a privacy perspective.

Figure 5.1, derived from research conducted by the Electronic Frontier Foundation (EFF), shows what the online ads ecosystem looks like.[1]

To understand figure 5.1, we need to establish some definitions:

- *Publisher*—Refers to a website that a user may visit and that can display ads. For example, the *New York Times* website is a publisher.
- *Supply-side platform (SSP)*—Refers to an ad network that helps decide which specific advertiser can place an ad on a website so that a user may see it.
- *Demand-side platform (DSP)*—Refers to companies that work with SSPs to try to display ads to a user who visits a web page (publisher).

For the purposes of this example, let's assume you run a website that will display ads, so you are a publisher. We will walk through the data flow from the perspective of a user who is browsing the internet.

1. The user visits www.website.com (see figure 5.1). Data flows from the user's browser to the ad networks, also known as "supply-side platforms" (SSPs). The advertising process begins when the ad networks collect data from the user's browser and device. This data inevitably ends up with the ad networks, which represent the supply side of this ecosystem. The reason behind this flow is that it helps facilitate the serving of a personalized ad to the user.

---

[1] Bennett Cyphers and Gennie Gebhart, "Behind the One-Way Mirror: A Deep Dive Into the Technology of Corporate Surveillance," part 3, *Electronic Frontier Foundation*, December 2, 2019, www.eff.org/wp/behind-the-one-way-mirror#Part3.

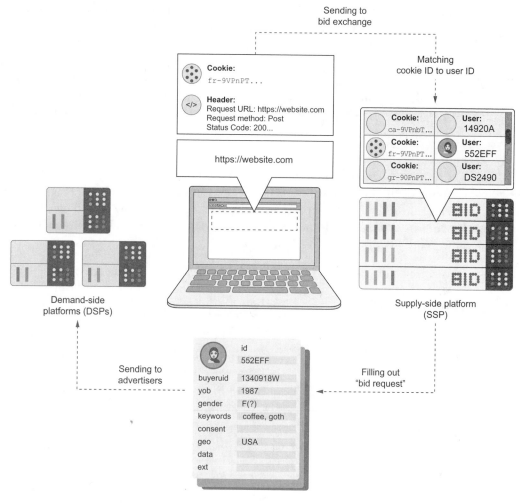

Figure 5.1 The online advertising ecosystem[2]

2. The SSP needs to personalize the user's ad experience and does so by way of the cookie, which contains identifiable information. This is where data sharing has begun in earnest, even though the user may not explicitly be aware of it. This point is key for leaders to understand, since many engineers often assume that data sharing refers only to conscious deployment of data. In reality, a significant amount of data sharing is triggered by software that works in the background.

3. The SSP needs to invite ads tailored to the user's information, and to do so it generates a "bid request." This bid request is akin to a call for proposed ads that are tailored to elicit user engagement based on the user's past behavior. By way of this

[2] Cyphers and Gennie Gebhart, "Behind the One-Way Mirror." The diagram is under Creative Commons License (https://creativecommons.org/licenses/by/3.0/).

bid request, the SSP is stating to advertisers that there is a user with specific features (based on information contained in the cookie) on www.website.com, and who could be served an advertisement.

4. The SSP sends this bid request to advertisers that have ads available to show, thereby rounding up the supply side of this data exchange. If there is a match and the web page is served an ad, the publisher earns revenue paid by the advertiser. Since multiple advertisers are competing to show the user an ad, the SSP conducts an auction, and the winner in that auction gets to display an ad for the user.

The ad that is served to the user, and whether an ad is served or not, depends on the contents of the bid request. The bid request enables potential advertisers to assess whether the user is worth serving an ad. A bid request contains several pieces of sensitive information, such as location, interests, and device data, and a unique ID that may universally identify a user (see figure 5.2).

Attribute	Type	Definition
id	string; recommended	Vendor-specific ID for the user. At least one of `id` or `buyeruid` is strongly recommended.
buyeruid	string; recommended	Buyer-specific ID for the user as mapped by an exchange for the buyer. At least one of `id` or `buyeruid` is strongly recommended.
yob	integer	Year of birth as a 4-digit integer.
gender	string	Gender, where "M" = male, "F" = female, "O" = known to be other (i.e., omitted is unknown).
keywords	string	Comma separated list of keywords, interests, or intent.
consent	string	GDPR consent string if applicable, complying with the comply with the IAB standard Consent String Format in the Transparency and Consent Framework technical specifications.
geo	object	Location of the user's home base (i.e., not necessarily their current location). Refer to Object: Geo.
data	object array	Additional user data. Each `Data` object represents a different data source. Refer to Object: Data.
ext	object	Optional vendor-specific extensions.

Figure 5.2   A sample bid request[3]

This information allows advertisers to decide whether the bid request, and the data it contains, is worth spending money on to show the user an ad. However, in keeping with the rising visibility around privacy, I like to remind people that the bid request is

---

[3] Cyphers and Gennie Gebhart, "Behind the One-Way Mirror." The diagram is under Creative Commons License (https://creativecommons.org/licenses/by/3.0/).

not an abstract entity. There is a real person behind that data, and that person deserves privacy and transparency as their data is shared.

That brings us to the end of the process, where the ad is served to the user. The advertisers now have a binary choice: they can either place an ad or not. Simplistically speaking, an advertiser who could potentially show an ad would normally examine the user's data and match that against the ad itself; in most cases, they will test the applicability of that ad and make a call, possibly using past metrics or an ML-based scoring system. They will then respond to the SSP with a bid if they wish to show an ad. The next step would involve the SSP picking the winning bid, which in most cases will be the bid offering the highest price, and display the ad.

This flow is captured in a somewhat simplified fashion in figure 5.3.

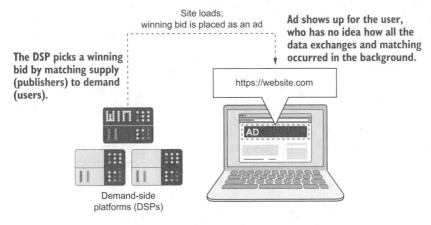

Figure 5.3   How an ad is finally served to the user[4]

There are privacy implications in this data-sharing activity. As the EFF indicates, the information in the bid request is shared before any money changes hands. Advertisers who don't win the auction still receive the user's personal information. Some companies may pretend to be interested in serving ads to a user but intentionally bid to lose in each auction with the goal of collecting as much data as possible as cheaply as possible.

Targeted advertising is critical for online businesses, since it helps match user preferences and identities with ads. However, from a user standpoint, there are some privacy risks involved. For any user who could be targeted for an ad, there are probably data brokers and other entities who maintain a data store about that user. That data is made available to players in the advertising ecosystem, and it helps set up the bid request. Most of these actions occur without direct approval by the user whose data it is. This lack of agency is the first privacy harm.

---

[4] Cyphers and Gennie Gebhart, "Behind the One-Way Mirror." The diagram is under Creative Commons License (https://creativecommons.org/licenses/by/3.0/).

The second harm involves the persistence and growth of this data about the user. Regardless of what (if any) ad is served to the user, the data that companies collect through the bid request remains with them, and it can be enriched with future data from other sources. This growth and dissemination of data makes it difficult to erase and extract that data. The user's ability to protect their privacy is reduced because their data is now in too many places.

5.1.3   *Privacy in advertising*

You saw in the previous subsection some of the privacy risks inherent to online advertising, so I want to provide some suggestions on privacy controls that could help companies use behavioral data to provide meaningful ads.

For many companies, their ability to target their users, or potential users, with ads depends on data. This data is a combination of behavioral data derived from user activity on the company's website as well as information about similar users. In the latter case, the logic is very similar to how Netflix provides a "movies watched by viewers like you" section when you view their web page.

Companies that serve ads typically build an *identity graph*, which is a list of identities associated with customers or users they wish to serve ads to. Consider this hypothetical user:

- User A has a Google ID of AAA@gmail.com, and A uses this ID to sign in to the New York Times website.
- User A also uses another email address, AAAA@yahoo.com, to sign in to their Facebook account.
- User A has an account on an online streaming service website using AAA@email.com.

Let's assume the streaming service wants to target user A with ads about upcoming movies on the streaming service when they browse the web. As in this example, a user may have multiple email addresses that they use as logins, so the streaming service will maintain an identity graph that links all of A's email addresses. This graph is important, because when the streaming service wants to serve ads to user A, it can use the graph to access all of A's online identities and the behavioral data associated with those identities. That way, when user A lands on either the New York Times app or website or on the Facebook app or website, the streaming company can target user A with an ad. This process of collecting a user's identities to build a graph and then targeting an ad involves copious amounts of data sharing.

Let's assume you are in charge of improving privacy protections for the streaming company. These are some actions you could take:

- You could create a hashed version of the ID on your website and map it to the original ID. In the preceding example, that mapping would be `AAA@gmail.com` to `hash(AAA@gmail.com)`.

- You could put the user into larger audience pools (such as users who search for thrillers, users who browse DVDs with Spencer Tracy, etc.) so that you can target ads that are not too specific while still being relevant. For example, if I am in my mid-30s and occasionally browse running shoes, being targeted with ads about shoes around new year's (when people make resolutions around health) may be perfectly fine if I am part of a cohort of similar users who are targeted. If an ad campaign identifies me specifically, that is both creepy and potentially illegal. The targeting needs to be cohort-based, such as users interested in running shoes, rather than profile-based, such as a specific user who bought shoes six months ago and is due for new ones.

- In the identity graph, you could build an opt-out flag, so that when the user opts out of receiving ads while signed in using a specific ID, the user's identity graph supplies that information as well, so that the user is not targeted with ads corresponding to data collected from that identity.

Hashing identities

You can find plenty about hashing online, but for the purposes of this discussion, hashing allows you to create a version of the original content (an email address in this case) that goes only one way. That is, with the right algorithm, you could derive the hashed value from the original email, but you could not obtain the original email from the hashed value.

For example, assume that you hash `nishant@hotmail.com` and end up with `22344`. From then on, each time you come across `nishant@hotmail.com`, you will be able to map it to `22344`. This means you can create a mapping between the version of the user's login that you use for their activities on your website and a more "privacy secure" hashed version, and you can use the latter for data transfers. As you can see, an ID like `nishant@hotmail.com` could be used to obtain other data about a user or even to contact them, whereas the transformed (hashed) version, `22344`, offers more privacy protection.

This approach enables you to create a wall between a user's activity on your website and their more global identity to help serve ads.

This list is not exhaustive, and the ads ecosystem is extremely complex. This example is vastly oversimplified and is just intended to demonstrate that you can both share data and build privacy controls into the sharing process.

In the next section, we will look at several techniques for safely sharing data that serves purposes ranging from public safety to advertising. Since each data share can be highly contextual, my goal is to equip you with several different techniques that you can adapt to the situation at hand and the relevant privacy risks.

5.2   How to share data safely: Security as an ally of privacy

We have so far discussed data as a key vector of business value as well as privacy risk. In order to protect data, you need to focus on the privacy harms that can be visited upon the data while it moves across your business network, while it moves to third parties, and while it is stored in your business system databases. Lest you think this is merely theoretical, let's first look at an example of how data in motion can help track, and therefore violate the privacy of, the most protected individual in the world.

5.2.1   Tracking President Trump

The *New York Times* has done some pathbreaking work as part of its Privacy Project.[5] Here we'll focus on the implications of the apps on your device sharing your location data.

The research conducted by the *Times* found that with apps on your phone sharing real-time location data, it is possible to track anyone. Yes, even the President of the United States. The *Times*, Privacy Project obtained a dataset with more than 50 billion location pings from the phones of more than 12 million people in the United States.[6] According to the *Times*, this was a random sample from 2016 and 2017.

Most online users understand that apps conduct some degree of online location tracking for personalization. However, it is often difficult to understand the big picture, so an example will be helpful.

As part of the Privacy Project, the *New York Times* was able to use publicly available information to deanonymize and then track the location and movements of President Trump.

If you are interested in visually following the president's movements that the *Times* tracked, that map is accessible at http://mng.bz/2joa.

The *Times* was able to create a trail of the president's movements because there was a cellphone in the proximity of the president, and that phone probably had an app that was broadcasting the phone's location coordinates.

On the map, the beginning of the trail represented the president's location at the Mar-a-Lago club in Florida. From this point forward, the president's location changes could be captured easily. The next stop was the president's golf club, and this is where the power of location tracking comes to the fore. The president's public schedule would typically list his meetings, and in this case, he was meeting with Prime Minister Abe of Japan. Combining the president's location data with his public schedule enabled the *Times* to track not just the president, but Japan's PM as well.

---

[5] Stuart A. Thompson and Charlie Warzel, "How to Track President Trump," *The New York Times*, December 20, 2019, http://mng.bz/2joa.

[6] Stuart A. Thompson and Charlie Warzel, "Twelve Million Phones, One Dataset, Zero Privacy," *The New York Times*, December 19, 2019, http://mng.bz/1j6q.

The *Times* was then able to track the president when he was having lunch at the Trump International Golf Club and finally when he returned for a working dinner with Prime Minister Abe.

As if this was not interesting enough (or unnerving, depending on your perspective), this tracking also enabled the *Times* to identify the device that was pinging location data. That device (more precisely an app on that device) had also broadcast location data at a nearby Secret Service field office.

This enabled the journalists to identify the device owner and map them to their place of work and residence with precision. That information, when combined with public information, helped identify the device's owner's family details.

This experience of involuntarily broadcasting location data, identifying yourself and further revealing biographical information, is not unique to this individual. It can happen to anyone using a mobile device that transfers data back to a server. This is why you need to use security controls to protect data from privacy harms.

The same security techniques that are used to protect your data from external hackers and bad actors can be used to prevent privacy harms from internal bad actors and maladroit employees. The rest of this section will focus on protecting your data while in transmission and at rest.

5.2.2 *Protecting data in motion*

As you have seen in previous chapters, more and more data that companies use and process tends to be unstructured. That presents a challenge in terms of being able to identify, detect, and protect data with privacy implications. It is therefore critical that you have clear privacy protections in place for data in motion (when data leaves your company's systems and before it lands in the hands of the recipients).

This is where there is an interesting overlap between security and privacy. If someone were to intercept data while it was in motion between two systems, that security violation would almost inevitably lead to privacy harms. We will discuss how to reduce the impact of this privacy harm by applying obfuscation techniques to the data before you transport it, but you will also want to reduce the likelihood of this data being intercepted by applying specific controls to your data.

You will want to come up with security strategies in partnership with your security team, but we'll look at a foundational checklist to get started. The following list is a starting point, but security experts may be able to recommend more updated or applicable tools.

For your most sensitive data being sent via electronic transmission, you should consider the following:

- The data must ideally be subject to end-to-end transit encryption at the service layer with mutual TLS where technically feasible. Where mutual TLS is not feasible, you must try to use regular SSL/TLS, since unencrypted HTTP could pose security risks.

- Prevent distribution via email because email is inherently insecure; this is a more common risk vector than many leaders appreciate, since in companies that have several products and millions of customers, it is common among engineers to share user details over email and chat programs while they build features, and especially when they troubleshoot bugs. This creates multiple copies of the data, thereby increasing the attack surface, and makes it that much harder to audit and trace where these copies live and to create privacy access controls. Additionally, even engineers who know better often use email to send sensitive business data when in a rush, thinking they will do it "just this one time." Over time, these instincts become habits. This is how phishing attempts succeed—external attackers can use emails as an entry point into company IT systems and exfiltrate data that is privacy-sensitive.

- Track and customize privacy controls based on the two points of motion for data. For example, as it undergoes processing and analysis, data can move

  - From your internal data center to another internal data center
  - From your internal data center to an external data center
  - From your internal data center to a public cloud instance you own
  - From a public cloud instance you own to another public cloud instance you own

  You will want to apply encryption techniques customized to each of these transmission paths.

The preceding checklist will need to be customized for your company, but you should use the following best practices:

- Classify the data before transmission, as we have discussed.
- Work with your security team to gauge the likelihood of interception when the data is in transit and when it is stored by a third party.
- Work with your legal team to understand any contractual or legal requirements stemming from the data transfer, especially if any of the data transfers are transnational in nature.
- Ensure that you have an understanding of how data replication will affect the transfers, since each copy of the data could add to your risk score.
- Ensure that all product and engineering teams have a seat at the table, since they will have more awareness about data movements than privacy and security teams whose job it is to monitor them and to build controls to mitigate privacy harms.

Remember, this list is a starting point. You should use the context from your data classification and inventory efforts to build a process that truly captures your risk cases and needs.

5.2.3   *Protecting data at rest*

Preventing privacy harms is critical when data is stored in the persistence layer—your databases. You will need to make sure that appropriate controls are in place before a user or an automated process can access stored data:

- Access controls and multi-factor authentication (MFA)
- Password-protected account or link

Let's explore these two requirements in detail, since managing access to data can help reduce unneeded access to it and thereby also reduce transmission privacy risks.

ACCESS CONTROL AS A PRIVACY TOOL

The following authentication and authorization tooling can help manage access to sensitive data:

- Mandate the use of a unique employer-provisioned identifier (such as email address or user ID) and password to authenticate to all employer-related information resources, networks, and data. The same password may not be used for more than one account (for example, the identity and access management password must be different than the GitHub password, unless single sign on [SSO] is in place).
- Any production user account passwords, secrets, cryptographic keys, tokens, API keys, or other sensitive material must not be logged or stored in cleartext, source code, or any other unapproved tool, including but not limited to wikis, Google Docs, spreadsheets, analytics events, or local development workstations.
- Passwords and authentication mechanisms must satisfy the following requirements, unless otherwise specified by regulatory, compliance, or legal requirements:
  - Not contain the user's account name
  - Be a minimum of eight characters
  - Contain characters from at least three of the following categories: uppercase letters of European languages (A through Z), lowercase letters of European languages (a through z), base 10 digits (0 through 9), non-alphanumeric characters (!@#$%^&*()_+|~=\{}[]:";'<>?,./), or any Unicode character that is categorized as an alphabetic character but is not uppercase or lowercase.
  - Passwords must not contain words similar to usernames, dictionary words, keyboard patterns, or character-to-number substitutions.
  - Lock out users for at least 30 minutes after six failed login attempts.
  - For the PCI environment or where multifactor authentication (MFA) is not enforced, passwords must be rotated at least every 90 days.
  - Break glass access (e.g., admin, root) to production machines must require multifactor authentication and be limited to no more than 20 hours.
  - Idle timeouts for information resources must be set to no more than 30 minutes and require users to re-authenticate to re-activate the idle session.

– Passwords and secrets on managed information resources must not use vendor-supplied default values and must adhere to the aforementioned requirements.

As previously stated, the democratized and highly siloed development process means that engineers are often free to collect and store data as they please. This data store is like a ticking time bomb, except that multiple copies of privacy-sensitive data means that you possibly have multiple time bombs. While it is prudent to not have such detonable devices, it is critical that you manage access to this data, lest someone inadvertently light a match. Access control helps you achieve that goal to a degree, and the preceding list represents a starting point that you will wish to add to, based on your exposure and risk.

ENCRYPTION AS A PRIVACY TOOL

Just as you can manage access to data using access control mechanisms, you can modify the data in a way that if someone were to access it, they could not do much damage. Encryption is one such tool, and while this privacy-focused book is not intended to build your expertise in encryption, this section will highlight how you can use encryption to prevent privacy harms.

Let's assume that the specific privacy threat you wish to negate is one where someone other than the intended recipient of sensitive data is able to decrypt and consume data in the clear. In order to execute upon this requirement, you will need to ensure that any compromise of a service account with access privileges to read or write from the bucket (where "bucket" refers to the storage unit on the cloud computing system like Amazon Web Services) or of the service account (at a third party, like a public cloud provider) with read access to the bucket, alone should not compromise the data.

To do so, you will want to ensure that the data is protected using client-side encryption; server-side encryption is insufficient, because the account at the server itself could be compromised. You will want to make sure the data is protected cryptographically before the data hits the server.

> **NOTE** Your security teams can provide more detail, but client-side encryption is the act of encrypting data before it is transmitted from a user device to a server.

This is a limited example for a specific use case. The larger point is that in order to prevent privacy harms arising from data sharing, you need to think about how to manage access to the data and the comprehensibility of the data. These controls ensure that even as data ends up being transported, the privacy impact can be managed.

The following list identifies some best practices for cryptography if you use it as a privacy device during data sharing. You will want to work with your security team and crypto experts to shape your specific strategy; this list is meant to be instructive rather than exhaustive:

- Ensure that cryptography accounts not just for data but also for metadata. Metadata could often prove to be a goldmine of information for an attacker. Metadata can provide information about the data, its relationships to other data, and its dependencies with external data, and creative attackers could use data lineage or links to identify users. They may even be able to use raw computing power to connect various aspects of metadata to infer the data itself without ever exfiltrating the data. This would be a silent breach, where no customer data ever leaves your systems, but the impact could be the same.

- Do not cavalierly share data just because it is encrypted. Cryptography is not a catch-all solution for data sharing. Cryptography-intercepting proxies do exist and can be used to mine data. Share only the minimum information needed to get the job done. Cryptography makes the process of data sharing itself safer, but it has limitations. We will look at techniques shortly to make the data itself safer for sharing.

- To make sure you cover some potential cryptography weak points, keep the following in mind:
  - Errors in architecture, policy, or coding can still reveal secrets.
  - Partners may not be completely reliable (due to rogue employees or contractors, or network configuration errors—intentional or unintentional).

- Ensure alignment with your business stakeholders, since encrypting and decrypting data takes time and will almost certainly affect throughput. Customers can also be fickle in that they often have the mutually incompatible expectations of complete security and negligible latency.

- Key management is "key" when it comes to encryption:
  - Encryption keys must be rotated on a regular basis, since cryptographic algorithms are continually being analyzed and vulnerabilities can be found.
  - Symmetric keys and private keys must be carefully protected.
  - If there's a public key, it needs to be distributed in a certificate to prevent interception attacks.

- As I have mentioned previously, you need to tailor your encryption to the state of the data:
  - Data at rest ideally requires envelope encryption—a key hierarchy is established. Never encrypt all data in a database with the same key.
  - Data in motion could require the use of HTTPS/TLS. Very sensitive data must still be encrypted, even over an encrypted connection. You may consider alternative ways to protect data, such as SFTP, IPSEC, etc.

Next, we will look at making the data itself less potent, should our security-centric tools like cryptography fail during data sharing.

5.3   *Obfuscation techniques for privacy-safe data sharing*

I used the example of data sharing by taxi or other mobility companies earlier to explain use cases where data may need to be shared so that these companies can operate with regulatory clearance. Having already looked at *why* such companies need to share data, it is now time to examine *how* such sharing of data could pose privacy risks.

If you are designing an app, and data sharing is part of the offering, you need to watch for the following red flags in the app:

- Uniquely identifying individuals without sufficiently anonymizing the data
- Placing individuals at a certain places and times for tracking
- Lacking consent for and visibility into how data is shared and with whom
- Identifying others connected to a user who may not consent to data sharing, even if the user did

If I were to evaluate a ridesharing app proposal that shared the following data, I would raise more than an eyebrow:

- Real-time tracking of a trip from start to finish
- Precise trip start and stop coordinates (later in this chapter you will see how a fitness app identified military service members with imprecise location data)
- Lack of privacy guidelines on the part of the entity receiving this data

There is no way to unshare data once it's shared. And when it comes to taxi companies, who you are and where you are may be all someone needs to identify and reach you. When a taxi company shares location and other identifying data with a third party, it is impossible to know what a recipient of your data will do with it, or how carefully they can protect it.

But this is not just about companies and how they may struggle with privacy and data sharing. Let's look at an example where privacy fell by the wayside when it came to the United States military.

5.3.1   *Data sharing and US national security*

Strava, the fitness tracking app, uses satellites to record its users' runs, bike rides, and other workouts.[7] It also makes many of these routes available for public view on its Global Heatmap, which shows where people around the world go running and cycling.[8]

This cool feature ended up creating headaches for Strava and the US military. US service members had been recording their runs around the compounds of their military bases. That information made it onto the Strava Heatmap and unknowingly revealed their locations.

---

[7] Joe Lindsey, "Strava's Heatmap Is Giving Away the Locations of US Military Bases," *Bicycling*, January 29, 2018, http://mng.bz/PWmR.

[8] Global Heatmap, *Strava*, https://labs.strava.com/heatmap/.

Twitter users figured out that they could identify outlines and activity patterns on US military bases in places like Syria, Afghanistan, and Somalia. The biggest potential threat was not the base locations themselves, which are public, but what went on in and around the bases. The map showed activity patterns within and around the base, giving away supply and patrol routes, as well as the precise locations of facilities like mess halls and living quarters. Further, users could get location-specific data, allowing them to link map activity to specific profiles. The result was that you could find out which service members were in which locations at a given point in time.

Strava responded, saying that all users have the ability to set activities to private so they're not included in the Heatmap. While that explanation is technically correct, when it comes to security and privacy, the companies building the products will own the outcomes, not the users.

As a former product manager, I understand what Strava was thinking when it built the Heatmap—it provides visibility into adoption and gives users a sense of belonging to a fitness-centric community. This, in turn, creates a positive motivation to run and then log your data. This was especially true in the early days of social media, when sharing was empowerment.

However, your feature is only as privacy-safe as the most creative invader of data privacy. If a privacy expert with an eye on the risks around data sharing had reviewed this app design, they may have raised questions like these:

- Who were these heatmaps visible to?
- What additional information can be inferred from them about Strava users?
- Could we alter the data to make it less identifiable when it comes to sensitive locations like military bases, refugee housing, etc.?

Here are some other lessons from this incident:

- Data sharing is not just about sharing data between one company and another.
- Whenever data you have collected from someone else leaves your company, you are essentially sharing that information with outside entities.
- In the age of social media, the combination of publicly available information, data on the dark web obtained by way of breaches, and ML-based tools that combine data make identifying people easier than ever.

For privacy, you need to think about data sharing any time data leaves your domain. This is true when you are a company collecting user data, and it is also true when you are just an individual broadcasting your data via your cell phone. This is not just about privacy, but also about safety.

It is therefore vital that anyone creating an app that shares data also builds in privacy techniques to anonymize this data and/or reduce access to it. Having set this context, let's look at some techniques to anonymize data for privacy before sharing it.

5.3.2   *Data anonymization: The relationship between precision and retention*

When it comes to data collection, I have built architectures with this key principle: the more precisely identifiable the data, the lower the retention period should be. This is a core privacy principle in action that drives the data classification conversations in many companies: precision and retention should have an inverse correlation. The more precise the data—that is, the more likely it is to identify specific users—the lower its retention period needs to be. In much the same way, precision and access control bear an inverse correlation. The logic behind this theory is that the more precisely identifiable the data is, the more likely it is that privacy harms can emanate from it, thereby shorter retention periods and more limited access are key to limiting the privacy harms.

This statement is equally relevant for data sharing. Figure 5.4 shows how you can split your systems in terms of how precise the data is that they contain and how you'd adjust the retention periods accordingly.

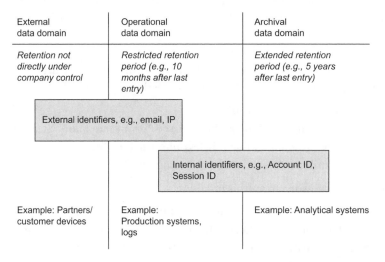

Figure 5.4   The more precise the data, the lower the retention period

Whenever I or my teams evaluate vendors with whom we share data, we categorize our data either as *operational* or as *archival*. The former is needed for regular business processes and is therefore extremely precise, whereas the latter is needed for more strategic research and therefore could be more aggregated.

For example, once a customer whose data it is cancels their account, we'd delete data that personally identifies that customer within a year; we then would have the option to retain a portion of less precise identifying data for longer. We'd ensure that any vendor that receives personally identifying data from us compartmentalizes their data storage units into two tiers, much like in figure 5.4. The operational data domain has precise data and a lower retention period, and the archival data domain has aggregated and therefore imprecise data with a higher retention period.

To continue our previous example of a taxi company, let's assume that the company shares data with a vendor that analyzes prices. This is what I'd recommend to a vendor before sharing customer data with them:

- Delete unique identifiers and precise times and geolocations after 90 days.
- Delete coarsened times and geolocations after 2 years.
- Internal, indefinitely retained data should be at least 5-anonymous or ε (epsilon) = 1.6 differentially private.
- Bulk shared data should be at least 100-anonymous or ε = 4.6 differentially private.

As you can see in the first two points, it is possible to tailor retention periods based on the precision of the data. The third and fourth points involve concepts that we will discuss later in the chapter. In short, however, as you coarsen data to make it less identifying, it is possible to measure the privacy impact of those changes. This is where *k*-anonymity and *l*-diversity come in; they are data-driven objective concepts to help protect privacy.

5.3.3   *Data anonymization: The relationship between precision and access*

Just as there is an inverse relationship between data precision and its retention, there should be a similarly inverse relationship between precision and availability.

When you share data with a partner, you should insist that they anonymize data in memory, especially if you share granular data with them. Some techniques include

- Not persisting data used solely for aggregation
- Keeping individual-level data in memory; only saving processed data to disk

This means that precise data is short-lived and less accessible, while more aggregated data is available to more people, since it is on disk, where you can also manage access more effectively.

To prevent personal identification, you should remove or replace any identifiers that uniquely identify someone. You will want to do this before sharing the data or have the vendor do this as soon as they receive the data and complete mapping it at their end.

There are two ways to dispose of personally identifiable data (like Social Security numbers, email addresses, etc.):

- Replace it with internal, uniquely generated values before sharing data.
- Replace it with values generated by a keyed pseudorandom function (such as HMAC-SHA256).

We have discussed, in the context of taxi companies, the potency of data that identifies a customer as well as their location. Just as we can delete IDs that personally identify customers and replace them with internal IDs, there are techniques available to obfuscate location data:

- Round times to the nearest 30-minute increment (for example, 12:25 p.m. would be rounded to 12:30 p.m.)
- Convert GPS coordinates to street segment start/center/end.
- Truncate GPS coordinates to three decimal degrees; this is critical, since fewer decimal points in a GPS location makes the location less precise.

To a reader who may not have dealt with the precision of location data, this may seem like a lot of work, especially considering the volume of data that apps generate and companies consume. It would be helpful to understand how this coarsening can alter the data and make it more privacy-safe.

Let's assume you have a table with two entries:

- Trip A: Started at 12:22 p.m., and ended at 1:09 p.m.
- Trip B: Started at 12:24 p.m., and ended at 1:11 p.m.

A key example of privacy harm is being able to uniquely identify an individual and/or an activity. If you needed to share this data for data analysis purposes, it poses a privacy risk, since you may be able to identify who took each trip based on the start and end times, and other public data. The goal of coarsening data is to make any two unique activities more similar, so that the ability of an engineer or automated process to identify them as unique decreases.

If we were to round the time in the preceding example to the nearest half hour, the entries would look like this:

- Trip A: Started at 12:30 p.m., and ended at 1:00 p.m.
- Trip B: Started at 12:30 p.m., and ended at 1:00 p.m.

These obfuscations make the trips less unique and therefore the individuals who took them less identifiable, without hurting the aggregate data analysis. Figure 5.5 makes the point more visually. The left column represents individual rows of data, with each row representing a specific ride based on the starting time. In this simple example, all the rides began at separate times, so no two rides have the same start time.

Let's assume we wish to perform analysis on rides for customer service, pricing, etc. In this case, we may not care about individual rides but rather about a cohort of rides broken up by some distinguishing features. We could create cohorts based on the hour (2 p.m., 3 p.m. and 4 p.m.) if there is no need to know exactly what the start time of each ride is. That data is not necessary as long as we know what cohort the ride belonged to. Also, having specific start times keeps open the risk that people taking those rides could be identified, especially with external data.

Therefore, when it comes to our analysis use case, rather than using the left column with individual trips identified with their start times, we could use the right column with trips grouped based on the hour of their start time. The left column represents the operational version of the data, while the right column represents an archival account of the data. The former can be used when you need more granular information (for example, you may need to know the specific start time of a trip in

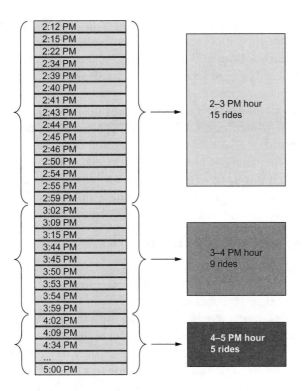

Figure 5.5 Aggregate data for privacy protection

case you need to look it up for customer support, refunds, etc.); otherwise the latter can be used.

These examples may be a bit simplistic, but the key message here is to avoid blindly sharing data that individually identifies the folks whose data it is.

If you thought access control was challenging within an organization, it is even more challenging when it comes to managing access granted to partners. When I evaluate data sharing protocols, I ask for access control to make sure that once a partner gets data, they manage who on their side can access it. Here is how I have accomplished this in practice: I ask that the partner ration the availability of their APIs to those who want to access the data.

My teams have implemented tools to check if engineers and data scientists who have access to sensitive encrypted data still need it. We have routinely sampled the data and audited it to see when it was last decrypted. Often, we have found that teams had requested keys but hardly or never used them to access data.

In those cases, we swapped the keys to check if the engineers ever complained. Seventy-five percent of the time, we never heard back. What this means is that people often think they will need more data than they do, and even if they don't use it, their ability to access it poses a privacy risk. You will want to use techniques like these internally and while sharing data as well.

You may have noticed that in previous chapters and sections we have looked at access control using tools, but when it comes to data sharing we have taken a more holistic view. We have deployed policies and altered data so as to reduce how much data and how precise the data is that vendors and partners have access to. This distinction is critical.

With internal stakeholders, you may feel more confident that your access controls plus audit checks can mitigate privacy harms. With external partners, it is possible that they may have access to other data that could uniquely identify a user and that their ability to audit who accesses the data and how they use it may be suboptimal. Therefore, rather than hang your hat purely on access control, you will want to coarsen the data so that even if someone were to gain access to it, and even if they combined it with other data, the privacy harm could be contained.

5.3.4   *Data anonymization: Mapping universal IDs to internal IDs*

Data sharing often presents interesting dilemmas. You may have some use cases where you want to identify someone internally, but you want to share their data in a way that the external partner receiving their data cannot identify them.

For those use cases, you may want to create a table that links their external identifiers (such as their passport number) to custom internal identifiers. If you do this, you will want to carefully manage access to this linking table, so as to prevent privacy issues. If you do not manage access to this table, it would be straightforward for internal and external actors to connect external data to internal data via this table.

Let's look at an example. Table 5.1 is an example of a taxi company that retains trip data mapped to the passport IDs of customers. I realize that cab companies do not normally collect passport numbers, but let's assume they do for this example.

Table 5.1   Trip data mapped to passport numbers

Passport number	Trip start	Trip end
5037678987	1 p.m.	2 p.m.
3239892821	2 p.m.	4 p.m.
2398753116	12 p.m.	4 p.m.
3873736111	11 a.m.	11:30 a.m.

Let's assume the cab company wishes to share this data with a vendor so that they can discern what times of the day demand is higher, so that they can adjust prices accordingly. It would be risky for the cab company to share passport numbers with this vendor, so in order to reduce the privacy risk, we could first create an internal mapping table—something like table 5.2.

Table 5.2   Passport numbers mapped to internal Ids

Passport number	Internal ID
5037678987	ghsvfydvbdv
3239892821	hgavdchgdfe
2398753116	dhbchchvhge
3873736111	wdjhpdjdiehf

In table 5.2, we have created internal identifiers that map to passport numbers. How this helps protect privacy becomes clear in table 5.3.

Table 5.3   Shared data with internal IDs

ID	Trip start	Trip end
ghsvfydvbdv	1 p.m.	2 p.m.
hgavdchgdfe	2 p.m.	4 p.m.
dhbchchvhge	12 p.m.	4 p.m.
wdjhpdjdiehf	11 a.m.	11:30 a.m.

If the cab company were to share the raw and personally identifying data (table 5.1 with passport numbers), that would pose a high degree of privacy risk. However, sharing the same data with internal IDs mapped to trip data (table 5.3) rather than passport numbers enables the kind of analysis and planning that's required without revealing exactly who took those trips. That way, the cab company can retain the data for marketing, retargeting, and discounts if necessary, without sharing that data with a vendor whose analysis does not require that data.

This is especially critical for several reasons:

- Any time data is shared, you need to protect it using encryption or other means of access control while the data is in motion, so as to reduce the risk of infiltration.
- Once the data reaches the vendor, you are vulnerable to any security mishaps that happen at the vendor; reducing the identifiability of the users whose data it is can help manage privacy risk.
- Finally, any time you share data, you are in essence making a copy of the data; the more copies of personally identifiable data there are, the more resources you need to expend to protect them. As any seasoned privacy pro will tell you, the best data protection is to not have that data to begin with. Making unneeded copies of data is foolish, especially when mapping tables like the preceding ones enable you to do the analysis without sharing personally identifying data.

In too many companies, data is collected, processed, and shared without any understanding of the attendant privacy harms. My emphasis on classification, inventory, and obfuscation seeks to help manage the risk every step of the way. Building these protections into this data will help you avoid a situation where algorithms and automated processes that work faster than humans cause privacy harms that are hard to detect until it is too late. These techniques should be seen as a progression, where each set of ideas builds on the ones that come before.

5.4   *Sharing internal IDs with third parties*

We have discussed how sharing internal IDs can be safer (relatively) from a privacy standpoint than sharing identifiers that are universally applicable, like Social Security numbers. As with all things data, this sharing is not entirely risk-free either.

External disclosure of users' internal IDs could create identification risks, even if these IDs are not linked to data that personally identifies a user. As some of these identifiers are long-lived and never change over their lifetime, exposing them to external parties could enable tracking of the same users across multiple datasets (either to the same party or, worse, to multiple parties if these datasets are shared or leaked) over an extended period of time.

As a general principle, internal identifiers should never be exposed in the dataset when sharing with external parties; they need to be pseudonymized in such a way that the original ID cannot be reconstructed from the pseudonymized identifier, while maintaining the consistency between the values of the dataset. Further, if hashed internal identifiers are externally disclosed and are subsequently subject to a breach, the hashing prior to sharing might enable you to determine which vendor was involved in the breach.

> **NOTE** *Pseudonymization* is a de-identification technique in which identifying data is replaced with surrogates (also known as tokens) in a consistent manner. This contrasts with other de-identification techniques, such as redaction or generalization, in that the surrogates retain their referential properties within the de-identified dataset. Furthermore, depending on which transformation is used to produce the surrogates, these surrogates may be reversed back into their original sensitive values by an authorized user. Encryption and secure hashing are examples of pseudonymization.

In short, do not share internal identifiers carelessly, just because they are less identifying of your customers than a Social Security number.

There are several variations in terms of datasets that contain internal identifiers, so we'll look at three distinct use cases to advise on how you can treat these identifiers in a sharing context.

Following the principle of data minimization, which stipulates that you should only use as much data as necessary to accomplish a specified purpose, an internal identifier should only have a given pseudonymized value within the intended session. Depending on the intended session boundary, a user could have multiple sessions within a dataset or a session spanning multiple datasets.

5.4.1 Use case 1: Minimal session (no linking of user activity is needed)

As a user of customer data, you'd use this approach if you are sharing the smallest data element within the dataset. For example, suppose you run an online retail website and you are sharing details with the delivery company to facilitate a transaction, like a single order. As there is no explicit intention to correlate sessions for each user within the dataset, an internal identifier should have different pseudonymized values in different sessions. Since the dataset you are sharing is very granular, you will need to obfuscate the identifiers accordingly.

SUGGESTED PSEUDONYMIZATION TECHNIQUES

You should use a cryptographically secure pseudorandom number generator (CSPRNG) to generate a 128-bit random number as the pseudonymized identifier. This number has the desired high-quality randomness and is length-compatible with the internal identifier (128-bit). This is the recommended technique. Note that I am assuming a 128-bit identifier for the sake of this example to keep it straightforward.

When CSPRNG is unavailable, a generic pseudorandom number generator (PRNG) can be used instead. Even though it is not as robust as CSPRNG, it is still acceptable for the purpose. This use is only a last resort, and it should require additional review and approval.

5.4.2 Use case 2: Single session per dataset (linking of the same user's activity within a dataset)

Unlike case 1, where we were sharing a solitary activity, this use case involves sharing a session that could have multiple actions. For example, suppose you run an online retail website. The user used your platform to buy merchandise and then save something else on their wishlist. You then share these details with an analytics platform that helps advise you on improving your user interface to improve the customer shopping experience.

In this case, each dataset is considered to be a single independent session. All data elements associated with the same internal identifier should have a deterministic and consistent pseudonymized value within the dataset. Typically this can be achieved by using a cryptographic or secure hashing function, or by utilizing a lookup table to maintain consistent pseudonymized internal identifier values within the dataset.

SUGGESTED PSEUDONYMIZATION TECHNIQUES

Apply the HMAC-SHA256 cryptographic function to the internal identifier with a unique, randomly generated 256-bit cryptographic key for the dataset. The 256-bit output hash value can then be used as the pseudonymized identifier. If it is desirable to maintain the 128-bit length as an internal identifier, the hash can be truncated to 128 bits. The HMAC key should only be used once and disposed of right after.

Alternatively, apply the SHA-256 secure hashing function to the internal identifier with a unique 256-bit randomly generated salt for the dataset. This method also produces a 256-bit output hash value, and it can be truncated to 128 bits if needed.

Another option is to generate a random pseudonymized value for each internal identifier as in use case 1, but to store each internal identifier and its pseudonymized value in a lookup table to maintain consistency. This option should be considered when a cryptographic or hashing function is unavailable. The lookup table must be secured and disposed of after use. This option has additional cost, either in memory consumption or external service dependency.

As different datasets are considered as separate sessions, the cryptographic key, salt, or mapping table should not be shared between datasets.

5.4.3   *Use case 3: Session spanning datasets (linking across datasets)*

To continue our example of the online retail store, let's assume you wish to share multiple examples of purchases and abandonment (when users add products to carts but do not buy) with an analytics company so as to help predict revenue. In this case, obfuscating identifiers requires some consideration. When a pseudonymized identity needs to be consistently maintained across multiple datasets for the same external party, it is an extension of use case 2.

SUGGESTED PSEUDONYMIZATION TECHNIQUES

The same cryptographic key (for HMAC-SHA256) or salt (for SHA-256) should be used when pseudonymizing these datasets. Proper care must be taken to ensure these keys or salts are properly protected internally, and each key or salt should be used only for one external party. HMAC-SHA256 performs two rounds of hashing, so it has roughly double the computation cost compared to SHA256. It has the benefit of using standard cryptographic primitives, which take care of key length and do not require the concatenation of the internal identifier and salt.

You should maintain one lookup table for each external party. Each lookup table contains a version of the ID linked to the internal dataset, so that in the event that the external party has a breach, you will know exactly which one was breached based on the internal ID that ends up getting exfiltrated. You can then notify the customers impacted by that specific breach rather than having to contact everyone. Also, the table must be encrypted according to best practices with minimally necessary access privileges.

5.4.4   *Recovering pseudonymized values*

In certain scenarios, the pseudonymized identifiers may need to be recovered internally after being shared with a third party. For example, a third party may return some of the data with their own metadata added. It would then be necessary to recover the original internal identifiers from the pseudonymized values. There are two possible ways to achieve this: utilizing a mapping table to cross-reference between raw internal identifiers and their pseudonymized values, or using a two-way cryptographic function to encrypt internal identifiers to pseudonymized values and recovering them through decryption.

MAPPING TABLE

Using a generic two-way mapping table to store every generated pseudonymized identifier with its original internal identifier will enable convenient lookup at the cost of storage space and maintenance overhead. This technique is advantageous for large-scale data processing, such as data warehouse operations and analytics, because the internal identifier values can be recovered with a simple table join. The table must be encrypted according to best practices with minimally necessary access privileges.

TWO-WAY CRYPTOGRAPHIC FUNCTION

Instead of using a one-way hashing function, a proper two-way encryption/decryption function can be used to generate a pseudonymized identifier with similar properties. Specifically, instead of applying HMAC-SHA256 to internal identifiers to generate pseudonymized values, you can encrypt the internal identifiers using AES with a 256-bit key (in CBC mode with null IV). The original internal identifiers can then be recovered by simply decrypting the pseudonymized values with the same key. Unlike one-way hashing, the generated value should never be trimmed. If a shorter length is desired, a 128-bit key should be used instead to produce 128-bit output value. This method incurs no additional storage overhead, but you will need to perform the decryption operation on every use.

> **NOTE** The use of a two-way encryption/decryption function is solely for the purpose of generating pseudonymized values, not for general data encryption. As such, some of the more robust modes of operation, such as AES-GCM are omitted because they either don't add value (e.g., feedback mode gains no advantage as key length is greater than or equal to the internal identifier's bit length), or they would significantly increase output length without obvious benefits (e.g., inclusion of nonce and authentication tag).

5.5 *Measuring privacy impact*

You have now seen several techniques to mitigate identifiability, and consequently the privacy harm, when data sharing. However, effort is not equivalent to impact, so it is vital that leaders use a data-driven process to ascertain the privacy impact of these obfuscation techniques. The use of privacy techniques will allow you to quantify this impact.

There are two techniques that can help you measure this privacy impact: k-anonimity and l-diversity. You could use them concurrently or individually, depending on your privacy context.

5.5.1   *K-anonymity*

The most exhaustive work on *k*-anonymity I have read comes from Professor Latanya Sweeney[9], but for this book, here is an intuitive explanation from Carnegie Mellon University[10]: In *k*-anonymity, attributes are suppressed until each row is identical with at least k-1 other rows. At this point, the database is said to be *k*-anonymous. *K*-anonymity thus prevents definite database linkages. At worst, the data released narrows down an individual entry to a group of *k* individuals.

K-anonymity is intuitive to implement, it's used by Google in their ad API, and it provides a minimum guarantee that you are one among a minimum cohort rather than being uniquely identifiable.

To see *k*-anonymity in action, let's walk through an example so you can see how user identifiability fluctuates based on data precision. We will look at thousands of rides, where each ride has a pickup and a drop-off location. We will vary the number of decimal points in the location GPS coordinates so that we can provide varying degrees of precision. If the GPS location is very precise, it may describe a specific address, like someone's home. If it is less precise, it may describe a block or a square mile, in which case a lot of different rides could be grouped together. This is similar to the earlier example where rounding off the pickup and drop-off times enabled us to group multiple rides and protect privacy more effectively.

K-ANONYMITY WITH IMPRECISE DATA

Table 5.4 shows how *k*-anonymity works when you have different precision levels of location data. In the table, the y-axis represents the number of decimal points in the location data, while the x-axis represents the *k*-anonymity value. To understand what the *k*-anonymity value symbolizes, here is a primer: Let's home in on the last row and the third column. When you have 5 decimal points in a GPS location, only 35.5% of location entries had 5 other trip values that were similar. This means that the other 64.5% of the entries had fewer than 5 values that were similar, rendering them identifiable. Removing one decimal point—allowing just 4 decimals in the GPS—means that in this sample 93.2% of data sets had other similar data, thereby reducing the likelihood of identification as compared to using 5 decimal points. This means that the more precise the data, the lower the chance that there will be other data that is similar, making each unit that much more identifiable. Correspondingly, the higher the *k*-anonymity value, the more private the data.

Two trips that have the same value would have to have the same pickup and drop-off points.

In the top row of table 5.4, based on GPS location data with 0 decimal points, you will see that for all users (100%), you can find at least 1 other trip (giving you a *k*-anonymity of 2), 4 other trips (giving you a *k*-anonymity of 5), all the way through 999 other trips (giving you a *k*-anonymity of 1,000) users with the same trip value.

---

[9] Latanya Sweeney, "*k*-anonymity: A model for protecting privacy" (May 2002), http://mng.bz/J1mZ.
[10] "K-Anonymity," www.cs.cmu.edu/~jblocki/Slides/K-Anonymity.pdf.

Table 5.4 *K*-anonymity with 0 decimal points

		K-anonymity value					
		2	5	10	50	100	1,000
	0	100%	100%	100%	100%	100%	100%
Decimal points in location data	1	100%	100%	100%	100%	100%	100%
	2	100%	100%	100%	99.9%	99.9%	99.1%
	3	99.9%	99.8%	99.5%	97.6%	95.3%	87.9%
	4	97.4%	93.2%	89.3%	73.1%	59.3%	17.3%
	5	68.4%	35.5%	18.3%	2.5%	1.5%	0.9%

When you share GPS location data with 0 decimal points, you have rendered the users less identifiable, with high *k*-anonymity. The reason this happens is that a lot of different pickup and drop-off locations have been made equal because of GPS rounding, just as the 11:21 pickup time and the 11:22 pickup time become 11:30 with time rounding.

Here your *k*-anonymity objective is met, but you have sacrificed data quality.

K-ANONYMITY WITH PRECISE DATA

Table 5.5 shows how *k*-anonymity works when you have very precise location data. The more decimal points you have in the GPS coordinates, the more precise the location of the user and the more identifiable the user is.

Table 5.5 *K*-anonymity with 4 and 5 decimal points

		K-anonymity value					
		2	5	10	50	100	1,000
	0	100%	100%	100%	100%	100%	100%
Decimal points in location data	1	100%	100%	100%	100%	100%	100%
	2	100%	100%	100%	99.9%	99.9%	99.1%
	3	99.9%	99.8%	99.5%	97.6%	95.3%	87.9%
	4	97.4%	93.2%	89.3%	73.1%	59.3%	17.3%
	5	68.4%	35.5%	18.3%	2.5%	1.5%	0.9%

Look at the bottom two rows in the table where you supply 4 or 5 decimal points for the GPS location for pickups and drop-offs. In this case, the *k*-anonymity is lower because the number of users who meet a precise GPS location is lower.

Therefore, as you go lower in the table, the percentage of the cohort that meets the corresponding *k*-anonymity threshold is lower, and it also decreases as you go from left to right. For example, when you display 5 decimal points, 68.4% of users have a *k*-anonymity of 2, meaning that for 68.4% of users, you can find one other user with the same trip values.

If we shave off one decimal point and offer GPS locations with 4 decimal points, we see that for 97.4% of users, you can find a similar ride, so they have a *k*-anonymity value of 2. As before, the less precise the data, the more anonymity you can provide for users.

On the far right, if we provide 5 decimal points and want to provide a *k*-anonymity of 1,000, meaning we can find 999 other similar rides, we can only do so for 0.9% of riders, so there is very little anonymity, given the precision of the location data. The numbers improve somewhat if we remove one decimal and round to 4, but we can still provide a *k*-anonymity of 1,000 for just 17.4%, so about 1 in 6 rides.

If we need a higher percentage of users to meet a particular *k*-anonymity value, we will need to provide fewer decimal points of location data.

K-ANONYMITY WITH INDUSTRY BEST PRACTICE

In the final view of this data, as shown in table 5.6, I will focus on a *k*-anonymity value of 5, since that is regarded as the industry best practice. In this case, you will have obfuscated the data such that for each record, there will be at least 4 others that are indistinguishable from it, thereby making that record more privacy-protected and less individually identifiable.

Table 5.6 *K-anonymity of 5*

		K-anonymity value					
		2	5	10	50	100	1,000
	0	100%	100%	100%	100%	100%	100%
Decimal points in location data	1	100%	100%	100%	100%	100%	100%
	2	100%	100%	100%	99.9%	99.9%	99.1%
	3	99.9%	99.8%	99.5%	97.6%	95.3%	87.9%
	4	97.4%	93.2%	89.3%	73.1%	59.3%	17.3%
	5	68.4%	35.5%	18.3%	2.5%	1.5%	0.9%

Take a look at the column for a *k*-anonymity value of 5, which suggests that for a specific trip there are 5 others just like it, thereby making an individual trip in that cohort less identifiable. As we work our way down this column, we can see what happens to *k*-anonymity as we add more decimal points to our location data. As we have already established, the more decimal points we add, the more precise our data, and the more identifiable the user whose GPS coordinates we are looking at. Thus, the number of users who have a k-anonymity of 5 will go down.

When we have 0 decimal points (a coarser location), we can find 4 others with the same values for all users (i.e., 100% of users have k-anonymity of 5). The same holds true for 1 and 2 decimal points—you could have GPS coordinates with up to 2 decimal points and still have k-anonymity of 5.

When you add a third decimal point, you hit an inflection point; this is the first time that not every user has a k-anonymity of 5. There are at least some users for whom there will not be at least 4 others with identical values. However, it turns out that even when we add a third decimal point while shooting for a k-anonymity of 5, we still include 99.8% of users.

So, if our goal is to have a k-anonymity of 5, we'd need to suppress only 0.2% of the data.

5.5.2 L-diversity

The industry best-practice of a k-anonymity of 5 provides a meaningful balance between privacy and usability. However, k-anonymity has its limitations, which is why there is yet another tool available to help you anonymize data before you share it: l-diversity. Let's consider a use case that shows the limitations of k-anonymity and how l-diversity can help.

Let's assume you end up with a k-anonymity of 5, but there is at least one pickup point such that every trip from that pickup point goes to the same destination. In this instance, using external data, you may be able to learn where any passenger from that source is going. This is where l-diversity can help. L-diversity will help ensure that there is a diversity of potential sources or destinations. Thus, for every trip that is reported in a time window, a pickup must have at least l different potential drop-offs, and every drop-off must have l potential pickups.

There may be situations where k-anonymity may filter out too much data, and in these cases, l-diversity may be a much better tool. Figure 5.6 helps make that point. In the figure, the dots on the left represent ride pickups, and the ones on the right represent ride drop-offs. If you apply a k-anonymity value of 2, you will filter out all the rides, since no two rides have the same pickup and drop-off. If, on the other hand, you separate the pickups and drop-offs and apply an l-diversity of 2, you can retain the entire dataset while preserving privacy as well.

In this specific scenario, let's assume you are trying to study the density of pickups. If a specific location is seeing an uptick in pickups, you may want to send more cabs there to reduce wait times.

In this case, it makes even more sense to disconnect the pickups and drop-offs, and not store them as one trip. You could even delete the drop-off portion of the data altogether. You will now be left with less data, which means lower storage costs; the data you do have is more germane to your use case, so you have better data quality; and by not having the entire trip stored, you have better privacy.

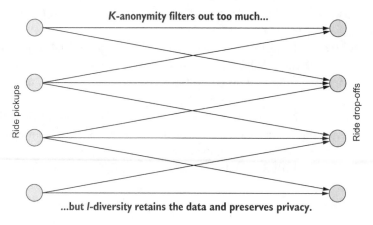

Figure 5.6   L-diversity in action

L-diversity is a win-win-win across the board *in this particular scenario*. You could apply it while storing data internally and while sharing data externally.

This is why I have shown you so many privacy techniques in the wider context of data quality and security. This is an art and a science, rather than a one-size-fits-all solution. I have used combinations of these techniques with varying degrees of data obfuscation and then iterated on them with different datasets. There were times when the privacy impact was easy to discern, while on other occasions we had to make a judgment call. The key takeaway is that you have tools to improve privacy protection and quantify impact. Use them before sharing data, and the *future you* will thank the *present you*.

5.6   *Privacy harms: This is not a drill*

I have spent a lot of time showing you how data can be used and shared online, and how you can manage the privacy risk and measure the privacy impact. A lot of business leaders and venture capital investors I speak to seem very relaxed about the likelihood of being impacted by the privacy harms of data sharing. Their attitude suggests they think companies that get into trouble with data sharing end up there due to negligence. Then, when a small mistake lands them in regulatory and PR hot water, they overcorrect and end up stifling even legitimate uses of data. This swing from nonchalance to zealotry can be detrimental to the business.

Here we'll look at some other real-life examples of how data sharing causes privacy issues, so that you understand the risks and deploy the techniques from this chapter prudently rather than reluctantly.

5.6.1   *Facebook and Cambridge Analytica*

By now, almost everyone has heard of the Cambridge Analytica issue. Cambridge Analytica, a political data firm hired by President Trump's 2016 election campaign, gained access to private information on more than 50 million Facebook users.[11] Cambridge, in its telling, had tools with predictive capabilities that could influence user behavior. Its desire to obtain that data from Facebook would, in theory, enable Cambridge to improve their predictive tools and deploy them on the users themselves. This would make their targeted messages more effective and possibly affect voting patterns and election outcomes.

The data included details on users' identities, friends, other connections, and user behavior by way of posts they had liked. Cambridge's big idea was to identify personality traits based on a user's Facebook activity, and then to target digital ads for that user based on their personality traits.

How Cambridge got this data, rather than how the data was used, is a key focus for this chapter and book. Users were asked to take a personality survey and download an app. The app then scraped private information from their profiles and the profiles of their friends. This mode of data extraction was not inhibited or throttled by Facebook then, but Facebook has since discontinued this level of access. This extraction and analysis capability had been developed at Cambridge University's Psychometrics Center. The center declined to work with Cambridge Analytica, but they found a willing partner in Aleksandr Kogan, a psychology professor in the university.

Harnessing this ability to extract large volumes of data from users and their contacts, Dr. Kogan built his own app and, in June 2014, began harvesting data for Cambridge Analytica. He ultimately provided over 50 million raw profiles to the firm. The privacy harm here impacted the users and their contacts. Only about 270,000 users, those who participated in the survey, had consented to having their data collected, under the condition that their data would be used for research and without any understanding that their consent would be used to collect their friends' data.

There are several lessons to learn from that episode, but here are the ones that stand out for me:

- Once data leaves your company, chances are you can exert very little control over what happens to it.
- The entities you share data with may not be as transparent and honest as you are.
- Whoever you share data with could have more sophisticated abilities than you do to process that data.
- It often takes a while to understand the full implications of data sharing, so in this case, no news is not necessarily good news.

Remember these lessons before you dismiss the risk inherent to data sharing.

---

[11]Kevin Granville, "Facebook and Cambridge Analytica: What You Need to Know as Fallout Widens," *The New York Times*, March 19, 2018, http://mng.bz/q21x.

5.6.2   *Sharing data and weaknesses*

As if we have not already seen enough attack vectors for data sharing, there is ransomware. Ransomware is malicious software that spreads quickly across computer networks and encrypts them, holding sensitive documents hostage until victims decide to pay the hackers.[12]

Ransomware has a significant impact:

- In 2019, ransomware hit 103 federal, state, and municipal agencies, 759 healthcare providers, and 86 schools and universities.[13]
- Four US cities were hit with ransomware in December alone.
- After seeing Atlanta spend $2.6 million to restore its systems rather than pay the $52,000 ransom, many officials have decided that it's cheaper to pay the hackers.[14]
- A ransomware attack cost the city of Baltimore $18 million.

These attacks have only increased in frequency as attackers realize how weak cyber defense capabilities are and how much sensitive data companies and governments hold.

The key lesson here is that when you share data with someone, you are also sharing their security and privacy weaknesses. And when those weaknesses are exploited, you will share in the consequences.

Summary

- In modern companies, data sharing is a key engine of growth, engagement, personalization, and just about every aspect of innovation.
- Companies share data with third parties for endeavors ranging from compliance to advertising to data quality.
- There are several techniques available for sharing data with privacy controls.
- Some of these techniques are inherent to standard data security requirements, in that they manage access to data as it leaves your organizational perimeter.
- Other techniques entail obfuscating data and processing it in ways to contain the privacy harm.
- There are also industry-acclaimed techniques (*k*-anonymity, *l*-diversity, etc.) available to measure the impact of your privacy techniques so as to assess whether you can safely share data.
- Data sharing is one of the most irreversible decisions a company can make, with discernible impacts upon the users whose data it is, so companies should share data very carefully.
- The techniques in this chapter are part of a larger data governance effort, and are successors to the previous efforts involving data classification and data inventory.

[12]Alfred Ng, "Ransomware froze more cities in 2019. Next year is a toss-up," *CNET*, December 5, 2019, http://mng.bz/7WYQ.

[13]Dan Patterson, "Four U.S. cities attacked by ransomware this month," *CBS News*, December 17, 2019, http://mng.bz/mxE8.

[14]Ng, "Ransomware froze more cities in 2019."

Part 3

Building tools and processes

This part will help engineers build point solutions using the data governance capabilities discussed earlier. Privacy engineering is aimed at delivering critical verifiable capabilities to customers of a platform. Many of these capabilities are technical incarnations of expectations put in place by regulations. This part will offer hands-on skills to help engineers meet these expectations.

Chapter 6 will help engineers set up a technical privacy review process to embed privacy as a technical feature for the company's products and services.

Chapter 7 will walk through a detailed architecture for data deletion, thereby providing a service-based framework for data erasure. It covers data deletion ranging from account data to streaming event data.

Chapter 8 will help readers design a data export capability so as to meet high-visibility "Data Subject Access Requests" or "DSARs."

Chapter 9 offers a sample design for a Consent Management Platform (CMP) so that businesses can meet this new requirement that is being enforced by regulators and corporations.

The technical
privacy review

This chapter covers

- What is meant by "privacy reviews"
- How companies can split privacy reviews between legal and technical teams
- How technical privacy reviews can be integrated into a company's workstream
- How the technical privacy review can become more automated and efficient
- Examples of both kinds of reviews (by lawyers and by engineers)

In earlier chapters of this book, you have seen how the modern development process empowers engineers to build products without the constraints of process. Adding to this innovative spirit is the flow of data and the inherent possibilities and risks. Add in impatient business leaders, complicated regulators, and a skeptical customer base, and you have a realistic possibility of products shipping with privacy issues.

The privacy review process is aimed at ensuring that privacy risks are addressed before a company releases products or features. Since the engineers who build the products do not always appreciate or have the time to understand the privacy implications of their work, it is vital that there be a process to ensure scrutiny of these products through a privacy lens.

Creating a privacy review process is a continuation of the work we have discussed so far, whereby a company has to manage how it classifies data, catalogs the data, protects it using access controls, and processes and shares it over the course of conducting business. While all the data-centric privacy controls are critical, ensuring that there is a specific stage in the development of products where these privacy controls can be validated and applied is critical. Just as we know that eating healthy and exercising is critical but often wait for an annual physical checkup to apply those lessons, the privacy review process is critical.

This chapter dives deep into this critical step and will provide tips on how technical leaders with limited resources can provide this service to their engineers.

Broadly speaking, this chapter is split into five logical parts:

- In part 1, you will learn what privacy reviews mean in the traditional sense. It helps to have this background even for smaller process-lite businesses, given regulatory scrutiny and customer expectations.
- In part 2, we will operationalize legal privacy reviews for two different kinds of development environments.
- In part 3, the reader will learn how to make the case for a technical privacy review to protect the customer and the company.
- In part 4, the reader will learn how to integrate the technical review more logistically, by way of automation.
- In part 5, scale and efficiency will be the focus so as to enable widespread adoption of the technical privacy review
- In part 6, we will look at hands-on examples to help train our readers in realistic technical privacy reviews.

Let's start with the fundamentals: what do we mean by "privacy reviews"?

6.1   *What are privacy reviews?*

Before diving deep into the kinds of privacy reviews and how to create a program to administer them, it would be helpful to understand what we mean by "privacy reviews." Modern interactive products and features are conceived by product managers, designers, and data scientists; they are built by software developers and architects; they scale based on work done by data platform teams and database operatives who manage data centers and cloud storage systems; and they are deployed by yet another team of specialists. As you can probably infer, the innovation process is owned end-to-end by individuals and teams that specialize in specific domain areas. In this modern, highly regulated, and risk-sensitive space, it is imperative that the work of vetting these products for privacy concerns be owned by privacy specialists as well.

Since there is no canonical definition of a privacy review, we'll define one for this book. A *privacy review* is the process by which privacy specialists assess a tech product (or feature) to ensure adherence to industry standards and customer expectations.

There are two basic steps in a complete privacy review process, and they are not always completed in any specific order.

First, the privacy legal team in the company, which is often just one attorney with multiple other responsibilities, needs to critique the products. This review will focus on laws like the GDPR, CCPA, Brazil's LGPD, etc., and help ensure that the products are in compliance with the requirements of applicable laws.

Second, privacy engineers, who in smaller companies often have other responsibilities such as security and IT, have to complete a more in-depth review that focuses on various aspects of data handling. This privacy review is tricky, since unlike attorneys, the privacy engineers cannot point to specific laws that may be violated. And since the technical review often occurs after the lawyers have given their go ahead, privacy engineers often have limited leverage and are accused of slowing down the product roll-out, making process the enemy of progress, and other heresies.

This chapter will explain how smaller and agile companies that lack the budget and staff of companies like Google and Apple can craft a privacy review process. These companies will need to lean on automation to help their innovative engineers through the privacy review process. This chapter will also provide several examples of products and features that can be put through the privacy review process. No book can teach companies how to come up with a foolproof privacy review, since innovation often moves faster than the guardrails; what this chapter will provide is a framework for a process and several examples to help you build a privacy muscle so you can prevent and spot privacy issues. This will help reduce the risk of privacy harms, and over time it will make the entire company better custodians of customer data.

> **DEFINITION** A *privacy review* is the process where privacy specialists assess a tech product (or feature) to ensure adherence to industry standards and customer expectations.

Before diving into the process and examples, it is key to establish some concepts. This book looks at the privacy review process holistically and covers both the legal and technical privacy reviews. To that end, we will first look at legal privacy reviews—the portion of the review process undertaken by the company's legal team or outside counsel. These reviews fall into two specific categories: the privacy impact assessment (PIA) and the data protection impact assessment (DPIA). The following subsections will explain them both in detail as well as how they fit into a company's overall privacy review process.

6.1.1   *The privacy impact assessment (PIA)*

For most companies, the only privacy reviews they conduct are the ones completed by the legal team. These are often attorneys with a background in privacy and security, but more often these are attorneys who have other responsibilities like litigation, employment laws, etc. As such, the scope and depth of such a review, called a *privacy impact assessment* (PIA), can be somewhat limited. Still, it is critical to come up with a definition of and criteria for a privacy impact assessment.

The PIA can be thought of as a decision tool for identifying and mitigating privacy risks along the following lines[1]:

- What Personally Identifiable Information (PII) a company and its employees may be collecting from customers and other users
- Why the data is being collected, with clearly identified and enumerated use cases
- The collection, usage, sharing, security, and storage of this data

A PIA should accomplish three goals:

1. Ensure alignment of design and functional aspects of the product or feature with the company's regulatory and compliance obligations.
2. Determine the possibility and impact of any privacy risks and the impact of those risks on the users or customers.
3. Evaluate protections and alternative processes to mitigate potential privacy risks and especially help ensure that privacy protections tied to specific geographies are applied. Quantify remediations and changes to the product design and requirements to minimize the likelihood and impact of privacy harms, and view these changes through the lens of countries, regions, etc.

It also helps to establish clear criteria for PIAs. For example, a company should conduct a PIA when it is

- Developing or obtaining any new technologies or systems that handle or collect PII. This distinction is critical, since companies often acquire and merge new tools due to mergers and acquisitions.
- Creating a new program, system, technology, or information database that may have privacy implications.
- Updating a system that results in new privacy risks. These updates could include building APIs or data crawlers that enhance data collection or loosening administrative controls that then result in more engineers having access to sensitive data. Software systems are rarely static and constantly change in how they process the user's data, so the PIA may need to be a continual process rather than a "once and done" affair.

---

[1] "Privacy Impact Assessments," *Homeland Security*, 26 November, 2020, http://mng.bz/8l7D.

- Issuing new or updated rules that entail the collection of PII. Governments and regulatory authorities often write and interpret new rules on data and privacy implications. The legal team will need to provide guidance to engineering teams accordingly.

The PIA is just one part of a company's process to check for privacy controls. Whether the PIA is conducted by in-house legal teams or outside counsel, companies need program or project managers to follow up on the remediation issues. This requires the ability to absorb a lot of the context around the initial gap and recommended remedy, privacy expertise to understand the options, and credibility to negotiate prioritization with the engineering teams. In many companies, there is simply not enough investment to fund this resource, so PIA teams often depend on an "honor system" when it comes to having engineering teams fix any privacy issues. That is why, later in the chapter, we will identify ways to embed technical privacy review checks, conducted by specialists outside legal, into the engineering workflow.

6.1.2 *The data protection impact assessment (DPIA)*

For many companies, the PIA may be sufficient, but for others a more elaborate process, the *data protection impact assessment* (DPIA), may be required.

According to the Information Commissioner's Office (ICO) in the United Kingdom, "A DPIA is a process designed to help you systematically analyse, identify and minimise the data protection risks of a project or plan. It is a key part of your accountability obligations under the GDPR, and when done properly helps you assess and demonstrate how you comply with all of your data protection obligations."[2] Under the GDPR, failure to carry out a DPIA when required may leave you open to enforcement action, including a fine of up to €10 million, or 2% of global annual turnover if higher.

Companies often relegate a DPIA to helping create legal compliance for a specific product. However, if DPIAs are conducted more strategically and their findings are used to improve the planning and design of the next set of tech products, it can help create organizational maturity. As the ICO points out, this maturity can help the organization as a whole adhere to a more global standard and avoid bespoke fixes.

There are four main questions that organizations should answer in the execution of a DPIA[3]:

1. How is the personal data being processed and for what purpose? Rather than answering with a simple high-level statement, the company should track what is collected, how the use of that data produces specific outcomes, how those outcomes map to the purposes initially identified, etc.

---

[2] "What is a DPIA," *ICO*, http://mng.bz/jyoe.
[3] Focal Point Insights, "Understanding the Differences between PIAs and the GDPR's DPIAs," *Focal Point*, January 17, 2019, http://mng.bz/doNw.

2. Why were specific pieces of data collected? Could the company have obtained the same benefits and insights through a different set of data, or fewer data sets? The goal is to make the case that data collection was fit for purpose rather than collecting voluminous data without a directly identified purpose.

3. What are the specific impacts on the user by way of rights, freedoms, vulnerabilities, and safety? This will force the company to look at the data from the perspective of the user rather than looking at the user through the lens of the data.

4. How will the company protect its users from privacy harms? The company will need to find a way to make the data accessible and usable but in a way that the privacy harms do not manifest. It is ideal to have defined controls, operational details, metric-driven descriptions of how these controls will address privacy harms, etc.

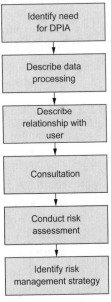

These four elements will help you focus on the type of data you are collecting and processing, the risks associated with data processing, and the likelihood of occurrence and their impact. A DPIA can help you determine the worst-case scenarios and prepare for or mitigate them.

> **NOTE** A DPIA is a risk assessment required by the GDPR depending on the nature, scope, context, and purpose of data processing, and especially for high risk activities and new technologies where the impact is unknown. It may only be required for activities that will target EU residents. You should seek advice from counsel on the applicability of the DPIA for your business.

The International Association of Privacy Professionals (IAPP) has provided a step-by-step DPIA process that can help small businesses conduct a DPIA in an expedited fashion. These steps are listed in figure 6.1. Let's look at each of these steps in turn.

Figure 6.1   The data protection impact assessment process

IDENTIFY THE NEED FOR A DPIA

Based on guidance from the EU authorities, "The GDPR does not require a DPIA to be carried out for every processing operation which may result in risks for the rights and freedoms of natural persons. The carrying out of a DPIA is only mandatory where processing is 'likely to result in a high risk to the rights and freedoms of natural persons' (Article 35(1), illustrated by Article 35(3) and complemented by Article 35(4)). It is particularly relevant when a new data processing technology is being introduced."[4]

---

[4] The working party on the protection of individuals with regard to the processing of personal data, "Guidelines on Data Protection Impact Assessment (DPIA) and determining whether processing is 'likely to result in a high risk' for the purposes of Regulation 2016/679," *EU*, October 4, 2017, http://mng.bz/9K7r.

Per the IAPP template, this is the time to "Explain broadly what the project aims to achieve and what type of processing it involves. You may find it helpful to refer or link to other documents, such as a project proposal. Summarise why you identified the need for a DPIA."

It is here that the privacy review process needs to be seen as part of a continuum, with a common understanding of data via the classification and inventory process and a common understanding of workflows. At this stage, a company has two choices:

- Have the engineers building the new technology explain what the project seeks to achieve.
- Have all-purpose technical leaders (or privacy engineers) shape the explanation at the design stage. This would be in an engineering requirements document (ERD) that would be co-authored by the engineers building the product and technical privacy specialists.

I advocate the latter approach, as you will see shortly. Either way, it is critical that there is a written understanding of the project, since, as previously discussed, teams that are focused on their remit often lack the big picture understanding necessary for a DPIA applicability evaluation.

DESCRIBE THE DATA PROCESSING

As described in the previous subsection, the engineers building the product should lay out specifics around the data processing inherent to the change by answering the following questions:

- Nature of data processing
  - How will you collect, use, store, and delete data?
  - What is the source of the data? Will you be sharing data with anyone? You might find it useful to refer to a flow diagram or another way of describing data flows.
  - What types of processing identified as likely high risk are involved? This is where lessons from chapter 5 are very useful.
- Scope of data processing
  - What is the nature of the data, and does it include special category or criminal offense data?
  - How much data will you be collecting and using?
  - How often will you be collecting the data?
  - How long will you keep it?
  - How many individuals are affected?
  - What geographical area does it cover?

Having a list of these questions is critical since, in my experience, it is often only when the privacy team asks questions that engineers and product managers assess the downstream impact of data collection. Often the data collection is conducted with a view to feature development and use engagement. The job of the privacy specialists is to create use cases and scenarios whereby the privacy implications are well understood.

DESCRIBE THE RELATIONSHIP WITH THE USER

Having understood the overall scope of the work and the flow or processing of the data, it is critical that the DPIA dive into the impact upon the user. As we have discussed before, privacy is highly contextual, so understanding each technology change and data flow in relation to the user is important.

Some questions to help assess this, as recommended by the IAPP, are as follows:

- What is the nature of your relationship with the individuals? This relationship could include customers, non-registered users, etc.
- How much control will they have?
- Would they expect you to use their data in this way?
- Do they include children or other vulnerable groups?
- Are there prior concerns over this type of processing or security flaws? Given the constant swirl around privacy concerns, it is helpful to draw parallels because they could help advise on mitigation efforts.
- Is it novel in any way? In other words, is this different from an existing expectation the user would have?
- What is the current state of technology in this area?
- Are there any current issues of public concern that you should factor in? There may be implications around fairness, for example, which is a topic of discussion at the present time.
- Are you signed up to any approved code of conduct or certification scheme?
- What do you want to achieve? It is helpful to itemize and quantify these outcomes, since engineers often have an approach loosely summed up as "let's collect data and we will find a use for it later."
- What is the intended effect on individuals? What are the benefits of the processing for you, and more broadly?

CONSULTATION

In this step, the engineers building the product and the privacy specialists will need to list specific steps they will take to manage the privacy risks. The following points should be addressed at this stage:

- Describe when and how you will seek individuals' views, or justify why it's not appropriate to do so. In other words, the innovators will need to explain how they have notified users impacted by the technology change. We will cover aspects of this in chapter 9.
- Who else do you need to involve within your organization? Do you plan to consult information security experts, or any other experts? This is a critical step, since many privacy harms can be mitigated using access control tools that security teams may already be using, such as multifactor authentication.

- Describe compliance and proportionality measures; in particular,
  - What is your lawful basis for processing?
  - Does the processing actually achieve your purpose?
  - Is there another way to achieve the same outcome?
- How will you prevent function creep?
- How will you ensure data quality and data minimization? What information will you give individuals?
- How do you safeguard any international transfers?

CONDUCT THE RISK ASSESSMENT

If you follow the data governance steps I have laid out so far, the risk assessment process should be relatively straightforward, since it is based on an understanding of the data in the abstract and the privacy risk posed by the specific change. The IAPP provides a handy template that I have modified in table 6.1.[5]

Table 6.1 Privacy risk assessment format

Describe the privacy risk and impact on users	Likelihood	Severity	Quantified risk on a scale of 1–100

The list of risks will provide the privacy team and engineers a clear-eyed, ranked, and quantified view of the privacy impacts of the innovation being proposed, thereby presenting clear choices on fixes and next steps.

IDENTIFY RISK MITIGATION MEASURES

Having enumerated the risks, you now need a similar template for the measures you'll take to manage the risks and remediate them. Table 6.2 provides such a template, courtesy the IAPP.

Table 6.2 Privacy risk management format

Risk	Mitigation options	Risk status post-mitigation	Residual risk	Outcome
		Eliminated/reduced/unchanged	Low/medium/high	Change approved or declined

---

[5] "Sample DPIA template," ICO, http://mng.bz/Nxdd.

Table 6.2 Privacy risk management format *(continued)*

Risk	Mitigation options	Risk status post-mitigation	Residual risk	Outcome

The last two steps, of conducting the risk assessment and identifying mitigation steps, are often deemed onerous by companies, especially since they are often the last step before going live. Engineers and product managers often believe that a consultation is enough, and they can be overly optimistic about being able to manage privacy harms. This dynamic makes these last two steps seem like a blocker, even though they are critical from a privacy and trust perspective. However, an existing data governance program can help accelerate them. Additionally, audits and other compliance activities will require such documentation, so it is helpful to build these processes and habits at least for high-risk projects. Finally, in the event that there is a breach or some other privacy incident, and questions like "why did we not see this coming?" come up, having risk assessment and risk management documentation can help accelerate the work of the incident response teams and post mortem.

6.2 *Implementing the legal privacy review process*

Let's now look at the privacy reviews conducted by the legal team. Figure 6.2 shows a traditional development process followed at many companies. Note that both figures 6.2 and 6.3 are oversimplified and may not cover all use cases.

In figure 6.2, you can observe how the needs of the customer feed into the company's core mission; the mission, in turn, helps define the quarterly goals. The goals enable product managers and business leaders to define the requirements and specs for the products, which in turn, the engineering teams build. The products, once built, go through testing and reviews and are then released.

Given the relatively smaller size of legal teams as compared to engineering teams, the legal reviews (including the PIA and the DPIA) can occur after all the development

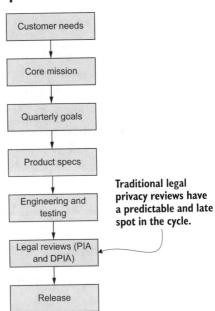

Traditional legal privacy reviews have a predictable and late spot in the cycle.

Figure 6.2 The legal privacy review in the traditional software development process

and testing is complete. That way, the legal team does not end up reviewing products that may end up changing anyway.

The process, as the figure illustrates, is fairly linear and predictable. The tight alignment between the customer, the company's strategic goals, and the engineering development could make the privacy reviews easier to manage and scale. Teams may be able to use some of the same processes and alignment to track the privacy reviews that they use for software testing, release management, and the like. The upshot is that the legal privacy reviews occur at the end of the development process.

However, with the onslaught of the agile and scrum revolution, the development process has become more susceptible and amenable to disruption. Figure 6.3 shows what a modern innovative development shop might look like.

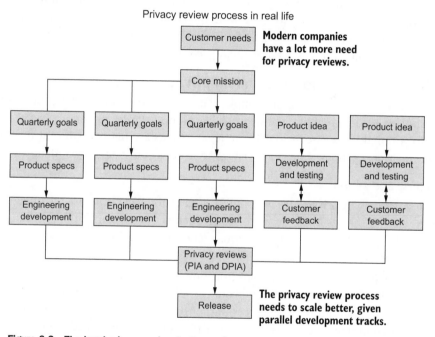

Figure 6.3 The legal privacy review in the modern agile software development process

Figure 6.3 shows how there may be several products being developed that follow the traditional development process. This does not change the legal privacy review process, since the attorneys may still wish to conduct their privacy risk assessments after product development is complete but before it ships. However, the collective volume of these products may overwhelm the review and testing resources.

Additionally, modern companies have adopted a startup mentality whereby developers are empowered to push their ideas and iterate in byte-sized increments. These may be ideas that deviate from, and over time help expand, the company's customer imprint and core mission. As you can see in the diagram, several ideas could eventually become products without adhering to the company's core mission in the traditional top-down way. When such features and products make it to the review stage, some of the assumptions that otherwise help accelerate testing and reviews may fall apart.

This poses several problems with the legal privacy review process:

- There are high volumes of proposals, and not all of them of consistent quality.
- There is a lack of context for attorneys, since not every product adheres to a top-down process.

You would be right to assume that there could be tension between quality and throughput in such a scenario, when it comes to privacy reviews.

As a company hits its stride in growth and user engagement, engineers building products and privacy reviewers alike may find that operationalizing the privacy review process at the end of the development cycle does not scale, either from a quality or a quantity standpoint. The volume of work means that it is vital to innovate the privacy review process. The next section will provide a business case for a technical privacy review as part of the development process rather than just depending on the legal review.

6.3   *Making the case for a technical privacy review*

Since privacy and its attendant compliance requirements are still fairly new, too many corporate leaders feel like the legal review alone is fairly sufficient. This section will help you make the case as to why the legal reviews are necessary but insufficient and why technical privacy reviews are critical to protect your company and customers.

6.3.1   *Timing and scope*

A key reason why privacy reviews orchestrated by the legal team are insufficient to protect your customers is the timing of when such reviews occur in the product development lifecycle. You saw in the previous section that legal privacy reviews occur at the end of the development process. This makes for two theoretical efficiencies:

- Engineering designs and specifications undergo changes, and attorneys often prefer to assess the finished product for privacy risks. This is seen as a more prudent expenditure of resources, rather than assessing in-flight products that may then undergo revisions that render previously dispensed advice redundant.
- Attorneys can look at several finished products at once and make judgments based on previous experience and current context (customers impacted, type of data, location where the product will be released, etc.) regarding which products they can review, while the others do not get reviewed. This methodology allows the company's attorneys to make sure that the most critical and sensitive products go through legal scrutiny, and possibly are blocked before they go out the door. It also means that some products will not get reviewed, given bandwidth constraints. This approach has a significant disadvantage: attorneys may make decisions on what to review without understanding all the technical details, since they were not part of the incremental development that occurred. It is often impossible to make a judgment about the privacy risk without knowing the context of how the product evolved.

The legal privacy review is inhibited not because attorneys or legal teams do not care about privacy. The timing of such reviews is governed by the ratio of engineers to attorneys, whereby there is a culling of what makes the cut for a review and when. The process is therefore not adequate, given the complexity of modern engineering and the ramifications of data-driven innovation.

Besides the timing of the review, there is also the matter of how the scope of the legal privacy review is somewhat circumscribed. Figure 6.4 shows how the legal PIA or DPIA is a subset of the overall work required when it comes to privacy reviews.

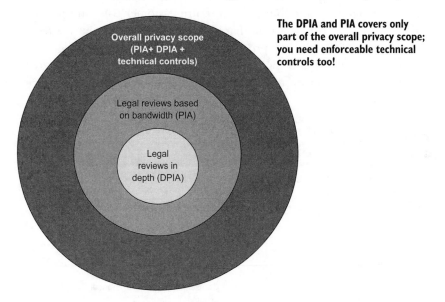

Figure 6.4 Legal privacy reviews and their limitations

In figure 6.4, the large circle shows the full scope of privacy issues that the review process should address, ranging from legal reviews to complex technical issues that must be addressed before products can ship. The second circle shows the number of privacy reviews a legal team may be able to undertake, based on their staff. The third, and smallest, circle shows the amount of technical depth the attorneys are able to bring to the projects they do review.

The questions cross-functional leaders need to ask are as follows:

- What if a high-risk feature doesn't get reviewed on account of bandwidth or technical depth?
- If an attorney were to find an issue with a feature at the eleventh hour, the only choices would be to block the release or ship it with the risks intact. Why not intercept the feature earlier in the pipeline and imbue privacy at that stage?

6.3.2   *What the technical review covers that the legal review does not*

As already stated, the recommended privacy process for today's companies requires a technical assessment as well. Whereas legal privacy reviews focus on regulatory compliance, technical privacy reviews focus on technical implementation details, data flows, and other aspects of how the tech products are built and designed. The goal for these reviews is to assess the downstream impact upon the user, look for potential harms, and put in place remediations.

Therefore, the legal privacy review—the PIA or the DPIA—is a useful resource from a due diligence standpoint, but to secure customer trust and provide technical coverage for privacy risk, it is vital that privacy engineers who have a technical background are part of the product process before development work begins.

Figure 6.5 explains at a high level the difference between privacy reviews when conducted by attorneys via the PIA or the DPIA process and the technical privacy reviews conducted by privacy engineers.

Legal privacy review vs. technical privacy review

Legal	Technical

• Owned and managed by attorneys
• Required by specific jurisdictions (e.g., GDPR)
• Governed by compliance-centric privacy checklist
• Output:
    ○ High level mitigations (e.g., educate engineers on retention policies)
    ○ Detect violation of laws (e.g., users not getting the privacy policies for their location)
	• Owned and managed by technical privacy
	• Provides engineering advice (pre-ERD) and analyzes technical documents (ERD)
	• Detects hidden PII flows
	• Examples of output:
	    ○ Ensure data is stored in line with risk
	    ○ Provide API for data deletion in a particular database
	    ○ Obfuscate data using differential privacy
	    ○ Measure identification risk prior to data sharing

Figure 6.5   **Legal privacy reviews versus technical privacy reviews**

The difference between the two reviews lies in the framework and depth. The legal team will use regulatory frameworks to ensure compliance. For example, during their review, the legal team may ask questions like these:

- Is the data to be collected to be used only for a specified purpose?
- Will the data collected be used for anything other than the specified purpose?

The goal behind these questions is to ensure that there is an unbroken link between the expectations of laws like GDPR, the privacy disclosures of the company, and the designs and specifications being put forward by the engineers. However, there is no way for the legal team to look under the hood and validate that some rogue engineer is not making multiple copies of the data, one of which is queried by a different team and another of which is available via an API to a third party that has not been vetted for privacy practices.

Often, engineers neglect to mention these details in documentation that they put together in a rush for the legal review, and just as often they forget to put in place controls to check for privacy violations after the product ships. Therefore, the privacy reviews conducted by the legal team are a necessary but insufficient resource for building privacy by design into your engineering and innovation processes.

The technical privacy reviews help address this gap. In the technical privacy programs I have shaped, the technical privacy specialists collaborate with engineers and product managers at the whiteboard phase—when the product or feature is being designed. The privacy specialists make sure that every blueprint, product specification, and engineering design accounts for privacy protections. So, for example, the technical privacy review may prompt questions such as these:

- What data is being collected?
  - How much of the data is structured versus unstructured (JSON blobs, XML, etc.)?
  - Where are you detecting it? At the edge layer? In in-memory databases like REDIS? In low-latency databases like Cassandra? Or at the tail end of the pipeline in the data warehouse?
- What does access control look like for each of these databases?
  - Are you using encryption? If so, is it point-to-point encryption? Or is it encryption at rest, while the data transport occurs in the clear with the data being unencrypted?
  - What does the key management system look like? Are we using keys such that ML algorithms and fraud analysis algorithms can access the data but others cannot?
  - Is there multifactor authentication? If so, are we using tools like Okta, OneLogin, or Ping? Or is there a homegrown solution?
- What does auditing for access to this data look like?
  - Are the audit logs written in real time or via batch processes? This can be critical in timely determination of inappropriate access and blocking insider risk and third-party risk?
  - Are the audit logs tamper-proof?
- What does the retention period for these audit logs look like? How is it consistently enforced?

The technical privacy review will look at the product design and specs in much more detail and elicit information that engineers often forget to specify in the documentation. This in-depth review is the connecting tissue between the legal compliance imperative, the customer trust imperative, and the engineering implementation.

A colleague of mine, who is an attorney, recently remarked that attorneys can offer "privacy by defense," while privacy engineers can offer "privacy by design." Attorneys can defend against discernible and visible privacy harms, while engineers can build privacy controls into the design. The upshot is that we need both kinds of reviews to protect both the company and the users.

NOTE The legal privacy review offers *privacy by defense* while the technical privacy review offers *privacy by design*. Both are irreplaceable parts of preventing privacy harms and mitigating privacy issues in products and features.

Figure 6.6 provides a condensed representation of the differences between the legal privacy review and the technical privacy review. As you can see, a given engineering product can get varying levels of scrutiny in the privacy review process depending on who is conducting the review.

Questions: Legal privacy vs. technical privacy

Legal	Technical

• Is the data to be collected to be used only for a specified purpose?
 	
• Will the data collected be used for anything other than the specified purpose?
	• What data is being collected?
	    ○ Structured versus unstructured
	    ○ Where are we detecting it?
	
	• What does access-control look like?
	    ○ Encryption?
	    ○ Key management system details
	
	• What does auditing for access to this data look like?
	    ○ Are the audit logs written in real time or via batch process?
	    ○ Are the audit logs tamper proof?

Figure 6.6   Legal privacy reviews versus technical privacy reviews

As figure 6.6 makes clear, you could have the same engineering product get varying levels of scrutiny in the privacy review process depending on who is conducting the review.

HOW TECHNICAL PRIVACY REVIEWS HELP The Technical Privacy Review is the connecting tissue between the legal compliance imperative, the customer trust imperative and the engineering implementation.

So far, we have examined the privacy review process conducted by the legal team by way of the PIA, we've looked at the DPIA, and we have touched on the technical privacy review.

Next we will look at how technical leaders can incorporate a more technical privacy review in the process and front-load it so as to ease the load on the legal privacy review and scale the overall process better.

6.4   *Integrating technical privacy reviews into the innovation pipeline*

Understanding how technical privacy reviews help fill the gaps left by the legal privacy review is helpful, but technical leaders need to understand how to fit such reviews into the workflow as well.

6.4.1   *Where does the technical privacy review belong?*

To help ensure that you can identify and remedy privacy gaps, the technical privacy specialists will enter the picture in two places:

- At the early stage, while the product is being imagined and designed. Here they will identify areas of possible privacy risk and embed technical controls like the ones we have looked at (classification, inventory, encryption, obfuscation, etc.) into the design and product features.
- Alongside the PIA and the DPIA, where they can ensure that the aforementioned privacy controls were successfully implemented as well as assist the lawyers in the legal privacy process.

In this fashion, the technical privacy review will help provide technical depth and scale to the overall privacy review process.

Figure 6.7 shows how technical privacy reviews can be added to the traditional development process. Technical privacy specialists can iterate on the product spec with engineers and ensure that privacy controls are embedded into the design before engineering and testing can begin. They can then partner with the attorneys for the legal privacy review prior to product release.

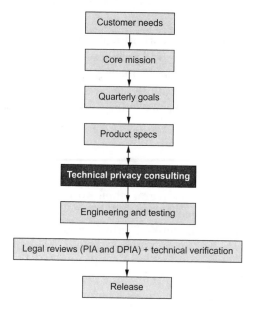

Figure 6.7   Technical privacy reviews in a traditional engineering flow

Figure 6.8 shows similar efficiencies available by incorporating the technical privacy review in the more agile development process.

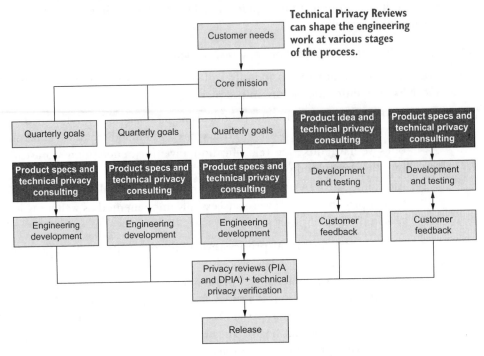

Figure 6.8   How technical privacy reviews could fit into an agile development process

As you can imagine, ensuring that multiple concurrent agile efforts are integrated with technical privacy controls at the design stage will help accelerate the subsequent verification prior to release and significantly accelerate the legal privacy review as well.

Now that you have a clear idea how a technical privacy review fits into the overall development process, we can now focus on the mechanics of how to incorporate products into such a review such that you can address privacy risks without creating unnecessary process burdens.

6.4.2   *How to implement a technical privacy intake?*

Engineers will need clear guidelines on how to integrate their work into the technical privacy review process. Given the heightened visibility around privacy, companies need to establish objective criteria to drive the level of scrutiny applied on individual requirements documents, often called *engineering requirement documents* (ERDs). Figure 6.9 shows what such a form could look like.

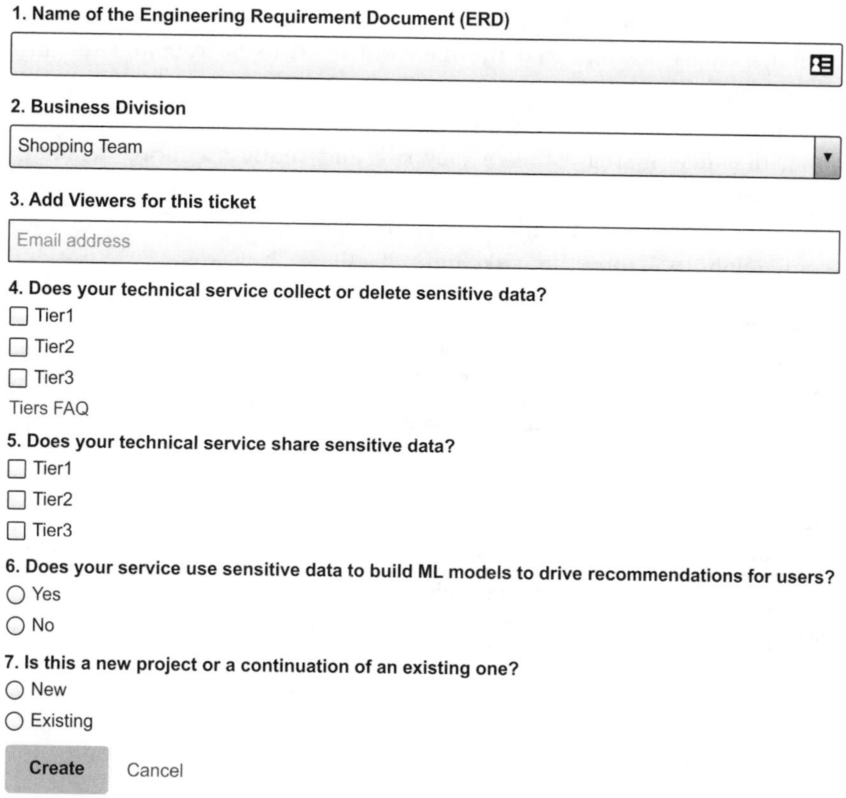

1. Name of the Engineering Requirement Document (ERD)

2. Business Division

Shopping Team

3. Add Viewers for this ticket

Email address

4. Does your technical service collect or delete sensitive data?
☐ Tier1
☐ Tier2
☐ Tier3
Tiers FAQ

5. Does your technical service share sensitive data?
☐ Tier1
☐ Tier2
☐ Tier3

6. Does your service use sensitive data to build ML models to drive recommendations for users?
○ Yes
○ No

7. Is this a new project or a continuation of an existing one?
○ New
○ Existing

Create Cancel

Figure 6.9 Sample technical privacy review questionnaire

As you can see in figure 6.9, a lot of information is requested in this questionnaire. This enables the privacy team to rank the privacy risk for a specific ERD based on variables like these:

- Business function
- Data collected, stored, and shared based on risk tiers
- Any vendors that may be in the picture
- Whether machine learning will be applied
- Regions where data will be collected or stored

Let's look at a few of these points in more detail to see how the privacy review process is part of an overall data governance strategy.

First, asking engineers to enumerate the data they intend to collect and use forces them to understand their own data flows and APIs, and it will help avoid the kinds of surprises that often elude legal reviewers. The effectiveness of this step depends on whether the company has correctly classified and catalogued its data, as we have discussed. At the backend, the entries from the engineers can be used to adjudicate the level of privacy review required.

Similarly, if the data being collected is to be used for machine-learning modeling and analysis, it is possible that the data will need to be retained for an extended period of time.

Finally, if the data is being collected from privacy-conscious regions like Western Europe, that may increase the privacy risk and require a more detailed technical review as well.

Once the engineers enter their values and click the Create button on the form, the outcome might look something like figure 6.10.

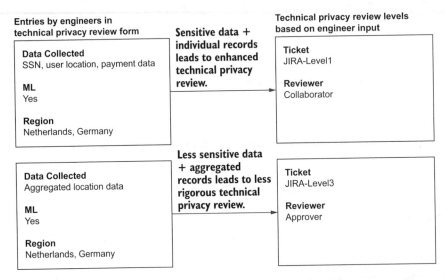

Figure 6.10   Technical privacy review questionnaire sample outcomes

Figure 6.10 shows two examples of how an engineer could fill out the sample questionnaire. In the first example, a large amount of sensitive data is collected and at the individual user level, with the potential of being used for machine learning. Accordingly, the corresponding JIRA ticket shows a high level of sensitivity.

I have configured my processes to allocate a privacy engineer to co-author the ERD with the engineer so that there is some privacy oversight in the entire design from the start. This is critical, since once data enters the system, you need to classify, catalog, and protect it, and that gets expensive. The technical privacy review is aimed at reducing this expense by limiting the collection of data to legitimate needs. This helps both from a compliance standpoint and a user trust standpoint.

This process can also be configured to create a privacy section in the ERD that the engineers and privacy reviewers can update on an ongoing basis, as risks are discovered and mitigated. Figure 6.11 shows how the technical privacy review process could work at the backend.

Technical privacy review ERD flow

Step 1: Technical privacy review trigger

3. Add Viewers for this ticket

Email address

This question triggers a technical privacy review.
Use of personal data could create privacy concerns.

If a technical privacy review is required, your flow must drive the creation of a ticket.

Step 2: Triage and JIRA ticket creation

5. Does your technical service share sensitive data?

☐ Tier1

☐ Tier2

☐ Tier3

6. Does your service use sensitive data to build ML models to drive recommendations for users?

○ Yes

○ No

This question helps evaluate the level of privacy review needed.

Entries into ticket should create a privacy section in the ticket for posterity and tracking.

Step 3: ERD privacy section

Personal data

Please fill in the table below (adding details about the UserProfile)

Collected / used personal data	Storage location (name of DB or 3rd party - if stored)	Source (Name of DB / user / 3rd party)	Retention (if you are storing data, when will data be deleted?)	Classification	Type of personal data	Type of data processing (storing/ reading/ sharing)
User Profile -Orders	Hive	dwh.fact_trip	6 months	Tier 2	shopper/ customer	storing/reading

The requirements doc now has a pre-filled privacy section for evaluation and ongoing reference.

This section is pre-filled based on responses to the form in step 2.

Figure 6.11 **Technical privacy review backend workflow**

The first question about data usage, "Do you collect, use, update, share personal data?" could trigger a privacy review, and the additional details could be used to populate the ERD privacy section. It stands to reason that answering "yes" would trigger a technical privacy review, so I often advise engineers to use synthetic data or fake data to conduct tasks that do not require product customer data. That way, they can still perform several activities without the added risk of collecting, accessing, sharing, and storing customer data. This discipline will help reduce overall privacy risk—after all, it is hard to misuse data you don't collect. It will also help reduce security risk—if there is a breach, it is hard to end up losing data you don't have. It will also help reduce costs in storing data and reduce the strain placed on your system by calls to delete this data.

The way you word the questions that drive the technical privacy review can help send subtle signals and offer soft training to your engineers. This is another opportunity to embed privacy by design in your company.

The second set of questions in figure 6.11, in the Triage and JIRA Creation section, will help determine the level of technical privacy review that the product or feature will undergo. In figure 6.10, you saw how individualized data led to a much deeper review than the aggregated data. The responses to questions in this section will help privacy engineers determine the level of privacy review required. Much like the first question, there is a subtle nudge to engineers here as well. Engineers can avoid using sensitive data or reduce the storage and sharing, and consequently reduce the intensity of the technical privacy review.

The third section of figure 6.11 shows the requirements document with the data entered in steps 1 and 2. This section captures the areas of the product that need to be scrutinized by the technical privacy team. Collecting the privacy findings in the requirements document serves several purposes:

- Engineers and privacy specialists can easily reference the document and debate the validity of any privacy concerns and proposed remediations from the same set of facts.
- Having a constantly updated privacy section helps avoid a disconnect whereby product features are neatly maintained while the privacy fixes are tacked on at the end. This section sends a message that privacy is on par with the remaining product features.
- When the legal team takes up the project for their PIA and DPIA, they can use this section and the context the privacy specialists have acquired as background. This greatly expedites the PIA/DPIA process and improves the relationship between privacy legal and engineering as well.

Based on my experience, I have two key insights to offer for the technical leaders at small companies who will champion privacy reviews. Readers may disagree or seek to improvise, but I wanted to offer them for consideration:

- It is critical that engineers not be pre-educated on how their input maps to the privacy review process. If engineers were to become aware that answering "No" to the data collection question could help them bypass the technical privacy review, you may run the risk of engineers trying to game the system so as to expedite their review.
- It is equally important that the ERDs have a privacy section, as shown in figure 6.11. This will help ensure that the privacy impact of the ERD will be catalogued

and managed on an ongoing basis rather than as an afterthought right before release. This will help avoid two problems that impede the legal PIA process. It will help accumulate all the privacy findings from the beginning, rather than creating chaos at the end and having privacy become a "blocker." Second, if there is a section dedicated to privacy in the ERD, it makes the engineers think of privacy as a feature rather than an add-on.

Let's now look at the end to end process for an ERD technical privacy review and see how the work can be tracked in a scalable fashion. Figure 6.12 shows the process.

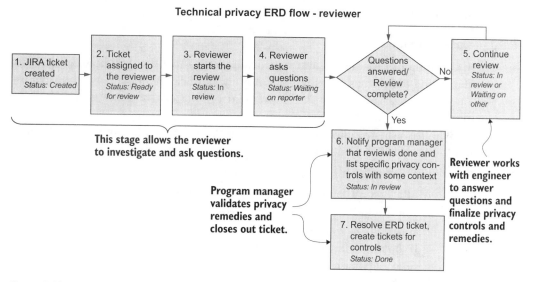

Figure 6.12   **Technical privacy review process workflow**

The process in figure 6.12 shows the essential steps:

- Creation of the ticket
- Initial reviewer questions
- Question-answer loop
- Reviewer outcomes with suggested privacy controls

This process is especially critical, because in a real workplace and in small companies, multiple engineers may iterate on the product coding, and multiple privacy reviewers could cycle through as well. Having this contextual continuity is critical so that your technical privacy review will produce consistent outcomes regardless of ownership. This provides a process that is easy to follow, is scalable, and will embed technical privacy reviews into the design of your products.

You have so far seen how to integrate the technical privacy review into your business. The fact remains, however, that small companies could find this burdensome and expensive. Engineers may try to work around this new expectation, and that may lead to privacy harms. It is therefore critical to find efficiencies when possible, and the next section will offer some ideas.

6.5   *Scaling the technical privacy review process*

Even with all the ingenious data governance in place, there may still be more ERDs than there are technical privacy reviewers. As such, it behooves cross-functional leaders to provide automated recommendations as much as possible for behaviors that are repeated across multiple ERDs.

This section will provide tips for automating recommendations based on information provided by the engineers.

6.5.1   *Data sharing*

If the author of the design and specification states that they will be sharing customer data with third parties, providing a handy checklist can help them avoid problems and make sure that any irreversible movement of data can be done correctly from the start.

The following example data-sharing checklist is purely for instructional purposes. It would need to be customized, based on context and use case.

- Use an approved tool for data sharing.
  - API/Box is the most preferred way of sharing.
  - You should not use Google Drive/Sheets/Docs for sharing unless it is approved on a case-by-case basis.
  - If you must share data with S3 (e.g., regulator requires it), then perform client-side encryption and limit retention periods.
  - You should never use email to share PII, like a Social Security number.
- For Box:
  - The file should not be publicly accessible. It should be password protected.
  - Retention is set to one week, unless client-side encryption is supplied.
  - You should use an employer enterprise account to share files, and not your personal Box account.
- For API:
  - Secure tokens are used for authorization.
  - Built-in authentication and authorization using oAuth 2.0.
  - Rate limiting and timeout need to be configured.
- For SFTP:
  - Encrypt personal data using CMS (RFC 6032) with the recipient's public encryption key. The receiving party may generate an RSA 2048 bit public/private key pair and share it with Uber using a X509 Certificate.
  - Private keys should be securely created and managed. Align with our crypto standard to create the keys. Keys must be rotated every three months.

6.5.2 *Machine-learning models*

As companies increasingly rely on efficiency and automation, they often create programs to perform tasks otherwise completed by human beings. Machine learning (ML) is an increasingly popular solution in automating tasks that previously required manual input by a human user. ML usually requires large quantities of data in order to develop properly trained models, so here I will briefly explore the implications of ML for privacy.

MACHINE LEARNING AND DATA

As an example of ML usage, governments may use ML to process appeals for traffic citations. If someone gets a traffic ticket (or a fine) for going over the speed limit, it is reasonable in many cases that they would appeal the fine by demonstrating past good behavior and promising better behavior in the future. Let's assume that a major metropolis were to implement such a system. The key ingredients of such a system would include the following:

- *Accuracy*—The data must be correct, in terms of the past records for the person appealing, the speed details, etc.
- *Latency*—The response must be quick, since the person appealing may call or email repeatedly if they don't get a response.
- *Equity*—If two people have the same chance of repeating (or not repeating) the offense, the outcome for their appeals must be the same.

This system would need to work at scale and produce results for vast amounts of data—remember, this is a big city with possibly thousands of appeals every day. In that context, data that the city collects would be used as a foundation for assessing the validity of future appeals.

Existing citations and appeals could be grouped into categories like the following:

- Folks who were 5 mph over the speed limit and repeated their offense
- Folks who were 10 mph over the speed limit and repeated their offense
- Folks who were 15 mph over the speed limit and repeated their offense

For any new driver who gets a citation, the system would match their appeal against one of the preceding categories. Then, within each category, the process of looking for the closest match would continue, based on other variables (for example, based on age, part of the city where the citation was issued, etc.). Upon finding the closest match, the system would check how that match fared upon appeal. And based on that outcome, the system would determine the likelihood of a future violation for the current appellant.

The system would then either

- Keep the existing fine
- Reduce the fine
- Waive the fine

This is a very simple example and I expect real appeals systems work differently, but any system where subjective and contextual human decision-making is replaced by automation will require a significant amount of data. Given the potency of personal data (in this case, driver's license number, car plates, location, etc.) privacy controls would need to be in place to protect the user's data privacy.

MACHINE LEARNING, DATA, AND PRIVACY

In order to collect data for ML in a privacy-centric framework, it is critical that the data be obfuscated so as to avoid identifying or profiling individual users. The following checklist provides some useful guidelines:

- *Remove attributes*—Any attribute that is not needed for the purpose should not be collected, read, or shared. For example, if date of birth is not needed for your service, do not collect or copy it.
- *Granularity*—Any attribute that is not needed at a granular level must be aggregated. For location data:
  - *IP address*—Zero out the last octet of IP addresses wherever possible. An IP address may have been collected from the vehicle's security system.
  - *GPS lat/long*—If possible, use a cell ID or landmark instead. If precise location is needed, minimize the decimals used (max 3 decimals). If 2 decimals or fewer are used, the GPS may not be associated with a precise location (thereby reducing the GPS data's privacy sensitivity). Three decimals gives about 100 meter accuracy compared to 5 decimals, which gives 1 meter accuracy. The less accuracy, the better.
  - *Timestamp*—Aggregate to 24 hours; if that's not possible, aggregate to 1 hour; if that's not possible (the worst case) aggregate to 15 minutes.
  - *Pre-aggregation*—Pre-aggregate data, and use a cohort size of 18, or at least 11–20 when aggregating trips to reduce the risk of re-identification. This means there are at least 11–20 individual trips that are indistinguishable from one another based on the combination of datetime and location.
- *Volume*—Use less data where possible. For example, if you can train your modeling data (for machine learning, for example) with 50,000 records, do not collect a million.

In order for these checklists to be useful, it may help to write bots or other programs that inject this content into the ERD JIRA tickets so that the engineers can check against them and then submit the ERD for privacy review. This will help create a consistent process and save time for the engineers and technical privacy reviewers alike.

Additionally, providing engineers with this information without them having to hunt for it in large databases will create a more agile training approach for privacy. For small companies that do not have training budgets and operate on lean margins, such economies are critical and over time will help build privacy not just into the design of the products, but into the company culture as well.

6.6   Sample technical privacy reviews

Having put in place a process to scale the technical privacy review process, it is now time to learn by example. This section will feature several use cases of real-world software development tools that can be improved for privacy risks by the review process. Given that this chapter touches on both the legal PIA and DPIA process as well as the more in-depth technical privacy review, we will first look at a privacy review through a purely legal lens and see what sorts of issues a PIA may uncover.

6.6.1   Messaging apps and engagement apps: Do they connect?

Let's imagine that your company is in the business of building applications that allow users to communicate and engage with each other. As your company grows,

1. It builds a messaging platform that lets users build profile pages for themselves or their businesses.
2. The platform then expands to let these users create groups and communities to engage with like-minded individuals. The engagement platform is geared toward users with high-speed internet and a culture where information-sharing is encouraged.
3. The company then acquires another smaller company that lets users send each other messages in an SMS-like fashion, except these are sent over the internet. The messaging app is geared towards locations and countries with possibly limited internet connections, and takes low bandwidth to operate.

NOTE   This example contains analysis based on my understanding of regulations, but it should not be construed as legal advice. The analysis here is for instructional purposes only.

The goal of the business is to have users on the engagement app eventually also use the messaging app, thereby competing with SMS and other methods of communication. Correspondingly, having onboarded users to the messaging app in other locations, the business aimed to gently nudge those users to its more engagement-driven app as well. The cumulative body of users would drive more data collection that could be used for analysis to help build other products and monetization.

As the company builds out its authentication protocols, the team building the identity database produces an ERD that makes a representation that it's technologies would not match accounts opened on the engagement platform with accounts opened on the messaging platform unless the users had provided explicit consent.

Upon the completion of the ERD, the identity team decided to complete the DPIA process. During this review, the privacy legal team found that the identity team was using phone numbers to validate the accounts for both the engagement platform and the messaging platform. Phone numbers can serve as a useful tool for multifactor authentication and thereby prevent attacks like fraudulent account creation or account takeover attempts. Collecting phone numbers as a precondition to letting users create these accounts is a valid security use case. However, the DPIA revealed that there was no restriction on linking the phone numbers in the databases for both these programs.

POTENTIAL PRIVACY VIOLATION!!

Engagement app

abc@mail.com
pre@woohoo.com
yuyu@coldmail.com
321-555-5555
hhh@woohoo.com
232-555-5555
444-555-5555

Messaging app

232-555-5555
444-555-5555
565-555-5555
322-555-5555

Common phone numbers will allow linking user data for at least some users between two apps.

Figure 6.13   Identity databases from engagement and messaging apps

As you can see in figure 6.13, there is overlap in the users who use the engagement app and the identity app. This is not a problem—in fact, it is a sign of success that the company has the same user using two distinct products. This presents several benefits:

- This affords the company customization opportunities by repurposing data collected from one app to personalize the user experience in the other.
- A specific user could connect with the same set of friends on both apps and decide which ones they wish to engage with in more detail and which ones they wish to just message once in a while.
- If the user gets locked out of one app, the company could use the other app to unlock them using the common identity. In figure 6.13, it stands to reason that 232-333-9092 could help unlock the same user for both apps.

The preceding benefits, ranging from user convenience to security, depend on the apps sharing data and user identities. Based on my experience, most companies may believe that they will keep user identities disconnected in two separate databases, as in figure 6.13. However, as the business grows, the opportunity to grow user engagement, sloppiness, or bad ethics result in creating "joins" or "connections" between the two databases. And once the two databases are joined, it is impossible to disconnect them, since a lot of downstream processes become acclimated to having the vast amount of data at their disposal. Often the join is done using automated scripts and APIs that are written to extract special insights from the data.

Given the vast amount of merger and acquisition activity occurring these days, and the vast amounts of data flowing between countries, EU antitrust regulators believe that consumer data use rights and promises are important in analyzing mergers and enforcing competition law. Inadequate transparency around data could affect a company's prospects adversely. It is vital that engineers understand that a simple query that runs in mere seconds could have far-reaching implications, depending on how the outcomes line up with user expectations.

Given that background, the DPIA findings came back as follows:

- The company needed to update its guidance to enumerate the use cases where the data present in the identity database for one app could connect with the identity in another database.

- The company must have a clear workflow to explain whether the messaging app users consented to their accounts being combined with their engagement accounts.

The DPIA process builds on the fact that the company has a data governance program with an understanding of what data lives in which database, the impact on user identifiability, and how that information needs to be furnished to users.

This example again brings home the point that privacy reviews, whether they are technical or legal in nature, need to be part of a systematic privacy program so as to protect both the business and its users. Here we saw a possible tension between privacy and security, where account linking could protect users but also hurt their privacy. In the next example, we will examine a similar tension between safety and privacy.

6.6.2 *Masks and contact tracing*

In this example, we will imagine a more contemporaneous situation whereby a care home for the elderly allows family members to visit only if they wear masks. Given the limited human contact possible, there are cameras and sensors outside the facility that will take a photograph of visitors. Upon detecting a mask, the visitor is allowed to enter. If no mask is detected, then the visitor is not allowed to enter.

Given the devastation caused by COVID-19, it is not hard to imagine care homes, schools, companies, and other entities using tools like these for public health and safety. However, at the backend, the information collected as part of this process needs to be handled with care. For example,

- Where will the photographs be stored?
- For how long will the photographs be stored?
- Who will have access to them?
- Will the software glean other data about the user? For example, will the company also store the timestamp of when the user visited the facility?
- What protections and controls exist to make sure the photo is only used to verify that the user is wearing a mask and not for other purposes?

As you may imagine, the problem space in this example is very new, and it is highly unlikely that there are prescriptive laws to guide a privacy review. Such an initiative needs a detailed technical privacy review to assess and then manage the privacy risk.

The technical privacy review could recommend changes such as the following:

- Any images are to be stored in operational databases like Cassandra for prompt verification and not in a data warehouse like Hive, where data is typically retained for a long period of time.

- Once an image is used to ascertain the presence or absence of a mask, the image should be deleted before any other algorithms can infer details like facial features that could then be used to identify the user. Remember, the goal here is not to identify the user or build a profile, but just to verify that they are wearing a mask. Part of the technical privacy review is to advocate for a user's privacy protection in a way that laws and regulations never can.

- If the images need to be transferred to cloud storage for analysis, the technical privacy review may insist on encryption, since it is possible that the image could be intercepted in transit, which could in turn hurt user privacy. This may have the effect of slowing down verification a bit, but having this negotiated ahead of time could help make decisions along the lines of image size. This will help balance privacy with image quality, thereby helping achieve both goals. This is the sort of check a compliance-centric DPIA can almost never conduct, and that is why a technical privacy review is critical.

- The technical privacy review could suggest a feature whereby a user could submit their photo before arriving, and once they receive validation that their mask is correct, they would then get a code that they could provide to secure entry. This would expedite their reunion with family and allow for health safety and privacy as well. Figure 6.14 shows what that UI could look like.

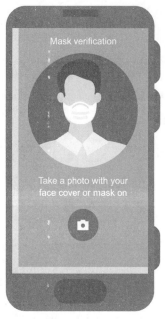

Questions to consider when validating user safety:
Where will the image be stored?
How will you validate user identity when masked?
How will you protect user against bias based on race?
How will you ensure images are destroyed after immediate use?

Figure 6.14   Mask verification software

This is yet another example of how the technical privacy review process can make for a better user experience, provide enhanced privacy protections, and avoid a situation where highly personal biometric data is collected or misused erroneously, leading to privacy harms and fines. It is almost impossible to make major design changes and implementation modifications at a late stage, once implementation is in full swing, and the deleterious impact on public confidence is irreversible if photos end up being leaked.

Having a culture of privacy governance enables cross-functional leaders to set initiatives like these into the larger business and societal context. That way, a business can balance physical safety on the one hand with privacy on the other.

Summary

- Modern companies innovate rapidly and are powered by data collection.
- As part of their overall data governance and trust offering, companies need to evaluate products not just from a regulatory perspective but also through a technical privacy lens.
- There are clear differences between traditional privacy impact assessments (PIAs) conducted by lawyers, and the more technical reviews conducted by privacy engineers.
- The PIA and DPIA reviews focus on regulatory compliance and map product and system level decisions to laws. The technical depth of such reviews is fairly limited, and these reviews occur toward the end of the development life cycle.
- The technical privacy review can start early in the process and shape the product design and technical architecture, thereby ensuring that privacy controls are baked into the product at the feature and data levels.
- There are ways to integrate and automate the technical privacy review process that will help build an overall culture of privacy, make the business more efficient, and build trust with users.

Data deletion

7

We have, so far, looked at privacy as a holistic business differentiator as well as a risk mitigator, involving processes such as classifying data, building an inventory, sharing data securely, and conducting technical privacy reviews. Another key concept in data privacy is *data deletion*; this is critical, since most security and privacy risks emanate from data misuse, leakage, and exfiltration. Chapter 5 provided some useful techniques for obfuscating data so as to mitigate privacy harms if the data is mishandled. However, in some cases, it may be more practical to delete the data altogether, since the best way to prevent data misuse is to not have the data at all.

This chapter will walk you through a system architecture for deleting data in a highly distributed environment. You will need to adapt what we discuss here to your systems, since all companies vary in their architecture and data, but this chapter will provide you with hands-on skills to start this complex but necessary initiative. You will learn how to approach operational and archival data from a privacy perspective.

First though, let's define data deletion. For the purposes of this book, deleting data means physically or logically destroying identifiable user data so that it cannot be recovered or anonymizing data so that it can not reasonably be re-identified by anyone, either at your company or anywhere else, even if it is publicly disclosed.

The act of deletion covers systems ranging from real-time databases to databases that hold archival data to backup systems where the company stores data. It is critical that the engineering coverage of data deletion—in terms of what data is deleted, how it is changed, and what systems are impacted—map to any representations (public commitments) the company makes on data deletion and retention.

> **NOTE** There are many other legal definitions and interpretations of deletion, but since this is not a legal book, I will focus on the end result of deletion as defined here.

Having defined what it means to delete data, let's move on to why a company would want to, and indeed must, go through the process of data deletion.

7.1   *Why must a company delete data?*

Companies need to delete data so that they can comply with regulatory requirements, like the ones spelled out in the GDPR and CCPA.

In Article 17, the GDPR outlines the specific circumstances under which the right to be forgotten applies.[1] An individual has the right to have their personal data erased if

- The personal data is no longer necessary for the purpose an organization originally collected or processed it.
- An organization is relying on an individual's consent as the lawful basis for processing the data and that individual withdraws their consent.
- An organization is relying on legitimate interests as its justification for processing an individual's data, the individual objects to this processing, and there is no overriding legitimate interest for the organization to continue with the processing.
- An organization is processing personal data for direct marketing purposes, and the individual objects to this processing.
- An organization processed an individual's personal data unlawfully.
- An organization must erase personal data in order to comply with a legal ruling or obligation.
- An organization has processed a child's personal data to offer their information society services.[2]

---

[1] Article 17, "Right to erasure ('right to be forgotten')," *GDPR*, https://gdpr-info.eu/art-17-gdpr/.

[2] Article 8, "Conditions applicable to child's consent in relation to information society services," *GDPR*, https://gdpr-info.eu/art-8-gdpr/.

The preceding list is not intended to be interpreted by engineers, but I've included it so that engineers have some context when they seek guidance from privacy legal on specifics regarding deletion.

For any company, the legal team typically maintains a *deletion and retention policy* that outlines how employees must implement data protection, retention, retrieval, and deletion/dissociation methods to comply with existing and anticipated regulations. The policy exists so that the company adheres to known regulatory guidelines and complies with the deletion rights outlined in the company's own public-facing privacy policy. This is critical, since companies often state in their privacy policy how they will delete customer data once that data is no longer needed.

However, deleting data just because that requirement is part of a law tends to be a myopic approach. Smart technical leaders will use privacy regulation as the floor to build on rather than a ceiling to cap their tooling for privacy. Beyond the mandatory deletion activities, companies will want to give users control of their private data. Companies should only hold private data so long as it serves a business purpose, and an approach to user privacy that focuses on data minimization can ultimately be a competitive differentiator.

Additionally, as companies seek efficiencies in data storage and improvements in data quality, it is critical that they identify, automate, and scale data deletion processes and tools. This chapter will dip into the deletion best practices that I have learned over the last decade—these range from how companies collect data to how they build deletion logic and tooling.

> **TIP** Don't come up with a deletion strategy just to meet the bar on regulation and compliance. Deletion offers the opportunity for additional privacy controls, like data minimization by eliminating spare or redundant copies of data. Deletion is an example of how you can use the possibility of privacy risk to help broader data discipline.

However, before we can take such a strategic view, you'll need to understand how modern distributed systems work. At the end of the day, engineers who build and use these architectures will make decisions that will influence deletion strategies. It behooves leaders to build these hands-on skills so they can make intelligent decisions around data collection and deletion, even if the leaders do not themselves own the data collection infrastructure or the deletion capabilities.

7.2 What does a modern data collection architecture look like?

Implementing a deletion process for a modern business is at once easy and difficult. Data deletion is easy because deletion is not a new concept. Getting rid of data is something that companies do all the time. However, locating that data, understanding how and why data ends up in different storage locations across the company, deciding how to prioritize the deletion based on the privacy risk of the data, and such other details can be extremely difficult for cross-functional technical leaders, since that information is not typically documented and not usually understood by a single person at a company.

Further, even as technical leaders try to locate a target data set for deletion, more data is being collected, which in turn makes deletion even harder, since the resources required to delete the data become that much harder to implement. Deletion is the quintessential example of a moving target, whereby how you delete, what you delete, and from where you delete change constantly.

This section, therefore, will look at modern technical data-collection architectures. This will enable you to work with engineers, data scientists, and architects to build a deletion strategy. These hands-on skills may not match up precisely with your company's architecture or processes, but this discussion should provide enough context for you to apply them to most situations.

First, we'll discuss how modern distributed architectures collect and process data using services, especially microservices.

7.2.1 Distributed architecture and microservices: How companies collect data

Every company will have its unique architecture and data storage capabilities, but most modern companies follow a microservices-powered architecture. To understand how a company is to implement deletion, it is critical to understand how modern data ingestion and storage works.

As you can see in figure 7.1, most companies build their capabilities not as a single chunk of code but as a combination of different services. On the far left of the figure is a load balancer (ELB) that decides how to handle incoming requests. These requests will include customers trying to use a company's website, its app, etc. All those requests come in real time, sometimes in the millions, and the load balancer has to line them up and map them to servers that can meet the needs of the customers.

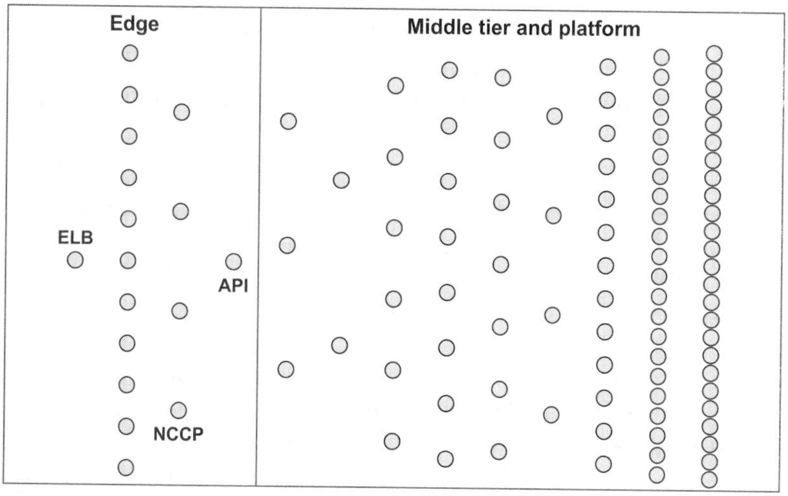

Figure 7.1 A modern microservices infrastructure

In this simplified use case, the load balancer transfers the requests to the main API—also often known as the *Edge API* or the *API gateway*—which then decides how to handle the request based on the nature and urgency of the request.

Typically, behind the Edge API are a series of other smaller services, called *microservices*, that handle the customer requests. For example, if a customer connects to a retail app, then behind the Edge API layer of the retail app will be microservices that conduct the activities like the following:

- Create a customer's account
- Verify the customer's identity (login and authentication)
- Show the customer the products available for purchase
- Display the customer's shopping history

As the customer performs additional activities, microservices like these collect and, in turn, generate additional data, and that data ends up in several data stores across the company's storage ecosystem.

As you build a deletion strategy and architecture, you will want to focus on all the services spread out across your system and perform a lineage analysis of these services and their owners.

Let's now look at how companies store and access real-time data for customer operations.

7.2.2   How real-time data is stored and accessed

A customer's account data (such as their login credentials, their most recent activities, their current transactions, etc.) end up on low-latency and high-availability databases like Cassandra. This approach renders such data accessible rapidly, should the need arise to serve the customer. The data stored in such databases is unstructured, a concept we discussed in detail in earlier chapters.

Let's consider how data can be stored in Cassandra. Cassandra data is stored in multiple nodes (storage locations). This helps create *redundancy*, in that if one node or storage location fails, the customer making the request (to search for products or make payments, etc.) can still get assistance.

The upside behind this approach is that if an engineer were to build a new capability that requires customer data (such as recommending new products to a customer based on the last few products they purchased), that capability can access the data from multiple possible storage locations. This is an important point, since it is possible that the new capability may need a dedicated data source because it needs a constant data refresh. Such a capability might saturate existing capacity, so redundancy can help prevent such failures. Additionally, even if a specific node were to fail or get corrupted, the new capability could still access the customer data.

Just as understanding the storage and collection of real-time data is critical, so is understanding the storage of aggregated data at the data warehouse level, where engineers working on machine learning and data science operate. These engineers use the warehouse to derive insights that could help guide future business decisions. This is why data tends to be archived for a protracted period in these data warehouses, and that is where privacy risks often hide. The next subsection will look at such storage.

7.2.3 *Archival data storage*

Companies often need to analyze the data they collect so that they can unlock deeper insights about the business. This data is often collected in databases that could either be data warehouses or data lakes, as illustrated in figure 7.2.

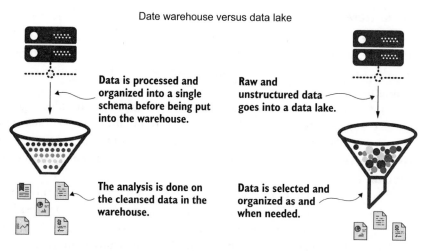

Date warehouse versus data lake

Data is processed and organized into a single schema before being put into the warehouse.

Raw and unstructured data goes into a data lake.

The analysis is done on the cleansed data in the warehouse.

Data is selected and organized as and when needed.

Figure 7.2 Data warehouses and data lakes

As figure 7.2 shows, data warehouses and data lakes are a rich store of data that can provide the company's data analysts and data scientists with the historical aggregated data needed to drive business decisions. Data lakes and data warehouses are both widely used for storing data, but they are not interchangeable terms.[3] A *data lake* is a vast pool of raw data, the purpose of which is not yet defined. A *data warehouse*, on the other hand, is a repository for structured, filtered data that has already been processed for a specific purpose.

The two types of data storage are often confused, but they are much more different than they are alike. In fact, the only real similarity between them is their high-level purpose of storing data. The distinction is important, because they serve different purposes and require different sets of eyes to be properly optimized. While a data lake may work well for one company, a data warehouse may be a better fit for another.

For the purposes of this book, the distinction between a data warehouse and a data lake is not as critical as the idea that these are both repositories where data collected

---

[3] See "What is a Data Lake," Talend, www.talend.com/resources/what-is-data-lake/ and "What is a Data Warehouse and Why Does It Matter To Your Business?" *Talend*, www.talend.com/resources/what-is-data-warehouse/.

by microservices is aggregated from real-time systems like Cassandra and MongoDB. These archival stores—be they warehouses or lakes—consolidate and centralize data that is collected upstream. They are a meeting point of various tributaries of data.

This is important from a privacy standpoint, because even if data stored in these archives is aggregated and anonymized, the combined data from several distinct sources could pose a re-identification risk. For example, aggregated shopping data from one database and specific refund transactions from another could end up identifying specific customers, and that data could then be used to perform analysis.

7.2.4   *Other data storage locations*

We have so far touched on real-time data access and archival data storage. These represent the bookends of the data collection process, the former being important for operational systems that support customers and the latter for analytics, research, and future insights.

We'll now consider other data storage that can serve specific needs germane to either accelerating the fulfillment of data requests or creating extra copies of data just in case a server goes down. This is a common use case; companies create caching layers that usually retain data for a short amount of time but that sometimes can persist information.

Here you have the same tension between operational efficiency and privacy that we have seen before. But before we look at these tensions, Figure 7.3 shows how caching works at a basic level. The user may think they are connecting to the main server and the backend database with all their data, but the reality is more complex. The main server itself has several copies to allow for scaling, in an attempt to meet traffic expectations.

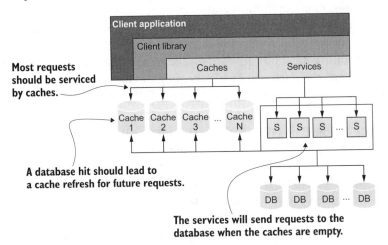

Figure 7.3   Caching and the spread of data

In figure 7.3, the user may think that they are connecting to the main server and the backend database with all their data, but the reality is more complex. The main server itself has several copies so as to allow for scaling in an attempt to meet traffic expectations. That is why you see the servers pointing to multiple databases.

Additionally, as figure 7.3 shows, before using the database to fulfill user requests, the infrastructure will use the caching capabilities that are maintained with backup data stores.

The details involved in caching are beyond the scope of this book. However, at a high level, when a user request causes a call to a database, the service first checks in the cache, and if the information is available in the cache, the service uses the cached values, even if they are outdated. This reduces the burden on the database and allows it to be used for more urgent use cases. This replication of data can lead to a more functional system in a modern infrastructure.

This is where the privacy vs. efficiency tension comes to the fore. The need for continuous availability and low latency is a key driver behind caching, and as I previously stated, replication of data opens up the risk of inappropriate access, leakage, exfiltration, and other privacy harms. Just as organizational efficiency leads to caching, the duplication that caching results in also leads to additional privacy risks. In this case, since caches constantly get accessed and refreshed, data is often harder to detect and its privacy risks harder to manage. Engineers may exchange data messages using chat channels, email, etc., and may even retain data in their laptops and other systems. Just as caching represents one kind of data persistence, such ad hoc storage represents the other end of the data flow. These and other potential data locations may need to be scrubbed in order to avoid privacy harms.

7.2.5 *How data storage grows from collection to archival*

The replication of data that you saw in the previous subsections poses a problem for privacy. We have discussed before the privacy governance challenge of dealing with the tension between reducing your company's data footprint to avoid privacy harms, while also making data available for business uses:

- *Operations*—Allowing customers, engineers, etc., to locate data on demand quickly.
- *Analysis*—Allowing data scientists and analysts to use the data to better understand the overall strategic direction of the business and help advise on next steps.
- *Holds*—Enabling the legal team, tax team, audit team, or law enforcement team to retrieve this data in case of litigation or other compliance activities.

In many companies, data is copied to different databases for these purposes, since each use case has varying retention and access-control requirements. This spread of data is often unregulated and unaudited, and that makes deletion very difficult.

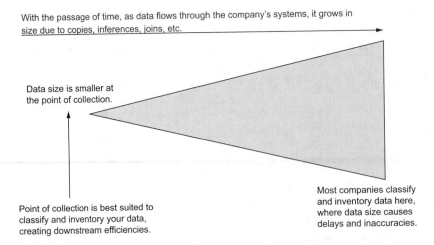

With the passage of time, as data flows through the company's systems, it grows in size due to copies, inferences, joins, etc.

Data size is smaller at the point of collection.

Point of collection is best suited to classify and inventory your data, creating downstream efficiencies.

Most companies classify and inventory data here, where data size causes delays and inaccuracies.

Figure 7.4   How the data footprint grows

Figure 7.4, which you first saw in chapter 4, illustrates how data grows once it enters the company. This is one of many reasons why I recommend that technical leaders classify, catalog, and inventory data toward the left end of the funnel. This will enable them to delete data faster when it is no longer needed. This is critical because companies may have to delete data either when the retention period for specific kinds of data expires or when a customer/user requests that their data be deleted.

> **NOTE**   In order for a company to be able to delete data meaningfully, accurately, and scalably, it is vital that the company classifies and inventories data early in the pipeline. Deletion is not a standalone activity but part of an overall data governance strategy.

Regardless of whether or not a company has classified and inventoried its data, most companies need to answer these questions:

- How will you delete user account data—data about customers such as registration and other operations?
- How will you delete warehouse data? This could include removing personal data from raw Kafka tables in Hive after a user requests an account deletion.
- How will you delete data that is extremely sensitive, like credit card data, that needs to be very accessible for the right teams (for example, the payments team) but needs to be deleted immediately when the time comes for deletion?

Subsequent sections of this chapter will explore these questions and suggest an architectural design you can use to implement a deletion system for a modern data-driven business.

7.3 How the data collection architecture works

We've looked at how data flows from the collection frontend to backend warehouses. Figure 7.5 shows a simplified picture of a typical microservice, represented by the box on the left. This service accepts user requests and writes user data to and reads it from some kind of data store, represented by the cylinder in the middle. This could be one of many supported data stores, such as MySQL or Cassandra. After data is written to this data store, it is ingested into the data warehouse, where it could be used for business analytics or machine learning. There's a lot of complexity within the data warehouse itself, but those details are beyond the scope of this book.

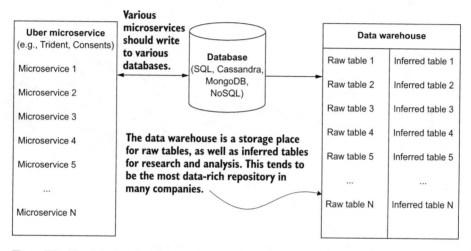

Figure 7.5   The data flow from microservices to database to data warehouse

The microservice in figure 7.5 would receive data to perform a specific function; for example, it might collect IP address data from someone who signs up with your company in order to ensure that they are a legitimate user and not a bot or attacker. Upon verifying their authenticity (or determining that they are a threat), the service could store their data to a Cassandra database containing information about legitimate users or to a different database that stores information about fraudulent users. Future login attempts by this user will prompt this microservice to call both databases. Depending upon which database returns a match, the user is either allowed to proceed or not.

Aggregated analysis of thousands or millions of such users would need to be conducted so that the business could meaningfully analyze usage and fraud patterns. To do that, a significant portion of the data will need to be transferred from the databases to a data warehouse.

This is an accurate but incomplete narrative. Technical and senior leaders need to understand the scale of the data that flows into their warehouse, so that they can harbor realistic expectations and make appropriate investments in data deletion infra-structure. Figure 7.6 paints a richer picture of this scale. In a realistic scenario, data flows from multiple data sources, is then transformed by extract, transform, load (ETL) processes, and is then funneled into the data warehouse. As companies buy other companies, ink deals with vendors, and empower engineers to create more data sources (microservices, APIs, etc.), the data flow to the warehouse will only increase.

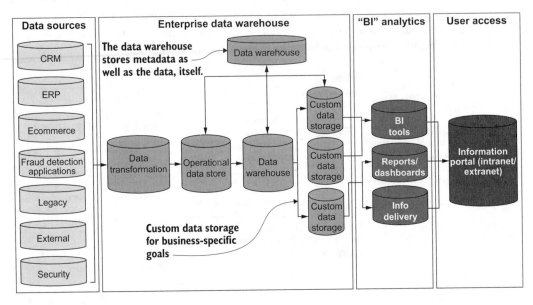

Figure 7.6   The data flow into the warehouse for modern businesses

In subsequent sections, when we discuss data deletion, we will be looking at deleting user data on request or upon the expiration of a specific time period from the middle cylinder in figure 7.5 (the database) and then from the warehouse at the far right in figure 7.5.

Deletion is at once very intuitive and yet very difficult to execute, so in this chapter we will design systems that collect and process data and use those systems to build a deletion architecture. That will enable technical leaders to execute deletion with a system as a reference and a privacy lens rather than understanding deletion purely from a conceptual standpoint.

7.4   *Deleting account-level data: A starting point*

When a fast-moving company has to create its first-ever deletion process, it can be difficult to come up with a list of areas to focus on. This section will help you build a basic process and then help drive automation efficiencies.

7.4.1   Account deletion: Building the tooling and process

In modern businesses, a common vector for account deletion tends to be a customer calling (or emailing or using social media) and requesting that their account be deleted.

Many companies struggle to implement a basic process for customer account deletion. A common early-stage deletion process, whereby you seek to delete data as early as possible once its use is complete, could follow these steps:

1. Upon receiving a deletion request, the customer's user record is tagged (marked with a flag), indicating that the record for this specific customer is to be deleted. You could come up with a machine-readable tag like "to_be_deleted".
2. The customer's credit balances (refunds) are changed to zero.
3. The customer's mobile number is marked as available for use by new customers.
4. The customer's profile pictures and other biometric artifacts are deleted from S3.
5. The customer is "deleted." This could include a list of actions such as the following:
   a. The customer's primary Personally Identifiable Information (name, mobile number, etc.) is overwritten with bogus or empty values.
   b. All "notes" are deleted. This is critical, since notes made by engineers and customer support specialists could contain personal data. I have seen many instances where engineers have entered information that identifies customers in comments and then forgotten to delete them. Many privacy incidents are the outcome of such carelessness rather than willful malevolence.
   c. All third-party identities (Facebook, Google+, etc.) and corresponding identity graphs are deleted, as is the data connected to the cookies for those identities. This is critical, since many privacy harms occur because of incomplete deletions where identity data is subsequently connected to activity data. Ensuring identity deletion is vital to avoid any surprises.
   d. All alternate emails (if any) are deleted.
   e. All behavioral and inferred data is deleted.
   f. All data tags are deleted. These tags could indicate the type of data or any details that provide context regarding the data.
6. All payment profiles are deleted. We will cover an example of payment data deletion in section 7.6.
7. The user is unsubscribed from any email lists so as to avoid any outreach to a user who has asked for their data to be deleted.

7.4.2   Scaling account deletion

Based on my experience, deletion often tends to scale poorly in companies because of the varying user data profiles and data types. Here are some examples:

- The process in the preceding section may not apply to all types of users and customers. For example, customers who have different profiles for subsidiaries could have a different deletion path. This could happen if a company provides banking services as well as retirement planning services, and both require customers to create separate profiles. That in turn could lead to complexity in building out the requisite deletion tooling.
- Derived and downstream data stores that replicate customer information will need to receive deletion notifications as well, so that any data they have stored about the customers is deleted.
- Append-only data stores like Kafka, and data stores that consume from Kafka (Elasticsearch, for example) may retain personal data in records that were emitted before the customer's profile was deleted. This could require the creation of more bespoke deletion processes.
- Deletion may not permitted in the following cases:
  - The user's account is exempted from the deletion process by someone with the right privileges.
  - The customer has been banned, in which case the company may end up needing to retain customer data even after the customer requests deletion.
  - The customer has an outstanding credit balance in the event of services not rendered after payment was received (for example, cancelling a service after an upcoming month was prepaid for).
  - The customer has an outstanding credit (refund).
  - The customer has an outstanding debit balance.

Quite a bit of this information often lives in databases that are append-only, which is to say that the database is "immutable." This means the database keeps the entire history of all completed transactions. This is useful for log data, and it is recommended for Kappa architectures.

The Kappa software architecture is used for processing streaming data. The main idea is that it can perform both real-time and batch processing, especially for analytics, with a single tech stack. It is based on a streaming architecture in which an incoming series of data is first stored in a messaging engine, like Apache Kafka. From there, a stream-processing engine will read the data and transform it into an analyzable format, and then store it in an analytics database for end users to query. This type of architecture has become widespread. In particular, HDFS, the bedrock of Hadoop, was designed in this fashion.

There may also be legal requirements to consider when designing this deletion infrastructure:

- You will need the ability to reach out to all tools and systems to delete records that are linked to internal identifiers like GUIDs. This is harder than you might think; it may be easier to correlate data between databases based on identifiers that are universal in nature, like Social Security numbers, whereas internal teams may have a variety of identifiers that may allow them to retain the data for longer. This process may allow for bespoke data storage for engineering teams, but it may make the data harder to eventually delete.

- Your infrastructure will need to block deletion requests for tables containing data that law enforcement might need. This would require some sort of tag to ensure that any attempt to delete such tables spares the tables subject to legal holds. This is an example of how data inventory can help policy enforcement.
- Teams will need to invest in verification methods to ensure the data is deleted but that also raise flags when it doesn't work.

A few points of clarification are in order so architects understand the roles and responsibilities on how this deletion system would work.

Let's assume we want to delete some data for Jack. To do this, a central deletion service will issue a request to the microservice that collects user data; the message will ask the microservice to delete Jack's data. That way, the central service can track deletion, but the task of deletion is handled by individual services. These individual services know best, or should know best, what they need to collect and for how long, and this approach will also avoid creating a central point of failure when deletion is executed by one central service.

This approach maintains the ownership model where individual services are responsible for their own data. I recommend this model because it can seamlessly inject deletion into your workflow, and it can create accountability as well.

The microservice ownership model offers yet another advantage. The deletion requests can be ingested automatically into the data warehouse such that the ingestion platform can overwrite the original records. There will almost certainly be some nuance to this, depending on which data store your company may be using, but generally speaking, when the central deletion service issues a deletion request, the resulting data deletions should propagate all the way to the data warehouse.

7.5 Deleting account-level data: Automation and scaling for distributed services

In this section we will create a high-level system design for the central deletion service, which we'll name "Destroyer." You can repurpose this design for your individual use cases if you choose.

In the most basic sense, Destroyer should support deleting personal or private data from a company's primary data stores upon customer request. This is accomplished through services that manage private data and their response to deletion calls. These deletion calls will be made from a scheduling service that will be part of Destroyer.

We will look at the scheduling service architecture shortly but before the deletion of user account data can be scheduled, there needs to be a check to ensure that there is no legal hold on the data. Destroyer should check for legal holds before initiating a delete of any customer data. This should be done using a Pull model: Destroyer should query a legal hold database (or service) to check for holds on the data targeted for deletion.

There are different ways a company could implement such a legal hold authority.

- A company could build its own separate legal hold authority service that would abstract information about customers that the company has collected. This abstraction could be in the form of a service (user interface, plus database) much like tax preparation software. Just as you get the data and guidance best suited to you from a government tax database without knowing all the underlying tax laws, the legal hold authority service could automatically return data that can be deleted without being subject to a legal hold.

- Alternatively, Destroyer (or the microservices that will actually delete the data) must be able to directly communicate with a legal hold database. This database would queue data fields whose legal hold has expired and therefore ensure timely deletion.

If an active hold is discovered during a deletion attempt, the deletion could be rescheduled, either by setting a specific postponement for the field you are attempting delete, or by using a default postponement period of 30 days.

Regardless of how this service is implemented, the basic underlying design remains the same. This service would need a unified source of legal hold information. For input such as an email address or a customer's internal ID, this service could expose an API that would answer questions such as these:

- Is an employee, contractor, or customer with the given email or UUID on litigation hold?
- What is the list of employees or contractors or customers on litigation hold?
- What is the retention policy associated with an employee or contractor or customer?

Every service that requires legal hold information would need to query directly from a legal hold database, which would normally be a service used by the legal team. This may turn out to be inefficient, since you want to avoid a situation where engineers and attorneys are competing for data from the same database. As a result, I strongly recommend building a legal hold authority service, which would serve as an abstraction layer on top of your legal hold database (which the legal team would maintain) and provide a RESTful HTTP interface. This will keep engineers and attorneys from competing for data from the same database.

Since deletion could be a key compliance metric, the legal hold service must account for some enforceable attributes and service level agreements (SLAs). The SLAs can either apply to all APIs, a specific API, or a category of APIs. You could measure the following metrics:

- *Accuracy*—What is the maximum permissible error rate for false positives and false negatives? This would include user records returned (so that they can be deleted) even if subject to legal hold, or records not returned even when legal holds are a non-factor. To be clear, user data should be returned for deletion only if there is no legal hold.
- *Capacity*—What is the minimum required throughput (requests/second)?
- *Latency*—What is the median response time, and what is the 99th percentile response time?
- *Availability*—What is the guaranteed uptime? Please add justification if it's less than 99.999%.

Once you validate that the data you wish to delete is not subject to a legal hold, you will need a mechanism to schedule the deletion.

7.5.1 Registering services and data fields for deletion

In order to manage deletion requests, service owners that manage private data should have to register those services and the private data fields they handle with the Destroyer deletion service. Destroyer would be in charge of initiating the deletion of those fields when a scheduled delete request is executed.

As I have mentioned previously, data collection occurs in a decentralized fashion among many teams that build tools and capabilities for customers. That is why the step of registering these services with the central Destroyer service is critical. If this step is not completed, you could have some services where data deletion occurs and others where it does not. Take it from me, you do not want to have to deal with a situation where you promised that data was deleted only to then find out that some fields were missed.

> **NOTE** In this design, we are optimizing for data deletion at the field level, which means we could deploy the service to delete data for customers on a field-by-field basis, and delete some accounts only partially if needed. For example, let's assume you run a retail website and wish to delete names and addresses of customers on transactions that are more than a year old, but you wish to retain their purchase history for subsequent analysis. You could use Destroyer to complete such a deletion.

When a service that collects user data and will subsequently need to delete it is registered with Destroyer, that service needs to help set the context for the future deletion to occur. The service will need to provide for each field a list of attributes that describe the field, its owner, and the relevant details for the API to be used when initiating a delete. The registration details could look like the following:

- *Field type*—The type of the private data field to be deleted, denoted by F, selected from a predefined list of types, which would determine which data retention policy applies to F. For instance, FIRSTNAME. This indicates the type of field that would need to be deleted and which retention policy would apply to this field. You could maintain a list of types, of which one would map to this field. For example, the types could include "firstname", "email", "location", etc. Supplying the field and type could also determine the type of deletion applied to the field itself.

- *Description*—Some text describing what data from the field is being deleted, for example, "First name deletion from MySQL."
- *Service name*—The service that "owns" F (that is, the service that contains the data field F), selected from a list of available services. The owners of this service would need to be notified in case of issues such as a deletion error or a test failure.
- *API type*—The type of the API that will be provided to and called by Destroyer for deletion.
- *Deletion and testing API templates*—I will provide below the details on the deletion APIs and attendant endpoints. They will assume the existence of a unique identifier to locate the user to be deleted.

There are three endpoints that could be provided, either via an HTTP or Thrift API. All endpoints could use the following parameters in any of their template URLs or headers:

- {user_id}—This is the internal identifier of the user to be deleted.
- {field_type}—We will match this field at runtime to the registered field type selected for deletion, such as "firstname". This approach would be useful if you wanted to utilize the same endpoint to delete multiple fields for the same UUID.
- {requestor_uuid}—This will match at runtime to the ID of the service that is making the deletion request.

Given that deletion is a mostly irreversible action, validating and matching the fields and services is important.

These are three recommended endpoints:

- DELETE—This is the main endpoint to support deletion of a field for a particular ID.
  - This field must allow passing of the three parameters we just looked at.
  - The deletion implementation can range from complete erasure to replacing the target fields with synthetic data to anonymization. This should be finalized by the team that maintains the Destroyer service and the engineers wishing to use Destroyer to delete data.
- GET_TEST_USER—This endpoint would return a user_id to be used for testing, so that you can test the delete endpoint
  - This user_id must be a valid user, with enough data to adequately test the first part of the deletion flow that provides an account for deletion.

- Upon calling to this endpoint, services should attempt to configure a user account that will "refresh" or "undelete" its data fields. The account would be seen as not-deleted, and the endpoint would therefore return its user_id on every call. That way, you can access a fresh record for deletion as part of this test.
- The alternative would be to generate a fresh test user on every call and return its user_id. Either way, the goal is to obtain a non-deleted user that could be deleted.

- IS_DELETED—This endpoint would ascertain whether data has been deleted for the given user_id. This endpoint would help test the second part of the deletion flow that executes the deletion process.
  - This endpoint should return whether the user is deemed as deleted, according to the deletion logic specified in the deletion policy.

The rest of the implementation details should be trivial for engineers, but this design offers a reliable foundation to build on.

A key part of deletion is creating a queue that ensures that accounts are deleted in an orderly fashion. To do so, you need a service or capability that orchestrates deletion among the thousands of microservices, engineers, and data stores that live at a company. The next section will offer some tips.

7.5.2 Scheduling data deletion

We can now look at high-level designs for the scheduler in our deletion service. The scheduler will serve as the backend for incoming delete requests and as the executor of scheduled deletes.

The scheduler will also be the *engineering* source of truth for your data retention and deletion policy, which is to say that the deletions that the scheduler orchestrates will need to line up with the retention periods in your policies (the assumption being that you may need to reference multiple retention policies to identify the one that is applicable). The policy would consist of two period definitions: the retention period for the data after a deletion request is submitted, and the extended retention period to apply if an active legal hold exists on the account, after which deletion could be reattempted. From an implementation standpoint, the receipt of a deletion request is tantamount to the expiration of the retention period for that customer's data. The logic flow would be similar if the retention period expires without any request from the user.

The process you follow in designing the deletion scheduling logic could resemble the following:

1. *Check for legal hold*—You would need to query the legal hold authority for any holds on the given user_id. If a legal hold exists, you'd need to pause deletion and reschedule the delete according to the legal hold policy and retry at a later time.

2. *Validate that the user remains deletable*—Once the legal hold expires, if there was one, you would need to verify that the state of the user's account has not changed between the scheduling and execution of deletion. For example, the user who requested that their account be deleted may have renewed their subscription, in which case it is not clear that the deletion request is operative.

3. *Initiate delete*—This step would execute the deletion (by erasing the data, obfuscating it, etc.).

Scheduling a deletion for a user account or checking the status of a deletion request would need to be managed centrally, so as to maintain an inventory of successful and unsuccessful deletions. This way, if the legal team needs to verify deletions across multiple services, they could just check one central source rather than chase individual service owners.

This section has provided an architecture for a deletion system for account data in operational databases. Next we'll look at how a company can delete highly sensitive data, like financial information, that is typically stored in a very secure database.

7.6   *Sensitive data deletion*

Every company will have its own unique payments system, and that will bring unique deletion challenges. For the purposes of this discussion, we will assume that our system has a database that stores customer data (called PaymentsDB, where Destroyer would operate) that contains some of the data required to charge the customer. We also have a second database (SecureDB) that contains payment-specific data that is protected using security tools to prevent exfiltration and misuse.

Let's also assume the following concepts, where "mop" is short for "method of payment."

- mop_token_id—This is a tokenized version of a 16-digit credit card stored in PaymentsDB and SecureDB, with the latter being the source of truth. Basically, this is a randomly generated ID assigned to a real credit card value. *Tokenization*, when applied to data security, is the process of substituting a sensitive data element with a non-sensitive equivalent, referred to as a token, that has no extrinsic or exploitable meaning or value. The token is a reference that maps back to the sensitive data through a tokenization system.

- mop_id—This ID can be owned by a payments engineering team. Every time a customer updates or enters a credit card number (even if it is the same as the previous credit card), payments creates a new mop_id (using a sequence generator, not sequential but distributed).

The Payments system typically uses an app, which we'll call COP (Cloud Online Pay) in this example, in order to handle customer credit card numbers in conjunction with SecureDB and the PaymentsDB.

- The COP app receives a request from another microservice to add a payment. When the request comes in, COP sends the payment info to SecureDB and gets a token (`mop_token_id`) from SecureDB, which COP stores in the PaymentsDB (`cass_seg_pay`). The Payments Cassandra database stores the following information:
  - The payment object (`mop_id`, `mop_token_id`, first name, last name, ZIP code) and status (primary/inactive/deactivated).
  - Transaction (activity) log with a time-to-live (TTL) of 10 months.
  - The mapping between `mop_id` and `mop_token_id`. The first of two upcoming examples in this section describes this in more detail.
- This token (`mop_token_id`) is stored in PaymentsDB regardless of whether the payment goes through or not.
- In SecureDB, we store the following:
  - The mapping between the token and the encrypted payment (possible schema: token, hashed payment ID, encrypted payment ID). That way, we supply both the hashed and encrypted version of the payment info. This is how SecureDB returns the token for a payment.
  - If a previously submitted credit card is reused, the app attempts to find the hashed and encrypted entry and return an existing token, but you may end up with a new token.
  - In the event of a soft delete, a longer retention period of 3 years could be set in SecureDB for `mop_token_id` and hashed payment when the API for the database that maintains the subscriber records informs the Payments service that the account has been cancelled for 10 months. The assumption at work here is that the account has to be cancelled for a specific period—10 months in this case—before formal deletion is initiated. This allows the cancelled customer to possibly return and resume their usage with their original data.

Figure 7.7 shows how a system like this would process deletions. Here are some salient points:

- The system is designed to delete customer payment data in batches, and that is true in many real-life situations as well, since companies are rarely able to delete data immediately. This is why companies routinely state that their systems may take a while to reflect a deletion request, and 401k account changes take more than one pay cycle.
- Payments systems check whether there has been recent activity on the account, in which case payments deletion can be halted.
- Deletion occurs in phases, whereby account data is delinked from payments data, after which Destroyer would delete account data, and then payments data would be deleted as well.

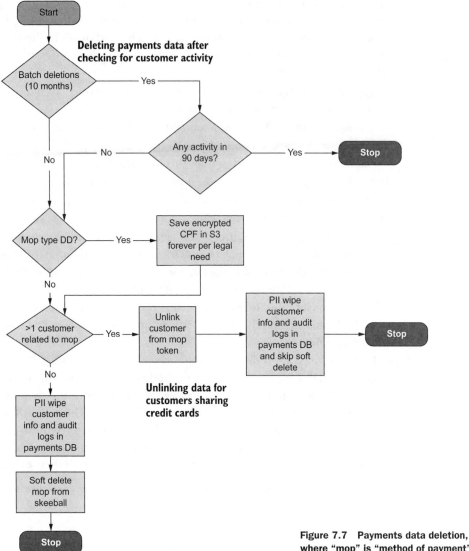

Figure 7.7   **Payments data deletion, where "mop" is "method of payment"**

A typical credit card wipe process could work as follows:

1. An upstream microservice calls Payments to the initiate wipe.
2. Payments goes into PaymentsDB and obfuscates all personal data by replacing their values with "PII_WIPE".
3. When the expiration date passes, at which point the customer data must be deleted, the Payments system undergoes what is called a "PII WIPE". This leads to the deletion of:
    - Activity logs that have credit card related information.

     – In the table that contains the link between `mop_id` and `mop_token_id`, the token is replaced with "PII_WIPE". As a consequence, payments cannot request the credit card from SecureDB and the customer cannot be billed.

4. When the Payments microservice sends a "PII_WIPE" request to SecureDB, the latter removes the encrypted credit card but retains the one-way hash of the card and its mapping to the `mop_token_id`, and it sets the TTL to three years for the token.

5. For a soft delete, the encrypted credit card is deleted in SecureDB, but the credit card hash and token are retained for a TTL of three years, besides being tagged as soft deleted. This will preclude the credit card from being used for payments.

6. For a hard delete, the deletion process removes `mop_token_id` as well. This is what happens when a customer requests full deletion of their credit card.

In the event that you wish to deal with multiple customers using the same credit card, and you have to delete the card for one customer, the payments team can do what is called *unlinking*. This will accommodate a situation where customers C1 and C2 (or potentially others) share the same credit card. The PaymentsDB would look like figure 7.8.

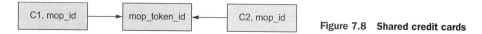

Figure 7.8   Shared credit cards

Also, the database contains a row that lists all the customers that a `mop_token_id` links to. For example, `[(mop_token_id), (C1, C2)]`. With `mop_token_id` being mapped to both `C1` and `C2` shows that both customers are using the same payment instrument.

    If C1 calls to have their credit card deleted, the aforementioned row will let the payments system know that the credit card is shared. The Payments system then does the following:

- Sets the `mop_id` to "PII_WIPE".
- Unlinks the C1 box in figure 7.8 from the `mop_token_id` box.
- The C2 box in figure 7.8 continues to be linked to the `mop_token_id` box.
- In the `[(mop_token_id), (C1, C2)]` example, the entry changes to `[(mop_token_id), (C2)]`.

Now let's look at data deletion holistically in terms of ownership and maintenance, so that the process can function smoothly as the company grows.

7.7 Who should own data deletion?

As you have probably figured out by now, data deletion can be very complex and time-consuming. As a result, companies often struggle to identify clear owners for the deletion logic and infrastructure.

In my experience, having a central privacy team owning the Destroyer service while having individual teams own the deletion APIs is the most scalable and efficient way to delete customer data.

Deleting warehouse data gets more complicated. It is vital that this work be someone's distinct responsibility, because otherwise you run the risk of non-compliance and also of having data exfiltrated by security breaches. Table 7.1 lays out the various options and tradeoffs when it comes to allocating deletion responsibilities.

Rather than identify a specific team, I recommend that a cross-functional Data Custodian team own the data warehouse deletion responsibility. The Data Custodian team may include a set of engineers from multiple teams, and a primary team that already owns Hadoop maintenance could build and maintain the Hadoop deletion service.

Table 7.1 highlights three possible approaches to who could own deletion responsibilities and their attendant tradeoffs.

Table 7.1   Deletion ownership options

Deletion execution API owner & data custodian	Pros	Cons
Each engineering team	Responsibility lies with the data producer and owner of the data's business use case. This way you can avoid erroneous deletions that could occur if a centralized team deletes data without the requisite context.	Shared tools (such as the Hadoop deletion libraries) would need to be supported in several languages, they would require a lot of documentation and education, and they would require continual maintenance.
Central privacy team	A single team is responsible for the service's implementation and maintenance. The Hadoop deletion library would need to support minimal clients.	Privacy engineering teams do not produce the majority of the Hadoop data, and do not maintain the health of or any aspect of the Hadoop system. Privacy engineering's role in data deletion projects is ideally that of scheduling deletion, not the executing deletion, since only teams that collect data know when deletion can occur in a way that does not disrupt permissible and necessary business activities.
Hadoop data collector and custodian *Preferred*	The custodian of Hadoop data is responsible for the service's implementation and maintenance, the Hadoop deletion libraries would need to support only minimal clients, and the Hadoop custodian would ideally already be involved in maintaining the health of Hadoop, if not all of its maintenance.	The Hadoop data custodian does not produce all of the Hadoop data, so this model leaves the responsibility of data deletion in the hands of the person who most benefits from its collection.

It remains to be defined exactly what the data custodian's responsibilities are, but they would include

- Setting standards and reviewing with other Hadoop teams for adherence
- Reviewing code across data warehouse teams and setting up monitoring for timely deletion
- Setting filters for data detection before egress of data that should be deleted

Using the custodian model would mean that companies wouldn't need to depend on each service owner doing the right thing. It would instead ensure centralized supervision for warehouse data deletion.

Note that the preceding approaches do not have any set formulas for applicability. Each company will work differently, and sometimes these models will have to evolve as deletion responsibilities evolve. The tradeoffs are critical, so it's important to understand the downstream consequences of each choice and which fits best with the company and its privacy journey.

Summary

- Data deletion is a key responsibility for a company and a vital component of its overall privacy and data governance strategy.
- To build a data deletion strategy, technical leaders and executives must understand a company's data collection infrastructure.
- Deleting operational account-level data involves the design of services and workflows.
- Deleting backend warehouse data will require considerations of scale and implementation for how the data is altered to satisfy deletion criteria.
- Companies may need bespoke practices to delete sensitive data that poses a high degree of privacy risk.
- Data deletion responsibilities can be split between various stakeholders in a company, but it is important to consider the tradeoffs of different approaches.

Exporting user data: Data Subject Access Requests

In this chapter, we will discuss Data Subject Access Requests (DSARs). As privacy laws like GDPR and CCPA become more entrenched in the public consciousness, leaders at all kinds of companies are seeing DSARs land on their desk, and they need to respond to them. Unless they are able to do so accurately and expediently, they risk reputational harm and possible fines. This chapter will help such leaders in three ways.

First, we will look at the DSAR workload and assess how companies are faring in the face of customer requests. This will help leaders and their executive supervisors make informed decisions around data governance, resourcing, training, and outreach. This part of the chapter is geared to a wide range of stakeholders.

Second, we will look at backend data and how those responsible for storing and extracting data to support DSARs can make decisions about architecture. These decisions are critical in both manual and automated fulfillment of DSARs. This section is geared more toward engineers but it could also be instructive for attorneys, since they need to understand the tradeoffs involved in various approaches to fulfilling DSARs.

Third, we will look at building an internal tool to manage the DSAR process, and we'll map the screens to backend data decisions. Many companies fail to build such a tool, and that may lead to inefficiencies in how DSARs are created and how user communication is managed.

As a whole, this chapter will provide you with best practices for designing your own DSAR platform, including both frontend and backend components, or enough understanding to purchase an external solution that meets your needs.

The DSAR obligation requires a company to be able to *collect, process, retain,* and *archive* customer data in a fashion that makes it possible to furnish that data at the customer's request. It is vital that the company be able to do so within a timeframe specified by law in the customer's jurisdiction, as well as in a manner that lines up with public sentiment.

This task would have been more straightforward several years ago, when companies had top-down structures that enabled them to regulate what was collected. In many companies, the data they collected then was more structured and defined, since storage was expensive and user experiences were not built to drive engagement and collect data. The data storage also occurred in a finite number of databases, tightly regulated by on-premises IT administrators

The modern innovation ecosystem represents a contrast to the world even half a decade ago. Modern companies tend to be heavily focused on expediency, innovation, and disruption, while their ability to meet customer data transparency requirements prioritizes consistency, aggregation, and explanation. The forcing functions that drive growth and engagement run contrary to the ones that drive privacy scrutiny and regulatory audits.

That is why this book has focused on data governance as a continuous effort, and this chapter will focus on creating a system and process to export user data. The sooner companies build in frontend and backend capabilities for DSARs the better, since locating data is easier once you have harnessed your data collection, cataloging, and export capabilities as one connected effort.

But before we delve further into the topic, let's start with the basics: what are DSARs?

8.1   *What are DSARs?*

Before explaining what DSARs are in detail, it will be helpful to understand their role in the overall privacy and governance landscape and to put DSARs into context in the narrative of this book. This context is useful, since DSARs are relatively new, and companies need to implement them correctly with a privacy focus.

I have so far explained how you can build in privacy data protection and governance from the point of data collection. Understanding a *distributed architecture* (the disparate services that process data as well as the various data stores that exist to persist data) is critical for technical leaders and executives alike, so that they can understand why privacy is hard to build into their systems. That investment across the company's tech stack is vital so that companies can meaningfully and scalably classify and catalog their data, share data with privacy controls, delete data, and conduct technical privacy reviews for new products and features.

However, a company's privacy obligations do not end with the governance of data within the walled gardens of its systems or in its data sharing with partners. Partly due to public sentiment, and partly due to legislation and regulation, there is also an expectation that companies will be able to provide a customer with a copy of the data those companies have collected about that customer. This is where DSARs come in.

A *Data Subject Access Request* (DSAR) is the means by which individuals request that your enterprise disclose the personal data it holds on them and how you use or intend to use it. Submitting DSARs is one of the data subject rights granted to consumers under data privacy laws such as the California Consumer Privacy Act (CCPA) and the European General Data Protection Regulation (GDPR). These laws not only give consumers an awareness of their rights over their personal data but also provide the tools necessary to exercise them.[1]

Just as the data deletion commitment is an outcome of the regulatory "right to be forgotten," the DSAR commitment is the outcome of the regulatory push to create greater transparency for customers on what companies do with customer and user data.[2] Figure 8.1 illustrates how DSAR requests are being shaped by the growth in privacy laws worldwide.

While technical leaders and executives at a company often do not need to understand the details behind the regulations, some understanding of the DSAR regulations is critical for the following reasons:

- The DSAR infrastructure is an extension of the work you should have done in data governance from the point of data collection. This infrastructure is not possible for a siloed team to create quickly.
- Several regulations tend to be fairly specific about what counts as a valid response to a DSAR request.
- The data you make available to customers in response to a DSAR request is now outside your company perimeter and in the public domain, and it's therefore open to scrutiny. A dissatisfied customer or persistent regulator could pose a serious problem for a company if an initial DSAR request leads to a deeper inquest into a company's broader privacy practices.

---

[1] Vivek Kokkengada, "6 Keys to Automating the DSAR Process Under CCPA," *Securiti blog*, April 29, 2020, http://mng.bz/Bx52.

[2] "Everything you need to know about the 'Right to be forgotten'," General Data Protection Regulation (GDPR) Compliance Guidelines, *GDPR*, https://gdpr.eu/right-to-be-forgotten/.

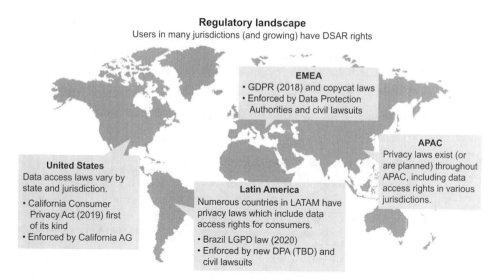

Regulatory landscape
Users in many jurisdictions (and growing) have DSAR rights

EMEA
• GDPR (2018) and copycat laws
• Enforced by Data Protection
  Authorities and civil lawsuits

APAC
Privacy laws exist (or
are planned) throughout
APAC, including data
access rights in various
jurisdictions.

United States
Data access laws vary by
state and jurisdiction.

• California Consumer
  Privacy Act (2019) first
  of its kind
• Enforced by California AG

Latin America
Numerous countries in LATAM have
privacy laws which include data
access rights for consumers.

• Brazil LGPD law (2020)
• Enforced by new DPA (TBD) and
  civil lawsuits

Figure 8.1 How privacy laws are providing customers DSAR rights

Since I am not an attorney, and going over these regulations in detail is beyond the scope of this book, I highly recommend that technical leaders and architects seek counsel or do their own research. It is important to internalize these concepts so as to tailor the company's system design and other business processes for DSARs.

Besides the regulations themselves, it will help company leaders to understand the stakes involved with DSARs. DSARs give consumers control over their personal information collected and stored by organizations; the information customers can request may include details around the access control to customer data, the duration for which the data will be stored, the safeguards the organization provides for customer data, who the company shares personal data with, etc. With the CCPA, consumers can request DSARs twice a year. Such requests can be hard to fulfill if companies do not have automation in place, and this chapter will provide broad architectural designs so companies can create systems that are suited to their needs for DSARs.

For businesses, timely and accurate fulfillment of DSARs could boost their trust relationship with key stakeholders while also ensuring compliance with regulations. However, the cost of fulfilling each DSAR could be nontrivial for some businesses, since DSARs require gathering data from multiple systems, putting all that data in one place, going through the data records, and compiling the findings in a single comprehensible report.

For leaders who feel like DSARs can be deprioritized and put on the back burner, ask yourself what would happen if a customer or some other entity organized a mass movement to request DSARs and flood your company with DSAR requests? It is critical to invest in these capabilities.

> **WARNING**   Executives and technical leaders need to consider the possibility that they could get DSAR requests not just from customers but also from others who wish to weaponize such rights to disrupt a company's business. In either case, it helps to have sound data governance and automation in place to fulfill DSARs.

Let's now look at some specifics on the regulatory details behind DSARs and privacy laws that codify DSAR rights.

8.1.1   *What rights do DSAR regulations give to users?*

You will need to check with your company's legal department or seek equivalent outside resources about the specifics of your DSAR requirements, but the following list outlines the broad categories of data that the DSAR response should contain:

- A copy of the user's personal data
- The reason the data was collected
- Checks and balances the company has in place to prevent privacy and security issues with the data

While it's not comprehensive, the following checklist outlines the sort of details a DSAR response should contain[3]:

- A confirmation that the company is processing the user's personal data ("processing" could mean "using," but you will want to confirm this with your legal team).
- A record or file that contains the user's personal data.
- An explanation of the lawful basis that the company has for processing the customer's data. This information will require alignment between the company's privacy, legal, engineering, and other teams that collect data.
- The period for which data will be stored. This requirement sets the tone for the new world, where companies can no longer collect and retain data for indefinite periods of time, but instead should tie collection and retention to specific time periods.
- Any details around data lineage—how this data was obtained, from what sources, etc.
- Any available details regarding how the customer's data was used for automated decision-making and profiling.
- The names of any third parties and other partners the user's information is shared with.

Given the fast-changing regulatory landscape of privacy and security, it helps to compare the rights afforded by some common laws already in place. In figure 8.2 you can see that the GDPR and CCPA may have some differences ranging from subtle to significant.[4]

---

[3] Eric Andrews, "DSARs: What You Need to Know," *Securiti blog*, January 1, 2021, https://securiti.ai/blog/dsar-rights-and-compliance/.

[4] This figure is based on one from Andrews, "DSARs: What You Need to Know."

DSAR under CCPA versus GDPR

	CCPA	GDPR
Application	The CCPA's deletion right applies only to data collected from the consumer. This excludes data from third-party vendors.	GDPR's deletion right applies to all data concerning a data subject.
Informed consent	Businesses must inform consumers at or before the point of collection of the categories of personal information to be collected and the purposes for which it will be used.	Businesses must inform consumers of their rights at the point of data collection.
Disclosure format	Disclosures must be delivered by mail or electronically. If delivered electronically, information must be portable and in a readily useable format.	Where the request was made by electronic means, and unless otherwise requested by the data subject, the information should be provided in a commonly used electronic form.

Figure 8.2 Customer rights afforded by GDPR and CCPA

As figure 8.2 shows, the CCPA could be seen as a more nuanced version of the GDPR with its deletion rights applicable only to data collected from the consumer, while the GDPR applies to all data. Whether it is data deletion, consent, or other aspects of privacy and data protection, all of these have an impact on what data and how data is exported for DSARs.

In the next subsection, we will look in some detail at how a company must strategically prepare for DSARs.

8.1.2 An overview of the DSAR request fulfillment process

Companies that have grown and prospered due to a process-lite, documentation-sparse, and democratized development approach often struggle with the processes required to scale their DSAR obligations. A checklist can help such companies as well as more mature companies new to the privacy space.

The following key steps cover the DSAR process[5]:

- *Make a record of and validate the DSAR requests*—It is critical for companies to maintain a record of the DSAR requests they receive, when those requests were received, and from whom. Accordingly, organizations must
  - Make a documented record of the DSAR requests you receive.
  - Make sure that the DSAR entries cannot be modified, so that they remain the source of truth.
  - Authenticate the user so that you have confirmation about their identity before you put your team through the process of collecting customer data.

---

[5] Andrews, "DSARs: What You Need to Know." Kokkengada, "6 Keys to Automating the DSAR Process Under CCPA."

Given the frequency of DSAR requests that many companies see, it may be worthwhile to authenticate via automation so that the process can scale.

Customers have options in terms of how they can request a DSAR: email, telephone, or other channels, but companies must also a provide a DSAR form that has the following features:

– It must be embedded into the company website, which could help make it easier for a vast majority of customers to find.

– It must be personalized, especially for companies that serve multiple geographies where DSAR rights are established. This may mean the company needs to manage multiple forms for consumers from different regions.

– Pending signoff from your legal partners, there may need to be options that allow consumers to select from a series of predefined choices. These choices could serve as a template where the backend automation can extract different versions of the data. While it is prudent to give the customers choices via these templates, you would need to make sure each template is compliant with application regulations.

– It must offer a way to spell out the customer request explicitly. Customers may wish to simply request a copy of their data (which they could accomplish by way of a DSAR request) or wish to close their account entirely (which they could accomplish by asking the company to delete their personal information). It is vital that the company understand the nature of the request before making irreversible decisions around user data.

▪ *Identify the user*—DSAR requests could be weaponized by bad actors to take over someone else's account, so you will need to collect enough user data to verify that the user requesting the DSAR is who they say they are. To do so, you will want to use industry-standard identity verification measures like multifactor authentication and others. These measures are critical to protect incoming requests, prevent fraud (like account-takeover scenarios or stealing someone's financial data), and eliminate incoming bots.

▪ *Collect, from internal databases and other data stores, the customer's personal information necessary for the DSAR*—For organizations to be able to respond to DSAR requests, they will need to discover and categorize the data they process and store. As mentioned in previous chapters, this data is often stored in multiple structured and unstructured databases, in-memory databases, and other locations within an organization, and some of this data may have been stored externally as well. Building a catalog of such data on an ongoing basis is critical for DSARs, and the data inventory techniques discussed in chapter 4 are a starting point for such a catalog.

▪ *Map user identities for accurate data collection*—It is possible that a user requesting a DSAR has used multiple identities on your website. For example, they may have used a Google ID as well as a Facebook ID. To collect all the data you need to furnish for a DSAR, you will want to build an identity graph that links all these identities and their data. The process of linking these identities cannot be done scalably on short notice, given the volumes and nature of data companies collect, so I recommend starting this work at an early stage, even before you get DSAR requests.

- *Review and approve the information*—After gathering the necessary information, companies (specifically, their legal and privacy teams) need to review the data and make sure it meets the DSAR requirements germane to the jurisdiction the company is located in without disclosing proprietary information or the personal data of any other user. Retaining this documentation is critical in the event that the DSAR is challenged for accuracy or completeness.

- *Safely deliver the customer information*—The completed DSAR must then be delivered to the consumer using appropriate security techniques. Companies may be liable for fines and penalties if data collected for DSARs is breached or exfiltrated. It is therefore vital that you classify your data based on risk and build in corresponding security protections during DSAR-related export, just as you should during retention and processing within your company.

- *Consider DSAR exceptions*—In addition to requesting access to their data, a customer request for a DSAR may also be accompanied by a request to delete their data. The DSAR rules provide for a range of exceptions and exemptions that businesses need to be aware of and validate the applicability of with their legal teams. This helps balance the individual's desire for privacy and a business's requirement to retain that data.

  The exceptions to erasure in the CCPA include

  a. Information required to complete a transaction.

  b. Security-related data that must be retained in order to detect fraud and prosecute the perpetrators.

  c. Personal information that may need to be retained to identify and fix program errors.

  d. CalECPA (California Electronic Communications Privacy Act) compliance. Businesses don't need to delete certain information when state law enforcement has requested personal information. Companies may need to set up another copy of customer data, stored in a secure database that only select employees can access, so that while the data is not deleted, it is retained under strict access controls.

  e. Personal information collated for the purposes of research in the public interest.

  f. Legal compliance. Any personal information that a business has to keep to satisfy a legal obligation is not subject to consumer deletion requests.

This checklist provides a high-level overview of how the DSAR process would work within a company. For a lot of companies, given the novelty of the privacy space and of DSARs within the privacy space, it will be very helpful to have a deployable and configurable workflow to help receive DSAR requests, track them, and execute them. The next sub-section will help you build such a workflow.

8.2   *Setting up the DSAR process*

This section will present some key steps for building a DSAR workflow. Given the diversity in how companies interact with their users, how they collect data, and how they could extract data for DSARs, I can't present a catch-all workflow, but what we discuss here will provide a start. Since the process of retrieving the data is fairly standard, and the systems where data is stored vary by company, this section will focus on the process of building a DSAR system in detail and then on the system itself at a more strategic level.

8.2.1   *The key steps in creating a DSAR system*

First, we will look at creating a workflow for the DSAR fulfillment process within a company. In the previous section, we looked at the workflow from an overall process standpoint; and in this subsection we will look at key steps in an administrator's interaction with the DSAR system itself.

1. *Accessing the DSAR tooling*—A company's privacy teams could pull user data for DSARs using queries that would run against its databases. However, in order to scale the DSAR capability, it may make sense to build a user interface that provides stakeholders the ability to retrieve backend data for the DSAR.

    Given the nature of the data that a DSAR could retrieve, it is prudent to manage access for such a tool. Access management for the DSAR UI would include the following:

    – Internal users responsible for compiling data for a DSAR should be able to access the DSAR tool by logging in with their work account information.
    – These internal users would have to complete two-factor authentication in order to access the tool.

    It would be prudent to establish more stringent controls if your company operates in a highly regulated environment or contains data that would be considered very sensitive.

2. *Building access control for the DSAR tool*—To prevent internal bad actors from abusing the DSAR system, special access controls may be needed:

    – You could set up controls so that the DSAR request can only be accessed by a limited group of people in the "allow list" for that request.
    – The controls could also be set up so that internal users are only authorized for a defined period of time, such as 30 days, so users would either need to access the DSAR and export the data to the user who requested it, or they would have to re-request that data.

– Additional security measures could be put into place, like rate-limiting the APIs that surface DSAR data and maintaining logs that indicate who accessed the DSAR data.

3. *Requesting the user data for the DSAR*—The internal engineer that retrieves the data for the DSAR will need to provide internal IDs that identify the customer requesting the data in the company's databases or a global identifier (email address, SSN, etc.) by

– Manually entering an identifier into the relevant field for a single user and manually entering a request to pull data for an individual user.

– Generating a DSAR for multiple users by making a "batch request"; you could implement this by enabling users to upload CSV/Google Sheets containing the identifiers (internal IDs, email addresses, etc.) for a group of users. This would help scale the effort rather than retrieving data for one user at a time.

4. *Set date ranges for DSARs*—By the time companies start facing DSAR requests, they will probably have accumulated data going back several years. While many DSAR requests may require the company to furnish all the data they collected from a user, it may also make sense to build capabilities to retrieve data based on a predetermined time frame so that the systems can respond to custom requests and not overwhelm the backend databases.

In such a scenario, the internal user creating the DSAR would be able to choose between two options:

– *Standard DSAR with lifetime timeframe*—The upside of this capability is that you can be reasonably certain that you have all the data for the user, assuming that you have tagged the data correctly.

– *Grouped and timeboxed DSARs*—In this implementation, you would come up with a DSAR where not every data field would cover the full duration of the user's association with your company. You could create groups of data fields, where each group has an adjustable timeframe (30 days, 3 months, 1 year, lifetime). For example, a customer for a retail website may want to get a copy of their entire shopping history, but only for specific products. Having filters set up for timelines or for specific products will help drive custom DSARs. Otherwise, you will need to run burdensome queries, retrieve more data than your customer has requested, and then filter out the specific data your customer requested. This is not just inefficient but will not scale well, given the number of competing queries that may run against the same databases (such as those from data scientists conducting data analysis) and the number of DSARs a company may have to service. This also becomes a problem as engineers grapple with legacy data as well as newly acquired data. Leaders at companies often fail to appreciate how the gradual trickle of accumulated data eventually leads to problems, so having the ability to extract a subset of data is smart engineering as well as a strategically savvy investment.

5. *Check for DSAR request frequency*—You should also configure the DSAR tool or UI or tag the user (using the same techniques we used for the data inventory in chapter 4) if the user has requested a DSAR in the past 12 months. The goal behind this configuration or tagging is to help recognize the user as having requested and obtained a DSAR if the same user requests another DSAR. In such an event, you may want to flag this for the company's legal team to determine whether certain users are attempting to overwhelm the system through weaponized (by frequently requesting, for example) DSARs.

The preceding list is not exhaustive, but it is intended to guide system design and usage for all manner of companies. This may seem basic, but when DSARs come in amid a busy schedule and oversubscribed resources, it helps to have a predictable and repeatable process to satisfy customer expectations without having to divert internal resources to compensate for process inefficiencies.

Next we'll look at maturing your DSAR offering with a dashboard that will help inform and advise the personnel working on DSARs, executives, and legal or audit teams.

8.2.2   Building a DSAR status dashboard

Given the number of DSARs a company may have to handle over time, it may behoove leaders to build a standard status template for how they will measure and track the progress of DSAR requests. This would be helpful for tracking specific DSARs as well as to identify how many requests have just begun, how many are under review, and how many are about ready to be sent back to the customer who requested them.

Table 8.1 provides such a template. This workflow will vary by company, but the intent of the template is to identify key milestones for tracking the progress of the DSAR requests. This template shows specific status values that can be attached to the tickets that track DSAR requests and the triggers that would lead to status changes. As the work proceeds to extract the data, the ticket status must be changed to reflect the state of the work. This is useful both for possible compliance reasons as well as to ensure that the same procedural rigor afforded to ongoing engineering development is made available to privacy projects.

Table 8.1   DSAR status possibilities

Status	Trigger
None	DSAR ticket has been opened but has not been worked on yet.
Verified	Customer has been verified. This step is critical, since it limits spammed requests from automated systems and confirms that the right person did in fact make the request.
Processing	The request has been successfully submitted to the DSAR tool, and the data export is being prepared. The ticket status will also be changed to reflect the progress.

Table 8.1   DSAR status possibilities

Status	Trigger
Ready for legal review	Once the data export file is ready, the privacy team can upload the file with customer data to a user-provided file-sharing system. The "user" in this case is the person who requested the DSAR.
Under review	Before the file containing the DSAR data is shipped to the customer, the privacy team could assign the ticket to the legal team for review.
Legal review complete	Legal reviewer completes the review and updates the ticket to "legal review complete" status. The legal reviewer then re-assigns the ticket to the privacy team.
Exported to data subject	The privacy team sends the export to the user and updates the ticket status to "closed" with a note saying "exported to user."

In order to explain the more linear flow of the DSAR between different teams within the company, a diagram tends to be helpful for cross-functional leaders who need multiple teams to follow a set process. Figure 8.3 helps explain such a flow. While figure 8.3 does not precisely match the status values in table 8.1, the general idea about how the DSAR process proceeds is the same.

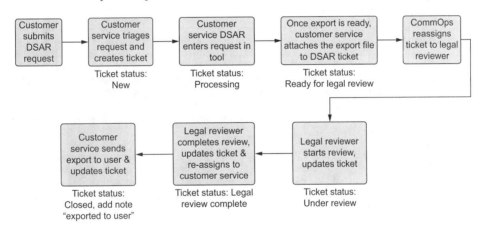

Figure 8.3   DSAR status change workflow

So far, you have seen a high-level flow of how DSAR service requests are handled once a user requests their data. However, the preceding workflows and processes assume the capability and backend logic to extract user data that you have previously tagged during the data inventory. Implementing this backend logic requires making choices to define templates for DSARs and schedule them. The next section will explore some of these hands-on skills so that technical leaders and leaders with other backgrounds who have privacy responsibilities can adapt those skills to suit their needs.

8.3   *DSAR automation, data structures, and data flows*

This section will provide architectural and data-design guidance on how to construct a system to furnish DSARs for users. These details will be most useful for privacy engineers who will create the data structures and scheduling algorithms. It will also be helpful for executives, legal teams, and regulatory leaders to understand some of these details so that they can get a sense of the complexity inherent in retrieving data. I am especially hopeful that teams in marketing, artificial intelligence, and other data analysis take an interest in this section, since they are the chief practitioners in data collection, and the work involved in extracting the data will hopefully give these stakeholders a renewed appreciation in being purposeful about the data they collect.

We'll first break up the DSAR logic into several components.

8.3.1   *DSAR components*

We will now design a basic DSAR automation capability that should serve as a reference for anyone seeking to automate their DSARs. Each company's architecture will vary, so this example is purely for reference and not exact replication.

Table 8.2 provides two key definitions we will need.

Table 8.2   DSAR terminology

Name	Meaning
DSAR template	For companies that have to run DSARs, it will help to create a template that will then drive the queries to fetch the data. Ideally, this template would cover as many use cases as possible. This template will identify, for a user requesting a DSAR, a group of related data tables. It will contain table names, column names for each table, the time period covered by the tables, and a column that lists the identifier for the user for whom the DSAR has been created.
DSAR cuboid	Instead of using a template, you could get a smaller dataset for the user. This dataset will have three dimensions: the user, the number of tables, and the time covered by those tables. Given the reduced three-dimensional nature of this dataset, we will call this dataset a *cuboid*. A cuboid will provide a subset of the data the template would provide for the same DSAR request.

With those definitions in place, let's break up the functionality of the DSAR delivery system into individual modules. Each module will provide specific functionality for whoever at the company extracts the data for DSARs. Building these and then stitching them together will help automate the DSAR process.

The composite DSAR automation service is comprised of five components:

1. *DSAR template module*—This service will enable standard DSARs to be created and provided to users who request a copy of their data. This service will provide two key capabilities:

– *List default DSAR templates*—Companies may need to define a finite number of DSAR templates to support specific contexts and geographies. This module would need to list all such templates so as to enable an administrator to support the template that is most appropriate for a specific user request.

– *Upsert DSAR template*—UPSERT is a DBMS feature that allows a Data Manipulation Language (DML) statement's author to atomically either insert a row, or if the row already exists, update the existing row instead, while safely giving little to no further thought to concurrency. This module should allow a DSAR administrator to modify DSAR templates to accommodate regulatory changes.

2. *DSAR batch request module*—Having selected a template for a specific DSAR, the administrator now needs to execute the template. This module will handle the execution. The module would have the following key capabilities:

– Execute a DSAR for a single user.

– Execute batch DSAR requests, where each batch would include multiple DSARs.

– Resume executing a DSAR request, in the case of data or dependency issues that may take time to fix. This capability would enable the administrator to resume and build on top of previous failed runs, leveraging intermediate results and not having to start again from scratch.

– Get a DSAR request status, which would then be used to update tickets, which you saw earlier.

3. *Combine/harvester*—This module will enable the DSAR administrator to combine and harvest data from HDFS, to group data by user and table, and to upload the data to a storage server for retention or transport to the user who requested the DSAR. The logic for designing this will be discussed shortly.

4. *Data pipeline*—The combine/harvester module will retrieve the data, but you'll also need a way to funnel the data back into HDFS so that it can be provided to the user who requested it. The data pipeline module fulfills that function. Given a table name, a set of selected table columns, a list of user identifiers, and time intervals, the pipeline would retrieve the data for the user and drop the result to HDFS. In a sense, the DSAR data that will be returned is three-dimensional (table/columns * user * time period).

5. *Audit trail*—Companies getting and fulfilling DSAR requests must maintain audit trails for subsequent audits, to verify the correctness of the DSARs themselves, or to ensure that the DSARs were created and accessed legitimately. Therefore, you will need a service that will create metadata for every DSAR request. This service will also publish logs in Kafka that will be consumed by HIVE through Hadoop. In the event of an audit, this library (the combination of the audit trails and logs) will provide core SQL queries to help query the relevant tables and gather information.

Having looked at the elements of an automated DSAR process, we will now proceed to practical implementations, starting with cuboids and moving on to templates.

8.3.2   Cuboids: A subset of DSAR data

As you can probably infer from the preceding components, automating the DSAR process can save resources and time, but DSARs are still fairly data-intensive and time consuming. Creating a template will help, but for many companies, it may be beneficial to start with a smaller dataset for three reasons:

- Many companies may have too many bespoke DSARs, and may end up investing resources in templates that end up not being used.
- It may also be beneficial to run DSARs that cover smaller datasets and to understand the data patterns before investing in the templates.
- Not all DSARs require the full dataset. For a host of reasons, it may make sense to request less than all available data for a user and their DSAR request.

In these scenarios, rather than start at step 1 in the previous 5-step process, it may help to skip the template step and create smaller datasets for DSARs called cuboids. As defined earlier, a cuboid will provide, for a given user, a subset of available tables for a portion of time rather than covering all tables for the entire period of the user's interaction with your platform.

It may be helpful to look at a real-world scenario where a company may benefit from such a limited extraction of data, rather than running a full extraction. Let's assume you run a retail website where customers can buy everything from groceries to pet supplies to furnishings. The website collects customer data in order to recommend products based on past shopping experiences. But then, as the business grows, you decide to acquire new data from third-party vendors to conduct behavior analysis. This data enrichment could help enable recommendations not just based on shopping history but on future behavior (for example, if someone buys weight-management dog food, the website could recommend other products for dogs who need to lose weight, like supplements, dental care for elderly dogs, etc.). You could buy data from websites based on research conducted by others who share similar characteristics to your customers.

Now, let's also assume that a customer has the following user journey:

- The customer adds grain-free food to their shopping cart, makes a purchase, and does no other research.
- Based on available data about the customer on your website, you can infer that the customer belongs to a specific age cohort.
- You also have information on the customer's address, based on where more than 90% of the customer's purchases are shipped.
- Your data analysis research shows that such customers (in that age group who order grain-free dog food and live in that specific ZIP code) also tend to be

yoga aficionados and order yoga mats. This analysis featured data you purchased from a third-party data company.

- You make other recommendations to the user based on information they provide you with, by way of product reviews, complaints, etc.

Now let's assume that the customer sees a product recommendation for yoga mats on your website. The customer is surprised, since they have not browsed any yoga-related products on your website. The customer submits a DSAR in order to find out what data about them in your possession enabled you to serve them an ad about yoga mats.

In this scenario, let's also make the following assumptions:

- Data about the customer's browsing history is stored in 50 tables in the Hive data warehouse.
- Data that you purchase about the customer from third-parties is stored in 30 completely different tables in the data warehouse.
- Data purchased from third parties covers a specific time span, and you can easily identify this data based on your transaction history with the third-party. All you would probably need to do is look at your transactions with this third party and filter out the transactions that fall outside this span.

In this scenario, pending approval from your legal team, you may be able to satisfy the customer's DSAR requirement by providing data only from the 30 tables that cover third-party data.

Too often, companies build DSAR capabilities that by default cover the full sweep of their data collection, since they want to play it safe and too many engineers simply do not understand what data they have and how it applies to the specific DSAR request. The cuboid approach will enable your company to run several parallel DSARs that more closely meet customer needs, without covering the full span of your data for every DSAR and taxing your system in the process.

Let's examine how you can create the three-dimensional cuboid data that the DSAR would contain and publish it to HDFS using the data pipeline. Each DSAR will focus on

- A specific user
- For that user, a specific set of tables
- For that user and corresponding tables, a specific time interval

Instead of running queries for the entire dataset for a specific user's DSAR, you may want to run queries for smaller Cuboids.

Let's assume we want to retrieve a DSAR for 1,000 users (using the same template for all users), with 10 tables for each user and for a period of 1,000 days. To run the queries on a more fragmented basis, one configuration for our cuboid could be trying to get data for 100 users at a time, with 1 table per user, and for a coverage period of 100 days.

Figure 8.4 shows how the cuboid approach can help you scale the DSAR automation process. In the figure, the three dimensions represent the three areas of DSAR coverage. In this specific example, each block in the cuboid represents a user for whom a DSAR request is being processed. Within each square, the vertical line represents the number of tables covered in the DSAR, and the horizontal line covers the time period covered by the DSAR.

The various combinations of red blocks offer some perspective on the coverage tradeoffs involved in processing individual DSARs as part of a larger batch. For example, in the case of some users, you will cover more tables but a shorter time window, and for others you will cover fewer tables but a longer duration.

Each square is a user, with the vertical line representing the number of tables, horizontal line representing the time interval.

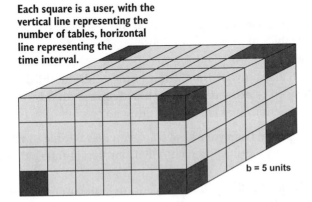

b = 5 units

Figure 8.4   Cuboid approach with DSARs

Having seen how DSARs can be partitioned, we can now look at designing a template for DSARs.

NOTE   Companies will need to make some tradeoffs when they support DSARs. Going the template route will provide repetition and reproducibility, but it may tie your hands in terms of getting all the data for a user. The cuboid approach offers more flexibility and may allow more targeted discovery by selecting how much data, based on the number of tables and the time period, you will export for each user.

8.3.3   DSAR templates

DSAR templates serve two primary purposes. First, they allow an internal administrator to use the template to retrieve the full data (or a subset of data, using the cuboid capabilities), and second, they allow the DSAR data to be written into a template to be sent to the user.

Table 8.3 provides an easy-to-use, hands-on template for creating DSARs.

Table 8.3 DSAR template

Primary Key: id; Partition key: Type

Field	Type	Description
id	User ID	This is a unique identifier for the user for whom the DSAR is being created. This will serve as the primary key.
datasources	Array of tables	A list of tables, columns, and time interval period.
created_by	User ID	This is a unique identifier for the requestor who created the DSAR on behalf of the user(s).
created_at	Date/time	This captures the time when the requester created the DSAR on behalf of the user(s). To maintain consistency, it should be encoded ISO-8601.
updated_by	User ID	This is a unique identifier for the requestor who has updated the DSAR on behalf of the user(s). The value would be the same as for created_by unless the record has been updated.
updated_at	Date/time	Time when the requestor updated the DSAR on behalf of user(s). Encoded ISO-8601. The value is the same as created_at unless the record has been updated.
is_active	Boolean	The default value of this field is false. The value will be true while the UI tool is processing the DSAR request. Once the DSAR is exported, reviewed, and completed, the field will be set back to false.

Listing 8.1 shows a sample query that you could use to create a DSAR template. You would need to update the fields to match your data schema.

Listing 8.1 Query for DSAR template

```
CREATE TYPEDEF type_struct (
    type int32;
);

CREATE TABLE DSARtemplate
(
    id            userID;
    data_attribute_name STRING(100);
    category STRING(100);
    datasources STRING(1000); **
    created_by        userID;
    created_at        DATETIME;
    updated_by        userID;
    updated_at        DATETIME;
    type        type_struct;
    is_active        BOOL;
) PRIMARY KEY ((type), userID);
```

The query should ensure that every template has the same basic construct, and each template can be identified by the userID of the person who created it. You may need to improvise if a user needs to create multiple templates, but that can get prohibitively expensive—there may end up being no limit to the number of templates a company may need to support—so I will assume no more than one DSAR template is created per user.

We will now look at the logic to define the source tables that will map to a given DSAR template.

8.3.4   *Data sources for DSAR templates*

In listing 8.1, you saw that each DSAR template identified specific tables to pull data from. For each table that a DSAR template supports, you will need to identify the fields the table will provide.

Each DSAR request contains a list of tables along with column details, UUID column or index column, and time covered. As stated earlier, you may not pull all the data from a given table, since the cuboid approach allows you to provide a partial dataset. Table 8.4 provides an insight into how you could define data source tables for the DSAR template.

Table 8.4   Providing data sources for DSAR templates

Data source

Field	Type	Description
table_name	string	Name of the table(s) included in the DSAR.
lookbackInDays	integer	Number of days you are looking back, from the day the request is created, to query the data. For example: A value of 365 indicates you are querying 1 year old data for a particular data source.
columns	array<string>	The list of columns to be exported from a table or data source for a DSAR.
userID	string	The userID column, primary key, or the user columns used to identify the user in context.

As you saw in table 8.3, the field that represents the data sources is one part of the DSAR template. How you store that value can be challenging, since the data source field has to specify the number of tables included in the DSAR as well as the columns on a per-table basis. These decisions will then

- Drive the queries that will extract data
- Affect the burden on the databases that will support those queries
- Determine the latency of the queries themselves

As such, you will need to consider the storage mechanism of the data source field carefully. Let's look at some options and their attendant tradeoffs. First, you could store all the data sources as one string in one field:

- This approach is easy to implement, since you can dump all the table and column names into one field.
- Each query for each DSAR (since you could use the same template for multiple customers) will require you to retrieve the list of tables stored in the single field.
- As a company onboards more new tables for DSARs, the length of each request increases, and this will greatly increase the time it takes for any future processing.

The second approach, where we store data sources as a user defined field, allows us to create a more enumerated approach to the data sources that form a part of the DSAR template:

- Each data source is an array of several individual data sources.
- An individual data source is a user-defined struct containing details about the table to be exported, the time period for the DSAR, the columns of the table to be included, and any attendant metadata.
- The columns field would also be defined as an array of strings.

Figure 8.5 illustrates how this could be structured. You could have a cascading set of arrays, and each query could optimize for the source tables and attendant columns per table in a way that makes sense.

This is a better approach than the previous one, where all the tables and all their columns would show up as one field, and that would require either

- A significant level of parsing and experimentation to investigate where all the potential data for the DSAR lives

  or

- A significant delay in getting the DSAR values back, since all the table and column entries in the DataSource field will be queried against

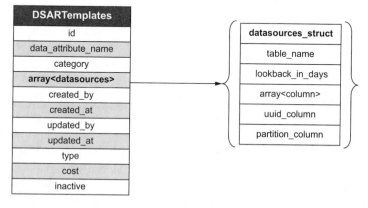

Figure 8.5 Defining data sources in enumerated formats

Before we close out the design of the DSAR system, it is worth examining where and how this data will be stored. You may wish to design a custom database, but it is worth examining a more traditional data store like Hive and evaluating its upsides and downsides, with a view to the performance expectations of such a system.

Hive may well be a suitable storage location for DSARs:

- It's easy and fast to insert data into Hive via Spark, using thousands of executors.
- When you store DSAR data in Hive tables, the output can be stored immediately, thereby enabling deletion once the DSAR request is fulfilled, saving money and avoiding security risks that might result from copies of sensitive data being stored for too long. This is key for leaders to understand, since DSAR data by definition is a copy of data that already exists elsewhere in your system. Therefore, writing, accessing, and then deleting this data expediently is critical.
- Since storage is comparatively cheap in Hive, size will not be a large concern.

It is also worth examining the downsides of Hive as a storage location for DSAR data:

- Inserts and updates can be slow. Hive does not natively support updates, so you will need to use other locations to do that. For each row to be upserted, the storage location will need to find out whether there is an existing row. You would need an internal index to help with such searches. As such, the effectiveness and performance of such searches needs to be considered, especially with data-heavy environments.
- Hive's read capability is slow. Read performance may not be critical for DSARs, since the data is transferred back to the customer in bulk, but you will need to carefully choose partition and bucketing schemes to ensure such queries finish within an expected time limit.

We've looked at the process flow and the architecture of DSAR systems, so let's now focus on some user-facing designs and screens that correspond to the processes and backend designs we have been discussing.

8.4   *Internal-facing screens and dashboards*

Companies can come up with easy-to-use dashboards and screens that will help them track, execute, and design DSARs. This may sound like overkill, and companies may eschew such an approach as overly bureaucratic, but having such designs is critical to scaling the DSAR process and meeting future auditing needs.

Additionally, it will help you logically connect the backend architecture and data decisions you saw in sections 8.2 and 8.3 to a user journey. If you were to buy an off-the-shelf, third-party solution, this combination of backend and frontend alignment is what you'd be paying for, so understanding how the two parts work together is critical to making an informed decision whether to build versus buy a DSAR solution.

The first design we will look at is a dashboard to track the progress of ongoing DSAR requests. Figure 8.6 provides DSAR administrators, privacy specialists, and legal teams with several bits of key information:

- It groups tranches of DSARs in one Request ID, which will enable the company to group all DSARs that correspond to a specific day or a specific lawsuit, etc.
- It indicates the date the specific group of DSARs was requested and when the DSARs are due.
- It provides a status for each group of DSARs.

Program managers and internal risk specialists could build filters that sort the DSAR requests based on any of the aforementioned criteria and could provide executive leadership and auditors with a clear sense of the company's performance and exposure when it comes to DSARs.

Requests

New request -

Request ID	Subjects	Request date	Deadline	Agent	Status
PROJECT-1234	14	12/09/2020	28/09/2020	Vivek Machiranju	Ready for export
PROJECT-1234	14	12/09/2020	28/09/2020	Vivek Machiranju	Ready for review
PROJECT-1234	14	12/09/2020	28/09/2020	Vivek Machiranju	Completed
PROJECT-1234	14	12/09/2020	28/09/2020	Vivek Machiranju	Processing
PROJECT-1234	14	12/09/2020	28/09/2020	Vivek Machiranju	Processing
PROJECT-1234	14	12/09/2020	28/09/2020	Vivek Machiranju	Under review
PROJECT-1234	14	12/09/2020	28/09/2020	Vivek Machiranju	Ready for export
PROJECT-1234	14	12/09/2020	28/09/2020	Vivek Machiranju	Ready for review
PROJECT-1234	14	12/09/2020	28/09/2020	Vivek Machiranju	Processing
PROJECT-1234	14	12/09/2020	28/09/2020	Vivek Machiranju	Ready for export

10 row ⌄

‹ Prev 4 ⌄ of 10 Next ›

Figure 8.6   DSAR status dashboard: for each list of DSARs, you will want a clear status so you know where the work stands and can communicate it to the user clearly.

The next set of screens will focus on supplying the DSAR tool with the user(s) for whom data is to be extracted and exported. For the purpose of this example, let's assume that our system lets employees do this in one of two ways:

- By entering email addresses (or internal identifiers) one at a time, for users who have requested DSARs
- By uploading a spreadsheet containing the email addresses (or internal identifiers) of several users all at once

Figure 8.7 shows how you can construct these options on a single screen so your admin, whether in engineering or legal, can specify how to extract the data.

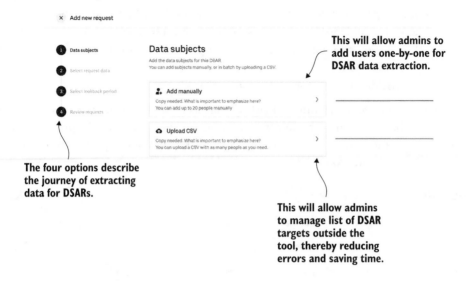

This will allow admins to add users one-by-one for DSAR data extraction.

The four options describe the journey of extracting data for DSARs.

This will allow admins to manage list of DSAR targets outside the tool, thereby reducing errors and saving time.

Figure 8.7   Two options for pulling DSAR data

Figure 8.8 shows what the path would look like for the case of specifying a single user manually.

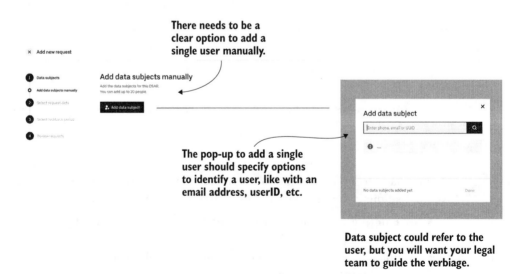

There needs to be a clear option to add a single user manually.

The pop-up to add a single user should specify options to identify a user, like with an email address, userID, etc.

Data subject could refer to the user, but you will want your legal team to guide the verbiage.

Figure 8.8   Option to add users to a DSAR request one at a time

You could then design a screen for selecting and adding matches as they show up, once the user starts entering an email address, as shown in figure 8.9. The matching users start to show up as you enter the email address. This capability assumes that you have the data inventory done, which in turn allows the data to be easily referenceable.

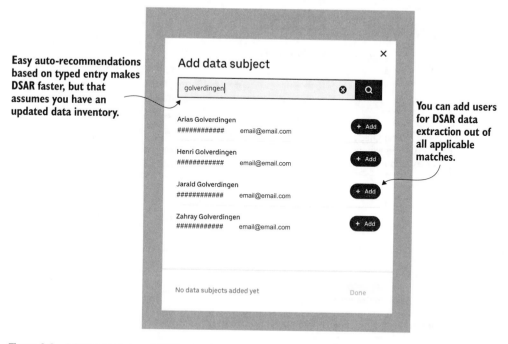

Easy auto-recommendations based on typed entry makes DSAR faster, but that assumes you have an updated data inventory.

You can add users for DSAR data extraction out of all applicable matches.

Figure 8.9 Adding users to a DSAR request one at a time—selection process.

The DSAR process can be error-prone, especially for companies that have millions (or possibly billions) of customers who carry out multiple discrete transactions. Some errors stem from sloppiness, where data from the wrong user is extracted for export. It is vital that there be a verification process after users are selected but before the data is extracted, as shown in figure 8.10.

We can now examine the process for adding users for DSARs via a spreadsheet (rather than one at a time). Figure 8.11 shows what that journey could look like. Note in figure 8.11 that we need to allow for different interstitial pages based on browser type, to upload the spreadsheet of users for whom we need DSARs.

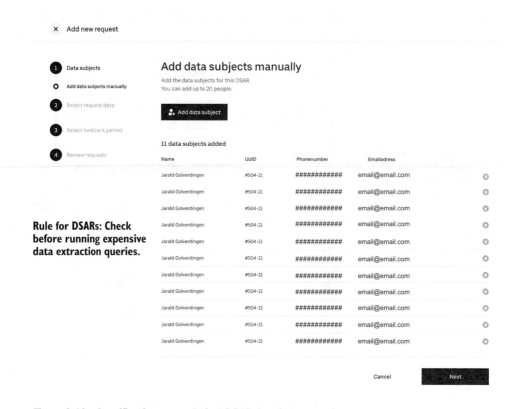

Rule for DSARs: Check before running expensive data extraction queries.

Figure 8.10   A verification screen before DSAR data is extracted

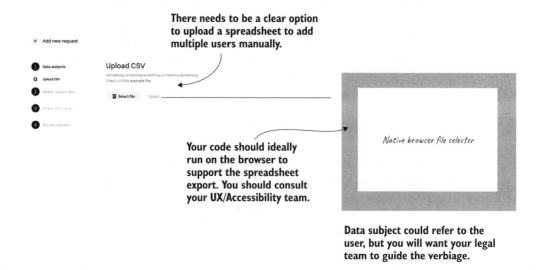

There needs to be a clear option to upload a spreadsheet to add multiple users manually.

Your code should ideally run on the browser to support the spreadsheet export. You should consult your UX/Accessibility team.

Native browser file selector

Data subject could refer to the user, but you will want your legal team to guide the verbiage.

Figure 8.11   Adding users to a DSAR via a spreadsheet

In figure 8.12, you can see that you might end up in the same place as you did (in figure 8.11) when you added users one at a time. You could have an Add feature on the right—or an X feature to remove selections—to perform a final verification check before running expensive DSAR queries against your backend databases.

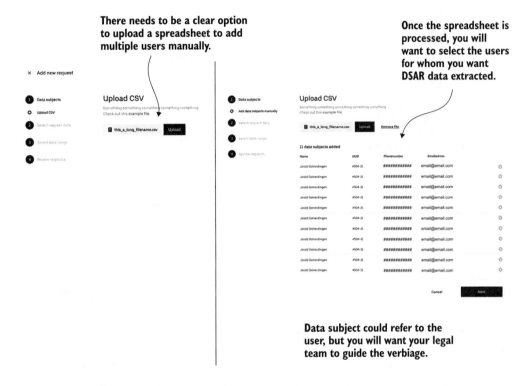

There needs to be a clear option to upload a spreadsheet to add multiple users manually.

Once the spreadsheet is processed, you will want to select the users for whom you want DSAR data extracted.

Data subject could refer to the user, but you will want your legal team to guide the verbiage.

Figure 8.12   Adding users to a DSAR request via spreadsheet—selection process.

Once you have established the users for whom you are requesting DSARs, you can now select

- The tables from which you want user data to populate the DSARs
- The period of time for which you want DSAR data

This is where the visual design aligns with our earlier cuboid approach, whereby you can get a subset of user data for DSARs rather than extracting all the available data, which may be unnecessary and therefore inefficient.

Figure 8.13 shows how you could create a selection screen where the DSAR administrator can select what tables to include in the DSAR. Having selected the tables, you could now select a lookback period to specify how far back in time you want the system to extract data for the DSAR request. I have found that, left to their own devices, DSAR administrators tend to request all the data even when it's not required. It is with that in mind that figure 8.13 includes a nudge, reminding the administrator that a

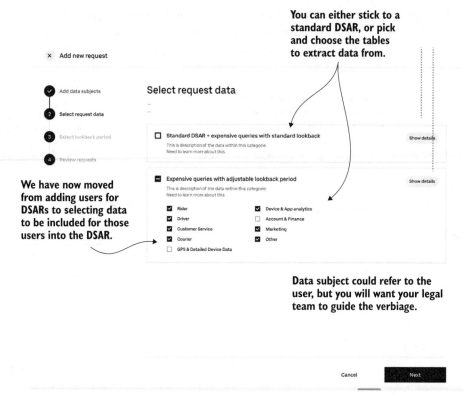

You can either stick to a standard DSAR, or pick and choose the tables to extract data from.

We have now moved from adding users for DSARs to selecting data to be included for those users into the DSAR.

Data subject could refer to the user, but you will want your legal team to guide the verbiage.

Figure 8.13   Selecting tables for a DSAR request

standard DSAR, which includes all the tables and the entire time duration, is more expensive. This may prompt them to select an adjustable lookback period with a subset of tables.

Even so, a DSAR may require all the tables for the entire duration of time. Figure 8.14 shows what such a screen could look like.

The standard DSAR template would obtain all data from all categories with all attributes. This tends to be an expensive set of queries, especially for large data stores with multiple parallel DSAR requests.

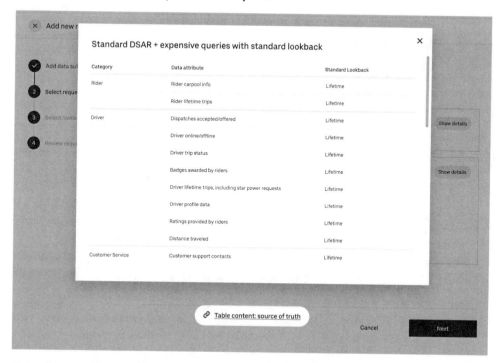

Figure 8.14 Creating a DSAR request for all tables and lifetime duration

The good news for program managers, privacy leaders, and anyone else designing a DSAR solution is that customizing the lookback period is fairly easy as figure 8.15 shows.

This provides you the ability to track and customize the DSAR creation process both at the backend and frontend.

We have now moved from selecting data to be included for users into the DSAR to customizing how much data to include.

Add data subjects

Select request data

3 Select lookback period

4 Review requests

Select lookback period

Category		Lookback period
Rider		Lifetime ⌄
Driver		Lifetime ⌄
Customer Service		Lifetime ⌄
Courier		Lifetime ⌄
Device & App analytics		Lifetime ⌄
Marketing		Lifetime ⌄
Other		Lifetime ⌄

Just as you can pick what categories to include, you can now choose how much data to pick per category based on timeline.

Data subject could refer to the user, but you will want your legal team to guide the verbiage.

Cancel   Next

Figure 8.15 Creating a custom DSAR request for varying durations per table

This chapter has provided the reader an understanding of DSARs as the next generation of privacy commitments. Having thus far focused on privacy governance internally, this chapter leaves readers with an understanding of how to build a process, automation, and presentation of a critical customer-facing privacy capability.

Summary

- DSARs are a key requirement for companies, as privacy regulations empower customers to seek access to the data that companies have about them.
- DSARs can become very onerous if companies do not plan well, but with sound data governance, companies can optimize for accuracy and speed in DSAR request fulfillment.
- Companies can design templates to help ease the DSAR process, and they can provide subsets of data to help scale the process better.
- It is critical to build an internal UI to help teams manage DSAR creation, and also to ensure that the UI aligns with backend data design choices.
- A stable and reliable DSAR process is critical for companies to demonstrate regulatory compliance and to secure customer trust, because sometimes the DSAR is the only tangible evidence a user will see of a company's sound privacy practices.

Part 4

Security, scaling, and staffing

Given the interconnectedness of privacy and security, it is critical that engineers address security gaps that could lead to privacy harm. It is also useful to have set milestones to help measure the maturity of a company's privacy offering. Building on governance and tooling, this part will help create a professional and mature privacy engineering offering.

Chapter 10 will take a technical deep dive into security incidents, their privacy impact, and how to remedy them. This chapter combines privacy and security into a data protection rubric, much like GDPR does.

Chapter 11 helps engineers plan maturity models for their privacy program. As privacy engineering becomes a discipline along the lines of software development, enumerating core capabilities and their completeness is vital. This chapter will provide a framework that engineers are otherwise too oversubscribed to build for themselves.

Building a consent
management platform

9

This chapter covers

- How collecting use consent became critical
- How a consent management platform (CMP) works
- A data model and schema for a consent platform
- Code structures for consent functionality
- Key capabilities that can optimize a CMP
- Integrating a CMP into the business workflow

You have seen so far how engineers, technical program managers, and other leaders in lean and fast-paced businesses can address privacy needs for their business and its customers. These strategies include using security tools to protect privacy, classifying and cataloging data, obfuscating it, and deleting it.

Besides protecting data, being transparent about how and why you collect data is becoming critical for privacy stakeholders and regulators. The former include customers, media, and activists, while the latter range from non-profits to governments. This sentiment led to the codification of Data Subject Access Requests

(DSARs), which we examined in chapter 8. This chapter will dive deep into consent management, which is another privacy expectation that is becoming critical for any company that collects and handles customer data.

The process of collecting user consent to manage customer data, connecting that consent to specific activities, and keeping that consent status updated are all becoming critical for businesses that collect customer data. Simultaneously, the nature of modern business and engineering makes these tasks more complicated. For simplicity, I will refer to all activities of this nature collectively as *consent management* and to the automation used to deal with consent management as a *consent management platform* (CMP).

Consent management is a relatively new area for many businesses, as well as for the engineers who work for these businesses and build the tools that collect customer data. It is also a new area for the customers themselves. For years, the exchange of data and services (that is, customers providing data in exchange for online tools), seemed intuitive. That has changed with laws like the GDPR and CCPA and a more privacy-aware atmosphere.

In order to ensure that businesses that depend on lawfully and transparently collecting and processing customer data have context, this chapter will first explain what consent management means for businesses from a regulatory standpoint. We will then dive deep into the implementation of a CMP. That will require looking into the backend database and relationships as well as some code examples, which when viewed comprehensively will help you understand how to design a platform that can manage user consent.

We will also explore other considerations involved in building CMPs. There are two challenges in this area for many companies. First, small, upcoming, and even some large businesses may not have large privacy, design, and legal teams, but they still need to follow global regulations regarding consent. Second, they need to ensure that customers who use their services consent in higher numbers. Lack of consent hurts the company's ability to use the data they collect. This is why consent management is one of the biggest challenges in the privacy and compliance space today. Privacy engineers need to ensure that they implement consent tools in a way that does not confuse customers, since that could lead to suboptimal customer retention outcomes.

The first section of this chapter will provide some context as to why businesses need to collect consent.

9.1   Why consent management is important

Let's begin by laying out the forcing functions behind consent management for businesses. As you will see shortly, there are regulatory and industry reasons behind consent management, and these forces make this requirement important for businesses to implement and plan for. Accordingly, we will look at the regulatory angle regarding consent and see how consent management has become important to business from a regulatory standpoint. However, in addition to being a regulatory or market-driven requirement, consent management could be a key driver for your business. In section 9.1.3, I will explain to engineers why that is.

9.1.1 Consent management and privacy-related regulation

In the text of the EU's General Data Protection Regulation (GDPR), it states that "The GDPR requires a legal basis for data processing." The following is their list of the legal bases[1]:

1. Processing is necessary to satisfy a contract to which the data subject is a party.
2. You need to process the data to comply with a legal obligation.
3. You need to process the data to save somebody's life.
4. Processing is necessary to perform a task in the public interest or to carry out some official function.
5. You have user consent.
6. You have a legitimate interest to process someone's personal data. This is the most flexible lawful basis, though the "fundamental rights and freedoms of the data subject" always override your interests, especially if it's a child's data.

One easy way to avoid large GDPR fines is to always get permission from your users before using their personal data.[2] Contrary to popular belief, the GDPR does not require businesses to obtain consent from people before using their personal information for business purposes. Rather, consent is one of the six legal bases outlined in Article 6 of the GDPR.[3] Businesses must identify the legal basis for their data processing.

> **NOTE** I want to remind you that this book is not offering legal advice. You should refer to legal counsel to determine the applicability of consent to your business as well as the completeness of any solution you implement.

The idea at work is that if the business collecting data has a legal basis (having user consent being one legal basis), the business is permitted to collect and handle the data.

The GDPR's definition of consent states that "Consent of the data subject means any freely given, specific, informed and unambiguous indication of the data subject's wishes ...." (article 4(11)). While the definition has more detail, engineers and technical program managers must ensure that their consent collection mechanism and the ensuing consent is

---

[1] "What are the GDPR consent requirements?" Complete guide to GDPR compliance, *GDPR*, https://gdpr.eu/gdpr-consent-requirements/.
[2] "What are the GDPR Fines?" Complete guide to GDPR compliance, *GDPR*, https://gdpr.eu/fines/.
[3] "General Data Protection Regulation (GDPR)," Complete guide to GDPR compliance, *GDPR*, http://mng.bz/oaVD.

- *Freely given*—Consent essentially means you have not coerced the data subject into agreeing to let you use their data. For one thing, that means you cannot require consent to data processing as a condition of using the service. They need to be able to say no. The one exception is if you need some piece of data from someone to provide them with your service. For example, you may need their credit card information to process a transaction or their mailing address to ship a product.

- *Specific*—When you collect user data, it should be clear what data processing activities you intend to carry out, granting the user an opportunity to consent to each activity. So if you want to collect a user's email address for marketing purposes and their IP address for website analytics, you must explain each data use case separately, giving data subjects an opportunity to consent to each activity individually. This requirement implies a very granular set of entities in the consent infrastructure so you can track and maintain consent statuses accurately.

- *Informed*—The customer whose data you collect must know your identity, what data processing activities you intend to conduct, the purpose of the data processing, and that they can withdraw their consent at any time. It also means that the request for consent and the explanation of the data processing activities and their purposes must be described in plain language.

- *Unambiguous*—There should be no question about whether the data subject has consented. Unambiguous consent "could include ticking a box when visiting an internet website, choosing technical settings, etc." (GDPR recital 32).

- *Revocable*—A user who has granted consent has the right to withdraw their consent at any time. Moreover, you must make it easy for them to do so. In general, it should be as easy for them to withdraw consent as it was for you to obtain consent.

So far I have leaned heavily on the GDPR, since its seminal nature could heavily influence other regulations that relate to privacy and security. However, each regulation will have variations and customizations, so the alignment between your legal and engineering teams is critical.

Regulations explicitly aimed at consent are not the only reason for sound consent management. Companies routinely get asked to delete customer data and provide customers with a copy of their data by way of DSARs. If you end up furnishing customer data via a DSAR and it turns out you collected data without consent, you may face unwelcome consequences.

In previous chapters, we connected data classification and data inventory as part of a larger governance strategy, and deletion and obfuscation as part of a larger data protection strategy. Similarly, privacy engineers should make DSARs and consent management part of a larger transparency strategy. This will help ensure that the tooling is strategic and maintainable, as well as help secure the resources necessary from an often myopic and skeptical executive leadership who may be unwilling to fund this work until it is too late.

Some of the push for consent management is coming from industry players, as you'll see next.

9.1.2 Consent management and tech industry changes

Besides governments, some tech companies that provide platforms and gateways for data collection have also started requiring consent from users before companies collect their data. For example, Apple recently announced that in order to submit new apps and app updates, app developers need to provide information about some of their app's data collection practices on their product page.[4] And starting with iOS 14.5, iPadOS 14.5, and tvOS 14.5, app developers will be required to ask users for their permission to track them across apps and websites owned by other companies.

This news is critical for several reasons:

- Apple's App Store is a key gateway for app developers and businesses to reach customers.
- There is an entire ecosystem built around online advertising, personalization, and behavioral analytics that depends on tracking users online.
- Even non-pecuniary causes like fraud detection require data collection.

As it stands right now, Apple enables iPhone owners to dig into their settings to disable this type of tracking. Now, instead of forcing users to be proactive about disabling it, Apple will demand that developers ask for permission first or risk suspension or removal from the App Store if they don't comply or try to skirt the rules.

Most of us, by now, are familiar with the online experience where we search and shop for a product but then do not buy it. We then go to a different website where an ad for the same product shows up. Even people who are not tech savvy understand that this connection between activity and advertising is not serendipity. This is the outcome of several automated actions.

First, the original website (or app) collects Apple's unique advertising ID (IDFA). The first app then associates the user's activities to the IDFA and then sends the IDFA to future apps the user visits. One of these future apps has on-screen real estate where it will display ads in exchange for money from advertisers. The IDFA and associated user context enables these apps to serve ads to users that are personalized. The IDFA also helps the apps track the effectiveness of the ads by providing metrics on how long the ad stayed on the screen, whether the user clicked on it, etc. This way, the combination of an ID, user activity data connected to that ID, and the ability to share that ID collectively allow an ads-funded internet to operate.[5]

The new requirement from Apple will require app owners (aka app developers) to seek explicit consent from users before their data is collected, attached to the IDFA, and shared with other entities. This means that everything from data collection to

---

[4] "User Privacy and Data Use," Apple App Store, http://mng.bz/nYxd.

[5] Nick Statt, "Apple's next iOS 14 beta will begin forcing developers to ask for permission to track you," *The Verge*, January 28, 2021, http://mng.bz/voOa.

usage and tracking requires an app owner to have user consent. This is a new challenge for app owners, since they have been conducting these activities with the user's implied consent—the user was opted in by default and had to opt out if they wanted to. That arrangement meant high participation rates for users and more performant ads for publishers and app owners. The new arrangement (where users are opted out and will need to opt in) opens the possibility of lower participation rates and lower revenues.

If app developers were to run afoul of Apple's definitions for tracking and proper bookkeeping, it is unclear what the penalties or remediations will be. For small businesses, getting kicked off the App Store and losing access to the customer base of iOS users would not be a financially desirable outcome.

With that context in place, it will therefore help you to understand Apple's requirements before we design a consent management backend. This will enable engineers to appreciate the granularity and complexity of consent.

As I noted, starting with iOS 14.5, iPadOS 14.5, and tvOS 14.5, app developers will need to receive the user's permission through the AppTrackingTransparency framework to track them or access their device's advertising identifier. Apple explains tracking in the App Store Developer documentation.

> *Tracking refers to the act of linking user or device data collected from an app with user or device data collected from other companies' apps, websites, or offline properties for targeted advertising or advertising measurement purposes. Tracking also refers to sharing user or device data with data brokers.*
>
> *Examples of tracking include, but are not limited to:*
>
> - *Displaying targeted advertisements in an app based on user data collected from apps and websites owned by other companies.*
> - *Sharing device location data or email lists with a data broker.*
> - *Sharing a list of emails, advertising IDs, or other IDs with a third-party advertising network that uses that information to retarget those users in other developers' apps or to find similar users.*
> - *Placing a third-party SDK in your app that combines user data from your app with user data from other developers' apps to target advertising or measure advertising efficiency, even if the app doesn't use the SDK for these purposes. For example, using an analytics SDK that repurposes the data it collects from your app to enable targeted advertising in other developers' apps.[6]*

9.1.3   *Consent management and your business*

For far too many engineers, consent management has been relegated to a tiny—often pre-selected—check box. This approach could be described as the "opt out" mode, where a user is pre-consented and has to proactively opt out by unchecking the box. Before news around privacy became mainstream in the media, and before privacy laws

---

[6] "User Privacy and Data Use," Apple App Store.

started being enforced, this model continued unabated. However, that could be changing.

First, many consumers may now notice a pre-checked box and uncheck it if they do not trust the company or are uncertain about the impact on their privacy. Second, the larger interconnected data ecosystem and governmental regulations may mean that pre-checking this box may not be an option. This means that your brand as a company in how you collect, handle, and protect data may determine the rates at which users choose to consent. To that end, all the technical tooling we have covered in this book so far is critical, but having a solid consent platform is vital as well.

A well-architected backend is critical for consent management so that you can accurately track which disclosure maps to which region and whether a user has accepted it or not. Given that customers can now check what data you collect about them, by way of DSARs, it is critical that your consent management be accurate.

Similarly, a confusing, overly wordy, or misleading frontend can lead to lower acceptance rates. In this scenario, you could have high utilization of services and high levels of engagement on your platform without the data to show for it. That will inhibit your ability to monetize your platform and add user-financed capabilities.

For any engineers who may still be skeptical, the results from a survey that studied Apple's aforementioned change could be helpful. According to a new analysis by Flurry Analytics, only 5% of US daily users with iOS 14.5 have opted in, as of late summer 2021.[7] Flurry Analytics, owned by Verizon Media, is used in more than 1 million mobile apps across 2 billion devices. It's collecting and updating data daily on the app, tracking opt-in rates, looking at the approximately millions of daily mobile active users who have the new operating system so far.

Worldwide opt-in rates are a little higher, the study, reported by Mashable, said.[8] It's sitting at 13% as of the time of writing. Flurry has data on 5.3 million global iOS 14.5 users.

Changes in the consent workflow will almost certainly have measurable downstream knock-on business effects. Companies can, however, address at least part of this challenge with a robust CMP. The next section will help you construct such a CMP and its critical components from the bottom up.

9.2 A consent management platform

A consent management platform (CMP) is an aggregation of capabilities that enables a website or app to

- Inform visitors about the types of data that will be collected from them
- Ask users for consent for specific processing purposes

---

[7] Estelle Laziuk, "iOS 14.5 Opt-in Rate - Daily Updates Since Launch," *Flurry*, May 25, 2021, http://mng.bz/4jvQ; Corinne Reichert, "App tracking has only 5% opt-in rate since iOS 14.5 update, analyst says," *CNET*, May 10, 2021, http://mng.bz/g4YG.

[8] Rachel Kraus, "After Update, Only 4 Percent Of iOS Users In U.S. Let Apps Track Them," *Mashable*, May 10, 2021, http://mng.bz/XWAE.

As stated earlier, CMPs encapsulate a lot of capabilities that have to do with allowing the user to manage their consent to handling that information at the backend. As such, they represent the culmination of privacy features that help you meet compliance requirements and privacy features that help build user trust. More specifically, from a feature standpoint, CMPs allow you to[9]

- Provide the user the opportunity to consent and then manage their data based on whether consent was offered.
- Offer a UI that lets the user consent (example: banners, pop-ups, etc.).
- Ensure that appropriate consent is in place before advertising tags can fire, so as to ensure that any serving of personalized ads is post-consent.[10]
- Link data collected to future DSARs. The data collected from users may need to be exported in a DSAR, so tying it together early on using a CMP is prudent in this climate.

A CMP fulfills the following specific purposes for a business by way of user-facing capabilities:

- Provides consumer notices for collecting and processing personal data.
- Provides consumer options to exercise consent-related privacy preferences at granular levels.
- Captures consumer preferences in an IAB-compliant consent cookie to share with approved partners. This context is vital for companies that derive revenue from or participate in the online advertising ecosystem. The Interactive Advertising Bureau (IAB) is a global business organization for online advertisers and marketers. The IAB Transparency and Consent Framework (TCF) supports publishers, advertisers, and tech vendors in meeting the transparency and user consent requirements established by the GDPR. Your CMP will need to align with the requirements in the IAB's framework.
- Enables a business to access the audit log that tracks user consent.

A CMP has two critical components, a frontend and a backend. The frontend of your CMP will most directly impact your users and customers; that is where they can select what data collection and usage they wish to consent to. The design and user interface of such a CMP will depend upon your business as well as the data you wish to collect, but an example CMP UI is shown in figure 9.1.

The CMP frontend in figure 9.1 explains the various use cases for data collection, ranging from analytics to testing, conversion tracking, marketing, and feedback. In keeping with the guidance from the GDPR, these are all individual toggle options.

---

[9] Joanna Kamińska and Karolina Matuszewska, "Comparison of 9 leading consent management platforms," *Piwik*, November 20, 2020, https://piwik.pro/blog/consent-management-platforms-comparison/.

[10] Tag Inspector, Lucas Long, "Marketing Tags and Pixels – What They Are and How They Work," *Tag Inspector*, May 24, 2016, http://mng.bz/y42e.

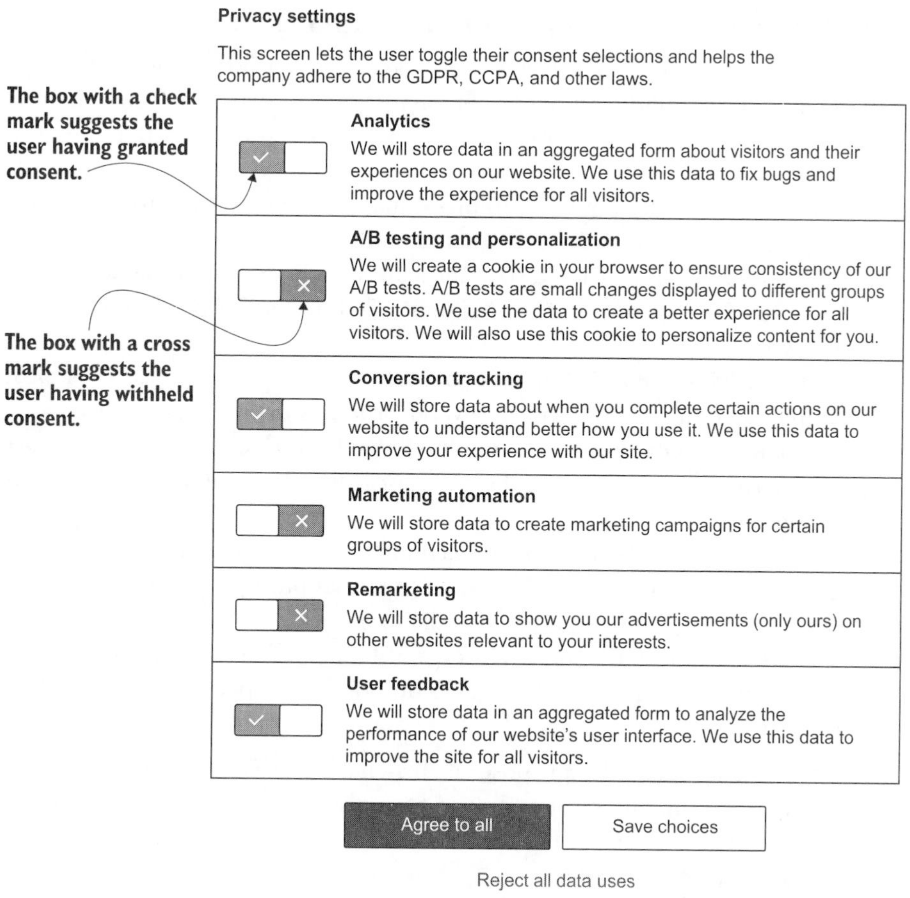

Privacy settings

This screen lets the user toggle their consent selections and helps the company adhere to the GDPR, CCPA, and other laws.

The box with a check mark suggests the user having granted consent.

Analytics

We will store data in an aggregated form about visitors and their experiences on our website. We use this data to fix bugs and improve the experience for all visitors.

A/B testing and personalization

We will create a cookie in your browser to ensure consistency of our A/B tests. A/B tests are small changes displayed to different groups of visitors. We use the data to create a better experience for all visitors. We will also use this cookie to personalize content for you.

The box with a cross mark suggests the user having withheld consent.

Conversion tracking

We will store data about when you complete certain actions on our website to understand better how you use it. We use this data to improve your experience with our site.

Marketing automation

We will store data to create marketing campaigns for certain groups of visitors.

Remarketing

We will store data to show you our advertisements (only ours) on other websites relevant to your interests.

User feedback

We will store data in an aggregated form to analyze the performance of our website's user interface. We use this data to improve the site for all visitors.

Agree to all   Save choices

Reject all data uses

Figure 9.1 A CMP frontend

From an engineering standpoint, building a CMP frontend may be relatively straight-forward; however, when the permissions are tied to multiple locations, devices, and languages, it can make the backend data management very complex. This is why it is vital that engineers build a mental model for consent management, and then work on the backend code.

As previously stated, the various forcing functions for consent—ranging from regulations to industry players to customers—require disciplined bookkeeping. The rest of this chapter will help engineers and technical program managers design such a backend.

As you design a CMP backend, you'll need to consider the data model and the endpoints code. We will first look at the relationships between different entities in the architecture, and then we'll dive into some code to help define the endpoints as well as their public APIs, the request objects, and the response objects.

The next section will define such entities and schemas.

9.3   A data schema model for consent management

For many companies, regardless of size, the idea of having to collect user consent and track it is novel. Building a system that maps consents based on versions and locations and then tracks acceptance rates involves a level of complexity that many companies simply are not prepared for. When such a business gets hit by an audit, a DSAR, or, worse, a lawsuit requiring them to prove that they had consent to collect and process user data, the company may struggle to handle it.

This section will provide a data model for such a consent management backend. The model I will provide will be instructive and not prescriptive, since every company has different needs.

In a real-life scenario, there could be many different types of disclosures. For example, a company could have several products or features, each of which would need to map to a disclosure separately. Global businesses will also have to account for their international presence and create disclosures for several different countries and locations.

In short, to disambiguate as well as update and access consents at scale, you'll need an *entity relationship paradigm* that establishes relationships so that disclosures and consents can be stored meaningfully in a database.

Before I describe this paradigm, it will be helpful to lay out some core concepts. Note that the following are not legal definitions but concepts, to ensure that the code samples make sense:

- *Disclosure*—For the purpose of this chapter, a *disclosure* is any legal document that a company can put forward in a customer-facing interface. This document could be a Terms of Use, Privacy Policy, etc.
- *Locale*—We will define a *locale* as the physical location that a disclosure is mapped to. We will review the granularity for locations, since in some cases you could have a disclosure that is country-specific, while in other cases you could have disclosures germane to a state and city, besides having one for the country that the state and city are located in.

With those concepts in place, let's lay out a paradigm that you can adapt to meet your needs.

9.3.1   The entity relationships that help structure a CMP

Figure 9.2 illustrates relationships that will drive some of the code that you will soon see, as well as database storage models, so that the backend of the consents platform can operate smoothly.

In figure 9.2, a specific feature (or product) sits at the top of the hierarchy. In a typical online experience, a user will use or access several products or features, and they may be required to provide an affirmative consent for those features or products before the company can use the user's data. Therefore, the entire consent workflow begins with a *feature*.

Entity hierarchy

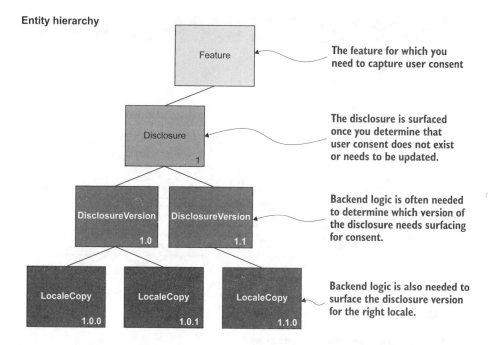

Figure 9.2 Relationships between different entities for storing consent details

Second, for each feature, you will need a *disclosure.* In this simple diagram, a disclosure maps to a feature, but in a real-life scenario you would almost certainly have multiple disclosures per feature. For example, on a pharmacy website, for the shopping feature, you may have a disclosure for privacy as well as for data sharing.

Third, each disclosure may have multiple *versions,* since disclosures are updated based on changes in laws and regulations. The relationship between disclosures and versions of disclosures is one to many.

Similarly, for each version of a disclosure you'd need a *copy for multiple locales* (or countries). As such, the relationship between a disclosure version and locale copy is one to many.

9.3.2 *Entity relationship schemas: A CMP database*

Now that we have relationships between the different entities, it will be helpful to sketch out a database schema. Figure 9.3 provides a sense of how you could define these entities and relationships.

We will be using the hierarchy described in figure 9.3 as our example as we look at the schema relationships.

Disclosure_Version		
UUID	disclosure_version_uuid	🔍
UUID	disclosure_uuid	
String	data_types	
String	business_purpose_name	
Boolean	mandatory_feature_update	
Boolean	is_per_device	
String (enum)	territory_granularity	
Datetime	updated_at	

Locale_Copy		
UUID	locale_copy_uuid	
UUID	disclosure_version_uuid	🔍
UUID	locale_uuid	★
String	rosetta_key	
Datetime	updated_at	★

LocaleTerritory		
UUID	localeUUID	🔍
String	territoryId	i
String	territoryGranularity	

Feature		
UUID	feature_uuid	🔍
UUID	disclosure_uuid	
String	owning_team	
String	feature_name	

User_Consent		
UUID	user_uuid	🔍
UUID	disclosure_uuid	★
UUID	locale_copy_uuid	★
String	device_id	
Int	compliance	
IP	ip_address	
time.Time	Timestamp	★

Figure 9.3   A sample schema for consents

THE FEATURE TABLE

We will now look at these tables one by one and get a sense of how they will be laid out in the database. First, we will look at the Feature table schema, shown in figure 9.4.

TIP   The example in this chapter is illustrative but open to permutations. In this example, you will see instances where capabilities and fields add significant value to the completeness. That said, a minimum viable product (MVP) may not require all the capabilities, especially since companies may need to ship a consents platform under duress. In those instances, engineers can use the following template and pick and choose the fields that make the most sense for their circumstances.

At the top of the hierarchy, the Feature table will contain attributes that define a feature. Each feature will have a team that owns (or maintains) it, and the owning_team field will store that value.

If you are in a smaller or budget-strapped company, or if time is limited, it may be helpful

Feature		
UUID	feature_uuid	🔍
UUID	disclosure_uuid	
String	owning_team	
String	feature_name	

Figure 9.4   Feature table schema

to think of an MVP without an `owning_team`. The upside of this field is that it will tie a feature to whoever owns it, so that you can audit the use of the data corresponding to that feature. This makes tasks like data deletion, encryption, etc. easier, and having this mapping between features and owners is something the future version of you will be glad the present version of you did. That said, if the goal is to collect consent for features to unlock markets or comply with regulations, this is a field that you could drop from the MVP version of your CMP.

Given that team names are (typically) non-numeric, the `owning_team` value will be a string, as will `feature_name`, which would describe the name of the feature. However, each feature will also need fields that are not strings, in that they can be used to uniquely identify the feature and serve as a primary key. The schema for a feature also allows for a `disclosure_uuid` that would uniquely identify a disclosure. Additionally, in most scenarios, each feature will have multiple disclosures (privacy policies, terms of use, marketing disclosures, etc.). You should think of the `disclosure_uuid` as containing many values, so a real-life database representation of a feature could look like the fields shown in table 9.1.

Table 9.1   Feature table sample values

Feature ABCD
feature_uuid ef42c910-981e-11eb-a8b3-0242ac130003
disclosure_uuid 0b712ee2-981f-11eb-a8b3-0242ac130003 16de1fe2-981f-11eb-a8b3-0242ac130003 1f1f0644-981f-11eb-a8b3-0242ac130003
owning_team "Marketing"
feature_name "communication opt-in"

This table shows a feature for the marketing team that would capture email addresses for users, so as to send them email offers. The feature has its own unique `feature_uuid`, but there may be multiple disclosures associated with this feature, so an array of `disclosure_uuid`s are present.

THE DISCLOSURE VERSION TABLE

The second table we will focus on is Disclosure_Version, shown in figure 9.5.

The Disclosure_Version table has the following key fields that should be part of an MVP consent offering:

- `disclosure_version_uuid`—The primary key. While you could, for example, have multiple privacy policy disclosures, you will only have one privacy policy v1. Therefore, this version UUID serves as a primary key.

Disclosure_Version	
UUID	disclosure_version_uuid 🔍
UUID	disclosure_uuid
String	data_types
String	business_purpose_name
Boolean	mandatory_feature_update
Boolean	is_per_device
String (enum)	territory_granularity
Datetime	updated_at

Figure 9.5   Disclosure_Version table schema

- disclosure_uuid—Serves as the UUID for the disclosure. You could have the same disclosure_uuid for multiple versions. We will take a look at an example shortly to explain this point.

The aforementioned fields are critical, since any disclosure needs to have a unique identifier for itself as well as for any versions. However, once you have a stable MVP, you may want to consider other fields like the following:

- business_purpose_names—Strings to store more descriptive information.
- mandatory_feature_update—Allows you to recognize whether or not a user has to accept that disclosure before they can get an updated version of a feature. For example, if an upgraded version of a video game were to contain more violence, you may want the user to accept a fresh liability waiver consent before they can access the updated version. In our example, this value is a Boolean to indicate whether or not acceptance of a disclosure should be made mandatory before the feature that the disclosure gates can be accessed.
- is_per_device—Another Boolean field that refers to whether this version of a disclosure should be mandated per device. This is critical, since different devices may have different versions or incarnations of the disclosure.
- territory_granularity—The geographic coverage for the disclosure version. For example, country, state, etc.
- updated_at—A timestamp that refers to the last time the disclosure version was updated.

Table 9.2 provides an example of what a Disclosure_Version table entry could look like.

Table 9.2   Disclosure_Version table sample values

Disclosure_Version ABCD
disclosure_version_uuid ef42u910-981e-11eb-a8b3-0242ac130003
disclosure_uuid 0b712ee2-981f-11eb-a8b3-0242ac130003
data_types "This disclosure covers "
business_purpose_name "communication opt-in"
mandatory_feature_update true
is_per_device true
Territory_granularity country
updated_at 2020/09/09

THE USER CONSENT TABLE

The third table is the User_Consent table, which contains a history of the user's consent. The schema for User_Consent is shown in figure 9.6.

The User_Consent table would ideally have the following fields as part of an MVP:

- user_uuid—Serves as the primary key. Since this table will contain one record per user, identifying each record with a unique ID for the user is an obvious choice.
- disclosure_uuid—Contains the UUIDs of all disclosures the user has consented to or declined to consent to. You can interpret and implement this design in

User_Consent		
UUID	user_uuid	🔍
UUID	disclosure_uuid	★
UUID	locale_copy_uuid	★
String	device_id	
Int	compliance	
IP	ip_address	
time.Time	Timestamp	★

Figure 9.6   User_Consent table schema

many ways, but here I am imagining a one-to-many mapping of users to disclosures, since one user will encounter several disclosures in web experiences and apps.

- locale_copy_uuid—Contains IDs for the locale-specific copies of a specific disclosure. As with the disclosure_uuid, there will be a mapping between a disclosure_uuid and a locale_copy_uuid. In other words, there could be multiple locale-specific UUIDs per disclosure UUID. You would also have an internal mapping where each user has many disclosures, and each disclosure has multiple locale-specific copies. Creating this data mapping will have ramifications in terms of your ability to store disclosure consents, update them, and provide evidence of consent functionality during audits. It is, therefore, critical that these schemas be built with care.

For a CMP to provide its core functionality, it is vital that you can map the user_uuid to the corresponding disclosure and its locale copy, so the preceding fields are strongly recommended in an MVP. As you build out the system, I recommend adding the following fields as well:

- device_id—This would be an ID associated with the device so as to uniquely identify it, and it would be mapped to locale_copy_uuid, since the device would not be accepting a disclosure, but the locale-specific version of the disclosure.
- compliance—This would be a binary true/false value or 1/0 to indicate whether or not the user accepted the locale-specific disclosure. You may have a situation where a user accepts a locale-specific disclosure with their iPhone but not with their Android device, so you could have multiple rows with device_id and compliance mappings.
- ip_address—This would record the IP address from which the consent was granted by the user, so that if you get audited, you can specify where the user was when they consented.
- time.Time—This would store the time to ensure you have, along with the location, the time when the user accepted the disclosure.

As someone who has been through my fair share of audits, I can tell you that the more granular your consents, the stronger your case that you have indeed captured an informed user consent. I will let you work out a schema for this table depending on your implementation details.

THE LOCALE COPY TABLE

The next table is Locale_Copy, which will hold information about a locale-specific disclosure (see figure 9.7).

The Locale_Copy table has a relatively straightforward schema, and it would have an MVP with the following fields:

Locale_Copy	
UUID	locale_copy_uuid
UUID	disclosure_version_uuid 🔍
UUID	locale_uuid ★
String	rosetta_key
Datetime	updated_at ★

Figure 9.7   Locale_Copy table schema

- `locale_copy_uuid`—The UUID for the locale-specific copy of a specific disclosure. This is a critical ID that will map back to the User_Consent table, since a user may consent to a specific document—a locale-specific copy of a disclosure.
- `disclosure_version_uuid`—An ID for the version of the disclosure. This allows additional granularity to the disclosure, since for each locale-specific disclosure, you could have a series of versions.
- `locale_uuid`—The UUID for each locale. This may not be the most critical mapping, but it will ensure that you have an accurate alignment between a specific disclosure and the locales it covers, as well as for locales and all the disclosures that correspond to those locales. For example, the privacy policy for the EU could cover all the countries in the European Union, while the United States would have several disclosures for several different states.

While not critical for the MVP, it may be vital for a company to provide an audit trail of a disclosure's updates. If that information is not constantly and consistently updated, crawling through logs during troubleshooting can be time-consuming. To avoid that, a field like `updated_at` would contain a timestamp indicating the last time a specific schema was updated.

THE LOCALE TERRITORY TABLE

The final table whose schema we will look at is LocaleTerritory, shown in figure 9.8.

The LocaleTerritory table has three fields that explain the granularity of the location so that a locale-specific disclosure can be mapped to it. The locale itself has a UUID, which serves as the primary key of the record. It maps to the same key in the Locale_Copy table.

LocaleTerritory	
UUID	localeUUID 🔍
String	territoryId i
String	territoryGranularity

Figure 9.8   LocaleTerritory table schema

The other two fields are optional in the MVP but could subsequently be introduced to provide additional detail about the location itself. Engineers implementing this solution could configure `territoryID` to be a numeric ID rather than a string to reduce errors, and could likewise set up codes for `territoryGranularity` to delineate the area the disclosure covers. If the two fields are made optional, it may make sense to add a name field, so that individual entries are better understood.

Part of the reason I have laid out this schema in such granular detail is personal experience. I once advised a company that retained my services after they served an incorrect disclosure to a customer. There was no malfeasance, just sloppy engineering, where the privacy policy for France in French was incorrectly mapped to users in Canada who had set French as their default language on iPhones. The user who got the incorrect policy flagged it to a local privacy authority, and that led to a major investigation into their privacy and data management practices. That investigation was extremely disruptive, delayed their engineering roadmaps, and created an odor of distrust in the court of public opinion. In short, when it comes to consent, as with all things privacy, getting the details right is critical.

Having looked at the data schemas and a comprehensive relationship model, we will next define some of the code, including public APIs as well as the attendant request/response objects.

9.4 Consent code: Objects

In this section, we will look at some Thrift code that will help define the key consent management capabilities we have just talked about. This section will show how you can map key data structures as well as request and response objects to the functionalities that you will need in order to obtain and maintain user consents. Note that while I identified fields that were critical for the MVP in the previous section, the code that follows is for a fuller system. You can customize it to your liking and needs.

> **NOTE** If you are interested in learning more about Thrift and the code you will see in this chapter, see the Thrift tutorial: http://mng.bz/M2W8. The code that follows should be intuitive to many engineers, but the tutorial could help accelerate learning, so I recommend a quick review of the tutorial if you're not acquainted with Thrift.

Let's consider a scenario in which we receive up to three calls (request/response interactions within seconds during the same visit) from a user who connects to our service. Each call will ask a specific question, and the response to that call will drive the next set of actions. Corresponding to the calls, there will be three endpoints that will provide the appropriate responses. In our scenario, let's assume a user connects to a retail website (or app), and based on how an interoperable internet works, data collection will start the moment the user consents. In that sense, the flow would look as follows:

1. Has the user already consented to the current set of applicable disclosures for the user's current locale?
2. Call 1:
   - If yes, let the user proceed and collect the appropriate data.

3. Call 2:
   – If not, surface the current, language- and locale-appropriate version(s) of the disclosures the user will need to consent to.
4. Call 3:
   – Update the consent status for the user for the corresponding current version(s) of the disclosures.

With that context in place, let's define the endpoints and public APIs. The next subsection will dive into the API to get the user's compliance status.

9.4.1 API to check consent status

The first API we will define will help you check if, for a specific disclosure, the user has a positive acceptance. This API may seem trivial—and from an engineering standpoint, it is easier to implement than others we will look at—but engineers and technical leaders should understand its importance to the business.

From a privacy standpoint, you will want to collect consent before you allow the user to access a feature or before you start collecting data. However, your business stakeholders will want to make sure that your privacy checks do not unnecessarily slow down the user flow. From the business standpoint, privacy checks should be expedient, since users get distracted easily, internet connections drop, etc. Therefore, you may need to balance privacy's role in securing user trust against its dependence upon the business for its existence. Remember, if your business fails because the customer bails, even the best privacy program will become surplus to requirements.

The following API should be seen as a critical part of the user consent workflow.

```
/** getCompliance returns a user's compliance status
*/
Compliance getCompliance(
1: GetComplianceStatusRequest getComplianceStatusRequest
) throws (
1: ValidationError validationError,
2: InternalServerError internalServerError,
3: NotFoundError notFoundError
)
```

The preceding API will help fetch the most updated consent status. However, as you have seen in the data model, the mapping between the user and consent for a specific disclosure can be complex. The corresponding objects must account for these nuances.

The request object for this API could be defined as follows:

```
struct GetComplianceStatusRequest {

1: optional UUID userUuid,                 // Requiredness enforced by
➡ service
2: optional UUID disclosureVersionUuid, // Either disclosureVersionUuid or
➡ featureUuid is required
```

```
3: optional string territoryId,          // Requiredness enforced by
⟹ service
5: optional string deviceId,             // Requiredness enforced by
⟹ service
6: optional string language,             // Requiredness enforced by
   service, IETF language code
7: optional UUID featureUuid,            // Either disclosureVersionUuid or
⟹ featureUuid is required
}
```

In the preceding request object, note that it requires the following:

- *A unique identifier for the user (*userUUID*)*—This would be an internal identifier rather than an external identifier like an email address or government identifier.

- *A unique identifier for that specific version of the disclosure*—The preceding code sample requires either a unique identifier for the disclosure or for the corresponding feature. I am assuming that a feature will have just one corresponding disclosure version, assuming all other fields are supplied, but you may make a different decision when you implement your service.

- *A unique identifier for the territory*—Disclosures are location-specific, so the need for a territoryID may seem obvious. However, there is an additional nuance at play here:

  - The user may try to access a feature from a location where the feature should not be available (for example, music videos licensed for a specific country may not be permissible to stream in a different country), so checking for consent against that feature based on location before the feature can be accessed is a way to ensure that the feature-location fidelity can be maintained. That way, if a user from territoryID X tries to consent to a feature meant for territoryID Z, you can block access while retaining the option to store a "Yes" consent, should the feature become available for territoryID X.

  - Note that I am assuming that asking for, and therefore updating, the compliance acceptance is a precondition for accessing a specific feature. This could be a way to manage traffic to a feature or to ensure that compliance status never lags feature access in the case of sensitivity around age, location, etc. To ease the friction, you could make the call to this endpoint in the background, rather than making the user accept the disclosure each time. The "By clicking this box, you accept the terms..." approach that companies often use to secure consent is the visual representation of such design decisions.

- *A* deviceID *field*—This may be critical for companies that need to map consents to a specific device, based on the needs of the jurisdiction.

- *A language code*—The user may access a feature in a specific language, or you may need to present a disclosure in a specific language based on the user's location.

The following code will define the response object:

```
struct Compliance {

 1: optional bool compliant              // Whether the user is compliant
}
```

The response object contains just one field—a Boolean response to whether the user accepted the disclosure or not. I will not be providing code for this Boolean response, since it is straightforward to comprehend.

9.4.2   *API to retrieve disclosures*

Next we'll look at the API for procuring an updated locale-specific disclosure in the event that the user's consent status comes back negative. In that case, the user would need to consent to said disclosure.

The following code shows the public API for the endpoint that supplies the copy for a specific disclosure.

```
/** getLocaleCopy fetches copy, retrievable by LocaleCopyUUID,
➡ DisclosureVersionUUID, or FeatureUUID */

 LocaleCopy getLocaleCopy(
    1: GetLocaleCopyRequest getLocaleCopyRequest
 ) throws (
    1: ValidationError validationError,
    2: InternalServerError internalServerError
    3: NotFoundError notFoundError
 )
```

As with the previous API call to check the compliance status, this API call will correspond to request and response objects. The code also allows for common errors, but otherwise the logic should be straightforward.

The request object for this API could be defined as follows:

```
struct GetLocaleCopyRequest {

    1: optional UUID localeCopyUuid,         // Either localeCopyUuid,
    ➡ disclosureVersionUuid or featureUuid is required

    2: optional UUID disclosureVersionUuid, // Either localeCopyUuid,
    ➡ disclosureVersionUuid or featureUuid is required

    3: optional string territoryId,          // Required unless the
    ➡ disclosureVersion territoryGranularity is GLOBAL

    4: optional string language = "en"              // Requiredness enforced by
    ➡ service, IETF language code,

    5: optional UUID featureUuid,            // Either localeCopyUuid,
    ➡ disclosureVersionUuid or featureUuid is required

}
```

This request to get the text for a specific disclosure requires information very similar to what was required in the previous request object. Just as the mapping in the data model affects how you check the consent status for a specific locale, it will affect how you locate the disclosure for a specific user:

- In the request object, you could map the copy of a specific disclosure to one of three fields: localeCopyUuid, disclosureVersionUuid, or featureUuid. This means you could retrieve a disclosure based on a specific version, a specific locale, a feature, or some combination of all three. I will leave those implementation choices to your judgment.
- The logic behind requiring the user's territory and language remains the same as before, although there is a nuance whereby the consent you surface may depend on the territory or language in the user's account settings or the user's device settings. You can make these choices depending on business factors and regulations.

We can now look at the response object for the API to get the disclosure copy.

```
struct LocaleCopy {

 1: optional UUID localeCopyUuid,
 2: optional UUID disclosureVersionUuid,
 3: optional string territoryId,
 4: optional string copy,
 5: optional string richText,
 6: optional DateTime createdAt,
 7: optional map<string, string> richTextMappingV2,
 8: optional list<DocumentDetails> documents

}
```

This response object for the disclosure retrieval API is fairly unremarkable, but it will still be helpful to look at an example. The request body could look like this:

```
{
  "getLocaleCopyRequest": {
    "disclosureVersionUuid": "2b2b33a7-1426-4a88-acc5-8bbebf50f265",
    "territoryId": "24",
    "language": "en"
  }
}
```

The corresponding response could look like the following:

```
{
  "ok": true,
  "head": {
    "$rpc$-service": "consents-staging"
  },
```

```
    "body": {
      "localeCopyUuid": "18873e56-a28c-4a79-87e7-1d0b55c42212",
      "disclosureVersionUuid": "2b2b33a7-1426-4a88-acc5-8bbebf50f265",
      "territoryId": "24",
      "copy": null,
      "richText": "This is the privacy policy.",
      "createdAt": "2019-09-12 20:51:44.706 +0000 UTC",
  "richTextMappingV2": {
        "BODY": "This is the privacy policy.",
      },
      "documents": null
    },
    "headers": {
      "as": "thrift"
    }
}
```

As you can see, in keeping with the response object, we allow for separate fields for the copy and a rich text version, but these are implementation nuances. The key takeaway is the mapping between disclosureVersionUuid, which was in part of the request, and localeCopyUuid, which is in the response. Mapping these correctly in the data model is critical, which is why we looked at the data models before looking at the code.

This may seem trivial in the context of this book, but I have seen real-life situations where incorrect or poorly scaled mappings led to content decrees simply because a user was provided with the wrong disclosure. If you fail to provide the user with the disclosure that applies to them, any consent you procure could be invalid as well.

This is an example of small decisions made during a company's early growth stages ending up having deleterious effects on their compliance posture. Having to resurface a new disclosure to re-acquire consent poses the risk that the user may not consent the second time around, which would lead to business risk. It is therefore critical to get these mappings right early, and to ensure alignment between these groups:

- The attorneys who draft these disclosures
- The privacy engineers who implement your consent management platform
- The engineering and product teams that use the consent logic

So far, we have covered the endpoints for checking the consent status for a user for a specific disclosure and for retrieving the disclosure. We will now look at the endpoint for updating the user's consent status.

9.4.3   *API to update the consent status for a disclosure*

Now we'll look at the code to update the user's consent status when a fresh or updated disclosure is presented to the user. Here is the API code:

```
UserConsent updateCompliance(

    1: UpdateComplianceRequest userConsentRequest
    ) throws (
```

```
    1: ValidationError validationError,
    2: InternalServerError internalServerError,
    3: NotFoundError notFoundError
)
```

As with previous APIs, we allow for errors.

Next, let's look at the request object for the API.

```
struct UpdateComplianceRequest {

    1: optional UUID userUuid,              // Requiredness enforced by
    ➥ service
    2: optional UUID disclosureVersionUuid, // Either localeCopyUuid or
    ➥ disclosureVersionUuid is required
    3: optional string territoryId,         // Required unless the
    ➥ disclosureVersion territoryGranularity is GLOBAL
    4: optional string deviceId,            // Requiredness enforced by
    ➥ service
    5: optional i32 compliance,             // Requiredness enforced by
    ➥ service
    6: optional UUID localeCopyUuid,        // Either localeCopyUuid or
    ➥ disclosureVersionUuid is required
    7: optional string language,            // Requiredness enforced by
    ➥ service, IETF language code, defaults to "en"
    8. optional string ipAddress
}
```

As with previous code examples, the fields validate specific design requirements:

- userUuid is required. We wish to update the consent status for a specific user, so the primary key is a non-negotiable prerequisite.
- disclosureVersionUuid or localeCopyUuid is required, since we need to record the acceptance for a specific one-to-one mapping. A specific user's consent maps to a specific disclosure.
- territoryId is required, since the disclosure version or the locale copy maps to a specific location, which we derive from the territoryId.
- deviceId is critical, since we may need to maintain an audit trail indicating on which device the user consented. Companies often need to maintain consent on a per-device basis or maintain a record of which device the user consented from.
- compliance is the binary value of the consent for the user (1 for when the user accepts, and 0 for when consent is declined).

The corresponding response object to update the consent could look like the following:

```
struct UserConsent {
/* Below we call out the fields that correspond to the user consent. Every
➥ consent will have the following fields for an update to occur*/
    1: optional UUID userUuid,
    2: optional string deviceId,
```

```
3: optional string ipAddress,
4: optional DateTime timestamp,
5: optional string language,          // IETF language code
6: optional string territoryId,
7: optional UUID disclosureUuid,
8: optional UUID localeCopyUuid,
}
```

By way of explaining the response object, let's look at an example of a specific request and the corresponding response body:

```
{
  "userConsentRequest": {
    "userUuid": "UserUUID",
    "disclosureVersionUuid": "",
    "territoryId": "1",
    "deviceId": null,
    "compliance": 0,
    "ipAddress": "203.0.113.1",
    "localeCopyUuid": "LocaleUUID",
    "language": "en"
  }
}
```

The preceding request, which indicates that consent was not granted, would produce a response that looks like the following:

```
{
  "ok": true,
  "head": {
    "$rpc$-service": "consents"
  },
  "body": {
    "userUuid": "UserUUID",
    "deviceId": "",
    "compliance": 0,
    "ipAddress": "203.0.113.1",
    "timestamp": "2021-04-22 03:21:43.218029116 +0000 UTC",
    "language": "en",
    "territoryId": null,
    "disclosureUuid": "DisclosureUUID",
    "localeCopyUuid": "LocaleUUID"
  },
  "headers": {
    "as": "thrift"
  }
}
```

So far, you have seen how to process disclosures and consents on a one-off basis, but given the scale of modern businesses, it may make sense to process several at the same time. The next subsection will explore how.

9.4.4 *API to process multiple disclosures*

In a real-life scenario, engineers must allow for the fact that they will need to retrieve multiple disclosures at once, rather than retrieving them one by one. They will need to verify or update multiple consent acceptances at once as well. This is where the need to get privacy right has to be balanced against the customer user interface design and business considerations.

If you make the customer accept four consents, one after the other, it not only makes for substandard design, but the customer may get weary, step away from the workflow, and not complete the purchase, for example. In this case, you will have achieved complete privacy at the expense of business success.

Therefore, we will now look at a way to get the consent status for multiple disclosures in one go. That way, in the example we just discussed, you could only surface the disclosures that require acceptance.

The API call for this capability could be as follows:

```
GetComplianceAndCopyForFeaturesResponse getComplianceAndCopyForFeatures (

    1: GetComplianceAndCopyForFeaturesRequest
       getComplianceAndCopyForFeaturesRequest

) throws (
    1: ValidationError validationError
    2: InternalServerError internalServerError
    3: NotFoundError notFoundError

)
```

In the following request object, you will notice the one-to-many mapping for the user to the disclosures. This call is like multiple `getCompliance` calls from section 9.4.1:

```
struct GetComplianceAndCopyForFeaturesRequest {

    1: optional UUID userUuid,
    2: optional list<UUID> featureUuids,
    3: optional string territoryId,
    4: optional string language,
    5: optional string deviceId,
    6: optional map<UUID, UserConsent> userConsentsToSync,
    7: optional string ipAddress
}
```

As with the previous calls, we check for location, language, and device IDs. However, in keeping with our intent to secure compliance status for multiple disclosures, we map the UUID to the `UserConsent` object.

The corresponding response object is as follows:

```
struct GetComplianceAndCopyForFeaturesResponse {

1: optional map<UUID, UserConsent> userConsents  // most recent userConsent
➡ for requested features, keyed by featureUUID
2: optional map<UUID, LocaleCopy> localeCopies  // localeCopy for any
➡ requested features WITHOUT UserConsent recorded

}
```

In order to understand what the practical functionality would look like, let's look at an example. In the following call, we are checking for acceptance for a user with UUID UserUUID for feature IDs covered by d6063933-161d-4134-abce-ff786db70193 and 13eaf184-b855-4a8d-8b84-7ded597f62a9. This approach allows us to check for user acceptance for multiple disclosures that correspond to multiple features.

```
{
  "getComplianceAndCopyForFeaturesRequest": {
    "userUuid": "UserUUID",
    "featureUuids": [
      "d6063933-161d-4134-abce-ff786db70193",
      "13eaf184-b855-4a8d-8b84-7ded597f62a9"
    ],
    "territoryId": "1",
    "language": "en",
    "deviceId": null,
    "userConsentsToSync": {
      "13eaf184-b855-4a8d-8b84-7ded597f62a9": {
        "userUuid": "UserUUID",
        "deviceId": "hailstorm",
        "ipAddress": "203.0.113.1",
        "language": "en",
        "territoryId": null,
        "disclosureUuid": "DisclosureUUID",
        "localeCopyUuid": "LocaleUUID"
      }
    }
  }
}
```

In our use case, a response to the preceding call could be as follows:

```
{
  "ok": true,
  "head": {
    "$rpc$-service": "consents"
  },
  "body": {
    "userConsents": {
      "13eaf184-b855-4a8d-8b84-7ded597f62a9": {
        "userUuid": "UserUUID",
        "deviceId": "hailstorm",
        "compliance": 1,
        "ipAddress": "203.0.113.1",
        "language": "en",
```

```
          "territoryId": null,
          "disclosureUuid": "DisclosureUUID",
          "localeCopyUuid": "LocaleUUID"
        }
      },
      "localeCopies": {
        "d6063933-161d-4134-abce-ff786db70193": {
          "localeCopyUuid": "769b6726-dcf8-41a1-a268-8b48f81cac89",
          "disclosureVersionUuid": "331b724f-a72d-4d47-9490-e034e6e3c442",
          "territoryId": "1",
          "copy": null,
          "richText": "test",
          "createdAt": "2018-12-27 00:30:15.78 +0000 UTC",
          "richTextMapping": {
            "BODY": "This is the first disclosure"
          },
          "documents": null
        },
        "13eaf184-b855-4a8d-8b84-7ded597f62a9": {
          "localeCopyUuid": "a878d99a-d817-43f1-9800-2879c652f1c4",
          "disclosureVersionUuid": "c0e80149-d3e2-440c-8cc3-ed401061122b",
          "territoryId": "1",
          "copy": null,
          "richText": "testing one two three",
          "createdAt": "2018-12-26 23:48:13.383 +0000 UTC",
          "richTextMapping": {
            "BODY": "This is the second disclosure"
          },
          "documents": null
        }
      },
      },
  "headers": {
    "as": "thrift"
  }
}
```

In the preceding response snippet, a few points stand out:

- Our check for disclosure acceptance for features represented by feature IDs d6063933-161d-4134-abce-ff786db70193 and 13eaf184-b855-4a8d-8b84-7ded597f62a9 yielded an acceptance for just one, "13eaf184-b855-4a8d-8b84-7ded597f62a9" as represented by the compliance value of 1. Since the other feature ID did not have an accepted disclosure, we had no values returned.
- Regardless of the disclosure acceptance, we are able to obtain the disclosures that correspond to the feature IDs we supplied.

This provides privacy engineers and business stakeholders with clear choices on how to proceed with data collection and usage based on consent statuses that correspond to multiple disclosures. They could make decisions on how to surface disclosures that had not been accepted yet and possibly make any changes accordingly. This is important, since you can imagine thousands (or even more) calls to the consents service, and even more calls to retrieve updated disclosures.

All of these decisions build on the data model and the Thrift code we have discussed in this chapter. It is therefore critical to have an appropriate data model as a starting point to prevent inconsistent capturing of consent status and audit failures, or worse, creating an impression that consent was disingenuously secured. Many a troubling headline has been born out of bad backend management of consent architectures with hard-to-undo architectural decisions.

Now that you've seen how to use the capabilities around the disclosures and acceptance status, we can look at how you would connect to (or onboard) this consent service.

9.4.5   *API to register with the consents service*

In this section, I will use the term *onboarding* to refer to a microservice or some other capability to utilizing our consents service. We will define the parameters that a service would need to support so as to use our consents capability.

The goal behind building a service is to allow multiple teams at a company to use this service. For example, if you run an online retail company, you would want the iOS, Android, and web teams to use the same service. We will look at how you could shape the code to allow other services to onboard the consents service. The request code is as follows:

```
struct OnboardingRequest {

    1: optional list<string> territoryIDs,
    2: optional TerritoryGranularity territoryGranularity,
    3: optional string owningTeam,
    4: optional string featureName,
    5: optional string businessPurposeName,
    6: optional bool mandatoryFeatureUpdate,
    7: optional bool isPerDevice,


}
```

In the preceding code snippet, a service owner would need to specify the applicability of the disclosure while registering their service with our consents service. They would need to address the following considerations for the disclosures for which they need to use the consents service:

- The territories or locations where the disclosure will apply
- Any information on location granularity—states, countries, regions, etc.
- IDs for the team and features that will map to the disclosure
- The business purpose for the disclosure
- Whether the disclosure will be mandated each time the corresponding feature is updated
- Whether the disclosure is mandated on a per-device basis

You can implement this onboarding/registration capability as you like, but this provides a template that you can adapt.

We have defined several core capabilities for a consents service. In the next subsection we will look at some foundational definitions to complete the service.

9.4.6 *Useful definitions for the consents service*

A significant chunk of the code you have seen thus far assumes certain accepted definitions. For example, you saw that a value of 1 meant that the user had provided consent for a specific disclosure. In this section, I will provide a template for some of these definitions.

The following code snippet creates a definition for the sorts of actions the user might undertake when they are given the chance to offer their consent to a disclosure:

```
enum UserConsentStatus
{
  ACCEPTED = 1
  DEFERRED  = 2
  INVALIDATED = 3
  DECLINED = 0
}
```

This code is fairly self-explanatory. It allocates intuitive values for consent acceptance and other actions the user may take.

We also referenced territory granularity for the locale that a disclosure is tied to. The following code provides a sample template for how you could define granularity.

```
enum TerritoryGranularity {

 CITY = 1001,
 STATE = 1002,
 COUNTRY = 1003,
 GLOBAL = 1004,
}
```

Besides defining those foundational values, it is vital that you throw meaningful errors in the event that the data in the call is not valid, or if there is a server-side error or a problem locating the data for the consent status or disclosures. The three snippets that follow should offer some ideas to build upon.

```
/** Validation Error, thrown when there's an issue with provided data*/

exception ValidationError {
 1: required string code,
 2: required string message
}

/** Internal Server Error -- thrown when unexpected errors occur during
➡ handler execution */
exception InternalServerError {
```

```
 1: required string code,
 2: required string message
}

/** Not Found Error -- thrown when entity is not found in the data store */
exception NotFoundError {
 1: required string code,
 2: required string message
}
```

While these represent a fairly strong list of errors and definitions for a CMP, the next section will help privacy-forward businesses plan for other scenarios as well. Throughout this book, I have aimed to build automation for privacy into the design as early as possible, so this will help smaller and growing companies to be as thorough as possible.

9.5   *Other useful capabilities in a CMP*

This section will identify features you can embed into your CMP to make sure there is no conscious asymmetry between the data you collect and the consent you possess. While the capabilities I will list here do not fall neatly into the frontend or backend buckets, they could still be useful to implement.

For starters, almost every website uses third parties such as pixels or social media platforms, but in many regions, until the user has consented, you cannot load those scripts. You will want your CMP to automatically block and unblock third-party scripts to ensure unsanctioned third parties don't collect user data without consent.

Several countries have visitor consent laws, but each country has its own nuances about what constitutes consent. In order to automatically display and enforce the correct consent requirement based on the geolocation of each website visitor, you will want clear guidelines on how to decipher user location. You could use the information in a user's account settings, but that may not account for unregistered users who still use your website or app. In that case, you may wish to lean on the user's IP address, but that may affect users connecting via a VPN. Regardless of how you decipher a user's location, having clear standards could help ensure your consent is valid.

Fast-growing companies often find themselves surprised when some part of their online infrastructure that's unaccounted for by their CMP nonetheless collects user data. This is especially challenging when the data is collected by a page that isn't searchable. You will want your CMP to be continually aware of hidden pages and keep you in the loop about what is loaded where on your site.

Given that small and even some larger companies do not always have cross-platform visibility, it will help if your CMP is equipped with A/B testing and reporting tools to track, manage, and optimize consumer consent.

Additionally, a CMP can be priceless if it enumerates all triggered cookies, trackers, and technologies by capturing all content executed via pixels, cookies, JavaScript, and API calls, and if it utilizes scenario emulation that mirrors user interactions (privacy preferences, login).

One of the lines of pushback that privacy engineers will get, especially in businesses that run lean and where privacy knowledge is not high, is that consent tooling will slow down the customer flow. Having to check those boxes will annoy customers and lead to missed conversion and cart abandonment issues. While it will help to educate those stakeholders on the cost of not getting consent, implementing a business-friendly consent solution will help. To that end, integrating identity solutions for a frictionless user experience across devices, and tracking user consent across the desktop and mobile web is helpful. This will avoid creating unnecessary speed bumps in the user's navigation path. Continually checking on the user's consent status and having a consent graph akin to the well-known identity graph will balance privacy and business imperatives. Finally, mapping your internal ID to proprietary or partner IDs could help ensure that privacy preferences can easily be recorded and shared as needed with partners.

Another area of consent management is third-party vendors. Business growth often requires, and leads to, vendor relationships. However, as Facebook found out during the Cambridge Analytica affair, data-sharing with third parties can be fraught with risk as far as consent is concerned. Therefore, you will want your CMP to flag privacy vulnerabilities that can lead to data leakage, non-compliance, and reputational risk, and to provide actionable insights to ensure compliance. You will want to consider the following specific capabilities:

- A page-scanning feature to monitor pages and add vendors to your list automatically
- Creating a comprehensive view of unauthorized vendors processing personal data—not just via cookies, but also via local storage and fingerprinting
- Detecting vendors creating fraudulent consent strings and sharing them with the ecosystem

Another useful capability in a CMP can be assigning roles and responsibilities for users who access a CMP. The configuration of the CMP impacts who can edit disclosures, map disclosures to locations, update versions, etc. Therefore, it is important to control who can edit, push, or check internal configurations within the administrative interface. Teams ranging from legal or marketing to IT need different levels of permissions.

A lot of these capabilities are not top of mind for customers who think a CMP is nothing more than a tiny check box on the login screen, so this section bears serious consideration for companies that are fast growing and that use data to fuel that growth.

So far we have looked at the capabilities and automation that drive the CMP. However, a lot of small businesses, and even some large established companies, struggle to build a practical workflow that integrates a CMS into their products. This is often because engineers and attorneys operate in different silos and lack shared context. It helps to have a practical example of the consent logic workflow.

9.6   *Integrating consent management into product workflow*

You have so far seen how consent management logic can be built to manage disclosures, consent collection, and status retrieval. In this section we will look at how a functional CMP can be used in a practical product workflow.

I want you to walk away with a specific use case so that you understand how the data model we reviewed earlier and the code snippets we looked at correspond to a realistic workflow. Privacy is not an abstract altruistic capability; when implemented correctly, it can play a critical role in enabling the business. This example will show you how the relationships between different entities and the capabilities of a CMP support a specific business need. Having an eye on the business need will help you craft a solution that drives business adoption, which in turn will lead to protecting the data privacy of the end user.

In this example, we will assume that our company is to host an online event. We will also assume that in order to collect data from the attendees of the events, we will need their consent. In the previous code examples, consents and disclosures were mapped to locations; similarly in this example, disclosures are mapped to specific events. The attorneys or planners in charge of the event would need to create the disclosures.

For this system, we will have two key microservices: the first, named NET, will govern the creation of events; the second, named NULL, will govern the creation of disclosures and record the user's consent for that disclosure.

To facilitate these capabilities, we will have three APIs:

- The first API will enable NET to send to NULL the parameters germane to the event and retrieve from NULL the relevant disclosure(s).
- The second API will periodically enable NET to send to NULL the RSVPs for the events (the list of attendees) and their corresponding disclosures with consent status.
- The third API will periodically enable NULL to send updated PDFs for disclosures to cloud storage and send corresponding URLs to NET with a mapping to the events affected by those disclosure updates.

In summary, the first two APIs will enable NET to tell NULL about the events and either

- Retrieve disclosures that require acceptance

  or

- Send accepted disclosures

The third API will allow NULL to keep disclosures ready so that when someone uses NET to create an event, they can create an event much faster.

Let's look briefly at each of the steps (I am taking for granted the step where attorneys create disclosures; this workflow starts with the event creation):

1. The creator of the event logs into NET to create the event. They will need to possess some baseline details about the event, including
   - Event name
   - Location
   - Start and end times
2. The creator uses NET to create the event. We'll assume the event is not marked as complete until there is a corresponding disclosure. Events without disclosures are marked as "not complete."
3. When the creator saves the event in NET, the backend logic recognizes the event as one with possible attendees and seeks out a disclosure that those attendees can consent to.
   - In order to get these disclosures, NET sends to NULL the same parameters that the creator provided (event name, location, and start/end times).
   - Any default values that NET creates, like event ID, are also passed to NULL so that NULL can map a location-specific version of a disclosure to that event.
   - NET may also supply NULL additional context on whether it needs a standard off-the-shelf disclosure or a customized one.
4. Before supplying a disclosure to NET, the NULL system will proceed with a workflow for standard or custom disclosures.
   - In the case of a standard disclosure, NULL fills the event details in an event-specific version of the disclosure and sends it to storage—an S3 location in this case. This generates a URL for the disclosure and marks the event as complete.
   - If a standard disclosure does not exist for a specific location, for example, or there is some other system error, the NULL service can send the legal or tech team an email.
   - If the event requires a custom disclosure (one that would need to be created by an attorney for this event), NULL proceeds to save the event but not mark it complete. NULL also generates an email to the legal team asking them to supply a custom disclosure.
5. The system used by the company's lawyers to create disclosures now has a shell disclosure with details about the event filled in. Once the lawyers fill in their details, the custom disclosure can be deemed completed.
6. Upon completion of the custom disclosure, the content management system (CMS) maintained by the legal team would need to notify NULL that an event-specific custom disclosure now exists. (Most companies I have worked for provide legal teams with some sort of CMS, but you may need to implement additional capabilities to enable the CMS to work with APIs as defined in this example.)
7. NULL transfers the newly generated custom disclosure to storage (again, an S3 location in our example) so as to generate a URL for the waiver. This is critical,

since every disclosure—be it standard or custom—could apply to more than one event, so having a URL enables you to link it to relevant events.

8. There is a call from NULL to send the URL of the newly created disclosure to NET, with information about the event the disclosure was created for. This enables NET to retrieve an event that is marked "not complete" for want of a disclosure.

9. The NULL service sends a notification to the creator of the event that the relevant disclosures have now been created and associated with their event. In a real-life scenario, this call may also be made by the NET service. Either way, the creator of the event needs to be notified that they can now proceed forward.

10. Having been notified of the disclosure completion, the event owner publishes the event. In real terms, this means that attendees can start registering for the event and accept the disclosures.

11. When an attendee clicks on the link to view the disclosure, the mapping logic (of the kind we viewed in the code examples earlier in this chapter) kicks in, and a call is made by NET to the storage layer to retrieve the disclosure.

12. The NET service registers the acceptance of the attendee for a disclosure and stores it in a table (using logic similar to what you saw earlier).

13. To maintain an auditable record of disclosure acceptances, the NET service may want to send batch updates to the NULL service so that there is a running list of who has accepted what disclosures. This ongoing inventory will allow companies to demonstrate that they have a way of verifying compliance.

14. This optional step allows attorneys to make edits to disclosures via their CMS, and to notify the NULL service that disclosures it tracks have been updated. The mapping between disclosures and locations, for example, is critical in executing these calls. This use case shows how the data model and code examples build a logical progression and are an irreplaceable part of a CMP that will need to accommodate several possibly concurrent permutations and combinations.

15. Upon being notified of an update to a disclosure, NULL publishes the disclosure update to the storage layer, generating a new version number and a new URL, if applicable.

As this use case shows, it is critical that a CMP must aspire for consistency (data schemas and code should stay in harmony) while also working seamlessly with other services (like the event service), platforms (like the CMS, where the legal team physically stores the disclosures), and a persistence layer (the S3 database).

It is important for privacy engineers to understand this, since many of them become privacy advocates rather than problem solvers and build solutions that are incompatible with existing technical infrastructure as well as business goals. When that happens, you end up with solutions that solve immediate problems (such as getting a new disclosure written and uploaded to launch a critical product) without providing auditable capability (ensuring the consent was recorded for automated retrieval).

Summary

- Consent collection and maintenance are critical for businesses to meet compliance requirements as well as to meet user trust and transparency requirements.
- In addition to governments, industry players are also using consent as a key metric for privacy rights.
- Consent management platforms are key to securing informed and granular consent and maintaining it in an auditable format.
- CMPs can have several key capabilities that enable businesses besides meeting the privacy use case.
- Privacy engineers building CMPs need to focus on how these platforms will play with the existing tech stack and infrastructure.

Closing security vulnerabilities

This chapter covers

- Privacy risks hidden within security risks
- How testing and development efficiencies can increase risk
- Building an enterprise risk model to identify, track, and address privacy risks
- How major privacy and security risks are cumulative and impactful in ways that are hard to predict and plan for
- Using authorization to reduce risk
- Privacy risks hidden in authorization implementations

Privacy controls are complicated for many companies to implement—particularly those with limited budgets or that are small or medium sized. Such organizations often face a critical question: "Where do we get started when it comes to building privacy into our technical infrastructure?" While prioritization questions are perennial, the much harder question to answer is *what to do first*.

In my experience, companies just starting out in the privacy space may find it daunting to start making their data privacy-safe. Practices like data minimization and data governance require significant changes that, in many cases, will affect all levels of the company. Data minimization, for example, requires engineers to collect less data. Implementing it at scale will require changes in culture, processes, and automation that may take time to scale, even as other vulnerabilities (around permissions management, affecting data you already have, for example) may remain unaddressed. Data governance may prove to be even more complicated for companies, since it requires understanding what is being collected, for what purpose, and by whom, and then implementing tools to enforce data privacy.

Companies may wish to consider an approach where they start not with an approach that doesn't focus on the data itself; a more forward-looking approach would entail protecting data privacy by safeguarding the infrastructure and reducing the attack surface. This would mean that the containers holding the data are more secure, thereby making the data itself more secure and setting the stage for the more granular privacy engineering approaches you have seen so far in this book.

Purely from a risk management perspective, it is critical for companies to secure their infrastructure, since any deficiencies in infrastructure open the company to not just external risk but internal risk as well. Applying security tooling to address privacy risks offers a definitive starting point, identifies key vulnerabilities, and helps create a knowledge base around data lineage as well as the organizational muscle necessary for data-driven prioritization. For many engineers and technical leaders, this work alone is both challenging and rewarding.

This chapter will offer insights into key considerations around their infrastructure and how users interact with it. The following are areas to focus on when engineers consider how effectively they can protect their data and systems:

- Attack surface reduction
- Perimeter protection
- Multi-factor authentication
- Mobile security
- Account takeover situations
- Weak password management
- Email compromise via malware and phishing

The preceding list represents a checklist for privacy engineers in that it mixes weaknesses and actions to prevent those weaknesses. It represents a starting point checklist for engineers as they seek to harden their defenses against attacks. These points would need to be mapped to services and endpoints before they are open for use by external customers.

Addressing these makes sense for all kinds of businesses, since that will help protect the company from losing not just customer data but also intellectual property and other business secrets. This chapter, in that way, will help you make progress on technical privacy by improving your security. That is a win both for your business and its customers.

In this chapter, I will walk you through real-life scenarios that demonstrate these vulnerabilities, how they were exploited, their attendant privacy impacts, and how companies can address them.

Note that this chapter will not cover every possible privacy security risk. My goal is to help you build an instinct so that you can use the guidelines and skills presented here as a stepping stone rather than a capstone.

Given that businesses with low margins and fast-moving releases are always stretched thin, they often have to prioritize where to start. I have found that reducing the attack surface is a win-win because expenditures on incident response and data protection could decrease, and the entire exercise tends to help the company become more mature in its overall data management. The first section of this chapter will explore this area in detail.

However, companies will still need to exchange data and context between their online capabilities and customers. This is where the risk of fraudsters and attackers pretending to be customers poses privacy risks. As such, the second section of this chapter will look at a more comprehensive access management regime by way of a deep dive into the famous breach at Target Corporation. I will show you how to account for such vulnerabilities in you own designs.

The third section of this chapter will focus on common access management risk-remediation strategies, since you will need to evolve your security stacks as attackers become more sophisticated.

10.1 Protecting privacy by reducing the attack surface

One of the reasons why data privacy suffers is the profligate spread of data in a company's systems. This is why I am advocating a comprehensive approach to reducing your company's attack surface.

In this section, we will first look at a traditional baseline approach for reducing a company's attack surface for security and privacy. We will then look at reducing the attack surface by examining the connections between data, infrastructure, and product development. Finally, we will build an enterprise risk model that will help you plan for innovation and growth while concurrently managing security and privacy risks.

First, let's look at how fast-moving companies can get started with attack surface management.

10.1.1 Managing the attack surface

Engineers who write customer-facing or customer-impacting tools need to account for attack vectors. Before you even begin to take a privacy-centric view of your security infrastructure, you will want to account for things like

- Vulnerable web components that are not fixed by appropriate software patches.
- Expired certificates and unused ports.
- Unsecured APIs that have access to customer or business data.
- Servers or networks that an attacker can flood with traffic in an attempt to disrupt and overwhelm a service and render it inoperable.

- Malware and phishing attempts that are targeted for maximal impact.
- Ransomware attempts that involve locking down your network and hijacking it.
- Lack of content filtering, due to which employees may visit unsecured websites, which in turn may lead to data loss.
- Lack of web server hardening, which is critical, since these servers often sit at the edge of the network. They could present an entry point for hackers, but proper hardening will ensure that you change default configurations and disable certain services.

Your attack surfaces are all the places where your organization is vulnerable to cyber-threats and attacks. Attack surfaces are not discrete and disconnected gaps that you can remedy. Given how quickly engineers build features, it is imperative that you look at your engineering practices, testing needs, infrastructure relationships, and organizational dependencies as an attack universe.

> **TIP** The typical company focuses on detection and remediation. A forward-looking security and privacy approach instead optimizes for prevention and, therefore, minimizes the need for remediation and its costs.

This is important for engineers and program managers to understand, since the attack surface in modern companies expands from the inside out. While the points in the preceding list are outside-in, the unaccounted for risks emerge from siloed teams making disconnected decisions that end up expanding macro risks. Such decisions create services and processes that impact the data platform and infrastructure. Looking at this holistically is critical to understanding what "reducing the attack surface" means.

To make this point clear, let's look at a specific example. In the next subsection, we will look at how well-intentioned engineering created a privacy risk, and how a good engineering instinct—more robust integration testing—inadvertently expanded the company's attack surface.

10.1.2 *How testing can cause security and privacy risks*

Companies that create customer-facing products and services need to test them extensively throughout the design, development, and deployment process. The goal behind this testing is to ensure that functionality is in line with the design. This process is complex because such products are composed of several smaller microservices; for example, a retail shopping app could have separate services like user experience, recommendations, payments, billing, shipping, and fraud detection. All of these capabilities require individualized or unit testing as well as integration testing. That way, engineers can ensure that the individual capabilities work as expected, and the aggregated product works as expected as well.

Given that different teams work at different cadences and often with varying tech stacks, it is common in many small companies to use real customer data for testing. In some cases, companies copy production data to a separate test server that is used for such testing. Such practices are understandable, since it saves engineering time, subjects the code to a more rigorous test process, and reduces costs. The following benefits flow from such testing:

- You can debug a problem that has only appeared in production.
- You can test the corresponding fix before applying it in production.
- You can allow people (such as customer support) to train on IT systems without the risk of impacting the live system.
- You can allow access to the data for easy end-to-end testing.

USING PRODUCTION DATA IN TEST

I once consulted for a company that followed a similar process for testing. The engineers in that company copied production data to test servers on a weekly basis. This process, called the "weekly refresh of Cassandra clusters," was handled by a tool that handled backup, token management, maintenance, and refreshes. All the Cassandra clusters in the production server were backed up by this process, which involved daily full snapshots and incremental data being copied to S3.

Another tool, using configuration settings, determined which test clusters needed to be refreshed with a copy of the production data, and a Jenkins job kicked off the refresh. The weekly refresh involved the copying of data files from S3 in production to the local instance in the corresponding test servers. The business goal was to enable any and all engineering teams access to production data without the access constraints enforced in production.

Once the refresh was complete on all the nodes, the fast property specifying the cluster name for an app was switched to the new cluster that had been refreshed so that the app teams could start using the new refreshed cluster. Figure 10.1 illustrates the workflow for the weekly refresh. The "CID" in the figure stands for "customer identifier," but it is really a placeholder for any internal identifier that identifies a customer or user.

Given that this book is not about testing, I will pass over the deep technical details in figure 10.1, but it does help to show why using production data in the test server was critical for this company.

- The company moved a significant number of its production accounts to the test server and then had a tool named TestTool identify accounts that could be used for testing. That way, the company could customize, on a weekly basis, which production accounts were to be used for testing.
- In steps 2–5, TestTool played the role of intermediary between the accounts and the services that needed those accounts.
- At the top right, you can see that since multiple services probably used the same accounts in the test servers, the data kept changing. This meant that TestTool had to repeatedly fetch accounts to find the right ones. This caused a lot of swirl, and avoiding that in the production server was key, since that server was used by paying customers.

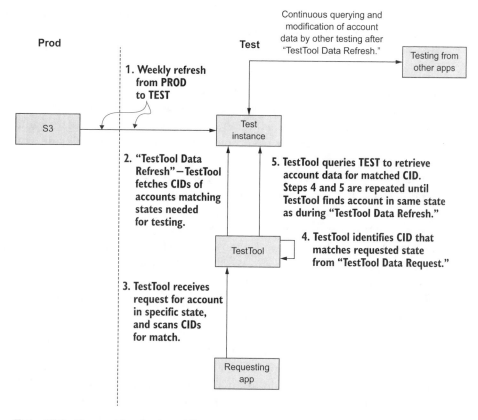

Figure 10.1 The weekly refresh workflow

This process, while technically efficient, caused privacy and security problems.

I was brought in when the company failed an audit primarily because the auditors faulted them for loose access control. The company was surprised at the finding, since they had never considered the privacy and security risks.

FLEXIBLE TESTING BUT WITH AN EXPANDED ATTACK SURFACE

Retaining personally identifiable customer data in more than one location is analogous to creating photocopies of your Social Security card and scattering them throughout your apartment, thereby increasing the probability of unauthorized discovery. Minimizing the number of copies of this data reduces the attack surface.

Retaining sensitive data in a test server could potentially make it harder to meet deletion requirements, since, for example, data could be copied to other locations from a test server. These other locations may not be known or accessible to automated processes that enforce other privacy controls, like anonymization.

Encrypting just the personal data in the test copy was explored as a solution but abandoned. In evaluating the encryption option, it turned out that different services were using their own subsets of fields that they'd need to decrypt in order to run their tests. This would require significant key-management infrastructure and logic to map tests, data, and keys. The cost for this setup was deemed too high, so the company explored an option where they'd continue the weekly refresh with more modest privacy protections.

POTENTIAL MITIGATIONS EXPLORED AND ABANDONED

The company attempted to encrypt just the sensitive fields, like email address, IP address, etc., in the test server. However, the infrastructure team that maintained the test server got many requests from engineers wanting those fields decrypted. The infrastructure team, already stretched thin, dropped this plan as well.

There was another attempt to scramble and obfuscate sensitive data from the production servers before a copy was transferred to the test server. This plan ran into trouble as well.

The weekly refresh was initiated on Thursday and culminated on Sunday so as to make the data available on Monday for testing. There was no easy way to modify the data files directly. The only way to modify or alter the data was to rewrite the mutations for the entire dataset, which would slow down the refresh and affect test schedules. Modifying terabytes of data in Cassandra generally would take weeks and not suit the weekly refresh schedules. In a choice between security and productivity, the latter once again won out.

As a result, the company ended up with real production data in a test server that was accessed by prototype apps; these apps had even more access than the release-ready versions of those apps did in the production server. Additionally, the test apps had other vulnerabilities endemic to fast-moving companies: reused or weak credentials, credentials in the code itself, verbose logging that may include sensitive data, limited security testing, and reduced alerting.

As new engineers joined the company, there was limited training and documentation on the differences between the test and production accounts, even as the use of production data in the test server increased. The testing server remained unprotected while the sensitive data gushing into it rose, and the attendant privacy risks increased.

This practice persisted even as the engineers using it found it suboptimal. For example, engineers who used the test server often had to run multiple queries before they found data that met their needs. This means they often wasted company resources and exposed and logged sensitive data that proved useless.

As you saw in figure 10.1, the data in the test server was constantly changing even as it was being used. This occurred because multiple teams were concurrently using the single copy of production data that sat in the test server. This led to failed tests and repeat attempts.

TAKEAWAY FOR ENGINEERS AND TECHNOLOGISTS

The lesson for engineers and technical program managers is simple: your company is almost certainly accumulating security risks because of habit and inertia. These risks will one day result in privacy harms, and when that occurs, you will be left with a paper trail of half-measures and the realization that enough people were aware of these risks and yet did not address them.

Your company may not have the exact same issues as the ones caused by this weekly refresh, but it may have others that are similar. Even as I helped this specific company migrate away from the weekly refresh, I helped them build a more strategic risk-reduction model.

In the next subsection, we will look at such an approach to strengthening security and improving privacy without alienating engineering stakeholders.

10.1.3 *An enterprise risk model for security and privacy*

Given the dissemination of data across companies, depending on perimeter security and detection capabilities alone is inadequate. Industry consensus is increasingly adopting a zero-trust model that focuses on always verifying the identity of users, devices, and applications within the network while upholding the principle of least privilege. Wide-open access to production data is one of the ways attackers can move laterally and breach a company's network and data.

The process of mapping user identities to access privileges is complex. An assessment of this requirement often covers all layers of a company's platform, including administration tools, hosts, containers, data stores, and even APIs.

Given that, I recommend that companies build a two-pronged strategy that starts with automated detection and closes with an evolving risk management matrix. We will first look at the automated detection approach.

AUTOMATED DETECTION FOR ATTACK SURFACE MANAGEMENT

In the weekly refresh example, you saw examples of security risk embedded into processes and infrastructure. The only way to stay ahead of these risks is the "thermometer and thermostat" approach—measure the status quo, much like a thermometer tells you the temperature, and then take action to alter the status quo, like a thermostat does by helping heat or cool the room. In the data protection analog, you'd want to build automation that detects these risks and proactively mitigates them.

Smaller companies may not have privacy specialists or engineers on their payroll, especially during early growth stages. But they may have invested in IT, application security (AppSec), or security operations (SecOps) specialists. These companies can leverage those specialists to fix security issues and in turn address privacy gaps.

Technical program managers could, for example, work with AppSec and SecOps to build a number of mechanisms to find code repositories that may be storing sensitive materials, such as credentials or private keys. These mechanisms would then feed a workflow that allows program managers to engage the repository owners and both remediate the issue and educate engineers on secure and supported methods for handling secret data. For companies using enterprise cloud services, these mechanisms could be further automated to detect and respond to misconfigurations and anomalous access of cloud storage resources.

Rather than creating multiple locations for sensitive data that, as you have already seen, create inefficiencies and risks, the company could take a different approach. Engineers could build a service for a number of security functions, including the secure storage of secrets, keys, and data. This service could be used to store not just privacy-related data but also business IP, and access would be restricted and audited. This approach would help win business support and funding, since it would be seen as a business enabler rather than a privacy imposition.

One of the reasons the aforementioned company persisted with the weekly refresh was credential management. They could not generate custom credentials for production access and felt like that necessitated data duplication with freer access. I helped drive a program that implemented an AWS capability called IAM roles for EC2 to access AWS resources from their EC2 instances. This service provides dynamic and ephemeral credentials that avoid many of the security issues associated with static and long-lived credentials. That way, the company was able to grant production access for many tests using credentials that were mapped to use cases and timelines.

As you also saw in the weekly refresh use case, the accumulation of risks was gradual, so it is likely that no one person internally could quantify the likelihood and impact of these risks. While we will shortly build a framework for such risk management, engineers and technical leaders at all types of companies may want to keep themselves honest with outside perspectives.

Your AppSec and IT teams should initiate a Bug Bounty program, which would allow external security researchers to responsibly disclose security vulnerabilities in your systems and receive appropriate compensation. Your internal technical leaders would need to work with these researchers to ensure any Bug Bounty reports involving access to personal data are handled appropriately and legally.

These ideas are by no means exhaustive, but they do point to several solutions that will stop the decentralized accumulation of risk by way of unaddressed bad habits. Left unchanged, those risks and habits will create technical debt that, while invisible on the company's balance sheet, will demand repayment. This is why the company will need a strategic approach to security, and an examination of such a strategy is up next.

SECURITY RISK MANAGEMENT IMPLEMENTATION

After addressing the most gaping security issues connected to the weekly refresh, I worked with the aforementioned company to build out their security and privacy apparatus. Before addressing data privacy, I helped them migrate to a more principled and intentional cloud and security infrastructure to scale their service.

The first step was to map services and applications that used data to the AWS accounts that housed the data. When I arrived, the company had dozens of separate AWS accounts to run its services and business. This growth and architecture began organically and was influenced by timing, resource constraints, compliance drivers, and varying business needs. As a result, their architecture was largely devoid of organizing principles, creating operational variances that made it impossible to operate efficiently and effectively.

For example, two distinct services with no shared objectives—payments and user interface personalization—used the same accounts and therefore the same test data. This made it impossible to provide security tailored to the specific service or to meaningfully customize the data itself for testing. The purpose of my initiative was to bring the company's AWS infrastructure in line with best practices for security. In order to achieve this goal, we sought account separation so that there was a tighter mapping between the storage account and service.

This is where the concept of *service residency* (which account a given application should be hosted in) is critical. The configuration of the account has implications on the robustness of the service itself.

If or when your company attempts to design such an architecture, you will notice that decisions about service residency are rarely completely deterministic. That said, I recommend using the following principles when determining the destination account for a given service or resource:

- *Business purpose*—What is the business purpose of the system or resource? This question will help you conduct a sort of service affinity by asking several follow-ups:
  - Is it part of the core service?
  - Is it part of a critical ancillary capability like payment processing, or other support applications like security monitoring, platform infrastructure, or big data processing?
  - Is it part of internally oriented services for internal employees like IT systems or expense management?
- You will want to consider the business purpose to be a primary mechanism for determining service residency.
- *Service and risk affinity*—Related to business purpose is the idea of service and risk affinity. Systems with the same business purpose (such as studio support) are likely to have dependencies on each other and have similar risk profiles and user populations. This affinity helps determine service residency.
- *Compliance requirements*—Is the service within the scope of regulatory compliance such as Payment Card Industry Data Security Standard (PCI) or the Sarbanes Oxley Act of 2002 (SOX)? Regulatory-sensitive systems may have restricted access requirements that are more easily facilitated by a separate and more isolated account environment.
- *Ownership*—Each account will be owned by a single team, even if the account is multi-tenant and the data and applications come from multiple owners. This team is responsible for defining the organizing principles of the applications and systems within their account. As such, the team that owns the account must agree that the service or data should be collocated in their account.
- *Absence of general purpose buckets*—Companies should move away from broad general purpose buckets and instead create buckets for applications and individual teams where appropriate. This will identify bucket and data ownership for teams that utilize S3.

So far, you have seen automation to detect homegrown vulnerabilities and account consolidation as security improvements. Now we will look at implementing parallel tracks to improve security across the board so as to accrue privacy benefits rather than technical debt and risk. For each track, we will enumerate

- *Principle*—The business and security impact of the specific track
- *What and why*—The business justification, so as to define the scope and business case
- *Suboptimal starting point*
- *Potential vulnerabilities*
- *Desired (end) state*
- *Capabilities*

I recommend three tracks that engineers and technical leaders can optimize: service segmentation, defense in depth, and supportability. We'll look at each of those in turn.

SERVICE SEGMENTATION

The implementation details of service segmentation are as follows:

- *Principle*—Limit blast radius and enforce "least privilege" access model.
- *What*—The goal is to limit the impact of critical events, such as security incidents (such as a data breach) or capacity limits (such as API throttling or resource exhaustion). Every service will only be able to access the information and resources that are necessary for its legitimate purpose.
- *Why*—This track will limit the number of avenues that an attacker might have to compromise critical systems or data and therefore reduce the impact of compromise.
- *Suboptimal starting point*—Because of chaotic growth, there is often no particular rationale with respect to the resources grouped within an account. Critical services are mixed in with non-critical services across various domains and with varying levels of security and access requirements (for example, core infrastructure services, OpenConnect control plane, and dashboards may be co-located). Services often have access to unneeded and unrelated resources, services, and data, and application owners are able to add access to arbitrary system resources. All virtual private clouds (VPCs) in the network could be peered with all other VPCs, enabling network connectivity and reachability between any system within the environment and any other system.
- *Potential vulnerabilities*—Because of these gaps, attackers have more straightforward access to valuable services and data given the broad access provided to most systems, and any security issue can rapidly spread beyond the initial compromise vector. For an attacker, getting an initial point of compromise is not as important as you may initially think, given that many companies have many entry points that will provide access to valuable data.

- *Desired (end) state*—The company should strive for a more purposeful account structure, into which applications are deployed based on affinity, ownership, and similar access requirements and configurations. Services should be able to access only the information and resources that are required for their purpose. Using automation and data analysis, the IT leads should strike a balance between delegating administration to improve operational efficiency while maintaining oversight over the infrastructure for security.
- *Capabilities*—The IT team should leverage separate accounts to help define boundaries and provide strong and natural blast-radius isolation. Ensure all services implement appropriate authentication and authorization protocols.

DEFENSE IN DEPTH

The utilization of data in modern services grows as more use cases emerge. This inevitably leads to more touchpoints and vulnerabilities. Therefore, building a defense mechanism that allows for granular risk assessment and remediation is critical.

- *Principle*—Have several layers of security.
- *What*—The company should implement multiple levels of security controls, placed throughout the stack.
- *Why*—The intent is to provide redundancy in the event that a security control fails or a vulnerability is exploited.
- *Suboptimal starting point*—Overly permissive security groups provide network access to services, with few services performing application-level authentication or additional restrictions. Broad peering relationships assume correct and complete functioning of other controls (such as security groups and host firewalls) to restrict network traffic. Some (not all) sensitive data is encrypted at rest and in transit.
- *Potential vulnerabilities*—Since smaller companies do not have a dedicated security or privacy function, one control tends to protect many different services and data stores. As a result, many controls are single points of failure and are overly broad (such as security groups). Compromising systems and data is easier, as fewer controls need to be subverted. Consequently, a data breach or AWS account compromise becomes that much more impactful.
- *Desired (end) state*—Implement multiple levels of security controls throughout the stack. For example, have multiple ways to protect against attacks on data in transit or attacks on endpoints or instances. Higher-level controls (such as TLS, service authentication, and authorization) would be broadly deployed to supplement lower-level controls (such as security groups). As a next layer, pervasive auditing and monitoring controls will facilitate faster and more comprehensive detection of issues early in the attack lifecycle.
- *Capabilities*—There will need to be several developer-focused capabilities at play. First, provide developers with tools and context to make timely decisions for their apps and to manage their security group ecosystem. Implement mutual TLS across the ecosystem to ensure secure communication between services. Implement robust and comprehensive monitoring of AWS activity across the environment.

SUPPORTABILITY

This area refers to an apparatus for across-the-board system visibility, ownership identity, and relationship management. That way, privacy and security experts can preempt attacks and mitigate impact.

- *Principle*—Visibility, ownership, and dependency management.
- *What*—Infrastructure teams should know what is present in the environment and how it operates. Data flows and dependencies should be understood and cataloged, as well as aligned with accepted availability and security patterns. Any special cases or exceptions should be known and documented.
- *Why*—This visibility reduces operational complexity and supports availability, continuity, and disaster recovery activities. This also helps with improved detection to support security and privacy needs.
- *Suboptimal starting point*—As with previous tracks, companies build services in a rush, start data collection to meet innovation needs, and then generate accounts to manage access. As a result, without central oversight, dependency management becomes hard to manage. There is often no authoritative ownership of accounts or of the services, resources, and data within them, and there is limited network and service-to-service visibility. This culminates in circular dependencies or dependencies that are not understood (and that therefore cannot be planned for).
- *Potential vulnerabilities*—This situation is akin to trying to reconstruct a building after an earthquake without images or blueprints. Outages and issues (security and other types) take longer to resolve than they should. Privacy regulations may be unmet because of the lack of data governance and maps. Data governance, discussed elsewhere in this book, will be hampered by this.
- *Desired (end) state*—As the company evolves its data protection stance, all dependencies and data flows need to be understood and aligned with accepted availability and security patterns. This could mean you need to include AWS dependencies, third-party dependencies, native service dependencies, cross-regional dependencies, cross-account dependencies, etc.
- *Capabilities*—Engineers and technical program managers will need to identify (and require) owners for all resources in the infrastructure and ensure that discovery of ownership-related metadata is simple and easy to integrate into solutions and tools. Second, I recommend that companies classify all resources on a number of dimensions, including business purpose, service and risk affinity, and compliance requirements. This classification helps to ensure that engineers dedicated to data protection are able to segment resources, improve their ability to appropriately secure sensitive data or resources critical to core services, and support availability, continuity, and disaster recovery activities. Third, it would be helpful to analyze dependencies within and across accounts (and regions). This insight will help accelerate the process of migrating accounts, and your system architects can take it into account when making decisions around service residency.

Based on all of this legwork, the company will need to define an intentional and deterministic account segmentation strategy and persist with it over time.

In this section, we have looked at reducing and managing the attack surface. Previously we have looked at reducing the company's data footprint by deleting and reducing data risk via anonymization. However, the fact remains that you will have data that, if it's accessed and processed unscrupulously, could lead to privacy harm. It therefore behooves companies to invest in access control at the perimeter level. The next section will dive deep into this concept with practical examples.

10.2 *Protecting privacy by managing perimeter access*

Reducing the attack surface area is critical, as you saw in the last section, since it helps scale data protection. Reducing the attack surface is like not keeping stacks of cash in your house and so reducing your loss in the event of a burglary. However, that does not rule out the need for a strong front door and security system that will prevent an intruder from getting in. For small and medium-sized companies, it is critical to have automated and scalable criteria set up to moderate access to their data and infrastructure.

It is often hard to create a framework for such access management, so I will offer one here: Companies must create contextual access policies that assess risk factors, such as device, network, location, IP address, and other contexts at multiple steps of the authentication process. Each time an access request is mapped to a policy, the company can assess the risk level for that access request. The next step is to pair the risk levels with appropriate access decisions, such as allowing or denying access or prompting for multifactor authentication (MFA).

To explain why such an investment is necessary, we will walk through an example where data security vulnerabilities caused business, security, and privacy risk. This example will serve as a guide for what not to do. After that, we will look at how to do things right.

10.2.1 *The Target breach*

In December 2013, Target released a statement confirming a breach, saying that 40 million credit and debit card accounts may have been impacted between Nov. 27 and Dec. 15, 2013.[1] The type of data stolen—also known as *data track*—allows crooks to create counterfeit cards by encoding the information onto any card with a magnetic stripe. If the thieves were also able to intercept PIN data for debit transactions, they would theoretically be able to reproduce the stolen debit cards and use them to withdraw cash from ATMs.[2] There cannot be a bigger example of a security breach that led to a privacy violation.

---

[1] "Target Confirms Unauthorized Access to Payment Card Data in U.S. Stores," *Target*, December 19, 2013, http://mng.bz/aD4X.

[2] Brian Krebs, "Sources: Target Investigating Data Breach," *Krebs on Security*, December 18, 2013, http://mng.bz/5KY8.

This story exploded in the cybersecurity and privacy circles when blogger Brian Krebs reported that hackers broke into the retailer's network using login credentials stolen from a heating, ventilation, and air conditioning company that did work for Target at a number of locations.[3] Since its initial disclosure, Target has made an argument that many others in its position have made before and since. The company's leadership sent two messages: their data-protection and threat-defense programs were reliable and solid, and the breach occurred because the attack was unprecedented and therefore not easily preventable.

Subsequent analysis painted a different picture. One of the counterpoints came from Jody Brazil, founder and CTO at security vendor FireMon. Brazil suggested that there was nothing especially sophisticated about the breach. This was an issue where Target paid a price for a lack of segmentation of its network, leading to an "all or nothing" approach. Giving Fazio access to do their job meant Target had given them a lot more access than was required, such as to Target's payment systems. This painstaking work of system segmentation allows for more targeted access and more focused protection. Too many companies fail to act on this until it is too late.[4]

For engineering and technical specialists at companies that handle large volumes of sensitive customer data, it may be hard to understand the underlying security vulnerabilities that caused this breach. This is especially the case since the amount of commentary and analysis on security and privacy has exploded, but readers are often more confused about the facts and necessary next steps at the end of the discussion than before.

Therefore, we will look at the workflow of the Target breach so that you can account for these vulnerabilities as you set up your own IT security.[5] Figure 10.2 shows how the Target breach was incremental, methodical, and, in the end, consequential.

As you can see in figure 10.2, the attackers were purposeful in their research and penetration of Target's systems, compromising applications within the systems and then stealing the data by first accessing it and then expanding their privileges. While the subsections that follow will offer more detail, the key point for engineers at smaller and fast-moving companies to understand is that ignoring or underestimating minor risks

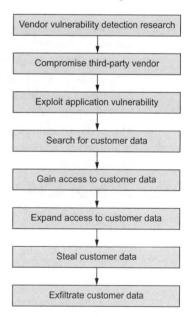

Figure 10.2   The sequence of the Target breach

---

[3] Jaikumar Vijayan, "Target breach happened because of a basic network segmentation error," *Computerworld*, February 6, 2014, http://mng.bz/6ZGp.

[4] Ibid.

[5] Thor Olavsrud, "11 steps attackers took to crack Target," *CSO*, September 2, 2014, http://mng.bz/oaVy.

can prove to be fatal. As we dive into the details, you will see that the tale of Target was one of missed opportunities and catastrophic outcomes.

RECON TO DETECT NETWORK VULNERABILITIES

As you have seen elsewhere in the book, data about you that is available elsewhere can lead to security and privacy vulnerabilities. The same is true for network infrastructure. In the Target breach case, research suggests that attackers may have gleaned information about Target's infrastructure in preparation for the breach. For example, according to researcher Teri Radichel, there was a detailed case study on Microsoft's website that described how Target used key Microsoft capabilities: virtualization software and centralized name resolution. The Microsoft documentation also described how Target used the Microsoft System Center Configuration Manager to deploy security patches and system updates. Microsoft's case study also described Target's technical infrastructure, and the description of the point of sale system may have been of significant value to the attackers.[6]

Thus, even before interacting with the Target infrastructure, the hackers had a blueprint of the attack surface. Engineers configuring your company's network access may wish to account for such freely available information.

As is often the case with modern distributed systems with different owners, it was not too difficult to unearth links between Target's infrastructure and its vendors. Krebs pointed out that Target's Supplier Portal was freely available on the web. The portal was aimed at educating new and existing vendors and partners on how to exchange information and conduct transactions with Target. That portal also contained a page that listed HVAC and refrigeration companies.[7]

The lesson here is that engineers who care about privacy and security must look at their vendors as a potential risk vector as well.

COMPROMISING THE THIRD-PARTY VENDOR

The attackers started with stealing the credentials of Target's HVAC vendor, Fazio Mechanical Services. According to KrebsonSecurity, which first broke the story of the breach, the attackers infected Fazio with general-purpose malware known as Citadel through an email phishing campaign.[8]

With Citadel in place, the attackers waited until the malware offered Fazio Mechanical's login credentials.[9] The attackers then used the stolen credentials to gain access to Target-hosted web services dedicated to vendors.

Companies with limited budgets or ones that lack targeted expertise are often tempted to use third-party vendors for specialized tasks, and that thinking may have

---

[6] Teri Radichel, "Case Study: Critical Controls that Could Have Prevented Target Breach" (SANS, 2021), https://www.sans.org/white-papers/35412/.

[7] Michael Kassner, "Anatomy of the Target data breach: Missed opportunities and lessons learned," *ZDNet*, February 2, 2015, http://mng.bz/nYxV.

[8] Brian Krebs, "Email Attack on Vendor Set Up Breach at Target," *Krebs on Security*, February 12, 2014, http://mng.bz/voOm.

[9] Kassner, "Anatomy of the Target data breach."

proved to be fatal in this case. Many such vendors themselves operate lean and hence take a dim view of security investments, doing the bare minimum in order to cut costs.

Fazio's leaders said the company did not perform remote monitoring or control of heating, cooling, or refrigeration systems for Target. In their telling, Fazio's data connection with Target was exclusively for electronic billing, contract submission, and project management.

The attackers now had access to an internal web application hosted on Target's internal network, but the application did not allow for arbitrary command execution, a necessity to compromise the machine.[10] Because of such design decisions, it is often assumed that access to a single application limits the privacy and security exposure. Target found out otherwise. The lesson for engineers and program managers is to vet third-party vendors that have access to your network.

EXPLOITING A WEB APPLICATION VULNERABILITY

Small-time and limited-purpose vendors often offer capabilities to upload documents. Either because of cost or gullibility, the vendors assume that this upload capability will only be used for documents and not malicious files. As such, no security checks are performed to ensure that executable files are not uploaded by outside bad actors.

The attackers used this gap to upload a PHP file, of the kind that is used for running scripts within web applications. The malicious script was probably a "web shell," a web-based backdoor that allowed the attackers to upload files and execute arbitrary operating system commands. The attackers made the file look like a popular PHP component to make it resemble a legitimate file and hide it in plain sight.

At this point, the attackers were inside the gates and had the ability to run scripts. However, what they still needed was the location of the customer data. There is a security and privacy lesson here for companies: what you permit into your ecosystem can determine what ends up leaving your infrastructure. Continuous monitoring of new entrants and their capabilities is critical.

SEARCHING FOR CUSTOMER DATA

It is at this stage that the security vulnerability became a privacy impact. The attackers, having penetrated the network periphery, needed to learn where the customer data was located before their intrusion was detected.

According to Thor Olavsrud, writing for CIO Online, the key vector the attackers homed in on was Target's Active Directory. The directory served as a data repository for users, members, and services. Using the standard LDAP protocol, the attackers were able to query Active Directory, and they may not have needed to know which service did what or served whom. It was quite possible that they searched for services matching the value "MSSQLSvc," and the names of the services helped identify the ones they wished to exploit, like the ones handling billing. Having obtained the

---

[10]Thor Olavsrud, "11 steps attackers took to crack Target," *CSO*, September 2, 2014, http://mng.bz/4jv5.

names and deciphered the functions of the target services, a simple querying of the DNS server was all it probably took to get their IP addresses.[11]

This is where behavioral analytics can help: if someone were trying to access your services for legitimate purposes, they should not need to retrieve all services. Having security monitoring helps protect privacy as well; engineers need to invest in algorithms that detect fraudulent and anomalous behavior when outsiders and insiders try to access sensitive data.

GAINING AND MAINTAINING ACCESS TO CUSTOMER DATA

Having identified the location of sensitive data, the attackers used a technique called Pass-the-Hash (PtH) to gain access to a hash token that would allow them to impersonate the Active Directory administrator. With PtH, a bad actor doesn't need to decrypt the hash to obtain a plain text password. PtH attacks exploit the authentication protocol, as the password hash remains static for every session until the password is rotated (until the administrator changes the password). Attackers commonly obtain hashes by scraping a system's active memory and other techniques.[12]

Fraudulently obtaining administrator access is ineffective if the administrator changes their password. Anticipating that possibility, the attackers used their stolen privileges to create a new account and add it to the Domain Admins group. This gave the newly created account the privileges the attackers required while eliminating the possibility that someone else would change the password.[13]

The lesson for engineers is clear: there needs to be more layered and continuous access control and authentication for anyone seeking a way into your network. Adding more friction to the intake process is worth it, given the risks to customer privacy should a bad actor find their way in and identify where your crown jewels are located.

PROPAGATING ACCESS TO CUSTOMER DATA

At this point, the attackers needed to bypass firewalls and other network-based security solutions that limited direct access to their targets, and then run remote processes on various machines in the chain toward their targets.

The attackers used their credentials in conjunction with the Microsoft PSExec utility (a telnet-replacement for executing processes on other systems) and the Windows internal Remote Desktop (RDP) client. Both tools use Active Directory to authenticate and authorize the user, which means Active Directory is aware of this activity if anyone is looking for it.

Once the attackers had access to the targeted systems, they used the Microsoft Orchestrator management solution to gain persistent access, which allowed them to remotely execute arbitrary code on the compromised servers.[14]

---

[11]Olavsrud, "11 steps attackers took to crack Target."

[12]"Pass-the-Hash (PtH) Attack," *BeyondTrust*, http://mng.bz/QWg1.

[13]Olavsrud, "11 steps attackers took to crack Target."

[14]Olavsrud, "11 steps attackers took to crack Target," page 2, http://mng.bz/4jv5.

At the risk of being repetitive: this additional vulnerability shows yet again how critical it is to ensure your monitoring capabilities are continuous and cover third parties, especially given Fazio's limited view of their data protection obligations. As stated before, Fazio's leaders said the company did not perform remote monitoring or control of heating, cooling, or refrigeration systems for Target. In their telling, Fazio's data connection with Target was exclusively for electronic billing, contract submission, and project management.

STEALING CUSTOMER PERSONAL DATA AND CREDIT CARD DATA

Section 3.2 of the PCI-DSS standard states: "Do not store sensitive authentication data after authorization (even if encrypted). If sensitive authentication data is received, render all data unrecoverable upon completion of the authorization process."[15] Since Target was PCI-compliant at the time of the breach, the databases did not store any credit-card-specific data. So while the attackers had managed to access the PII of 70 million Target customers, it did not have access to their credit cards.

However, as discussed in the "Searching for Customer Data" and "Gaining and Maintaining Access to Customer Data" sections previously, the attackers had obtained access to Target's point-of-sale machines. They also had the ability to execute programs remotely on these machines. They used these combined capabilities to install malware that they then used to scan the memory of infected machines and save any credit cards found to a local file.

The lesson for engineers here is that smaller security vulnerabilities that are not top of mind often accumulate to pose serious privacy threats, and they can lead to the exfiltration of sensitive customer data.

Researcher Tal Be'ery, whose work I have cited throughout this discussion, states that "The initial penetration point is not the story, because eventually you have to assume you're going to get breached.... You cannot assume otherwise. You have to be prepared and have an incident response plan for what to do when you are breached. The real problem arises when malware is able to enable an attacker to penetrate deeper into the network."[16]

SENDING THE STOLEN DATA OUTSIDE THE COMPANY'S NETWORK

Once the malware obtained the credit card data, it created a remote fileshare on an FTP-enabled machine using a Windows command and the Domain Admin credentials. It would periodically copy its local file to the remote share. These activities would have been authorized against Activity Directory, making it aware of the activity. Had there been any monitoring of data leaving the company, all previous mistakes notwithstanding, the company and its partners may have been able to prevent the loss of this data.

Thor Olavsrud, whose analysis this section has cited (published by CIO and later by CSO), provides several hands-on techniques for engineers wishing to protect their

---

[15]Olavsrud, "11 steps attackers took to crack Target," page 2.
[16]Olavsrud, "11 steps attackers took to crack Target," page 2.

company's privacy and security. I have drawn from and added to these techniques, but you may also wish to look up Olavsrud's original article.[17]

- Create a more robust access controls regime. This is where privacy and security engineers need to work with data scientists by categorizing data access requests. You will need to define "normal" and "expected" access requests and block the ones that deviate from that norm.

- Given the rapidity with which access can result in exfiltration, multifactor authentication (MFA) is a critical "friction point" for managing leaks of user authentication data.

- Just as you would want to first categorize and then inventory, you will want access to networks to be tiered as well. That way, how someone connects to your services and data stores determines the fine-grained access they have. Free-for-all access to data is unwise, and broad access to networks can similarly be problematic. Researcher Teri Radichel states that limited administrative privileges may have prevented inserting software to get into the deployment process used to infect the POS systems with malware.[18] This is a cultural shift more than an engineering challenge; one that may need to walk back engineers' sense of entitlement to ubiquitous and perpetual access to sensitive data.

- Given the prevalence of shadow IT and distributed service ownership, you will want to assess whether new users and their privileges are in line with demonstrable needs. You will also want to check for irregular activities performed by user accounts with the ability to grant other users access. This is especially important in companies without top-down command-and-control shops where rigid adherence to policy drives the addition of user privileges. This may add initial latency, but you will avoid a "power user" situation, where a rogue account with strong access extricates data without any guardrails.

- Since attackers often come sniffing for low-hanging fruit (small security vulnerabilities) before attacking sensitive data, you need to monitor any queries that seem optimized to gather intelligence. If you see a user making such requests to services or for data, that could be an indication that something suboptimal is afoot.

- For servers that are dedicated to specific services or users or that hold sensitive data, you will want to maintain an explicit list of users who are permitted access. The default access response should be "no" unless the user seeking access belongs to that list.

- Anti-malware solutions can be effective if the attacker is using homegrown tools, but most sophisticated attackers tend to use off-the-shelf enterprise tools to fool anti-malware solutions. You will want to diversify accordingly.

- Active Directory can serve as both the gateway as well as the vehicle for outside attacks, so your automated controls will need to track its use for the life of any attack.

---

[17]Olavsrud, "11 steps attackers took to crack Target," page 2.
[18]Radichel, "Case Study: Critical Controls that Could Have Prevented Target Breach."

Besides the preceding tips, experts that I speak to recommend enforcing MFA on everything that is internet-facing (VPN, email, chat programs, etc.). Given distributed SaaS and data storage, the infrastructure perimeter has become more porous, and network access has become more global, so continuous MFA is important and will help reduce the chances of account compromise.

> **TIP** The old approach that optimized for perimeter-based access control is insufficient, given the spread of data and infrastructure and the ability of attackers to hijack systems to gain additional access once they penetrate the perimeter. Access management, therefore, needs to be continuous and intelligent.

Additional hands-on best practices from researcher Teri Radichel include maintenance, monitoring, and analysis of audit logs.[19] These logs could help you watch for anomalies like malformed packets and packets with unexpected sizes or data. While voluminous, these logs could flag the egress of large amounts of data. These logs could also record unexpected traffic to and from critical systems. An example of an anomaly would be a payments system shedding data outside of its normal cycle. These anomalies are often signs that someone unwelcome is committing unwanted acts upon sensitive data.

Radichel also suggests that companies "profile accounts for normal activity and usage periods to spot anomalies." Account privileges should be limited to need to know. The company's IT and security engineers must "segregate account access across network tiers. Disable and delete unneeded accounts."[20] The Target and Colonial Pipeline issues both highlight the risks of broad access as well as those of unmaintained dormant accounts. This is another cultural change moment, where companies need to optimize for the quality of their user engagement rather than just the quantity.

When it comes to vendor portals, Teri Radichel recommends "Penetration Tests and Red Team Exercises: Since this system is on the perimeter at the first layer of defense...."[21] Just as preventing entry to bad actors is critical, it is equally critical that you ensure that data stored in specific locations does not leave the network perimeter. As such, URL filtering for egress capabilities may help limit outbound access. Target's response to the breach included the implementation of many of these ideas.[22]

The vendor vulnerabilities we have seen thus far are important, but they're hardly exclusive to low-tech single-purpose vendors. The next subsection will show why.

10.2.2 *MongoDB security weaknesses*

MongoDB was a popular choice for developers during the transition to cloud-based servers, such as those hosted by Amazon AWS. I had to become conversant overnight

---

[19]Radichel, "Case Study: Critical Controls that Could Have Prevented Target Breach."

[20]Ibid.

[21]Ibid.

[22]"Updates on Target's security and technology enhancements," *Target*, April 29, 2014, http://mng.bz/XWAl.

in MongoDB during my time at Nike, when I led the identity management team. That age represented significant adoption of the MongoDB technology.

MongoDB is particularly useful in storing unstructured data; its document data model stores all related data together within a single document, making it much more flexible than the rigid structure of the relational database model.[23] However, MongoDB has been subjected to more high-profile attacks than any other database platform.

Early releases of MongoDB allowed the installation of a database server with no authentication mechanism enabled. In simple terms, the default MongoDB installation was insecure. This meant that anybody who had access to the database port would be able to connect to the database with unlimited authority. It is possible that the central purpose of MongoDB—low-latency access of massive volumes of data—caused this vulnerability. However, given the proliferation of sensitive data across companies, this is not purely a security risk but a major privacy risk, and one that is inside the perimeter, not one that emanates from a vendor.

The period from 2014 through 2017 was significant because during this time there was an expansion of both the online identity space and the amount of unstructured data that companies were accessing. Databases like Cassandra and MongoDB were beneficiaries of this change. They were also targets of attacks, with MongoDB databases being routinely attacked and with some attacks succeeding in exfiltrating data. In 2017 there were several ransomware attacks targeted at MongoDB cloud databases. Given the nature of ransomware attacks, the data was not recovered in many of these instances.[24]

As data protection laws ramped up and breaches became common, MongoDB made changes.[25]

- MongoDB 3.6 (2017) closed external access by default, resulting in low discoverability by potential attackers. This did not fix every vulnerability, but it did reduce the likelihood that default installations were attacked.

- MongoDB 3.6 also introduced IP allowlisting, which meant that access was not automatically granted and the default behavior was to deny access outside of approved IP addresses.

- In version 4.0, the Atlas cloud server's addition of LDAP authentication support meant that there was a higher bar to initial entry. On the storage side, the disk storage was encrypted with the customer in control of the keys. This helped reduce the likelihood that loss of storage was tantamount to loss of data. Version 4.2 built on the encryption progress by way of client-side encryption as well as field-level encryption. All these changes, put together, made it difficult to execute an attack and exfiltrate data.

---

[23]"Unstructured Data Management," *MongoDB*, https://www.mongodb.com/scale/unstructured-data-types.
[24]Guy Harrison, "MongoDB Security Improves in the Face of Increasing Attacks," Database Trends and Applications, September 29, 2020, http://mng.bz/y427.
[25]Ibid.

- MongoDB 4.4 added x509 authentication and integration with the AWS Identity and Access Management (IAM) system, thereby juxtaposing encryption with AWS's access-control regime.

In spite of these improvements, as of July 24, 2020, thousands of MongoDB databases were destroyed by the Meow attack.

After seeing how consistently database breaches were occurring, researchers planted honeypots to find out how these attacks happen, where the threats are coming from, and how quickly thay take place. A *honeypot* is "a computer or computer system intended to mimic likely targets of cyberattacks."[26] The researchers set up a number of unsecured MongoDB honeypots across the web, each filled with fake data. They monitored network traffic for malicious activity; if password hashes were exfiltrated and seen crossing the wire, that was an indication that a database was breached.[27]

The research showed continuous attacks on MongoDB online databases. The attacks seemed automatically configured toward newly online databases, and were high volume so as to exploit vulnerabilities. In one sample, unsecured databases were compromised in less than 24 hours on average.[28]

During the research, at least one of the honeypots was successfully attacked and held to ransom within a minute of being online. In a modus operandi that seems all too familiar now, the attacker erased the database and left a ransom note, asking for a Bitcoin payment in exchange for the data. Note that in such situations there is no guarantee that the attacker still has the data or is willing to return it after money changes hands.

The researchers set up other honeypots, and in that research, an exposed Mongo database was breached within 13 hours of internet connectivity. One breach, which the researchers believe to be the fastest recorded, was carried out nine minutes after the database setup was complete.[29]

Researcher Chris Wallis states that responding to such attacks before nine minutes may be hard, and this is especially true for smaller companies. Wallis points out that there are two challenges that companies face: first, detecting an unsecured database and assessing the risk level; and second, troubleshooting the issue and closing the security gap. Completing both these tasks in 13 hours is hard enough, Wallis says, making nine minutes a much bigger challenge.[30]

As security expert Guy Harrison states, "MongoDB's own Atlas database as a service platform is fully secured and immune from such attacks. Only systems configured manually on cloud-based virtual machines will exhibit these vulnerabilities."[31] In that

---

[26]Steve Symanovich, "What is a honeypot? How it can lure cyberattackers," *Norton*, May 26, 2020, http://mng.bz/M2WE.

[27]"MongoDB is subject to continual attacks when exposed to the internet," *Help Net Security*, July 8, 2020, http://mng.bz/aD4x.

[28]"Ibid.

[29]Daniel Andrew, "9 minutes to breach: the life expectancy of an unsecured MongoDB honeypot," *Intruder*, July 7, 2020, http://mng.bz/g4YZ.

[30]"MongoDB is subject to continual attacks when exposed to the internet."

[31]Harrison, "MongoDB Security Improves in the Face of Increasing Attacks."

sense, only those systems that were configured manually on cloud-based virtual machines exhibit these vulnerabilities. So all a business has to do is use MongoDB Atlas to achieve a high level of cloud database security.

Herein lies the risk for small businesses with limited budgets. They may not have the funds to procure the top-of-line Atlas database, and their manual configurations may rely on MongoDB defaults, thereby inheriting privacy and security vulnerabilities. It is also possible that most unsecured MongoDB databases are development or test instances using obsolete versions of MongoDB code. However, as you have seen, test and development instances can contain production data with limited access and audit controls. Such instances, and accounts to access them, are often not retired by small businesses. Therefore, while this issue is not endemic to MongoDB, the progression of default settings and lax security practices could create a data exfiltration possibility and therefore a privacy risk.

The lessons for small and medium-sized companies and the engineering community are clear: enterprises running MongoDB should review their installations to ascertain they are secure and not exposed to the internet.

The examples we have looked at so far have offered defensive hands-on techniques for engineers to protect their infrastructure. The next subsection will provide some proactive best practices in authorization management.

10.2.3 Authorization best practices

Many companies set up their authorization design during their early growth stage. Mistakes from that growth phase tend to haunt companies at a time not of their choosing. In this subsection, I will provide some best practices that will serve as a checklist for such companies as they evolve their authorization posture.

The real challenge companies face is that of fine-grained authorization. Authentication has been discussed for long enough that it has standards based on OAuth 2, SAML, and OpenID Connect. By contrast, there is no analog for authorization in terms of how it may be consistently implemented across different services. As a result, each service owner is free to customize permissions, privileges, and roles. This results in a bespoke access-control regime rather than a fine-grained authorization architecture that can be mapped to risk and usage.[32]

According to security researcher Omri Gazitt, your approach to authorization needs to adhere to certain best practices.[33] We will consider some of these practices in detail in the following subsections.

---

[32]"Authorization is Broken," *Aserto* blog, January 28, 2021, http://mng.bz/endw.

[33]Omri Gazitt, "5 Ways to Fix Your Broken Authorization System," *The New Stack*, March 18, 2021, http://mng.bz/p2gE.

ENFORCING SEPARATION OF AUTHORIZATION POLICY FROM CODE

Engineers may be tempted to decentralize authorization policy and customize it for their service just as they do other features, but this will pose problems as the service usage and threats grow. For example,[34]

- Even if individual services have bespoke authorization policies, there may be a time when you need to harmonize those policies across all services. Making those changes on a per-service level will get more expensive.
- Given the rapid turnover in engineering and security teams, it is often hard to understand why authorization policies were set a certain way for a specific service.
- As companies grow because of mergers, they may inherit services written in different languages. This makes onerous not just the task of modifying the authorization policy, but also potentially the rest of the service as well.

Based on insights from Omri Gazitt, here are some recommended best practices for delineating between policy and code:[35]

- There is a risk in joining applications and the authorization policy, since it could breed confirmation bias. You will be better off implementing authorization policies using languages or tools that are separate from the service they govern. This could help address the issue where engineers have an incorrect risk-assessment of their services and tightly couple the functionality of the service to the authorization threshold to access the service.
- Even as you separate the authorization policy from the application itself, it is appropriate for the application owner to have easy access to the policy. You will want to apply the same rigor when it comes to versioning and quality control. Since the code and authorization logic are to remain decoupled, you should map the policy version to the code version for automated implementation and auditing.
- You may often need to change the authorization policy without impacting application capabilities. In this case, you will want to be able to make these changes seamlessly. Otherwise, your policy could be outdated, and that could lead to compliance or other issues. Planning for this at an early stage may help you respond to changes in laws, enterprise customer needs, and security patches.

Additionally, I strongly recommend that, as a transition to this separation mode, you create a first principle whereby in cases where services have varying authorization policies, you ensure that the strictest policy applies to all the services. That way, as new services come online with more advanced authorization policies, those policies would then apply to the older services as well. This will help ensure enforcement of policies at the account level rather than the app level. This will also help you avoid a situation where an ingenious engineer deploys a service without an authorization policy.

---

[34]Gert Drapers, "Why separate policy from your code?" *Aserto* blog, March 4, 2021, http://mng.bz/OG22.
[35]Gazitt, "5 Ways to Fix Your Broken Authorization System."

If Target had these protections, they might have been able to patch their vulnerabilities at scale. Many breaches and privacy violations come down to insufficient enforcement of authorization policies because services make their own policies, and that makes scaling any fixes next to impossible.

MAKING AUTHORIZATION SECURE, SERVICE-BASED, AND EASY TO INTEGRATE

Security and IT engineers and program managers at small businesses must approach authorization with two assumptions. Most engineers, if given the right tooling and context, will do the right thing for privacy and security. The same engineers, often because time is short and instructions are confusing, may end up making sloppy mistakes.

To show how this could play out, let's look at how bugs in John Deere's code base created a vulnerability. Engineers often think of bugs in code as being distinct from how their data can be protected. In this case, the bugs served as an open door to the data of customers who owned John Deere equipment and vehicles.[36]

The vulnerabilities, if exploited, would have exposed personal data about John Deere's customers, including their physical address. According to the researcher, "on newer farm equipment he was able to see the vehicle or equipment owner's name, their physical address, the equipment's unique ID, and its Vehicle Identification Number or VIN, the identifying code for a specific car."[37]

The researcher said that "the first vulnerability allowed anyone to list all usernames on the John Deere Web Portal." This would be the equivalent of visiting a retail website and being able to see the usernames of all the shoppers. If this vulnerability were to go undetected, an attacker could easily find out how many users had subscribed to the online portal. This could be prevented if the website or the mobile app were able to detect such requests. However, this is where the second vulnerability was to become even more critical.

A remote unauthenticated attacker, which is to say someone who was not even signed in, could simply remove the cookie from the original request, so that each successive request would seem like a new one. The attacker could make the same request multiple times. Besides the weak authentication protocol, the absence of a rate limit would allow the attack to persist unabated. This limitless ability to find usernames, coupled with being able to obtain personal data on newer equipment, represented a strong attack vector.

These gaps could be used by attackers to dox all John Deere's owners. According to the researcher, this vulnerability was accessible via the John Deere Operations Center Mobile app for Android and iOS and the corresponding web version.

An attacker could obtain the requisite API cookie by just signing up for the app without having purchased John Deere equipment. They could then "expose any vehicle or equipment owner's name, physical address, equipment GUID (permanent

---

[36]Lorenzo Franceschi-Bicchierai, "Bugs Allowed Hackers to Dox John Deere Tractor Owners," *Vice*, http://mng.bz/YgPe.
[37]Ibid.

equipment ID) and the status of whether the Terminal is remotely accessible via the RDA protocol via the Vehicle Identification Number (VIN) API," according to the vulnerability report.

Cases like this one could be addressed by several techniques recommended by researcher Omri Gazitt:[38]

- *Make policies secure by default*—The danger in using authentication tokens for policy decisions is that the token may be outdated, or someone else may be accessing the account. This is why your policy needs to be conservative in that the default policy outcome will be to disallow access, followed by a real-time assessment of the credentials, the account, and the privileges to which access is being sought. This is akin to deeming users as having opted-out of data collection by default and respecting their privacy by having them proactively opt in.

  Lest you think this is a theoretical exercise, recently the Venmo account of President Joe Biden was revealed. It took researchers at Buzzfeed less than 10 minutes to find it once they started looking. Not only were they able to find the President's account, but also a network of his private social connections. The lesson here for app developers is that engagement and privacy can be inversely related if the app is not built carefully. The features that drive engagement—the ability to pay connections easily and invite friends to subscribe in exchange for incentives—create a graph that makes data leaks more impactful. In the case of President Biden, this could have been a national security issue. For regular everyday users, this represented a major privacy concern because there was no way to predict how they might be impacted by this gap. "Customers always have the ability to make their transactions private and determine their own privacy settings in the app" said Venmo in response.[39] This led to a demand by privacy influencers to make transactions and friends private by default. So "privacy by default" is an idea whose time has come.

- *Delivering authorization as a service, rather than a library*—Delivering a developer solution as a library instead of a service is an idea that works in theory, not in practical adoption. Instead, if you deliver a developer service, it may help provide a central point of control and handle the work necessary to scale the solution. Gazitt identifies this as a critical reason why developers trust services like Stripe for payments or Auth0 for authentication.

- *Make authorization services easy to integrate*—In many (if not most) cases, authorization services will need to adapt to the services that drive engagement and make the business money. Your company's CEO can extol their commitment to security and privacy ad nauseum, but integrating an authorization tool is akin

---

[38]Gazitt, "5 Ways to Fix Your Broken Authorization System."

[39]Ryan Mac, Katie Notopoulos, Ryan Brooks, and Logan McDonald, "We Found Joe Biden's Secret Venmo. Here's Why That's A Privacy Nightmare For Everyone." *BuzzFeed News*, May 14, 2021, http://mng.bz/GGWV.

to cleaning up after a party where everyone imbibed and celebrated without restraint.

As such, Gazitt recommends, you will want to build an authorization service that integrates with your existing identity and directory providers and offers a variety of hosting models. It would need to have bindings and samples for every language and framework, so service owners can get it integrated in minutes.

Your authorization system must be flexible and extensible. It should ideally integrate with standard authentication systems so that the "AuthN to AuthZ" transition is seamless. This implementation would require that the authorization system accepts identity information in a cryptographic token such as a JavaScript Web Token (JWT). Authorization systems are required to provide broad coverage ranging from platform identity providers like Google and Azure to federated identity providers like Okta to enterprise directories like Active Directory.

In order to be comprehensive, the system should align various kinds of identities, such as universal identifiers like a Google ID, federated identities like Okta, and enterprise identities like LDAP. That way, you can maintain all the overlapping identities that map to a single user. This will ensure that your authorization policies provide the same outcome regardless of what identity is used.

Additionally, the authorization policies must be available quickly for any application-identity combination. If the policy discovery and enforcement takes too long, there is a danger that a less-than-ideal default setting gets used. Measuring and testing for this is key.

Finally, Gazitt points out that this system must support "REST and gRPC APIs for authorization, SDKs and language bindings for popular languages and frameworks, [and] simple conventions for organizing and authoring policies for resources that are accessed using standard architectural patterns (e.g., REST, GraphQL)."[40]

This is more important than many privacy newcomers may realize: rapid integration will help you build models that track user behavior, fraud attempts, and anomalies. Therefore, ease of integration is critical in driving developer adoption and consequently in minimizing privacy risk. It will help make your business safer, smarter, and cheaper.

VERIFYING THE STRENGTH OF DATA LINKS AND VALIDATING AUTHENTICITY OF IDENTITY

You have so far seen how we can better protect the perimeter, layer protections inside the perimeter, and make those protections more applicable for adoption. But how do we make those protections more effective so that we achieve our main goal—protecting the customer's data and privacy?

---

[40]Omri Gazitt, "Authentication != Authorization," *Aserto* blog, April 18, 2021, http://mng.bz/zQMr.

Identity expert Robert McKay points out the risks in the confined verification processes companies follow.[41] This is especially true for fast-moving companies that are desperate for customer engagement. Companies often verify user identities by validating information that in theory only the real user would know, like your pet's name or your mother's maiden name. Traditionally, identity verification is a linear process where the person trying to authenticate provides verifiable artifacts as proof. Depending on a company's workflow and risk appetite, the number of artifacts requested could be high or low. The most intuitive example is when we provide a Social Security number (SSN) or tax ID number (TIN) to avail of financial services. There are many avenues to verify that the SSN is linked to the person providing it. The user may further need to provide a utility bill as proof of residence.

However, those approaches have limitations as bad actors become sophisticated. McKay says that "rather than performing authentication through a series of data point verifications, they should instead examine the linkages between all the identity markers holistically over time."[42] The reason behind the need for a new approach is that the sequential pieces of data that drive the verification process are becoming more easily obtainable by bad actors.

McKay describes an attack known as the man-in-the-middle attack. While it's possible to mitigate if mutual TLS is correctly applied, this attack could be highly impactful given the potency of phishing attempts, the insufficient application of MFA, and the profligate presence of credentials in the dark web. Figure 10.3 below shows how such an attack works conceptually.

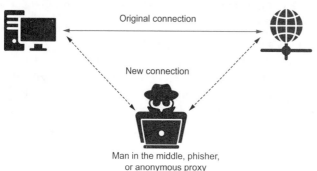

Man in the middle, phisher, or anonymous proxy

Figure 10.3   A man-in-the-middle attack

This attack is executed as follows:

1. The attacker sets up two parallel conversations between a business and its customer.
2. The business believes it is connecting with the customer, and the customer thinks they are talking to the business. In reality, it is the attacker interacting with both parties.

---

[41]Robert McKay, "It's time to shift from verifying data to authenticating identity," *Help Net Security*, May 28, 2021, http://mng.bz/0wWm.

[42]Ibid.

3. The attacker might initiate the scheme by requesting the issuance of a one-time passcode via a session on the business's website. This has become easier because people's email addresses tend to be more freely available online, and other credentials are available due to other breaches on the dark web.

4. In parallel, posing as the business, the attacker calls the unwitting customer and, using social engineering, convinces the individual to read off the one-time passcode sent by the business.

5. The attacker then uses this information to log in to the customer's account and perform unauthorized transactions.

6. Since the attacker was able to provide all requested data to pass each point in the verification process, access is granted.

Such attackers can also create fake identities using a combination of genuine data that belongs to a customer and fake data that may plausibly belong to that customer.

To get a sense of human engineering that drives impersonation attacks, consider this: if you or I find that our Social Security number is being used by someone else, it is likely that we'd immediately take action. This is why some attackers may use personal data belonging to children, the elderly, and folks who are homeless. A stable or even average credit history coupled with simple identity checks (using information freely available on the internet) may satisfy the verification threshold for many institutions.[43]

This occurs partly because of the number of transactions and volume of data at play, and the dynamics where engagement and low latency are the coin of the realm. This state of affairs is suboptimal across the board—both for the person whose identity is misused and the institution that gets defrauded. An incident where security and privacy harms occur almost always has more than one victim.

Even more dynamic techniques like location verification have limitations, McKay correctly points out. Companies have smartly incorporated the use of location data to verify identity. One example is a bank adding extra layers of verification if you happen to use their app from a brand new location. In such cases, the application may send a one-time code to a verified email or phone number. However, this approach has loopholes ripe for abuse by wannabe attackers. An attacker could be physically close to the address of the customer so as to come up with a GPS location that is close enough to fool the verification process.

This is where privacy protections are often in conflict. I have stated elsewhere in the book that companies could abridge the number of decimals in GPS coordinates they store for location data. Doing so protects data privacy by making users hard to identify in a cohort; on the flipside, the limited precision of such data hurts the preciseness of the location and leaves an open door for attackers.

Given these risks, what are engineers and technical program managers to do when verifying user identity? McKay recommends that they adopt a holistic view of identity

---

[43]McKay, "It's time to shift from verifying data to authenticating identity."

across online, offline, and device-based data and behaviors over time. Such a process entails the following near-real-time assessments:

- Do not treat data points individually but correlate them to each other and derive a single view of the user's identity. This way, you have a greater chance of detecting an attack, since the attacker now has to meet a higher verification threshold.

- The validity of identity depends upon the connection between individual data points. You will need to look at each grouping of data points, their age, how frequently they connect to one another, etc. Examining the strength of these various permutations could help you detect attacks faster when those attacks use either legitimate data points or a combination of real and fake data.

- You could look at risk as not being attached merely to the attacker but also to the device they use. You could consider the recent usage of the mobile device as well as whether SIM swapping or spoofing have occurred. This individualized assessment of the device is the next logical step after assessing data points individually and collectively.

- Assign a risk factor to the person's identity and device collectively before moving forward with the interaction. This step is about answering the following question: Is this action appropriate from this user using this device? This could help address the attacks directed at low-tech users like the elderly who do not frequently use their online accounts and are the targets of attackers.

In the preceding four points, we start with an aggregated set of data points, move on to groupings of individual data points, followed by focusing on the device itself, and finally considering a combination of the individual's data points and the device's. In the progression of these ideas, you have risk values affixed to each of these steps. You can now allow or disallow access depending on your benchmarks and risk appetite.

Building this intelligence over time is critical for companies, since they have to balance the business need for rapidity, the engineering need for simplicity, and concerns around fairness and bias as well. The preceding criteria will enable engineers to make risk-driven deterministic decisions around letting users validate their accounts.

The company's algorithms can then make decisions, with close calls possibly escalated for human decision-making. A continuous audit trail will allow engineers to revisit past decisions, change the preceding criteria, and also adjust risk value calculations.

So protecting privacy for your customers goes beyond protecting data you have about your customers. You need to think about processing that data en route to verify customer identity as well.

Of course, the other key tension here is the need to often collect data for security purposes (fraud detection, DDOS prevention) and the privacy risk if the company were to suffer a breach. It is imperative that engineers, especially those who focus on security and privacy, emphasize the need to collect only what is needed and retain it only for as long as it is needed.

TIP It is imperative that data collection geared toward security adhere to data minimization (collect only what is needed) and retention only for as long as needed. Given the propensity and potency of modern breaches, companies need to avoid turning a security initiative into a privacy problem.

In the next section, you will see how gaps in your authorization logic can allow users more access than they are supposed to have. The privacy risks in such a situation are obvious.

10.2.4 Why continuous monitoring of accounts and credentials is important

There are those who believe that engineers have gotten wiser about the need for data protection, given the time that has passed since the Target breach and the fact that the stakes are now much higher. Their optimism seems unwarranted in the face of recent evidence.

In early 2021, one of the nation's largest pipelines, which carries refined gasoline and jet fuel from Texas up the East Coast to New York, was forced to shut down after being hit by ransomware. This was the latest example of how vulnerable America's energy infrastructure could be to cyberattacks. The operator of the system, Colonial Pipeline, said that it had shut down its 5,500 miles of pipeline, which it said carried 45 percent of the East Coast's fuel supplies, in an effort to contain the breach.[44]

You would think that a breach of this scale would emanate from a compromise of equal magnitude. This would especially be the case given the carnage that ensued: there was a shortage of fuel and long lines across the East Coast. However, this hack, at its core, was the outcome of a single compromised password, according to a cybersecurity expert. According to a Bloomberg report,[45] hackers were able to access the Colonial Pipeline networks because of a vulnerability that should not have existed, given the lessons that should have been learned from breaches at Target and Equifax. The hackers used a virtual private network (VPN) account that was set up to allow employees to remotely access the company's computer network. The part that should be especially concerning is that the account was dormant but had still retained its access to the network of the company.

We have seen a few times over the course of this book that the combination of data points can significantly magnify vulnerabilities. In this case, the aforementioned account coupled with the discovery of the account's password inside a batch of leaked passwords on the dark web was all it took. It is impossible to know for certain how that credential ended up on the dark web. Charles Carmakal, a security expert interviewed in the Bloomberg article, surmised that an employee of Colonial Pipelines could have used another account with the same credentials, which then got hacked. The number

---

[44]David E. Sanger, Clifford Krauss, and Nicole Perlroth, "Cyberattack Forces a Shutdown of a Top U.S. Pipeline," *New York Times*, May 8, 2021, http://mng.bz/KB14.

[45]William Turton and Kartikay Mehrotra, "Hackers Breached Colonial Pipeline Using Compromised Password," *Bloomberg*, June 4, 2021, http://mng.bz/9KOa.

of identities and their mappings to privileges is hard to update and protect, and one failure is sufficient for attackers to swoop in.

Additionally, the VPN account did not use multifactor authentication (MFA). In hindsight, an account that allowed for remote access and had not been authenticated for a while should have been a prime candidate for multifactor authentication. The absence of this hurdle reduced any friction from the attackers' path. An investigation into possible phishing attempts directed at the employee whose account it was came up empty.

This means that the breach could have been the outcome of

- A VPN account that may have been lying dormant for a while
- Lack of monitoring for account dormancy and password reuse
- Credential reuse, whereby someone used the same password elsewhere on the internet that they used for the VPN
- Lack of MFA, due to which the failure of the basic authentication layer led to a security failure

This exact set of events could occur in a hospital, grocery chain, clothing store, fitness enterprise, gaming company, etc. The privacy implications there would be staggering. Therefore, it is vital that engineers follow best practices like the following:

- Enforce MFA as a best practice, especially each time someone needs additional access or data. If you are not certain how much access control to apply, you could reply on behavioral analytics and anomaly detection. With all that said, being conservative and escalating the scrutiny is the safer bet before granting additional and more powerful privileges.
- Disable accounts that are no longer in use and change passwords for those accounts. That way, even if an employee is naive enough to reuse the same credentials elsewhere and that other account is compromised, that failure does not become a gateway into the business.
- Search code repositories for plain text secrets (passwords, identities, etc.), which all too often lead to sensitive data that should be protected.
- Keep an eye on credential leaks on the dark web. This is critical, since your adversaries will search email, intranet sites, etc., for credentials.

Of course, this list is not exhaustive, but it gives you a sense of how, even as the attention on security and privacy has risen, business preparation has not. At a minimum, the contents of this chapter should serve as a starting point for sensible access control.

10.2.5 *Remote work and privacy risk*

As I write this, there is a raucous debate occurring in corporate America. Employees who have been working from home for almost a year and a half have gotten accustomed to the flexibility and the lack of commute. Companies are confronting the possibility of rising attrition in the event that their return-to-work arrangements are deemed to be not responsive to this changed environment. What challenges might this pose to infrastructure security and, consequently, to privacy?

The possible risk presented by weak data protection became real on January 15, 2021. The target was a water treatment plant that served the Bay Area. Not only did a bad actor get in unauthorized, they tried to poison the water, directly connecting the vulnerability to public health in a direct way. The mode of entry was an open door: the username and password of a former employee's account for a software program that enabled remote access. As we have seen before in this chapter, the combination of easy access and privileges can be consequential. Sure enough, the hacker tried to delete water treatment programs upon logging in.[46]

This incident is an example of how cyberattacks are now being aimed at water infrastructure. Just a few weeks after the Bay Area attack, there was a similar one in Oldsmar, Florida. The second attack was similar to the first one in that the access path involved a TeamViewer account. The attacker used their privileges to raise the levels of lye in the drinking water to poisonous levels. Detection came not via controls or automated monitoring but via an alert employee noticing that the computer's mouse was moving on its own. Fortunately, that employee was able to undo the hacker's changes.[47]

The NBC news report about the Bay Area incident points out, correctly, that the decentralized nature of the water supply inoculates it from centralized outages. Just as elections are localized, so are most water supplies. This inhibits an attacker from exploiting a central point of failure.

And that blessing is also a problem. The lack of a central managed authority in our infrastructure also aligns with a lack of central cybersecurity and privacy law.

"'It's really difficult to apply some kind of uniform cyber hygiene assessment, given the disparate size and capacity and technical capacity of all the water utilities,' said Mike Keegan, an analyst at the National Rural Water Association, a trade group for the sector."[48]

The electric grid in the United States mostly consists of for-profit corporations, which could be more tightly regulated. On the other hand, most of the drinking water facilities in the United States are nonprofits. Their cybersecurity muscle depends on how large their customer base is, which in turn determines the funding available for cybersecurity. When local governments cut funding, it is likely that the cybersecurity functions suffer, leading to upgrades being delayed and staffing levels being slashed. This has echoes of the HVAC vendor whose vulnerabilities formed a key breadcrumb in the Target breach almost a decade ago.

---

[46]Kevin Collier, "50,000 security disasters waiting to happen: The problem of America's water supplies," *NBC News*, June 17, 2021, https://www.nbcnews.com/news/amp/rcna1206.

[47]Kevin Collier, "Lye-poisoning attack in Florida shows cybersecurity gaps in water systems," *NBC News*, February 9, 2021, http://mng.bz/jyOy.

[48]Collier, "50,000 security disasters waiting to happen."

The NBC News report cites a specific anecdote that I find especially troubling.

Small rural water facilities tend to be reluctant to share their vulnerabilities, said Daryn Martin, a technical assistant at the Kansas Rural Water Association, a trade organization for about 800 Kansas water treatment facilities, including Post Rock.

"Generally, they're not reporting to the federal government. There's some distrust, you know, in small-town, Midwest USA," he said....

"Remote access makes it so you don't have to man a facility 24 hours a day," he said. "We have a lot of remote water districts that cover hundreds of miles. To pay a guy to drive 30 miles to turn a pump on and then he might have to turn it off in 3 hours when the tank gets full? He can do all that remotely. That saves money."[49]

Replace intergovernmental distrust with organizational disconnect, and you have the makings of a major business with data about healthcare, travel, and finances being susceptible to cyberwarfare and privacy harm.

While remote work and service segmentation are here to stay, the implications on data protection keep getting more serious. Just as a bad actor can sabotage a water supply by altering programs and data, the damage they could do to personal data is unimaginable and unquantifiable. There is a reason ransomware and cybersecurity are thought of as a key component of national security.

Russian and Chinese spies have sneaked into numerous federal government networks, sometimes going for months undetected. Criminals have hacked into every industry and extorted companies at will, including those that occupy important parts of U.S. supply chains.

While there is no guaranteed fail-safe plan, companies and organizations can take steps to contain the risk, as you will now see.

10.3 *Protecting privacy by closing access-control gaps*

No discussion of access control can be complete without discussing insecure direct object references (IDORs). IDORs are a type of access control vulnerability that arises when an application uses user-supplied input to access objects directly.

Let's first look at how an IDOR vulnerability works, and then we can look at mitigation options.

10.3.1 *How an IDOR vulnerability works*

Before we look at IDORs and ways to test for and remedy them, understanding the core concepts can be helpful:

- In the case of IDOR, *object* refers to data and/or functionality. For example, as an e-commerce shopper, I have access to objects like my shopping cart but not the backend inventory of the website that sells the merchandise.

---

[49]Collier, "50,000 security disasters waiting to happen."

- *"Vertical access control* aims to control the restrictions to access functions according to the user roles."[50] In our e-commerce example, while I as a shopper can change the items in my cart, modifying items in the backend inventory that are available to all shoppers is only possible for the admin.
- *"Horizontal access control* aims to control the restrictions to access resources by users who have the same capability level."[51] For example, I should be able to remove items from my shopping cart, but not from the cart of another user who has a different account.

Put simply, an IDOR "occurs when an attacker gains direct access by using user-supplied input to an object that has no authorization to access."[52] This occurs when either authentication (the mechanism that allows user entry into the system) is not sufficiently tethered to authorization (the mechanism that allows user access to objects in the system). In other words, in the context of an IDOR weakness, my access as a user to objects is not tied to my identity.

It is also possible that weaknesses in the authorization implementation are weak enough that attackers can bypass the authorization mechanism and access resources in the system.

In most web applications, an object is represented with an ID. For example, in an e-commerce app or website, my identity and the product I buy will have IDs. And if these IDs are easy enough to guess or can be accessed by an attacker by bypassing access controls, you have the telltale signs of an IDOR.

Let's look at an example to understand how such an attack can work and then we will look at mitigation strategies. Figure 10.4 shows an object schema for an e-commerce backend. As you can see, a `users` object has attributes like an ID, name, and creation date. Similarly, the `orders` object has attributes like ID, creation date, user ID, and product ID. Both objects have as primary keys their own IDs, but they point to other IDs as well. For example, an order maps back to a specific user ID, since normally one order maps to one buyer. However, one order could map to multiple products, so it is possible that one order ID maps to several product IDs. Let's assume that two users are shopping on the website and have orders as shown in table 10.1.

Table 10.1 Two example orders

User ID	Order ID	Products
1234	A1	Food products
5678	B1	Home furnishings

[50]Ayşe Bilge Gündüz, "Everything You Need to Know About IDOR (Insecure Direct Object References)," *ayşe bilge gündüz*, April 19, 2020, http://mng.bz/W7ax.
[51]Ibid.
[52]Ibid.

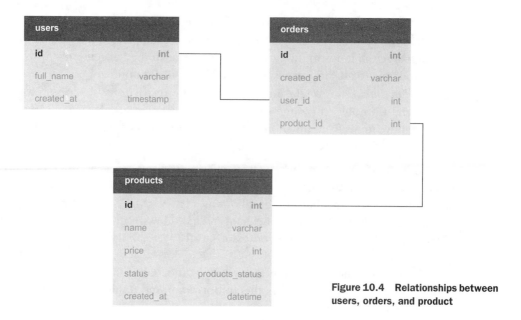

Figure 10.4   Relationships between users, orders, and product

Let's also assume that the backend query to display the orders is as follows:

```
http://www.buyproducts.com/order_details?order_id=A1
http://www.buyproducts.com/order_details?order_id=B1
```

If the backend function does not verify that the user that is logged in is the same user whose order is being displayed, this counts as an IDOR vulnerability.

In this example, the order ID is used directly as a record index in queries that are performed on the backend database. If no other controls are in place, an attacker can simply modify the order ID value, bypassing access controls to view the records of other customers. This is an example of an IDOR vulnerability leading to horizontal privilege escalation. If a user can change the order ID and get information about another user's purchase history, or if the page listing the details of the order contains the user's name and address, you have a severe privacy violation leaking one user's purchase info to another.[53]

According to the PortSwigger blog, "an attacker might also be able to perform horizontal and vertical privilege escalation by altering the user to one with additional privileges while bypassing access controls. Other possibilities include exploiting password leakage or modifying parameters once the attacker has landed in the user's accounts page, for example."[54]

There are other ways for IDOR vulnerabilities to manifest themselves. For example, IDOR vulnerabilities often arise when sensitive resources are located in static files

---

[53]Gündüz, "Everything You Need to Know About IDOR."
[54]"Insecure direct object references (IDOR)," *PortSwigger,* http://mng.bz/8lJ2.

on the server-side filesystem. A website might save user purchase receipts to disk using an "incrementing by 1" filename, and allow users to retrieve these by visiting a URL like the following:

```
https://www.buyproducts.com/static/12144.txt
```

In this situation, an attacker can simply modify the filename to retrieve a receipt belonging to another user and potentially obtain user credentials and other sensitive data.

To make this risk even clearer, if an attacker does not like the coverage of newspapers like the *New York Times* or the *Wall Street Journal*, they could write a script to look at the IDs of subscribers, if the IDs were publicly obtainable or guessable. They could then obtain the credentials of such subscribers via the dark web and put their subscriptions on hold, or worse, cancel them.

Given today's hyper-polarized atmosphere, it is possible that bad actors will use cyberwarfare to make their points as well. To be fair, it may be unlikely for there to be a breach at a national newspaper where someone would update info to escalate privileges to cause geopolitical issues, but it is possible for a more local paper to be at risk here.

10.3.2 *IDOR testing and mitigation*

There are no easy ways to foresee every possible attack method for IDOR, but there are some effective techniques that researchers recommend:[55]

- The challenges to make sure that you can test for situations where a user can access more applications than they should, as well as whether a user can obtain more privileges than they should for a specific application. In short, you will need more than one user account for testing purposes. When you do this at scale, you should be able to, for example, test various access-levels for different concurrent access requests by users with varying levels of privileges.

- To protect individual features, you should try to discover as many features as you can. To avoid confirmation bias and false negatives, you will want to use the role with the highest privilege.

- You may remember how intuitive service names assisted the Target hackers. You could similarly try to identify a naming pattern for all your endpoints. You could then come up with new names and patterns that are not quite as easy to guess.

- To cover all your endpoint-role combinations, you will want to test each time you create/register a new role. Whether you do this manually or in bulk will depend on the maturity and reach of your tooling.

---

[55]"IDOR explained – OWASP Top 10 vulnerabilities," *Thehackerish*, April 22, 2021, http://mng.bz/8lJ2.

There are also coding best practices that engineers can deploy to avoid IDOR gaps in the first place:[56]

1. Given that the IDOR is borne out of combinations, unit testing is insufficient. Integration tests that cover IDOR use cases are a must have.

2. The testing for IDOR is not confined to roles; at the DevOps stage you will want additional integration tests to check once more before services are deployed.

3. Developers should not display private object references. The goal here is to minimize how publicly visible keys or filenames should be.

4. For any kind of access, all parameters and referenced objects should be continually validated.

5. There should be a tight coupling between users and tokens, and neither the tokens nor the mappings should be public.

6. At render time, you should store data values in session and not in a database where subsequent access is possible; given the number of times we have seen sensitive data be accessed by attackers, you should prevent persistence, which in turn will mitigate the risk of later leaks.

7. When the user submits data, you will want to validate the data, with one eye on latency. For example, if the user submits a Social Security number, you could join the table that stores financial data and the table that stores user account data. This will serve as access control enforced by the data itself, unless your backend data itself has been corrupted.

This chapter has provided engineers and others with some insight into how inefficient security controls can lead to privacy harms. It is vital to understand that there is no exhaustive list of security weaknesses that, once fixed, can mitigate privacy impacts. Just as combinations of data can lead to privacy risks, security gaps can work in concert as well.

As a checklist-type resource for businesses, the guidance from the Center for Internet Security can be a good place to start.[57] Their guidance provides a list of data protection controls and their components. If companies adhere to these, there is a good chance they will avoid or detect any gaps in their data protection posture.

---

[56]"IDOR explained – OWASP Top 10 vulnerabilities." "Insecure Direct Object Reference (IDOR) Vulnerability," *GeeksforGeeks*, 12 September 2021, http://mng.bz/NxA2; "Parameter Tampering," *Hdiv*, http://mng.bz/DxV9.

[57]"CIS Controls Navigator," *CIS*, http://mng.bz/lapM.

Summary

- Companies too often optimize for privacy by focusing on the data, but security risks around infrastructure and IT are just as critical. For many companies, these areas could be a starting point to manage privacy.
- An expanded risk surface and a porous access management posture pose real risks to a company, its data, and customer trust.
- A risk-management model and proactive access management for the company and its vendors is critical.
- Many security (and therefore privacy) harms are the denouement of smaller risks and their collective impact, so proactive and gradual risk-mitigation is critical.

Scaling, hiring, and considering regulations

At this point in the book, you have learned how to build privacy into data, tooling, and business review processes. Chapters 3 and 4 dove deep into data management once data enters the company, by classifying and cataloging it using automation and metadata. Chapter 5 offered scalable privacy techniques for data sharing, given how much online computing and commerce deals with data transfers.

You will have also understood how to scale those architectures and processes as your company grows. You will have also understood how to operationalize your privacy tooling and processes, since companies cannot keep throwing hardware, software and staff at these issues. Chapter 6 aimed to repurpose the traditional privacy review process by front-loading it into an advisory and consultative capacity. Using automation, companies can build in privacy for their features rather than bolting it on after the fact.

Given the energy around customer-facing compliance, chapters 7 through 9 took a deep dive around deletion, data export, and consent.

Given the need for both security and privacy in data protection, we have also spent a fair bit of time in addressing security gaps that could lead to privacy harms. Chapter 10 looked at security through the lens of privacy, and offered hands-on skills for companies that many may use as a starting point.

However, after having put all these tools and processes into practice, companies face a critical choice:

- Will they operate by making improvements as needed but otherwise tread water? In this case, privacy and data protection will remain reactive and tactical.
- Alternatively, companies could choose a different course and plan on a privacy engineering offering that is not just operationalized but also optimized.

This chapter will help you plan for the latter course.

Having such a mature program has several benefits. You will be able to staff intelligently, make data-driven prioritizations, and avoid building up technical debt. I am advocating for this choice based on my experience advising many startups and venture capital firms. Companies that fail to mature their program often find that their plans for "hockey stick" growth, instead, end up with a broken stick. Their product roadmaps freeze and atrophy; rolling out features becomes difficult, due to privacy audits and data leaks. Instead of a unicorn, the company becomes a camel.

In companies that fall into this trap, privacy engineers and program managers keep having to go to their leaders for funding without a framework or metrics to back them up. This sets up the company for failure, both in privacy strategy and in operational efficiency. In this chapter, we will look at how you might avoid such an outcome.

First, I will help you build a capability maturity model for your privacy engineering program. I will be offering you a template that will not just help you scale your offering, but also help you:

- Segment your data protection capabilities into dimensions like identification, protection, detection, and remediation
- Conduct a gap analysis for key aspects of your data protection capabilities
- Build tiers for your capabilities to track their evolution from *foundational* to *mature* to *advanced*

This approach will help you measure your program against the backdrop of the threat model, compliance commitments, customer obligations, and feature roadmaps. In the absence of such a data-driven model, privacy and security engineers will always end up scrounging for scraps rather than partnering with and enabling the business.

Second, I will help you build a staffing model, which will be important in the event that your program grows. Even if your company remains on the smaller side, you will want to develop equivalent skills either in-house or via third parties. Just as software development requires experience in frontend, backend, platform, and infrastructure, privacy engineering has its own subdomains of expertise; we will look at the various skills required to develop the tools and metrics we have discussed throughout this book.

Third, we will look at the larger regulatory ecosystem that affects companies and technical staff. It is not enough for engineers to merely understand the basics of laws like GDPR; engineers need to be able to interact with regulators and other influential bodies. This will enable engineers to influence new and existing laws.

As a technologist, I have always believed that it is wrong and bad business practice to pigeonhole engineers as order-takers. Keeping privacy and security technologists away from the regulatory process is counterproductive, just as it is when engineers are kept away from sales conversations. In the latter case, you see churn and unmet expectations, and in the former case, you may see privacy laws that fail to provide customers with meaningful protections and create unneeded burdens for businesses.

Before we dive in, I want to offer a word of caution: this chapter, like the book as a whole, is the beginning of a journey. I will offer frameworks and architectures that you can customize to your liking. Given the scale of modern technology and data, no book can offer simple step-by-step instructions to achieve enterprise-level privacy engineering maturity.

First we'll build a maturity model so you can track the effectiveness of your privacy engineering. To maintain consistency and provide a recognized starting point, I have used the NIST Cybersecurity Framework (www.nist.gov/cyberframework) and lessons learned from audits/assessments conducted by large firms as a reference for my work in this chapter.

11.1   *A maturity model for privacy engineering*

Something I have learned over a decade in cybersecurity and privacy is that these disciplines are like doing improv (improvisational theatre). The golden rule of improv is that you never say "No"; instead you say "Yes, and...."

Far too often I have seen privacy practitioners who have deep domain knowledge but lack business finesse. They see themselves as user advocates and purists, and they try to block any products that are not completely privacy-safe. They find themselves initially feared but eventually sidelined, since the business sees them as intractable. This is not a sustainable approach.

As you begin your data protection practice within a company, you will run up against headwinds like immature processes, resistance, lack of focus, and, often, people just prioritizing revenue over data privacy. To entrench your work and win allies, you will need to resist the urge to say "No" and find a way to help the business get to "Yes, but without violating user trust."

This approach is a great one to start with, but it's also not a durable one. Over time, you will need to secure and ring-fence resources and create objective success criteria. This section will help you build that framework, which will serve as a maturity model for your privacy engineering efforts.

As we build this maturity model for privacy engineering, we will look at four key dimensions. For each dimension, we will look at assessments and actions that will help you gauge effectiveness. The following subsections will look at each of these dimensions in more detail.

- *Identification*—In this dimension, you are assessing your privacy risk identification capabilities. Rather than detecting a risk in real time, you are exploring possible risks before they occur by investigating the following:
  - Can your program rapidly identify privacy risks and gaps?
  - Can this identification of risks occur at scale?
  - Is the identification occurring consistently via a combination of process and tooling?
- *Protection*—In this dimension, you can assess the reach and maturity of your data protection capabilities by checking for the following:
  - Can you protect the data in motion between endpoints and at rest in multiple storage locations?
  - Are you conducting activities like vulnerability scans and dynamic testing to address any gaps?
  - Are you managing access to assets, data, and systems in a risk-driven and auditable fashion?
- *Detection*—Since not every risk can be proactively identified and protected against, your program will need to be able to detect risks as well. In this dimension, you should consider the following questions:
  - Is your data protection coverage comprehensive in that it covers all key systems and tools?
  - Are you detecting anomalous behavior both for the ingress and egress of data?
- *Remediation*—Even the most mature privacy engineering program may not be able to prevent all risks and harms. In this dimension, it is therefore critical that you test your program's ability in the following areas:
  - Does your program offer resiliency and business continuity capabilities to remedy a privacy harm?
  - Does your incident response team have established service level agreements (SLAs)?
  - Is there a dashboard that tracks incoming incidents, SLA status, and patterns?

This list is an outline around which a growing and maturing company can build its framework.

We will now look at each dimension in detail and assess your program's readiness. First, though, it will be helpful to set readiness milestones like *foundational* to *mature* to *advanced*. That way, when your company performs a gap analysis, you can use these levels as stepping stones and targets.

Since there is no industry definition for these milestones, we can define them here:

- *Foundational*—The program has core capabilities but they still need to scale and increase their coverage. This is common in startups and companies that have made a major shift.
- *Mature*—The program has iterated and adapted and can scale to meet privacy compliance goals in most cases.
- *Advanced*—The program is not just in line with existing best practices but also has progressed in a way that demonstrates how other companies can evolve and grow.

11.1.1 Identification

To identify privacy risks, you will want to look at your infrastructure and systems as individual units as well as collective systems that interact with and impact each other. Just as engineers need to perform unit testing and integration testing prior to code deployment, privacy engineers need to look at the entire business through a similar inside-out lens. This dimension is about looking at your tech stack and business processes across the board to identify possible risks.

Given the decentralized nature of modern engineering, identifying privacy risk involves several component activities. These are not activities that you can suddenly perform on demand. Additionally, it may take a while for their impact to be felt. That is why it is helpful to examine the three levels of maturity and plan your evolution accordingly. We will now look at these activities in turn.

ASSET MANAGEMENT

Given that your IT infrastructure will serve either as a pipe for transfers or as a container for data storage, asset management is critical to identify privacy risks. In particular, you will need to track the status and ownership of any assets that affect your data. This is critical so that you can then focus on applying the data privacy techniques discussed throughout this book on the assets based on their prioritization.

Table 11.1 provides an example of the sorts of activities you will need to perform under the aegis of asset management and how your execution must evolve for maturity.

Table 11.1 Asset management maturity evolution

Foundational	Mature	Advanced
Capabilities optimize for tracking and listing assets, so as to start a basic list of possible risks.	Capabilities optimize for tracking, listing, and ranking, so that preemptive remediation provide high value in risk reduction.	Scope focuses on automation and orchestration improvement.

Table 11.1   Asset management maturity evolution *(continued)*

Foundational	Mature	Advanced
Roadmaps and quarterly plans build on this informal list of business processes and information assets, such as data stores, IT (corporate engineering) assets, etc. Engineers have an intuitive albeit undocumented understanding of which systems contain which information. As with data, the criteria for classifying information assets are foundational but have buy-in from leadership.	Roadmaps and quarterly plans leverage a prioritized database of all business processes and information assets; this evolving list is a combination of architectural designs and technical workflows. Assets are tagged to indicate ownership, data sensitivity, and business criticality; this helps provide accountability and quantifiable KPIs. The inventory of digital assets covers the entire tech stack with no initial opt-outs, so as to build a baseline of risk identification.	The process of discovering and cataloging assets is automated with minimal errors. The asset inventory lists business value, privacy risk, and associated owners; this inventory and its continually updated versions have executive approval with technical mitigations as a fast-follow.
Information assets are represented as specific nodes in a network architecture diagram and workflow. Existing workflows and data flows are continually mapped in response to and in preparation for inappropriate access of sensitive data by insiders and vendors.	A majority of third-party information systems are catalogued, and they are prioritized based on the company's internal risk appetite. The most privacy-sensitive assets are mapped to business risk to facilitate analysis and prioritization.	All third-party systems are catalogued and regularly refreshed to reflect external updates, and they are prioritized based on the company's risk appetite. A dollar value is assigned to each business process and asset to determine the impact and likelihood of privacy harm.
KPIs are tracked at the team level so as to set up a light-touch process and get teams started on this maturity journey.	KPIs are tracked by clustering related teams or ones that belong to the same business lines.	KPIs are tracked and reviewed bottom-up across the organization's scope.

For table 11.1 and subsequent tables, the following two points apply:

- Each offering attains more maturity as you move from left to right. For example, the scope (row 1) in the Mature column requires that you prioritize the cataloging of assets rather than just tracking them ad hoc, as companies are likely to do at the Foundational stage of relative immaturity.
- Additionally, each entry assumes the work in the box to its left is already accomplished.

GOVERNANCE

Regardless of size, companies need a governance structure to help identify risks. This means having standards and guidelines that can be used to monitor operations and flag risks. Table 11.2 lists the activities you need to perform and how the maturity levels evolve.

As you can see in table 11.2, improved privacy governance can help detect privacy risks. At the foundational level, you see standards and policies that are vertical in

Table 11.2 Governance maturity evolution

Foundational	Mature	Advanced
Employees sign on to acknowledge disclosures and standards during onboarding and then annually (i.e., with a defined cadence but after the passage of non-trivial amounts of time).	Employees do not just sign on to disclosures and standards but are trained on an ongoing basis with assessments to help ensure understanding rather than just awareness.	Employees do not just sign on to disclosures and standards but are trained on an ongoing basis, and they need to meet a minimal assessment score, as a condition to retain data access, for example.
Teams are able to evaluate policy exceptions on a case-by-case basis.	A committee comprised of data privacy specialists reviews the risks by applying policies and standards.	A committee comprised of data privacy specialists partners with businesses to review risks and build metrics around policies and standards.
Privacy standards are defined for all risk areas, such as identity and access management and data encryption, but no clear enterprise standard needs to be in place.	Enterprise-wide privacy standards are in place in some but not all of the risk areas; for remaining risk areas, foundational standards exist.	Scalable and flexible enterprise-wide privacy controls address privacy risks including architecture, endpoints, access management, change management, vendor management, etc.
Each business function establishes its own privacy risk metrics and KPIs to measure its compliance.	The company maintains a central scorecard to measure privacy risk reduction using a complete set of KPIs.	Besides the central scorecard, the company maintains and updates privacy risk appetite thresholds for each business area.

nature, in that they apply to a specific business unit. A more mature governance offering creates company-wide controls, while the advanced governance posture shows a more collaborative and itinerant process.

The likelihood of timely risk identification grows as you move from foundational to advanced, but a caveat does apply: as your privacy governance capabilities grow, possibly so do new business units, mergers, and cavalier behaviors among employees. Therefore, any maturity of your privacy governance is not to be seen as an absolute gain but as a moving target.

RISK MANAGEMENT

It is critical that businesses have mechanisms to manage assets and govern them to discover risks. However, another key vertical of the identification capability for privacy is risk management. Once risks are identified, businesses can end up on one of two extremes. They could either be overly tactical and miss out on efficiencies or be overly strategic and get caught in analysis. Therefore, developing a maturity framework for risk management is vital. Table 11.3 lays out such a framework.

As you can see in table 11.3, the foundational risk management strategy is very team-specific. It is possible, even likely, that teams develop such strategies for themselves while being oblivious to dependencies and redundancies with other teams. There is a substantial evolution as you move to a more mature model, where there are more sustained

Table 11.3 Risk management maturity evolution

Foundational	Mature	Advanced
The privacy risk management strategy is seeded by teams in disaster recovery and incident response based on past incidents or ones that have occurred elsewhere. As such, the strategy leans into a more defensive and backward-looking mindset.	The privacy risk management strategy aggregates input from technical and non-technical stakeholders, so as to provide broader business coverage. As such, the strategy is dynamic and evolving but in a more scattershot rather than collaborative manner.	Business leaders evaluate and quantify risk and remediation options (backed up by KPIs and risk appetite mappings) as part of privacy strategy development.
The strategy includes input from upstream stakeholders like heads of business lines and markets, but these insights don't always affect technical outcomes and decisions. The non-technical leadership may or may not have veto power over the emerging strategy, since the company is typically optimizing for growth and market penetration/expansion instead of risk assessment maturity.	The privacy risk management strategy aggregates input from technical and non-technical stakeholders; however, the aim for this engagement is awareness rather than explicit endorsement or formal sponsorship by those stakeholders.	The privacy risk management strategy is developed in close collaboration with business and technology stakeholders, and there is a formal sponsorship by those stakeholders. The business stakeholders are accountable for the success of the strategy, sort of like how executive leaders are increasingly tying their compensation to diversity and inclusion.
There is quasi-mandated consultation between privacy engineers and strategic leadership, but alignment is not a prerequisite for roadmap planning and execution.	Consultation between privacy engineers and business leaders is a prerequisite for planning and execution; whether acquiescence and alignment is a blocker is determined on a case-by-case basis.	Business leaders are initiators of the privacy risk management strategy; they provide formal review or sign-off and serve as escalation points for internal and external audits.
The management of strategy development and execution is often not documented because the risk management conversations tend to be embryonic, transactional, and tactical.	Risk management strategy development and execution is fueled by metrics, tooling, and automation, as well as growing coverage of business units.	The privacy risk management strategy managed by the tools is routinely consulted before key business decisions.

partnerships with the business. There is a gentler evolution in the advanced model, where the business uses the privacy risk management strategy more proactively.

We have seen how a company can evolve in its identification and management of privacy risk. In the next subsection, we will examine how a company can protect itself from such risks after having identified them.

11.1.2 Protection

The tools for protecting data range from security techniques like multifactor authentication, encryption, anomaly detection, and monitoring to privacy techniques like anonymization, obfuscation, and deletion. However, a program's evolution in maturity requires an approach that helps drive these tools in coordination rather than as isolated point solutions. In this section, we will look at the various parts of an ideal protection strategy.

IDENTITY AND ACCESS MANAGEMENT

The best data protection strategy would be to limit collection from the start, but the data you do need to collect requires protection. Table 11.4 shows how you can build a framework to manage the identities for those who access the data and build in access management tied to those identities. These identities would typically be employee identities, but over time could refer to partners or even customers. Note that some of the specifics may need to be adapted for your company, its sector, geographic presence, etc., so the table is to be used as a starting point.

Table 11.4   Identity and access management maturity evolution

Foundational	Mature	Advanced
In keeping with a growth mindset, the IT administrators can provide access credentials for employees, partners, and others. There is potential audit coverage as part of an embryonic access control system.	The company drives identity and access management based on informal but quantifiable standards so as to avoid falling behind competitors or failing audits. As such, access management follows a "do no harm" approach.	The company routinely stress-tests its access management policies via bug bounties, audits, and industry benchmarking.
The management of identities is governed by zero-trust but also low-friction access. This leads to an identity management strategy that does not comport with industry standards but provides a solid starting point. Key stakeholders, vendors, and regulators are set up for short-term access, but there are often minimal controls to prevent abuse..	The coupling of zero-trust access and scalable controls means that identity management and governance tends to have an upward arc. There is also tooling to auto-provision and auto-rescind. This leads to upwards of 50% identity coverage across all systems and assets. User identities are closely tied to systems based on documented need, and their access is constantly monitored so as to allow for renewing access or discontinuing it. New identity-based access systems help monitor usage. Such access is renewed in response to need and not provided in expectation of future need. The company begins to factor into its overall risk score the continual reduction (or right-sizing) of cumulative access across all teams and data assets. The company also starts investing in automation that can assess access requests expeditiously.	The company has such an advanced state of access management that they can quantify the need for access for users (internal and external) and for systems. By way of automated tooling, user-system access requests are evaluated and granted (or denied). There are impenetrable controls that prevent privileged users from growing their access without administrative approval. For example, a privileged user may not amplify their access and also may not create another identity of equivalent privilege.

Table 11.4 Identity and access management maturity evolution *(continued)*

Foundational	Mature	Advanced
Systems that store sensitive user or customer data need to use authentication tooling that is constantly monitored.	Most systems, at a minimum, rely on single-factor authentication but increasingly need to use multifactor user authentication and additional verification for specific systems that contain sensitive data. This progression represents the fusion of asset management and identity management.	Using a combination of data inventory, asset management, and identity, the company can strategically deploy access management at scale in a targeted fashion. There is ongoing improvement in these mappings based on shifts in data collection and usage as well as regulatory expectations.

You can see in table 11.4 how access management is multifaceted given the sprawl of data, systems, and identities. There is a risk-multiplier aspect to the privacy risk given the amount of online activity that companies and governments capture. It is vital that companies try to evolve their maturity across the various facets of access management so as to reduce the pressure on downstream activities like deletion and encryption.

VULNERABILITY MANAGEMENT

Protecting data requires patching any gaps in your systems. As you have seen in earlier chapters, bad actors have exploited vulnerabilities ranging from access control to leaked credentials to third parties. While you may not catch every gap, building a framework to track and manage these vulnerabilities, like the one shown in table 11.5, is critical.

Table 11.5 Vulnerability management maturity evolution

Foundational	Mature	Advanced
Vulnerability scans are continuous and comprehensive. Vulnerability identification tools need to be managed outside of teams that own assets, data stores, or services so that there are no bespoke exceptions that then lead to increased risk. Remediation of vulnerabilities is managed at the team level. This could lead to reliable and targeted remediations but also to a lack of central visibility into overall organizational remediation maturity.	Central privacy and security teams define SLAs for vulnerability remediation based on business impact as well as regulatory risk. These SLAs are binding for teams across the company unless explicit exceptions are granted. Testing and fixing of vulnerabilities should follow a set template so as to maintain consistency and create a paper trail for future audits. The company uses a documented risk framework to prioritize vulnerability remediation based on data sensitivity and business risk (in terms of money at stake, should the risk materialize).	The SLAs for vulnerability remediation are made more aggressive with the passage of time and heightening of scrutiny. Security and privacy teams compare the results of vulnerability scans so as to assess risk across the tech stack. Product lines are asked to improve their risk-reward ratios. As such, vulnerability management helps set business direction rather than being an after-the-fact cleanup job. There is a tight coupling between vulnerability scans and parts of the tech stack so that risks are targeted for elimination rather than unknowingly replicated.

Table 11.5   Vulnerability management maturity evolution *(continued)*

Foundational	Mature	Advanced
	The company maintains a central CMS (or other system) that inventories all known vulnerabilities and their applicability in systems other than the ones where the vulnerability was first detected. Risk vectors are updated automatically and continuously in line with changes internal and external to the business; this insight then feeds into the implementation of the vulnerability scanning.	Vulnerability reporting is stored in tamper-proof logs and maintained both for audit reporting and to demonstrate compliance to enterprise customers.

After high-profile privacy breaches, I am often asked why companies and governments fail to provide the basic steps for data protection. As you can see from table 11.5, the leap from foundational capabilities to more mature coverage is non-trivial. The sooner you start to close these gaps, the less effort it will take to close them.

SOFTWARE DEVELOPMENT SECURITY AND PRIVACY

Investing in protecting your data and infrastructure will only go so far if you don't also protect the product development process itself. Your engineers make many micro-decisions on design and implementation that, left unguided, could lead to privacy risk. Table 11.6 shows how you can create a software development process that balances engineering throughput and privacy.

Table 11.6   Software development security and privacy maturity evolution

Foundational	Mature	Advanced
Vulnerability identification is conducted in code (to spot loose credentials, for example) and at runtime, but teams may prioritize one over the other in the absence of top-down guidance or industry standards. Privacy reviews act as a final potential blocker before code deployments to production, but there are no workflows or mandates to compel engineering participation in the review process.	Development and testing need to proceed with synthetic and/or anonymized data. Code migration—from development to production environments or vice versa—would require approvals and impact analyses. Change-management systems provide for documenting the impact on high-touch systems and blocking for approvals if applicable. There would be a callout to privacy engineers to review changes that impact sensitive customer data. Emergency changes trigger warning notifications to impacted entities with an option to revert.	Additive changes like new systems, tech stacks, or mergers should proceed only after integration and unit testing is conducted for privacy risks. Individual systems as well as cross-functional combinations of systems should have controls built in to identify vulnerabilities emerging from new changes; for example, ingesting more data from a new API could trigger tests to recalculate k-anonymity, which you learned about in chapter 5. The engineering and privacy/security teams should continuously update threat models based on industry insight and standards, and then adapt those changes to product design, code environments, and transfer mechanisms.

Table 11.6   Software development security and privacy maturity evolution *(continued)*

Foundational	Mature	Advanced
Only authorized engineers and DevOps personnel can deploy code, and there is a tamper-proof audit trail of all deployments and review requests. Penetration tests are conducted annually for all critical applications and processes. These tests simulate the activities of an attacker to validate that discovered vulnerabilities can be exploited.	Systems, code, and access configurations are subject to sudden reviews to validate compliance. This guardrail can be repurposed for privacy as well. Penetration tests are conducted for critical applications.	Automated vulnerability scans are buffered by manual testing so as to avoid an over-dependence on automation. Teams utilize testing techniques that attempt to find bugs in code by randomly feeding invalid and unexpected input so as to find coding errors and security loopholes. Done continually, teams are able to identify patterns of new vulnerabilities and treat them as training opportunities. Access to deployment and environments is restricted to people with verified or verifiable use cases. There is a document approval process that engineers can follow before services can egress data to outside the network perimeter (such as the public cloud, third parties, etc.).

The critical takeaway from table 11.6 is that companies need data protection capabilities as an accompaniment to the software development process. Given the number of variables at play, companies need to help their engineers do the right thing. Companies that fail to do so are the ones who end up pointing their fingers at an engineer whose simple mistake ended up with outsized ramifications. The framework in table 11.6 will help protect the company, its engineers, and its customers.

CLOUD-BASED DATA PROTECTION

Given the vast amount of data that already lives in the cloud, as well as the number of companies migrating data to the cloud, cloud-based data protection is a key component of overall data protection. The chasm in data protection skills between cloud-first or cloud-native companies and companies playing catch-up is significant. This is critical, since cloud infrastructure is now a key part of the engineering development process. Table 11.7 provides a framework for making sure that data protection is woven into your usage of the cloud.

Table 11.7   Cloud data protection maturity evolution

Foundational	Mature	Advanced
The company has a list of cloud service providers and their services that have been "allowlisted" by finance, compliance, requisitions teams, etc. Data protection is actively managed for public cloud programs and workloads.	Data protection is considered explicitly in all cloud programs. There is a proliferation of controls applicable to data, whether in storage or transit.	Data of varying levels of sensitivity are often processed in a cloud, and this data is often unstructured.

Table 11.7   Cloud data protection maturity evolution *(continued)*

Foundational	Mature	Advanced
A security-driven process is in place to verify and test hypervisor configuration settings. A mix of security and business specialists periodically review hypervisor configuration settings and document findings and gaps. There is a need-based and metric-driven process to grant and withdraw access to hypervisor management functions and administrative consoles for systems hosting virtualized systems. If access is granted, the validity of the usage is continually monitored to compare against the predefined need. Engineers use secured and encrypted communication channels when migrating physical servers, applications, or data to virtualized servers. Engineers must be strongly incentivized to use a network distinct from production networks so as to avoid data leakage during the migration process.	This standard should be further entrenched based on the sensitivity of the data and the volume of the data. Data is encrypted from end to end and exemptions must be clearly enumerated. All server interactions occur via encrypted channels.	When that happens, engineers must configure distinct cloud accounts to provide appropriate levels of privacy or the level of protection is optimized for the highest level of sensitivity.

INFRASTRUCTURE-BASED DATA PROTECTION

Just as protecting the cloud is critical, taking the same view toward the overall infrastructure is key. Given the segmentation of the modern tech domain into endpoints, services, etc., taking a holistic view of the infrastructure is non-negotiable. This will also increase the chances that a bad actor gets detected, since your data protection controls will be broad and deep rather than consolidated in a single layer. Table 11.8 provides a framework.

Table 11.8   Infrastructure-based data protection maturity evolution

Foundational	Mature	Advanced
Network and endpoint security is governed by policies that define remote access, segmentation, email security, network and endpoint security monitoring, and device hardening. The universal and consistent application of these policies may not be present.	There has to be a direct correlation between the sensitivity of the data and the security offered by the containing network segment. Such security, regardless of implementation details, should adhere to the principles of zero-trust, continuous monitoring, and rapid adjustment in the event of an anomaly.	It should be possible to isolate system components from other components of the system so as to provide enforceable access limitations. This isolation can occur based on threat identification, detection, or on regulatory changes.

Table 11.8   Infrastructure-based data protection maturity evolution *(continued)*

Foundational	Mature	Advanced
The company will segment networks to drive protection based on risk. The success criteria is the quantifiable reduction of discovery and exfiltration of critical information assets. Segmented networks for systems open to third parties do not have the same lineage and access to production assets that internal networks do. Remote access is often necessary for employees but is configured such that secure communication and data transfer can occur over publicly accessible networks with minimal risk. There is enterprise email security filtering with anomaly detection and third-party "allow" lists and "block" lists.	There must be proactive and continuous monitoring of adherence to access control policies. This must be upheld for every network segment as well as remote access. Such approval must also require scrutiny of the business case for such access. There must be a baseline set for services in terms of network traffic and data flows they will generate. These metrics evolve with changing adoption levels, so acceptable thresholds must be regularly refreshed for the entire enterprise. Access to websites, especially ones that may lead to content injection or data extraction, should be restricted through web content filtering. Remote wipe capabilities and data loss protection must be offered by the mobile device management (MDM); the MDM must also offer lost device tracking for hardware with access to sensitive data. In the event that "Bring Your Own Device" (BYOD) is permitted, the administrators must facilitate a ring-fenced environment for enterprise applications and data. The security controls to detect sensitive data egress should cover email, chat programs, and other data mobility tools. Detections of unauthorized data sharing via all possible channels should be used to update the risk score as well as threat models. This finding is then fed into roadmaps for risk identification when new systems are conceived.	There is a constant automated comparison of data flows across network segments to an acceptable baseline. Deviations from this established baseline will immediately lead to access being blocked. The mobile device management (MDM) mandates the highest and most potent encryption; BYOD devices are not allowed access to systems with sensitive data unless there are exceptional circumstances. There is little, if any, difference between monitoring, quarantine, and deletion controls that apply to internal email and messaging and the corresponding controls for external communications. Only select users with privileges can make changes to the firewall rules when those changes are to apply immediately.

A key observation from table 11.8 is that the use of endpoints is not all there is to infrastructure protection. Since privacy is contextual and is often compromised by data aggregation, the mobile nature of today's workforce and customers should be a consideration, as should communication via email, given the risk of targeting and compromise.

Given the number of companies just migrating to the cloud or struggling to update their legacy protocols, it is possible they are vulnerable to email-powered attacks. These range from spoofing and phishing to domain squatting. These attacks tend to be aimed at companies with antiquated email configurations. Their targets tend to be busy executives or other leaders who may be increasingly susceptible.

Client-side attacks can be equally effective. Malicious content, by way of an email attachment, could easily lead to a ransomware situation. This is just a flavor of infrastructure-related vulnerabilities that, when combined with a hyper-mobile and connected workforce, form a combustible cocktail. Having continually evolving infrastructure security is vital for detecting and remedying these gaps. I hope that you will see the shadows of recent headlines and mistakes in the recommendations in table 11.8.

11.1.3 Detection

The third dimension of privacy engineering is detection of risks or actions that could pose risks. However, the traditional detection model optimizes for damage control via timely detection and remedial action. I am proposing that we lean in and build preemptive capabilities that detect risks upstream and help build products that are risk-resistant.

THREAT INTELLIGENCE

Bad actors who wish to gain access to customer data will either hew to existing risk patterns or identify new ones. Companies that wish to thwart them need to act likewise and gather threat intelligence so they can prepare a defense strategy. Table 11.9 provides a sample framework.

Table 11.9   Threat intelligence maturity evolution

Foundational	Mature	Advanced
The collection and interpretation of threat information and corresponding updates occurs in an ad hoc fashion. These updates may not be uniformly enforced like they should be, since they exist, in many cases, at the service level rather than the infrastructure level. The company updates security tools and their configuration settings based on threat intelligence that is a superset of several threat models and vectors. There is a very rudimentary prioritization mechanism for threats that are newly discovered. There are limited risk indicators and KPIs for threat intelligence, and these KPIs vary by team and service (i.e., the KPIs for a specific service may not reflect the network exposure or data sensitivity).	The organization has an evolving threat profile that identifies potential threat actors, motives, intent, capabilities, and targets. Rather than relying on internal assessments that carry the risk of confirmation bias, the company regularly refreshes threat intelligence from free and paid sources, such as benevolent hackers and other experts. The company prioritizes and addresses threat information sources; these sources are regularly validated to confirm completeness and currency. While the Key Risk Indicators (KRIs) and KPIs may not be finessed for all edge cases, they are tracked to ensure organizational coverage. The company can track whether the threat intelligence is comprehensive as well as adaptable. For example, incoming emails are continually monitored and intercepted to detect phishing attempts or SQL injection attempts.	The organization has an evolving threat profile that covers the full perimeter and constantly imbibes insights from the team/service level. Responses to detected or identified threats trigger pre-planned processes and mitigation workflows.

As table 11.9 shows, threat intelligence requires not just an agile understanding of data and identity, but also a tight alignment organizationally. This will help build an understanding of upcoming attacks and gaps that would amplify the effectiveness of those threats.

CONTINUOUS MONITORING

As you build out privacy engineering maturity, ensuring that you monitor for threats and anomalies is critical. Monitoring should optimize for both coverage as well as depth. That means you want a capability that covers a large and expanding surface area as well as to probe in depth for specific silos. Table 11.10 provides a sample framework.

Table 11.10   Continuous monitoring maturity evolution

Foundational	Mature	Advanced
It is possible to identify privacy incidents, policy violations, fraudulent activity, and potential breaches based on logging activity and signals sent to system owners. There may not be a centralized monitoring system that enforces identification SLAs. There are the beginnings of a mapping between monitoring resources and corresponding remediation workflows. Alert escalations tend to follow an ad hoc process that is optimized for resolution rather than formal documentation. In order to discern the impact of privacy and security events, alert thresholds are programmed based on incident severity and blast radius. Engineers create and prioritize logging sources with a myopic and service focus rather than extrapolation to organizational monitoring needs.	Engineers fine-tune, test, and run QA for alerts prior to and during production, so as to ensure continual monitoring. Owners of mission-critical services create runbooks for advanced use cases; these runbooks provide guidance for triage and "stop the bleeding" steps. Log generation and storage are configured for easy access and rapid response. Any sensitive data (IP addresses, device IDs, etc.) are aggregated and/or obfuscated to serve monitoring needs but to also avoid granular use profiling.	All logs are monitored with high frequency to observe anomalies such as when a source system generates discernibly more or less data than normal. Automated network scanning tools continuously identify log sources that could help identify threats and even new services that may process sensitive data.

There is obviously more to mature monitoring than I have provided in table 11.10. However, the key observation is that you will want to check more places for logs, check more often, and watch for anomalies in those logs. Patterns in those entries and timely identification of those patterns will help identify security risks that, left undeterred, could cause privacy harms.

INSIDER THREAT

Companies may have internal associates who end up compromising the protection of its data. This threat may stem from malfeasance or incompetence or even carelessness. This creates a need for sophisticated granular and tiered access control and in-depth monitoring and response capabilities. Table 11.11 provides a sample framework.

Table 11.11   Insider threat maturity evolution

Foundational	Mature	Advanced
There is continuous monitoring of insiders whose services access and process sensitive data. There is a lack of continual education and training on data management and processing best practices or on the outcomes if these best practices are violated. The team relies primarily on existing applications, generated alerts, and user reports, and these efforts are often siloed. Privacy and security engineers correlate and analyze a defined set of data such as log information, IP addresses, and data movements to identify potential insider threats. There could be more invasive monitoring for employees identified as likely insider threats. When anomalies are identified, remediation is often localized to the team. Policies and controls for insider threats tend to not be defined clearly, nor is their application consistent.	There is continuous monitoring of third-party vendors whose services access and process sensitive data. The security team monitors behavior analytics to simulate a set of use cases that a malicious insider may execute. These behavioral analytics are compared to defined baseline profiles and legitimate behavior. These comparisons help drive escalations, remediations, and sanctions.	The access to sensitive data is granularly segmented so that there are specific risk focus areas. An example would be insiders who have access to a customer's mobility data and could use it to track an ex-spouse. Varying levels of insider sophistication drive response workflows; this will help cover insiders ranging from the sophisticated to ones that are dilettantes. Employees with granular access to sensitive data are made aware of the additional scrutiny and monitoring that will apply to them. Rather than looking for deviation from a baseline, the insider threat modeling evaluates how the baseline must evolve as data, network segments, and service engagement levels change.

As you can see from table 11.11, privacy controls for insider risk require monitoring based on the data and infrastructure. However, they also require an insight into human behavior. While I understand the data protection imperative, building a baseline of acceptable behavior and predicting future behavior could land you in some sensitive areas. I advise you to take a consultative approach so as to avoid a process and outcome tainted by prejudice or false positives.

11.1.4   *Remediation*

Even if companies do everything in their power and then some, there will be privacy incidents. These could range from inadvertent logging or access of sensitive data to incomplete deletion to exfiltration. These will require an incident response management capability that cannot be spun up on the fly. This resource (or team) will need to work cross-functionally and quickly. This is a challenge for small and growing companies, since these businesses are segmented to optimize for rapidity. Table 11.12 provides some context on how you can scale this dimension to complete your overall data protection rubric.

INCIDENT RESPONSE MANAGEMENT

Companies need to understand that insider risk is often the most underrated risk vector to security and privacy. Either out of malevolence or incompetence or something in between, insiders and their ability to process data could cause privacy harm. Therefore, preparing for that risk is critical. Table 11.12 presents a framework for evolving your insider threat offering.

Table 11.12   Incident response management maturity evolution

Foundational	Mature	Advanced
System owners must complete incident response training and detailed assessments when they get access to a system and data store; there is limited clarity on training refreshes.	System owners are required to participate in incident response training and assessments every six months. The training and the assessments have owners who continually update them.	System owners are required to participate in incident response training and testing quarterly. Privacy and security engineers help improve the incident response runbook based on lessons learned from high-visibility and high-impact incidents; training and targeted testing emerge from these insights as well.
The security and privacy engineers create bespoke response runbooks that speak to different services with the goal of creating a more universal process.	The security and privacy engineers create response runbooks that become more comprehensive and representative because of half-yearly reviews. A response workflow automatically sends an alert to service owners and impacted parties with information and timelines that are driven by severity and blast radius.	The security and privacy engineers create response runbooks that become more comprehensive and representative because of quarterly reviews. There are capabilities to disable the system partly or entirely in the event of an incident of a certain impact level or magnitude. Engineers and program managers have access to a dashboard with updated incident status; there are templates for communicating mission-critical details to executives, regulators, and customers.
Incident prioritization is driven by the "squeaky wheel" approach.	Incident prioritization is based on IP address, time of day, or day of the week, business vertical that is impacted, compliance obligations, enterprise customer expectations, etc.	In the event of incidents above a specific prioritization level, the responses follow a defined checklist, including alerting administrators and applying stringent security controls.

Now that we have built an understanding of organizational and infrastructural maturity for privacy engineering, we will explore the skill set required in your team.

11.2   *The privacy engineering domain and skills*

I have aimed this book at companies that run fast, operate lean, and where engineers and other technical leaders often have to multitask. Such companies don't always have the luxury and resources to hire privacy engineering specialists. Even so, companies often grow enough in revenue and scrutiny to make such hires possible and necessary. It may also be that existing personnel need to absorb the work and develop the skills to build privacy tooling.

In this section, I will provide a synopsis of the sorts of skills that make up the privacy engineering domain. Some of these skills can be found in one person, while others require a level of domain specialization. The degree to which you will require and be able to afford to hire individuals with these skills will depend upon several factors about your business:

- Scale
- Geographic reach
- Regulatory scrutiny
- Engineering depth

Regardless of how you staff your privacy engineering function, it will help to have an understanding of these skills. Cybersecurity, data protection, and privacy engineering are novel enough that there is still plenty of incorrect information around domain expertise. I'd rather companies with finite resources make more informed staffing decisions. With that background, let's do a quick runthrough of privacy-related skills.

PRIVACY SOFTWARE ENGINEERS

Privacy software engineers are engineers who may not have privacy domain expertise—for example, cryptography, anonymization, etc.—but who build privacy-preserving tooling. Their tools could detect data using crawlers that deploy regular expressions, enforce access control using behavioral analytics, delete data while maintaining service continuity, etc. These engineers understand data, system architecture, data warehousing, and query efficiency. They contribute to the attainment of privacy goals and can build privacy skills gradually. This book is primarily aimed at existing internal engineers with this skill set who can go on and become your privacy engineers.

COMPLIANCE SPECIALISTS

It is helpful to understand the difference between privacy engineering and compliance. Compliance is the act of ensuring documented due diligence—showing that you followed known rules. Compliance is reactive in that it is aimed at satisfying rules borne of previous failures. Compliance specialists are often not engineers, but experts at mapping rules to engineering outcomes, performing gap analysis, and helping drive prioritization for the gaps creating most risk. Just as an actuarial analyst could provide insurance rates based on risk, compliance specialists can recommend the next course of action based on a company's need to meet a specific standard.

PRIVACY ANALYSTS

Chapter 6 and its focus on privacy reviews was aimed at privacy analysts. These privacy experts should look at your products and features (or preferably, the designs for these features at an early stage), ask questions, identify risks, and help you redesign in a privacy-safe fashion before you make irreversible technical decisions. For example, rather than making a copy of data and encrypting it for limited access, a privacy analyst could help drive access from a centralized source. This would allow for consistency, reduce duplication, and cut down on the work involved to manage encryption keys and access logs. These experts don't just look at technical artifacts on their own, but at how human ingenuity or malfeasance could lead to unpredictable outcomes. They are privacy engineers by trade.

PRIVACY PRODUCT MANAGERS

Privacy product managers have two key responsibilities. First, they design and finalize requirements for privacy-specific products, like deletion, data extraction, etc. These designs are used by privacy software engineers to then build the products, which are then used by the rest of the company. This way, you don't end up with bespoke privacy tooling on a team-by-team basis in the company. Second, these product managers should also build privacy features that are user facing, like consent capture tools, privacy settings, dashboards, etc.

Privacy product managers should also try to build privacy features into the company's core products that aim to drive engagement and revenue. In so doing, they would be consultants to other product managers whose remit focuses on building features that drive engagement and revenue. That way, the company's privacy maturity is not dependent solely on the adoption of central privacy tools.

DATA ANALYSTS

Data analysts have a deep background in mathematics and data querying. They can help provide data-driven guidance; quantifying re-identification risk and k-anonymity, which you saw in chapter 5, are examples. Well-resourced companies can hire mathematicians and then SQL analysts to provide support. More nimble companies hire mathematicians and then teach them how to query databases; this approach scales better, since it helps ensure that an understanding of the data as well as the ability to retrieve it will reside in the same individual.

PRIVACY INFRASTRUCTURE SPECIALISTS

All the tooling we have discussed in this book needs to account for scale and the segmentation and distribution of the tech stack. Implementing deletion at scale requires knowledge about data warehousing, caches, availability zones, and adjusting all these for business continuity. Allowing for scale will require that privacy infrastructure specialists focus on validation and verification at scale as well. In my opinion, this role can repurpose existing systems architects and does not require privacy domain knowledge, although such expertise can help build credibility with stakeholders ranging from privacy attorneys to the rest of the engineers who may have zero privacy expertise. Given the reality of cloud-based computing and trans-national data transfers, this role is critical for growth companies.

PRIVACY UX DESIGNERS

Privacy UX designers act as user advocates, so they will need at least some formal privacy expertise. Their remit ranges from

- Writing copy for public-facing privacy tools that needs to account for regulatory needs yet must be clear enough for the layperson to understand
- Deploying quantitative and qualitative methods to understand how users (internal and external) could react with privacy products
- Advising privacy product managers on why adoption of privacy products may differ from expectations based on observed user behavior patterns

For companies that operate with diverse populations or deal with very personal data, this skill is vital.

PRIVACY ARCHITECTS

When I am not leading global privacy teams at major companies, this is the domain I occupy at companies. Privacy architects have aggregated and accumulated expertise in privacy regulation, public policy, software development, and system architecture. Their role is to drive internal alignment around privacy and security standards. They need to thread the needle between writing policy that is aspirational and capturing the status quo on data handling at a company. The former requires privacy and regulatory expertise, and the latter needs engineering and architectural chops. This role requires the ability to manage relationships, build bridges, and create privacy champions out of skeptical executives. Among other things, this book aspires to help companies create homegrown privacy architects.

Finally, let's take a look at the larger regulatory climate that privacy operates in.

11.3 *Privacy and the regulatory climate*

I have long believed that regulation is downstream from popular sentiment. It is no accident that laws like the GDPR, CCPA, and others have arrived just as resentment toward the tech sector has grown. Simultaneously, it is no accident that institutional distrust of governments and businesses has led to populist movements worldwide.

What does this have to do with engineers, whose aspiration in life is to build products and solve problems? Engineers have had to live downstream from decision makers for far too long. In the days of waterfall development, they lived downstream from product management and sales and were often glorified order-takers. Today, in a more agile and bottom-up phase, they find themselves downstream from privacy regulation, which re-examines decisions that were made under an environment that was vastly different.

This book is aimed at solving a part of that problem; it will help engineers deploy a "build in" model for privacy rather than a "bolt on" model. The former embeds privacy into the design, process, and architecture of the company. The latter, by contrast, tries to close gaps as they emerge, with containment as its ceiling. However, engineers need to form alliances outside the company with industry influencers, privacy commentators, media, and others so as to make sure that privacy regulations are meaningful.

In my opinion, privacy regulations have three key objectives:

- Hold bad actors accountable when they misuse data.
- Provide customers and users with meaningful protections.
- Create quantifiable expectations that companies can meet.

To that end, I want to provide two examples of the macro-political picture to help you understand why the engineer's already difficult job regarding privacy is about to get harder. In 2006, then Chair of the Senate Commerce Committee, Senator Ted Stevens, was expressing his thoughts on Net Neutrality. In part of his speech, he said the following:

> *There's one company now that you can sign up [with] and get a movie delivered to your house. Daily. By delivery service [...] This service is now going to go through the Internet. And what you do now is go to a place and order your movie, and guess what? You can order 10 of them delivered to you and the delivery charge is free, right?*

> *10 movies streaming across that Internet. And what happens to your own personal Internet? Just the other day an Internet was sent by my staff at 10:00 in the morning on Friday—I got it yesterday. Why? Because it got tangled up with all these things going on the Internet commercially.*

> *And here we have this one situation where enormous entities want to use the Internet for their purpose to save money for doing what they're doing now. They use FedEx, they use deliver services, they use the mail. They deliver in other ways, but they want to deliver vast amounts of information over the Internet.*

> *And again, the Internet is not something that you just dump something on, it's not a big truck. It's a series of tubes. And if you don't understand, those tubes can be filled, and if they're filled, when you put your message in, it gets in line it's going to be delayed by anyone that puts into that tube enormous amounts of material.*[1]

Sen. Stevens was, in all likelihood, discussing the upcoming business model for Netflix. The senator's remarks have been widely mocked on the internet for years due to the errors they contain. For example,

- He uses the words "email" and "internet" interchangeably.
- There was no evidence to suggest that video streaming led to delayed email in this specific case.

That said, a report from Canadian networking equipment company Sandvine found that more than a third of all North American internet was generated by Netflix alone during peak hours.[2] Even though the senator's statement and the Sandvine findings were almost a decade apart, there have been other examples that suggest that even as the tech industry is impacting the world at levels not seen before, the sophistication

---

[1] Evan Dashevsky, "A Remembrance and Defense of Ted Stevens' 'Series of Tubes'," *PC Magazine*, June 5, 2014, http://mng.bz/BxDg.

[2] Stephanie Mlot, "Netflix Dominates Web Traffic as Cord Cutters Gobble Data," *PC Magazine*, May 14, 2014, http://mng.bz/doPX.

and understanding of political leaders with regulatory power has not made much progress.

This poses a critical problem for engineers and the tech industry. Regulations are being pushed by advocates, including many in government, whose strong point of view about online commerce is unaccompanied by an equal immersion in the technical details. Engineers are always expected to write code, deliver products, and not violate such complicated laws; the lack of connection between the regulatory apparatus in government and the productivity apparatus in industry hurts the very customers the laws are intended to protect.

At this point, you might wonder if things have changed in the 15 years since the Stevens speech. In early 2018, as the U.S. Senate held hearings on the Cambridge Analytica episode, Facebook CEO Mark Zuckerberg had an exchange with then Senator Orrin Hatch. Sen. Hatch asked Zuckerberg if Facebook was still committed to offering its service for free. The transcript of that exchange is as follows:

> *ZUCKERBERG: Senator, yes. There will always be a version of Facebook that is free. It is our mission to try to help connect everyone around the world and to bring the world closer together.*
>
> *In order to do that, we believe that we need to offer a service that everyone can afford, and we're committed to doing that.*
>
> *HATCH: Well, if so, how do you sustain a business model in which users don't pay for your service?*
>
> *ZUCKERBERG: Senator, we run ads.*
>
> *HATCH: I see. That's great.[3]*

The fact that one of the most experienced sitting senators did not do his homework on Facebook's business model prior to a televised hearing was disconcerting. The video of this exchange has prompted mockery among many engineers around politicians' lack of technical knowledge.[4] Many engineers in online forums use this video as an example of their superiority over those who are far less tech savvy.

My reaction is the exact opposite. If someone with more power than you knows less than you about a critical domain, that problem is yours to fix. Engineers can no longer assume that functional fidelity, engagement, and adoption are the sole metrics for success. To the extent that data is the fuel of the information superhighway, regulators will control the speed limits and enforce detours. The lack of technical sophistication of these regulators could lead to unhelpful laws that stifle innovation, hurt competition, and fail to protect consumers.

I cannot sign off without another recollection, one from my own memory. I was once at a four-person panel that featured two cybersecurity industry experts (me and another person) and two individuals who advised governments on privacy law. The

---

[3] "Transcript of Mark Zuckerberg's Senate hearing," *The Washington Post*, April 10, 2018, http://mng.bz/raBZ.
[4] "Senator Asks How Facebook Remains Free, Mark Zuckerberg Smirks: 'We Run Ads'," *YouTube*, http://mng.bz/VlqO.

exchange was mostly off the record, but during a portion of the event open to the public, the following exchange ensued:

> *GOVERNMENT EXPERT: We need more privacy laws because the tech industry is out of control.*

> *BHAJARIA: Well, we have two laws already on the books with wide applicability and open to emulation. Would it not be better to study their effectiveness and use them as a baseline? That way we know the laws are producing intended protections for users.*

> *GOVERNMENT EXPERT: There are not very many good actors in industry to partner with, and besides, why not have 50 privacy laws in 50 states? The cream rises to the top, and we will have a superset of protections that way.*

The exchange returns to me every time I argue for privacy budgets and projects to be prioritized. The lack of technical sophistication among privacy regulators in government is matched only by their desire to regulate companies that monetize user data.

This book will help engineers and companies front-load privacy engineering into their businesses. This is critical, since emerging and growing companies have two choices. They could continue business as usual and surrender their future to someone who will gradually regulate them into the ground. Unlike the big tech giants, newer companies lack endurance to deal with punitive laws.

They could, however, make a second choice. This book lays out the engineering tools companies can build for privacy, but it is just as critical that engineers engage more widely to educate and influence. The future of data protection will depend on the healthy tension as well as collaboration between innovation and regulation. Both need to inform rather than cancel each other. This will be the subject of my future endeavors and authorship.

For now, I want to close with a word of advice. I hope the engineers and other technologists who are this book's primary audience will use this book aggressively as a starting point. Use it as a framework to build out privacy technology into products, tools, and processes. You have a baseline now available that you can customize for your technical implementations.

I also want to reach out to company executives who are often disconnected from the details and often surprised by suboptimal privacy outcomes. While you may not understand every detail, this book is aimed at conveying the risk and scope related to privacy, but also the efficiencies and benefits as well. This book is aimed at helping you, as a leader and decision maker, to prioritize and drive maturity within your businesses.

Finally, members of the media and regulatory apparatus have focused on privacy with increasing intensity in recent times. This book should help you understand the complexities and interdependencies when it comes to privacy engineering. The media often act as thermometers, in that their coverage provides a sense of how well or poorly things are going. Regulators then act like thermostats in that they turn up or down the heat, depending on customer impact and sentiment. Things often move quickly amid the flurry of news without appropriate context, and this book is aimed at healing that. Technical journalists, lawmakers, and regulators should also benefit from this book and be enabled to fulfill your roles more prudently.

Whatever your background and the angle with which you have approached this book, thank you for coming on this journey with me. It is my hope that we will see a future in which privacy is increasingly built (engineered!) into all that we do, to the benefit of users and in turn the businesses who prove to have their users' interests in mind. Good luck!

Summary

- Companies need to gradually and continuously mature their privacy engineering systems and tools.
- Given the wide scope of privacy, there are several dimensions and choices for companies to track program maturity.
- Companies also need to understand the diversity of privacy engineering skills, all of which come with varying levels of criticality.
- The disconnect and knowledge imbalance between the tech industry and the regulatory authorities is the next risk/challenge for government and industry to solve.

index

RELATED MANNING TITLES

Secure By Design
by Dan Bergh Johnsson, Daniel Deogun,
and Daniel Sawano
Foreword by Daniel Terhorst-North

ISBN 9781617294358
400 pages, $49.99
Fall 2019

API Security in Action
by Neil Madden

ISBN 9781617296024
576 pages, $69.99
Winter 2020

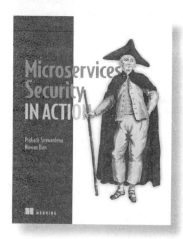

Microservices Security in Action
by Prabath Siriwardena and Nuwan Dias

ISBN 9781617295959
616 pages, $69.99
Summer 2020

For ordering information go to www.manning.com